History
of the World's
GLIDER
FORCES

Patrick Stephens Limited, part of Thorsons, a division of the Collins Publishing Group, has published authoritative, quality books for enthusiasts for more than twenty years. During that time the company has established a reputation as one of the world's leading publishers of books on aviation, maritime, military, model-making, motor cycling, motoring, motor racing, railway and railway modelling subjects. Readers or authors with suggestions for books they would like to see published are invited to write to: The Editorial Director, Patrick Stephens Limited, Thorsons Publishing Group, Wellingborough, Northants, NN8 2RQ.

History
of the World's
GLIDER
FORCES

—Alan Wood—

PATRICK STEPHENS LIMITED

First published in 1990

British Library Cataloguing in Publication Data
Wood, Alan,
History of the worlds glider forces.
1. Military gliders, history
I. Title
623.746

ISBN 1-85260-275-9

Patrick Stephens Limited is part of the Thorsons Publishing Group,
Wellingborough, Northamptonshire, NN8 2RQ, England.

Typeset by Burns & Smith Ltd, Derby

Printed in Great Britain by Mackays, Chatham, Kent

1 3 5 7 9 10 8 6 4 2

Dedicated
to
The Glidermen and their Tug Crews

Contents

Acknowledgements

I EXTEND my grateful thanks to the following regiments, associations, government bodies, museums, and persons, without whose help, advice, research, information and encouragement this book could not have been written:

The Museum of Army Flying, Middle Wallop, England, in particular Colonel Nick Nichols, MBE, Major John Cross, Major 'Chips' Clifton Moore, the urbane archivist Flight Lieutenant Harry Foot.

My friend and master of statistics David Hall, GPR, and his wife Olive, and Brandy.

And the following in alphabetical order: Jean Alexander, Border Regiment (Colonel R.K. May); David Brook, Editor of *Eagle*; Dr Peter Bowen, National Army Museum; BBC, Berlin; M.J.F. Bowyer; Bundesarchiv, Germany; Dan Campbell, 82nd Airborne Division; Brigadier G.J.S. Chatterton, OBE, DSO, Commandant Glider Pilot Regiment; Major Bob Cross, Secretary of the Glider Pilot Regimental Association; Charles Case, Master Photographer; Bill Chambers, GPR; Ron Driver, GPR; Joe Dabney, USA (author); John M. Davies, USA; DR&B Ltd, Syrencot House, Wiltshire; Susan and James Francis, artists; Dennis Galpin, DFM, GPR; Major-General Joseph Harper, US Army, and Maria; Captain A.P.M. Griffiths, 6th Gurkha Rifles; Dr Adrian Groenweg, Arnhem Museum; General James M. Gavin, 82nd Airborne Division Commander in the Second World War, for his observations and best wishes; Daniel Hagedorn, Texas, USA; Jim Halley of Air Britain; Mr Hibbs of the 12th Devons; Staff Sargeant Roy Howard, DFM, for his efforts on my behalf. Major John Howard, DSO, for his Foreword and proof-reading on the *Coup de Main* Operation; the Imperial War Museum (Alan Williams) for their help with photographs; Major Alan Jefferson, 9th Battalion, Parachute Regiment, for his help on Merville; the Lockheed Aircraft Company, Georgia, USA; Joe Michie, GPR; Janac Milan, Czech Glider Pilot; the late Will Morrison, GPR, for his encouragement; Don Middleton, author; Museum of Army Transport, Beverley; Ministry of Defence (Air), London, (E.A. Munday); *Daily Mirror*, London; Ted Noble, 2nd Ox and Bucks; National Air and Space Museum, Washington, USA; John Potts, GPR; Colonel Wayne Pierce, 325th Glider Infantry Regiment, US Army; Alan Richards, DFM, artist; Royal Army

Medical Corps (Roy Eyeions); Royal Army Ordnance Museum, Deepcut; Royal Air Force Museum (Peter Elliot); Royal Corps of Signals, Blandford; Lieutenant-Colonel G.J. Rudd, RAOC; Staff Sergeant Harry Rathband, GPR; Edward Siergi, 17th Airborne Division, US Army; Staffordshire Regiment (Captain N.J. Hitchings); Silent Wings Museum, USA; Slingsby Aviation; Terry C. Treadwell, JP, for his great practical help; 13th Airborne Division, US Army; Charles N. Trask, USA; Major Ian Toler, DFC, TD, Squadron Commander, GPR; Captain C. Turner, Commander of Operation 'Bunghole'; Major R.A.J. Tyler, MBE; United States Air Force, United States Air Force Historical Research Center for permission to use maps and charts; US Embassy, London; United States Marine Corps HQ Washington, USA; United States Navy (Captain Richard Knott); Lieutenant-Colonel Ken Vines, Royal Engineers; John Willoughby, 2nd Ox and Bucks Regiment; Waco Historical Society, Troy, Ohio, USA; Staff Sergeant Len Wright, DFM, for 'Turkey Buzzard'; Martin Wolfe, 81st Squadron, USAAF; John Wickenden of Air Britain; Walter Wrzeszczynski, 17th Airborne Division, US Army; Ivan Worrel, 101st Airborne Division, US Army, and the 101st Association for permission to use *Rendezvous with Destiny*; Geoff Yardley, 2nd Ox and Bucks Regiment; and to the Controller of Her Majesty's Stationery Office.

Lastly my long suffering wife, Rita Ann.

                                                                    Alan Wood

I
The History of Gliding
1709–1940

For centuries man had looked at the birds of the air and envied their effortless flying, soaring and gliding prowess. Unaware of the principles of flight, he strove to copy their example by devising feathered wings of a like nature. He flapped them without result, for his body was too heavy and did not possess enough muscle power to sustain flight, let alone to take off.

Leonardo da Vinci pondered the problem and drew many designs, but they were still based on the wing-flapping theory. A Portuguese priest, Lorenso de Gusman, did design a flying machine in 1709 which he called Big Bird; it looked just like one, and is reported to have flown like a glider, making it the first in the field. He also built the world's first hot air balloon, which achieved flight many years before the Montgolfier brothers' hot air balloon of 1783. For good or ill, man had how achieved flight.

The first recorded man-carrying glider flight was in 1853, at Brompton Hall, near Scarborough, Yorkshire, England, when a glider built of wood and canvas designed by Sir George Cayley (1773–1857) flew, carrying a small boy and, on later flights, Sir George's coachman. Although the flights by the coachman were successful, he left Sir George's employment. He was employed, not to fly, he said, but to drive horses.

Cayley was a scientist, making many worthwhile inventions, and has come to be regarded as the father of the aeroplane for his pioneering work on heavier than air gliders and other aircraft. His 1853 glider had a kite-type wing, which supplied lift, and a tail with both vertical and horizontal flying surfaces, which gave direction.

In America, research and invention was also being carried out: in 1883 an American, John Montgomery, built and flew a glider from the hills near San Diego, California. In 1894 the French-born American railway constructor, Octave Chanute (1832–1910) published a book, *Progress in Flying Machines*, and in the same year built a glider which became the first of many such manned gliders to carry out a large number of successful flights.

The German civil engineer Otto Lilenthal (1948–1896) published his book *The Flight of Birds as the Basis of Aviation* in 1889, his thesis being that flight would have to be modelled on that of the bird. Between 1891 and 1896 he built five

monoplane and two biplane gliders with bird-like wings and made flights of up to
250 metres. Control of the gliders was effected by his hanging beneath them and
using his body weight and movement to steer. Many of his flights were made in
1895 at the Rhineower Hills, Stollen, Germany, but unfortunately, on 9 August
1896, he lost control of a glider and crashed, suffering such serious injuries that he
died.

Scotland too had its glider pioneer: Percy Sinclair Pilcher (1866–1899) a naval
architect and lecturer at Glasgow University. Pilcher designed and built the Gull
and Hawk gliders, and made a glider flight of 250 yards, but crashed in a Hawk
and died on 30 September 1899. Pilcher's designs, of monoplane construction
with a separate tail plane, controlled by his body movements like Lilenthal's
gliders, were somewhat similar to the hang gliders of today.

The Americans Wilbur (1871–1912) and Orville (1871–1948) Wright flew their
No. 1 glider in 1900. This was an unmanned biplane glider with a wing span of
165 feet controlled from the ground like a kite. Realizing that control of the aircraft in the air was vital, they invented rudder control and wing warping, thereby
giving control of the flying surfaces for the first time. On their No. 2 glider, flown
in 1901, they added a horizontal front elevator for ascending and descending. To
lessen air resistance the pilot lay prone and controlled the wing warping by control
cables attached to his body; his hands were thus left free to control the front
elevator. Later they added a movable rudder in place of the fixed one, which the
pilot operated in conjunction with the wing warping. This made turns possible,
and the design later became their 'Flyer', which, with an engine, flew 120 feet at
Kill Devil sand dunes on 17 December 1903 and gave man successful powered
flight.

In Australia, George Taylor made the first Australian man-carrying glider flight
in December 1909, and his wife became the first woman in the world to become a
glider pilot when she flew his glider in December 1909. The same year, British officer Lieutenant John Dunne – who was attached to the Royal Engineers Balloon
Section, formed in 1890 – designed and built a viable glider which flew
successfully.

The years between 1903 and the twenties were full of men with vision and
foresight who took to the air in gliders mostly of their own construction. In
America, Glenn L. Martin (1886–1955) began building gliders in 1907 and then
turned to powered flight, which later produced some outstanding aircraft. In Germany, the glider pioneer Frederick Harth worked with the later-to-be-famous
Willi Messerschmitt and built gliders between 1910 and 1914. The British
pioneer airman Flight Lieutenant Pashley started glider flying at Hockley in 1908
and later became a Naval Flying Instructor who taught the famous pilots Mick
Mannock and John Alcock to fly. Russia produced Alexander Yakolev, the aircraft designer of later years, who began by building a glider in 1923. In Britain,
the nearest approach to military gliders was on 1 April 1911, when the first Air
Battalion of the Royal Engineers was formed with a strength of 14 officers and 150
other ranks. The battalion used aircraft, balloons and man-carrying kites as an aid
to Army Observation. Kites had been used in the Boer War and as far back as
1806 by the Royal Navy.

During the First World War, whereas increasing attention had been paid to powered aircraft, no one had yet seen a use for the unpowered glider. Afterwards, under the terms of the Versailles Peace Treaty concluded between the Allies and Germany in June 1919 all German military aviation was prohibited, only civil aircraft being allowed. The Germans then began building and flying gliders, turning it into a national sport. By 1929 the *Luftsportverband* had a membership of 50,000. Gliders like the Vampyr, built in 1921, and the Grief in 1922 led to the graceful Olympia and Minimoa sailplanes which could sustain gliding flight rather than the launch and quickly descend early types. Many of Germany's famous pilots of the Second World War, like Adolf Galland, learned to fly at this time. In the autumn of 1931 Galland won his gliding certificate in a Meyer 2 glider, which had a wingspan of 60 ft.

Parallel with the Germans' interest in the glider was that of Russia: there, glider design was improving and interest was being shown by the military. In 1932 the Russians built the world's first transport, or passenger, glider, the Groschev TSK Komsula four-seater, to be followed in 1934 by a five-seater. Designs and prototypes of still larger gliders were made, but the real interest lay in parachute troops.

In the United States, gliding grew into a civilian hobby, though the US Navy did conduct experiments, as did the US Army. Still, no one had yet realised the concept of the assault glider. In a few years time the Germans would. In 1925 a group of gliding sportsmen in Germany formed the Rhon-Rossitten Company at Wasserkuppe to build gliders and research glider flight. On the rise to power of the Nazi Party in 1933 the German Gliding Research Institute (*Deutsche Forschungsanstalt Fuer Segelflug* – DFS) took over the company's activity and further engaged in glider research which produced a high-altitude meteorological research glider. From this glider the world's first military assault glider was evolved – the DFS 230 – and put to stunning use in the first glider assault at Eben Emael, Belgium, in May 1940. The glider had now gone to war.

II

German Military Glider History 1932–1945

O N 1 March 1935, the German Air Force – the Luftwaffe – officially came into being with a strength of 20,000 men who had received their training either in civil aircraft gliders or clandestinely abroad.

At first the Luftwaffe had a command structure of squadron (*Staffel*), wing (*Gruppe*), and group (*Geschwader*). Three wings (*Gruppen*) formed a group (*Geschwader*) and later air fleets (*Luftflotten*) were formed. Each air fleet contained two or three flying divisions and when war broke out in 1939 there were seven air divisions. As the Luftwaffe increased in strength some of the air divisions were up-rated to flying corps (*Flieger Korps*).

In 1932 an experimental glider, the OBS meteorological observation glider, had been built in Germany for research. This was taken over by the German Gliding Research Institute (DFS) in 1933. From this research a Dr Hans Jacob, assisted by others, designed the DFS 230 military assault glider in a top-secret project. The glider was demonstrated to a gathering of the German High Command and Government at Darmstadt in 1937. The observers included the German Secretary for Air, Erhard Milch, the Air Ministry Director of Technical Department, Ernst Udet, and Generals von Greim, Kesselring and Model.

The DFS 230 glider, carrying eight troops and towed by a Ju 52/3m aircraft, was flown by Air Captain Hanna Reitsch, who carried out a successful dive and landing in front of the observers. Impressed by the concept, the Germans put the DFS 230 into production.

The German glider force was born in the autumn of 1938, under Lieutenant Weiss, as part of 7th Airborne Division of the 11th Flying Corps and comprised a small unit using the recently developed DFS 230 assault glider. Under the command of the Flying Corps commander, General Kurt Student (1890–1978), the embryo unit grew quickly with the increase in production of the DFS 230. In November 1939 a special unit, Storm Unit Koch was formed under Captain Walter Koch at Hildesheim, Germany, and early in 1940 No. 1 Wing of the 1st Air Landing Group came into being. After the success of the Koch storm unit at Fort Eben Emael in May 1940, Nos. 2 and 3 Wings were created with further operations in mind.

From their Eben Emael debut until 1941, the air landing units were employed on freight-carrying duties but on 26 April 1941 No. 1 Air Landing Group was used in the capture of the Corinth Canal bridge in Greece.

The group was next used in the invasion of Crete, Operation 'Mercury' (*Merkur*), but the German airborne forces suffered such appalling losses (271 Ju52s destroyed out of 493 engaged and 6,500 dead and wounded men) that Hitler ordered that no more large-scale airborne operations were to be undertaken in spite of the fact that Crete had been captured. Gliders were to be used for freight and small-scale operations only.

The German glider designers and the Gothaer Waggonfabrik Company (Gotha) produced the Go 242 large transport glider, the first of which was delivered to the Luftwaffe in August 1941. Cargo Carrying Squadrons Nos. 1 to 6 were formed by February 1942, and engaged in delivering vital supplies to the encircled German forces at Kholm on the Russian Front in the spring of that year.

The Messerschmitt Company had also produced the enormous Me 321 Gigant glider, originally designed to carry tanks and guns for the projected invasion of Britain in 1940 and first flown on 25 February 1941, and by June 1941 a Heavy Cargo Glider Wing of three squadrons, each with six Me 321s, was created. Shortly afterwards this unit was enlarged to four squadrons, each with five Me 321s.

By September these squadrons were operational on the Eastern Front at:

Riga (North)	No.	1 Squadron Air Fleet No.	1			
Orsha (Central)	"	22	"	"	"	" 2
Kherson (South)	"	4	"	"	"	" 4
Orsha (Central)	"	2	"	"	"	" 2

The Me 321 No. 1 Squadron was used in the capture of the Baltic islands of Muhu, Hiiumaa and Saarema in late 1941 but this did not prove entirely successful and its Me 321s were mostly withdrawn, although a few remained in isolated use on the Eastern Front. The bulk of them were transferred to the south of France but were not used on operations.

However, the motorised version of the Gigant, the Me 323, was more successful and in November 1942, two wings were formed as Special Duty Battle Group 323 and operated in the Mediterranean theatre of operations in support of the German Africa Corps by carrying much-needed fuel and supplies. At the end of 1942 most Gigants were ordered back to the Eastern Front for the Stalingrad airlift for a short time, then returned to the Mediterranean.

In April 1943 Special Duties Battle Group 323 was renamed Transport Group 5 and was heavily engaged in re-supply missions from Italy to Tunis with fuel for the retreating Africa Corps. On 10 April the RAF shot down three of the group's gliders, and on 22 April sixteen Me 323s of the group loaded with fuel were en route to Tunis when they were bounced by RAF aircraft. In spite of the gliders being heavily armed and making a fight of it, 14 out of the 16 gliders were shot down. The two surviving gliders reached Tunis but one was destroyed on the ground on 25 April and only one glider returned to Italy. Transport Group 5 had ceased to exist.

On 12 September 1943 twelve DFS 230C-1 gliders were used by SS Captain

Otto Skorzeny to rescue the Italian dictator Mussolini from his mountain-top prison perched on the 9,050-foot-high Gran Sasso Massif, in order to fly him out in a helicopter or light aircraft.

By November 1943 Transport Group 5 had been reformed and saw extensive service in Hungary, Poland and Rumania but in the spring of 1944 production of the Me 323 was stopped and its use petered out.

On 25 May 1944, in an attempt to kill or capture the Yugoslav resistance leader, Marshal Tito, the Germans launched a glider and parachute assault on his Head-quarters at Drvar in Yugoslavia. Preceded by a bombing attack by the Luftwaffe, the 500th SS (Penal) Battalion under SS Captain Rybka assaulted the HQ. Tito managed to escape to the hills and on 3 June was flown to Bari, Italy, by a Russian Dakota.

In France, after the landings of the Allied Forces in June, 1944, 3,000 men of the Free French Forces of the Interior (FFI) raised the French Tricoleur on the thirty by twelve mile Vercours plateau near Grenoble, France. Commanded by Colonel Huet, they were supplied with weapons by the USAAF in a 1,000-container daylight drop on 14 July 1944. At first the Germans were unable to take the plateau but on 18 July SS troops landed there by glider and after two days fighting eliminated the Resistance.

The DFS 230 and the Gotha 242 gliders continued to be used on the Eastern Front on re-supply missions, as the Russian steamroller continued inexorably on. Both glider types were used to re-supply German forces in Budapest in December 1944, but by February 1945 twelve Go 242s and thirty-six DFS 230s had been lost. In March 1945 the end was near but Go 242s and DFS 230s transported guns and ammunition into the encircled city of Breslau. Six gliders made the trip, but two DFS 230s and one Go 242 were shot down by the Russians. Two Go 242s managed to land with two field guns, and one DFS 230. More DFS 230s loaded with ammunition were flown in but nothing could stem the advance of Marshal Koniev's 5th Guards and the 6th Army of the 1st Ukrainian Front and surrender soon followed.

With the disintegration of Hitler's Reich and the final surrender on 8 May 1945, German airborne forces ceased to exist – their place in history secure as the first to launch a gliderborne assault.

III

German Military Glider Operations

The First Glider Assault: Fort Eben Emael

Between 1932 and 1935 the Belgian Government had built what was then thought to be an impregnable fortress at Eben Emael on the west side of the defensive line formed by the Albert Canal. Eben Emael occupied a strategic position near the Dutch and German borders and commanded the Vroenhoeven and Veltesvelt bridges over the canal, the roads from Maastricht to the west, and the canal itself.

Eben Emael was built on top of the western side of the 125-foot-deep canal cutting at Caster and covered an area of 750 yards east to west and 950 yards north to south. The outer perimeter on all sides was protected by trenches, anti-tank guns, rapid-fire cannon, machine-guns and searchlights.

Inside the perimeter were six turrets with 7.5-cm cannons, two turrets with 12-cm revolving twin cannons and 7.5-cm revolving twin cannons; two forts with heavy machine-guns, and five positions with anti-aircraft machine-guns. All the installations were linked by underground tunnels to an underground stores and accommodation complex, with only one entrance, on the south side perimeter. Fort Eben Emael was considered impregnable to ground attack and plans were in hand to render it likewise to airborne attack. By 10 May 1940 nothing had been done.

As the fort stood in the path of the German 6th Army in the sector allotted the 16th Panzer Corps, German High Command (OKW) considered it was vital to eliminate it and to capture intact the bridges it commanded, in order that the invading forces could pour into Belgium and drive for the coast. Hitler himself devised the daring plan to capture the fort and bridges, using – for the first time in history – the recently developed DFS assault glider, which would be towed to the German border, released over German airspace and glide to land just before the intended ground attack by the 6th Army.

The force chosen for the history-making glider assault was Storm Unit Koch, formed at Hildesheim, with Captain Walter Koch, a 29-year-old former policeman, in command. For the assault Storm Unit Koch would consist of the 1st Company of the 1st Parachute Regiment, a parachute engineer unit of the 7th Airborne Division, a freight glider unit and a tow unit of Ju 52/3m tow aircraft.

Thirty-one DFS 230 assault gliders were to be used in the attack, to be made by four assault groups with the following objectives:

Assault Group 'Granit'
Commanded by Lieutenant Rudolf Witzig, with 85 troops, to capture Eben Emael.
Assault Group 'Konkret'
Commanded by Lieutenant Schacht, to take the Vronhoeven Bridge.
Assault Group 'Stahl'
Commanded by Lieutenant Altman, to attack the Veldvezelt Bridge.
Assault Group 'Eisen'
Commanded by Lieutenant Schachter, to take another vital bridge, the Kanne.

In November 1939 training began for the Koch unit under the greatest secrecy, with practice attacks on similar forts in Germany and demolition trials in Poland.

Essential to success was the breaching of the fort's steel and concrete fortifications and emplacements. For this purpose special 110 lb explosive charges had been devised to crack open the casemates. These charges gave a shaped-blast effect and had been developed from a principle discovered by an American scientist, C.E. Monroe. Fifty-six of these 'cavity' charges were to be used, with ten-second fuzes, to penetrate ten inches of steel. Several charges placed in the same position would penetrate deeper. Over two tons of explosives were to be carried and used in the assault.

For the Eben Emael assault eleven of the thirty-one DFS 230A gliders were to be used to carry eighty-five troops, each glider carrying seven or eight assault engineer sappers including the pilot who, on landing, would fight with the rest of his section. Each man and section was heavily armed with sub-machine guns, smoke and fragmentation grenades. Six light machine-guns were to be carried by six of the eleven sections together with several flame throwers.

On the afternoon of 9 May 1940, with the Koch storm unit assembled at Cologne's Ostheim and Butzweilerhof airfields, word was flashed from OKW that the operation was on for the next morning. At 04:30 on the morning of 10 May 1940 thirty-one DFS 230 gliders were towed off from the two airfields by Ju 52/3m tug aircraft led by the air commander, Lieutenant Schweizer. Circling to gain height, the combinations formed into their assault groups. A few minutes later the tow rope of Witzig's glider broke and the 'Granit' force commander and his men were forced to land south of Cologne. Radioing for another Ju 52 tug to land and tow the glider off, Witzig and his men had to wait for another three hours. Another glider was also forced to land shortly after lift-off and the troops were unable to take part in the assault but they later joined the ground forces in their attack.

The remaining twenty-nine gliders were towed to the German border at 8,000 feet. Nearing the Dutch town of Maastricht, still in German airspace, they cast off their tow ropes. Gliding silently and descending slowly they arrived over their targets. First to land, at 05:15, was the 'Konkret' group, followed ten minutes later by the other three groups.

Nine gliders containing the sapper engineers crashed into Eben Emael, meeting with anti-aircraft fire as they approached. As Lieutenant Witzig and his men had not arrived, command was taken over by Sergeant-Major Wenzel and all the landed sections went into the attack against the 750-man garrison commanded by Major Jean Jottrand. By now Major Jottrand's garrison was fully alerted and resistance was being offered. Cavity charges were exploding on seven casemates, cracking five of them. Nine 7.5-cm guns in three casemates were put out of action and a twin 12-cm cannon was spiked by throwing small charges into the barrels. Sergeant-Major Wenzel reported by radio to Captain Koch that the attack had been largely successful.

Belgian infantry launched a counter-attack and their artillery fire was directed onto the fort, causing the Germans to take cover. In spite of this the attackers managed to blow up three ascent shafts with 56 lb charges.

Fighting continued all day as the assault troops awaited their relief ground force from the 51st Sapper Battalion trying to cross the Albert Canal in their rubber boats. Part of Eben Emael was still in Belgian hands and the defenders were able to repel the German ground attack until darkness fell. During the night no further Belgian attacks were made against the 'Granit' group and at 07:00 the next day, 11 May, part of the ground relief force managed to cross the canal and capture the casemate overlooking it. With this casemate in German hands more and more Germans were able to pour over the canal and engage the Belgian defenders, till at noon that day the garrison surrendered.

The 'Eisen' group at the Kanne bridge landed under heavy fire and its commander, Lieutenant Schachter, was killed. The Belgians blew the bridge and resisted until almost midnight. Assault Group 'Stahl', attacking the Veldvezelt bridge, found it intact but had to fight all day against the Belgian defenders, and it was not until the late evening of 10 May that they were relieved by strong ground forces. The 'Konkret' assault group seized the Vronhoeven Bridge intact and held it until relieved by the advancing ground forces. The 'Granit' assault group had suffered six dead and fifteen wounded out of the original force of eighty-five men – but they had achieved their objective within thirty hours. Later, Hitler personally congratulated the officers and men of Koch's unit on their operation.

The first military gliderborne assault in the world had been made with success, and it set the pattern later to be copied by the Allies in their gliderborne operations.

The Corinth Canal Bridge Assault

On 13 December 1940 Hitler issued Führer Directive No. 20 for the invasion of Yugoslavia and Greece to secure the Aegean Coast and enable his Wehrmacht to advance on Crete and later Cyprus. Codenamed Operation 'Marita', the plan was to use ground and airborne forces in eight main thrusts from Bulgaria, where the Wehrmacht had been moved from Rumania. On the 18th Hitler's 21st Directive was issued for Operation 'Barbarossa', the invasion of Russia, scheduled to take place early in 1941. This would take place if Operation 'Marita' was successful and the Wehrmacht had gained control of the Aegean coastline.

Allocated for Operation 'Marita' were twenty-seven divisions under the 12th Army commanded by General List and seven armoured divisions of a Panzer

Group commanded by General von Kleist. Air strength was provided by Air Fleet No. 4 with 1,200 aircraft, which included 270 Ju 52/3ms and a squadron of 7th Airborne Division, 11th Flying Corps, equipped with DFS 230 assault gliders.

Opposing the Germans were thirty-three Allied divisions: three British, six Greek and twenty-four Yugoslavian. In the air the Allies could only muster some 200 aircraft in total.

At 05:15 on 6 April 1941 Operation 'Marita' began and the Germans poured into Yugoslavia and Greece. Within ten days it became clear that Greece would fall quickly. By the 24th the airfield at Larissa was in German hands and the 7th Airborne Division flew in from their base at Plovdiv, Bulgaria, where they had assembled. Each of the 270 Ju 52s had to be refuelled by hand pump from petrol drums, there being no other means of refuelling available.

The Allied forces pulled back across the Corinth Canal bridge which linked the south of Greece with the Peloponese. The bridge was the only road route across the deep gorge-like Corinth Canal and a small rearguard of three tanks and some Australian troops were left behind to defend it. Demolition charges were rigged at each end of the bridge to enable it to be blown on the approach of the Germans.

In an attempt to take the bridge intact to enable the German forces to stream across, a hastily contrived plan was made by the Germans. DFS 230 gliders would land troops at each end of the bridge and storm it, assisted later by parachute troops who would be dropped nearby. The parachute troops would be from the 2nd Parachute Regiment, commanded by Colonel Albert Sturm. Two battalions, No. 1 led by Captain Kroh and No. 2 led by Captain Pietzonka, would be airlifted in forty Ju 52s to drop and form a defensive perimeter to hold the bridge against any Allied counter-attack.

The *Coupe de Main* bridge assault party would be thirty troops carried in six DFS 230 gliders and include sapper engineers led by Lieutenant Haffner. Three of the gliders, piloted by Lieutenants Fulda, Brendenbeck and Mende would land on the north side of the bridge and the other three, piloted by Lieutenants Phenn, Lassen and Raschke, simultaneously on the south side. Phenn's glider would carry Lieutenant Haffner and Fulda would be in overall command of the glider operation. The Luftwaffe would strafe the bridge with cannon and machine-gun fire just before the gliders were due to land.

At 04:30 on 26 April the six DFS 230 gliders were towed off from Larissa airfield by six Ju 52s, the lead tug pilot being Lieutenant Schweiser, and made for the Corinth Canal accompanied by forty Ju 52s carrying the assault paratroops. At 06:58 the Luftwaffe began to strafe the bridge to make the defenders keep their heads down.

Arriving over the bridge at 07:00 the glider pilots cast off their tow ropes and the three north side gliders dived to a crash-landing near the bridge. The assault troop passengers quickly took the northern end, capturing eighty Allied troops. On the southern side of the bridge the action had been repeated – Lieutenant Phenn's glider, with the engineer Lieutenant Haffner aboard, had crashed into a buttress of the bridge, injuring one of the troops on board, but the others quickly overcame the defenders.

Haffner's men disconnected the wires leading to the bridge demolition charges but left the actual charges in place in case of an Allied counter-attack. By this time the paratroops of the 1st and 2nd Battalions were dropping around the bridge and quickly formed a defensive perimeter. So far the assault had gone according to plan, and the bridge, still intact, was in German hands.

Controversy rages as to what happened next, but beyond dispute is the fact that Allied troops opened fire on the bridge with small arms and a Bofors gun. The demolition charges were hit and exploded. Photographs taken at the time show explosions at both ends of the bridge simultaneously which lifted it up bodily into the air, then dropped it into the canal. Several Germans were on the bridge at the time, including Lieutenant Phenn, and were killed. In all the Germans suffered 237 casualties, including 63 killed. For his part in the operation Lieutenant Fulda was awarded the Knight's Cross of the Iron Cross by Hitler.

The Germans erected a temporary bridge over the canal over which their 12th Army advanced and by 30 April had occupied the whole of the isthmus from which the Allies had withdrawn to Crete.

The gliderborne *Coup de Main* part of the assault had been one hundred per cent successful, but the failure to remove the demolition charges rendered their efforts in vain. The Allies did eventually profit from the German operation, using the idea successfully in their capture of the River Orne and the Caen Canal bridges in Normandy on D-Day.

Operation 'Merkur'

The first large-scale airborne assault in history
The capture of Greece completed, Hitler's attention was now fixed on Russia, but his attention was drawn to the fact that the island of Crete was still in Allied hands – and the RAF could strike from there at the vital Ploesti oil fields essential for the Wehrmacht's fuel needs in Russia.

General Kurt Student, the airborne forces' commander, put before the OKW on 15 April 1941 a plan to take Crete by using airborne forces. Göring put the plan to Hitler on the 21st, and four days later Führer Directive No. 28, Operation 'Merkur' (Mercury), was issued for the capture of Crete, with the date for the assault 17 May.

The plan was to take Crete by a combined air and sea invasion using gliderborne, paratroop and air landing troops followed by seaborne troops. The airborne forces would drop and land on the northern coast of Crete at Maleme, Canea, Retimo and Heraklion airfields. The seaborne troops would land at Suda Bay after the airborne landings and would link up with the airborne.

The role of the glider force was to land in the morning at Maleme and Canea and seize ground under cover of bombing by the Luftwaffe. They would then provide covering fire for the paratroops' descent. With these two forces on the ground and in control, Ju 52s would then fly in air landing troops to expand the air head gained.

For the assault the Germans had 22,750 men: 750 glider troops, 5,000 air landing troops, 10,000 parachute troops, 7,000 seaborne troops and two Flying Corps.

Order of Battle

11th Flying Corps
Commander General Student
Composition
1st Air Landing Assault Regiment: Major General Meindl
1st Battalion: Major Koch
2nd Battalion: Major Stentzler
3rd Battalion: Major Scherber
4th Battalion: Captain Gericke
7th Airborne Division: Lieutenant-General Sussman
1st Parachute Regiment: Colonel Brauer
1st Battalion: Major Walther
2nd Battalion: Captain Burckhardt
3rd Battalion: Major Schultz
2nd Parachute Regiment: Colonel Sturm
1st Battalion: Major Kroh
2nd Battalion: Captain Pietzonka
3rd Battalion: Captain Wiedeman
3rd Parachute Regiment: Colonel Heidrich
1st Battalion: Captain Heydte
2nd Battalion: Major Derpa
3rd Battalion: Major Heilman
5th Mountain Division: Major-General Ringel
85th Mountain Regiment: Colonel Krakau
1st Battalion: Major Treck
2nd Battalion: Major Esch
3rd Battalion: Major Fett
100th Mountain Regiment: Colonel Utz
1st Battalion: Major Schrank
2nd Battalion: Major Friedman
3rd Battalion: Major Ehall
95th Mountain Artillery Regiment: Lieutenant-Colonel Wittman
1st Battalion: Major Sternbach
2nd Battalion: Major Raithel
95th Motorcycle Battalion: Major Wolte
95th Pioneer Battalion: Major Schatte
95th Reconnaissance: Major Castell
95th Anti-Tank: Major Bindermann
7th Airborne divisional artillery; anti-tank, machine-gun and pioneer battalions.
Luftwaffe Flying Corps No. 7
Commander Lieutenant-General Freiherr von Richthofen.
Fighters
Nos. 2 and 3 Wings of 77th Fighter Group
No. 1 Wing of 2nd Training Group
Heavy Fighters
No. 1 Wing of 76th Heavy Fighter Group (Messerschmitt Me 110).

No. 2 Wing of 26th Heavy Fighter Group (Messerschmitt Me 110).
Bombers
No. 2 Training Group (Junkers Ju 88).
No. 2 Wing of 26th Bomber Group (Heinkel He 111).
2nd Bomber Group (Dornier Do 17).
Transport Command: Major Conrad
Nos. 40, 105 and 106 Wings of 1st Transport Battle Group (Ju 52/3m).
Nos. 60, 101 and 102 Wings of 2nd Transport Battle Group (Ju 52/3m).
No. 1 Wing of 1st Air Landing Group
Gliders
80 DFS 230 assault gliders
Reserve
Nos. 1 and 2 Wings of 172 Transport Battle Group with four squadrons of Ju 52s
Staff of 1st Air Landing Group
Aircraft

Bombers	280	Fighters	180	Gliders	80
Dive-Bombers	150	Reconnaissance	40	Transports	493

Total 1223 aircraft.

Operational Headquarters would be at the Grand Bretagne Hotel in Athens, Greece, with General Student in full command. Even with 493 transport aircraft and 80 assault gliders it would be impossible to air lift all of the troops in one lift, so two became necessary. Student divided his force into three elements: Group West (Meindl), which would attack Maleme in the morning with glider and paratroops; Group Centre (Sussman), which would attack Canea also in the morning with glider and paratroops; Group East (Ringel), the second lift, which would attack Retimo and Heraklion in the afternoon with paratroops.

The overall plan was for these forces to link up after landing and form a continuous 'air head' along the north coast of Crete to allow reinforcements to land behind them from the sea and air.

Defending Crete were 28,500 British, Commonwealth, Greek and Cretan troops. The bulk of the defenders were the 6th Australian Division and the 2nd New Zealand Division, both recently evacuated from the campaign in Greece. On 30 April General Wavell, Commander-in-Chief Middle East, flew into the island and appointed the New Zealander Major-General Freyberg as General Officer Commanding. Freyberg's troops were short of weapons having had to leave most of their equipment behind in Greece. Wavell supplied them with what he could spare from other theatres, which included sixteen light tanks manned by C Squadron, 3rd Hussars, and six infantry tanks of B Squadron, 7th Royal Tank Regiment. Forty-nine field guns also arrived together with the 2nd Battalion Leicestershire Regiment as reinforcements on the 16th May.

Knowing that the Germans were likely to attack by air, Freyberg did all he could to fortify his airfields: trenches, mounds of earth and barrels were placed to obstruct aircraft landings and such guns as were available were placed to cover the airfields.

Air defence was but one squadron of the Fleet Air Arm equipped with obsolete

Gladiators and Fulmars. The remnants of 33, 80 and 112 Squadrons, RAF, with a few Hurricanes, which had seen much action in Greece, were the only modern fighters available. These squadrons could at best only muster twelve serviceable aircraft to oppose the Luftwaffe. By 18 May only four Hurricanes and three Gladiators remained. Their position hopeless, they were withdrawn to Egypt the next day. The Luftwaffe now controlled the skies over Crete.

At 06:15 on 20 May Operation 'Merkur' began. For an hour the Luftwaffe pounded the Crete landing grounds to prepare the way for the glider and parachute troops landings. On the Greek bases of Corinth, Dadion, Eleusis, Phaleron, Tanagra and Topolis the airborne troops were air-lifted off and headed for Crete, where they were due to land between 07:00 and 07:15. The glider units were lifted off from Tanagra, Megara and Eleusis; three detachments from the 1st and 3rd Battalions of the 1st Air Landing Assault Regiment, some 288 men, were lifted off at 05:03 from Tanagra in forty-eight DFS 230 gliders towed by Ju 52s, which some two hours later cast off over Maleme, with the Luftwaffe still strafing the defenders. Another force in twenty-six gliders was lifted off from Megara and Eleusis.

Specific tasks had been assigned to this force. One detachment, led by Major Braun, in nine gliders was to take the River Tavronitis bridge, which spanned the dried-up bed of the River Tavronitis. Another, commanded by Lieutenant Plessen, was to land at the mouth of the River Tavronitis and eliminate defending anti-aircraft guns there. The other, under Major Koch now famous for Eben Emael, was to take a hill, known as Hill 107, which commanded the Maleme airfield.

Immediately behind this force came the bulk of the 1st Air Landing Assault Regiment, some 2,000 troops carried in Ju 52 transports who would drop by parachute and link up with the gliderborne troops. As Major Koch's unit was landing, they came under heavy fire from the defending New Zealanders of the 22nd Battalion. Many were killed and Koch himself was wounded. The survivors made for the Tavronitis bridge, which had been taken by Major Braun's detachment. Plessen's men had, under fire, overrun the anti-aircraft guns at the river mouth, but were now pinned down and their officer killed by the New Zealanders. The glider troops had suffered heavy losses and had only achieved one of their objectives: the bridge.

Paratroops landed near Hill 107 and surrounded it but failed to capture it from the New Zealanders, though more and more paratroopers dropped west of the River Tavronitis and began to attack Maleme. Group Centre (Sussman) had attacked Canea at the same time as Group West had attacked Maleme. Sussman, riding in an overloaded glider at the head of the glider stream, was already dead; the wings of the glider had buckled and it had crashed onto the island of Aegina killing all on board. The rest of the glider stream had carried on towards Crete.

With Sussman dead, Colonel Heidrich took command and his glider force landed south of Canea and along the east coast of Crete. However his units were dispersed over several miles and had taken such heavy casualties that his force was reduced by a third. More and more casualties were sustained as the Allies counter-attacked. For the Germans, the assaults at Maleme and Canea were proving disastrous. Nevertheless more paratroops were dropped into the battle, suffering heavy losses. The Group West commander, Meindl, was himself seriously wounded. The afternoon drop on Heraklion went ahead into a hail of fire. Many of the 1st Parchute Regiment were killed while still descending. Only five men out of two companies survived.

Night fell on the battlefields with the situation desperate for the surviving paratroops and gliderborne forces, though the 1st Air Landing Regiment did manage to take Hill 107 during the early hours of the next morning. During the night, however, Cretan partisans moved among the German dead and wounded, killing and mutilating all they found. Later the Germans responded to this by savage reprisals, which to this day still rankles with Cretans. Colonel Brauer was held to be responsible for the reprisals and was tried, convicted and executed in 1947. A distasteful tactic used by the Germans was to use captured defenders as a human screen whilst advancing. Any prisoners of war who did not advance were shot in the back.

The seaborne force which had set sail after the air landings was intercepted by the British Navy. The 3rd Battalion of the 100th Mountain Regiment and the 2nd Battalion of the 85th Mountain Regiment were wiped out almost to a man. Of the two battalions, only fifty-three men survived.

General Student, studying the German battle reports at his HQ in Greece, saw that ground had been gained at Maleme and ordered into battle the remaining troops of the 5th Mountain Division, who had been held back. Disregarding losses to men and aircraft, the Germans poured in troops, as Ju 52 pilots crash-landed their aircraft on and around the airfield and the dried-up river bed of the Tavronitis.

By 27 May the defenders were beaten by these tactics and began to evacuate Crete. A gallant rearguard action was fought, and ships of the Royal Navy managed to carry 14,800 men to Egypt; Freyberg himself left aboard a Sunderland flying boat of the RAF. On 31 May the last 1,500 were embarked. Operation 'Merkur' had succeeded, but at a heavy cost.

German casualties were 30 per cent of the total – some 3,500 troops were killed and 3,400 wounded. Two hundred and seventy-one Ju 52 transport aircraft were lost – 54 per cent of the transport fleet – and another 148 were badly damaged. The gliderborne part of the operation had not been a great success, except at Maleme. Losses had been heavy, owing to heavy small-arms fire from the defenders.

Hitler, on receiving news of General Student's costly victory, was appalled at the heavy losses suffered by the airborne force, and forbade any more large-scale airborne operations. From now on the airborne troops would fight on the ground and not be carried to battle by air. Crete proved to be the graveyard of German airborne forces; their run of successes had ended.

Operation 'Eiche'

The rescue of Mussolini on 12 September 1943

With the Allied Forces' invasion of mainland Italy imminent, after the successful Allied landings in Sicily in July 1943, the Italians began to negotiate an armistice with the Allies, contrary to the wishes of the German leader, Adolf Hitler. Part of the Allies' demands in the negotiations was that the Italian Fascist dictator Benito Mussolini, was to be handed over to them to be put on trial for alleged war crimes.

To meet the Allies' demands the then King of Italy, Victor Emmanuel, ordered the arrest of Mussolini, and at 17:20 on 25 July 1943, this was carried out by Police Captains Aversa and Frigani at the Villa Savoia, Rome, after Mussolini's leaving an audience with the King.

Hitler, on hearing of Mussolini's arrest, ordered his airborne forces commander General Kurt Student to effect Mussolini's release so that he could be used as a figurehead leader in a puppet Italian Government which would continue the war in Italy. General Student summoned SS Captain Otto (Scarface) Skorzeny of the SS Friedenthal (Special Forces Unit) to Hitler's Headquarters in East Prussia on 26 July 1943, and directed him to locate and rescue Mussolini, then bring him back to Germany.

After his arrest, Mussolini had been moved several times by his captors to different places in Italy in case an attempt might be made to rescue him. On 8 September 1943, the Italians surrendered and signed an armistice with the Allies, and by then Mussolini had been moved to what was thought to be an impregnable location, the Albergo Rifugia ski resort hotel perched on top of a 9,050-foot-high peak of the Gran Sasso Massif in the Apennines, sixty-five miles north-east of Rome. The only access to the hotel was by cable car as the ground dropped sharply away on all sides. In front of the hotel was a small rocky plateau, behind the hotel a sheer drop. It was guarded by 250 carabinieri, commanded by General Mario Gueli, and the only contact with the outside world was by radio to the Italian Government and the cable car.

Skorzeny, having learned of Mussolino's location from intercepted Italian radio traffic, studied aerial photographs of the mountain where he was held and saw that there was what appeared to be a small, flat, triangular piece of land behind the hotel which he estimated could be used for a landing area.

General Student and Skorzeny debated as to the method of landing a rescue force: a parachute landing was ruled out due to the altitude and small proposed DZ behind the hotel. A ground assault would require a large force of mountain-trained troops, probably with heavy casualties, which left the choice between helicopters or gliders or a combination of both. Finally it was decided that the assault troops would use DFS 230C-1 assault gliders fitted with nose-braking powder rockets to reduce their landing run and one Focke-Angelis FA 223 helicopter to fly out Mussolini.

Skorzeny moved his assault force, the Skorzeny Sturm Abteilung (Storm Troop) to Practica di Mari Airfield, near Rome, which was still in German hands. As Mussolini was guarded by Italian carabinieri it was decided to include an Italian army officer, General Antonio Spoleti, who might be able to prevail on the guards not to fight and give Mussolini up without bloodshed to their former allies.

By 12 September, Skorzeny's force was ready for the rescue, but the FA 223 helicopter went unserviceable and a Fiesler 156 Storch (Stork) had to be used instead. The Storch could carry two passengers and a pilot (the normal payload was 870 lb) and this remarkable aircraft could fly as slow as 32 mph and land in from 5 to 18 yd depending on terrain and head wind. The take-off run depended on load but could be as little as fifty yards. In a strong head wind the aircraft could almost hover on landing.

At 13:00 on 12 September the rescue force was towed off from Practica di Mari in twelve DFS 230C-1 gliders with the Storch piloted by General Student's personal pilot, Captain Hans Gerlach, flying behind. A short time later the assault force arrived over the moutain-top hotel where Mussolini was being held. As they approached, however, Skorzeny saw that the intended LZ behind the hotel was not flat as shown in the aerial photographs, but steeply sloping and useless as a LZ. Making a rapid decision he decided to crash-land his force on the rocky ground in front of the hotel. One by one the DFS gliders crash-landed on the rocky plateau; the Sturm Abteilung Skorzeny rapidly emerged from them and raced for the hotel with Skorzeny and Spoleti in the van. Spoleti was shouting at the top of his voice for the guards not to shoot and the stunned captors did not open fire. Skorzeny crashed into the hotel, smashing the radio set on the ground floor before running to Mussolini's room. Neither the Italian guards nor the German attackers had fired a shot in the storming of the hotel.

Skorzeny, standing stiffly to attention, informed Mussolini that Hitler had sent him to rescue him and take him forthwith to Germany. The bemused Duce accompanied Skorzeny to the front of the hotel where Captain Gerlach had landed the tiny Storch, and he and Skorzeny squeezed their ample figures into the two passenger seats. Gerlach held the Storch on full throttle with the brakes on, and twelve of Skorzeny's men held onto the wings and tailplane as he chose the best take-off run he could. Releasing the brakes and signalling the troops away, Gerlach took the Storch off and staggered off the edge of the plateau and dived steeply into the valley below. After a few moments he managed to get the aircraft into level flight and set course for Practica di Mari airfield.

On arrival at the airfield, Mussolini was taken by the Luftwaffe to Vienna, then Munich, and finally to Hitler's HQ, the Wolfschanze (Wolf's Lair) near Rastenburg in East Prussia, to be met by the Führer. Skorzeny was promoted to major and awarded the Knight's Cross of the Iron Cross.

Mussolini established a puppet Italian Government in northern Italy, the Republica Sociale Italiana, to continue the war against the Allies which was being fought in Italy by the Germans. But by April 1945, the Germans were beaten and retreating northwards to Austria, and Italy was in the hands of Italian partisans. Mussolini and his mistress, Claretta Petacci, were captured by partisans and on 28 April, 1945, both were shot by Walter Audisio of the Volunteer Freedom Corps. The next day their mutilated bodies were hung upside down in the Piazzale Loreto, Milan. The daring rescue mission by Skorzeny and his men in their gliders had merely gained the Duce nineteen more months of life and puppet power before his end at the hands of his fellow countrymen.

IV

German Military Gliders

Blohm & Voss BV 40

Bomber interceptor glider fighter. Designed to combat Allied day bombers over Germany by being towed to high altitude – then released to glide against the bomber formations at high speed, making only one attack with its two cannon before gliding to the ground.

Description: High wing monoplane constructed of wood and metal, with a fuselage 18 ft 8 in long. Cockpit section of welded metal sides, and floor with 120-mm armoured glass glazing to protect the pilot against defensive gunfire whilst making his sole attacking pass. The centre section was also made of metal sheeting but the rear section was of wooden construction as was the tailplane. The pilot lay in a prone position with his chin on a rest and his outstretched feet controlling the rudder pedals behind him. This position caused a strain on the neck and was not popular. The 26 ft wings were of wooden construction with flaps capable of being lowered to 80 degrees to give a short landing run but a flap angle of 50 degrees was normally used. The undercarriage was a simple two-wheeled trolley used for take-off and was jettisoned when airborne. Landing was on an extendable skid under the cockpit. All up weight was 2,100 lb and the normal tug aircraft was either a FW 190, Bf 109 or the twin-engined Bf 110.

At the end of 1944 the first production order of 200 was stopped. As far as is known, the glider was not used in combat and very few were made. The first BV 40-V1, PN-UA, made its maiden towed flight in May 1944, and there was a pre-production order of nineteen. However, the glider crashed on landing on its second flight in June. Another prototype BV 40-V2 made two test flights. The BV V3 was used for static tests only but the BV V4 and V5 were used for air testing. The BV V6 made the only flight of any towed duration in July 1944, but with the last prototype – the V7 – production was stopped.

It was calculated that the glider would attain a diving speed in an attack pass of 559 mph, but that speed was never reached. The concept of a glider fighter was novel; the pilot, though, would have had little time to fire the 35 rounds from each of his two cannon in a single diving pass.

DFS 230

The first military assault glider in the world and the first to be used as such on operations at Fort Eben Emael, Belgium, on 10 May 1940.

Developed from an experimental meteorological research glider design of 1932 by the Rhon Rossitten Company and taken over by the German Gliding Research Institute (DFS) in 1933, the DFS 230 had a 37 ft fuselage of rectangular section welded steel tubing covered with fabric. Troop entry was by a door at the rear of the high wing on the port side. Eight troops plus 600 lb of equipment could be carried, or an equivalent payload. The single pilot gained entry through a hinged cockpit cover. The 72 ft span wings were of plywood construction fabric covered with ailerons and trim tabs; a panel underneath the starboard wing could be used for equipment stowage. Both wings were single braced and strutted. A machine-gun could be fitted behind the pilot's seat and on the front fuselage.

A simple two-wheeled trolley undercarriage, which could be jettisoned after tow-off, was fitted under the fuselage, with landing on a central sprung skid extending from the fuselage nose to the troop cabin. All up maximum weight was 4,630 lb. Towing speed was 180 mph maximum with a normal towing speed of 112 to 130 mph.

The towing tug was usually a Ju 52/3m, either with a 130 ft tow rope or a small rigid tow bar (*Starrschlepp*). The rigid bar enabled both night and bad weather flying when normal tow rope towing was unsafe.

About 1,569 DFS 230 gliders were produced in Germany and Czechoslovakia during the war and various marks of the glider were made.

DFS 230A	Dual controls.
DFS 230B/FA	Focke Achgelis 225 rotor glider. Fuselage of a DFS 230B with the wings removed and unpowered rotor blades.
DFS 230C-1	Fitted with braking rockets in the nose to reduce landing run. Used in Operation 'Eiche' to rescue Mussolini from captivity.

DFS 230 V7

Military assault or freight transport glider, designed by Hunerjager to improve the capacity and speed of the DFS 230 series, but not a direct descendant, rather a new design completed in 1943.

It was similar in appearance to the DFS 230 series, but designed to carry fifteen troops and their equipment plus two pilots. A freight cargo could be loaded through a removable hatch on top of the fuselage and through two more smaller cargo holds on both sides of the fuselage, to hold a total weight of between 2,530 and 3,850 lb.

The wing span was 63 ft 8 in, and fuselage length 41 ft. Gliding speed was estimated at 200 mph and towing speed 185 mph.

A prototype was built and test-flown, but the glider did not go into production; it would have been designated the DFS 230 F1.

DFS 331 V1

Designed by the DFS 230 designer Dr Hans Jacob to meet a requirement for a larger glider. Construction similar to DFS 230 but with a load capacity of

5,500 lb. Twin braced tailplane with tail skid and twin landing skids and trolley lift-off undercarriage. Wing span 75 ft. Fuselage length 52 ft. The pilot's canopy raised to port above transparent nose section for greater visibility and to mount a machine-gun. Gliding speed of up to 200 mph and towing speed of 160 mph.

Only one prototype was built and flown in 1941 and the programme was abandoned in favour of the Go 242.

Messerschmitt Me 321 Gigant

Conceived with the invasion of Britain in mind – design work on the Me 321 was started by Messerschmitt in 1940. The prototype Me 321 V1 first flew at Leipheim on 25 February 1941, towed by a four-engined Ju 90 tug which however was found to be underpowered for the heavy 75,840 to 86,860 lb load.

The specification originally issued to Messerschmitt was as a heavy cargo or troop transport glider designated the Me 263 but this was altered in December 1940 to the Me 321V-1.

Description: Fuselage 92 ft long, of rectangular section welded steel tubing, fabric-covered. Nose section loading doors opening outwards hinged to each side of the fuselage to give direct access to a 36 ft × 11 ft cargo hold with a $19\frac{1}{2}$-ton maximum load. A special wooden deck could be fitted to carry up to 200 troops. Two 7.9-mm MG 15 could be fired from mountings in the nose doors; other gun positions were through the side windows of the fuselage.

Five – later six – aircrew members were carried: one – later two – pilots, a radio operator, two gunners and a loadmaster.

The undercarriage consisted of a four-wheel jettisonable trolley for lift-off. Landing was on four sprung-steel skids under the nose and centre of the fuselage. A braking arrester chute was fitted to the rear fuselage to shorten the landing run.

Both high wings were single braced, each with two V struts. The 180 ft 6 in wing was constructed of welded steel tubing and wooden formers covered with fabric and plywood. The whole of the trailing edge was used for flying controls – the inner sections as ailerons and the outer sections as flaps. Four – later six – assisted take-off rockets could be fitted under each wing, each rocket giving 1,100 lb thrust for a short time. The tailplane was of wooden construction and hinged to change the flying incidence by 7.5 degrees.

Owing to the weight of the glider, a special tug, the Heinkel Zwilling, was evolved by joining together two He 111s. A new constant chord centre wing section with an additional engine was inserted between the two fuselages, making a powerful five-engined tug of unusual appearance. Twelve of these tugs were built and saw operational use. Until the He 111Z was available to tow the Me 321, three Bf 110 twin-engined aircraft were used to tow one Me 321 in a triple tow arrangement. The three tugs took off in V formation; the lead tug had a 328 ft long tow rope and the other two ropes, 262 feet in length, were attached to the other two aircraft taking-off line abreast. The 66 ft difference in the lead tug's rope was supposed to give a safety margin to avoid collisions on the runway on tow-off.

The Me 321 went into production as the Me 321A, and later as the Me 321B-1, the latter being the dual control mark. A total of 200 were made in both Marks and were used on operations on the Eastern Front until 1943, when the surviving gliders were moved to the south of France for use as troop and fuel transports.

Messerschmitt Me 323 Gigant

Developed from 1941 as a motorised version of the Me 321 B1 Gigant.

Me 323 V2	Prototype with six Gnome Rhône (French) engines for non-towed take-off and free flight under own power. Designed as a prototype for the Me 323D Series.
Me 323 D	Developed from the Me 323 V2 and adapted in preference to the four-engined Me 323 C. Built as a powered aircraft rather than an adaption of the Me 321. Two machine-guns in nose door and two dorsal gun turrets on top of fuselage behind the wing line. Three machine-gun mountings either side through fuselage windows. More machine guns were later added to the series. Six to eight fuel tanks and a capacity of 1,568 gallons gave a range of 620 miles depending on load and speed. Up to 120 troops could be carried.
Me 322 V13 and V14	Prototypes for the Me 323 E1.
Me 323 E	Improved fuel capacity. Increased firepower with a 20-mm cannon in a gun turret fitted to each wing.
Me 323 E-2 W/t	Weapon carrier escort. (*Waffentrager*). Heavily armed to act as escort for other Me 323s but only one aircraft built. Carried eleven 20-mm cannon and four machine-guns. Four of the cannon in two gun turrets on each wing – one in nose turret and three each side forward and rear of fuselage.
Me 323 F	Development of the Me 323 E with more powerful engines and an increased load carrying ability.
Me 323 G	Further development with redesigned air frame – partly constructed only.

The Me 323 series saw service in North Africa and on the Eastern Front and performed well, but owing to its large size and low speed was vulnerable to antiaircraft fire and fighter attack. Production stopped in 1941, with 198 of the series being delivered to the Luftwaffe.

Gotha: Kalkert KA 430

Cargo and troop carrying glider, put into production but after a few were built the design was abandoned.

Description, KA 430 A0: High wing monoplane with a 64 ft wingspan of plywood and fabric covering. 43 ft fuselage of welded steel tubing, fabric-covered and extending into a single boom to the single tailplane. Permanent tricycle undercarriage. Rear bottom hinged loading ramp door at end of upswept fuselage. Machine-gun turret mounted on top of fuselage behind cockpit. Armoured floor for dual control cockpit. Twelve troops or 3,000 lb load could be carried.

Junkers Ju 322 Mammut

In November 1940 the German Air Ministry issued a joint specification to Junkers (*Warschau-Ost*) and Messerschmitt (*Warschau-Sud*) for a large troop- or equipment-carrying glider to be used in the projected invasion of Britain. Junkers' specification was for an all wooden construction glider and Messerschmitt's for a welded steel tube and fabric-covered glider.

Junkers' design was for a 203 ft span flying wing with the cargo or troop hold in the central section; access to the hold was from the front. This central 'fuselage' also carried the raised and offset to port pilot's cockpit as well as two machine-gun barbettes on the leading edges of the wing. A short extension of the 'fuselage' carried the single tail plane. The 'undercarriage' consisted of four steel skids under the central section. A multi-wheeled trolley was used for lift-off, then jettisoned. A test flight of the glider was made in April 1941, with a Junkers Ju 90 being used as a tug. The glider handled badly and had to be landed in a field. Further trials were made but the project was abandoned in May 1941.

Gotha Go 242 A-1

Designed in 1940 by Albert Kalkert of Gothaer Waggonfabrik as a heavy transport and assault glider.

Description, Go 242 A1: High wing monoplane with twin booms extending to a twin tailplane. 52-foot-long fuselage of fabric covered steel of boxcar type section. Top-hinged loading door at rear end of fuselage giving whole-section access to cargo hold, with a maximum loading of 9,000 lb cargo or twenty-one troops with their equipment. Two pilots were used, carried side by side in the large cockpit, with provision for a machine-gun to be mounted on the fuselage roof. Three more light machine-guns could also be mounted – one on each side of the fuselage and one at the rear end through the loading door. Eighty-foot wing span, constructed of fabric-covered wood and plywood and with normal flying controls. Twin-wheel take-off trolley jettisonable; landing was on three steel skids, one under the nose and two under the central fuselage, fitted with shock-absorbing struts.

Production of the glider commenced after the test programmes of the two prototypes, the V1 and V2; first deliveries being made to the Luftwaffe in August 1941, and by December 1941 some 250 had been delivered.

Various Marks of the Go 242 were made:

Go 242 A-2	Assault glider. Fitted with arrester parachute at rear and different loading door arrangement.
Go 242 B-1 and B-2	Fitted with permanent undercarriage and stronger cargo hold deck.
Go 242 B-3 and B-4	Adapted for paratroop dropping via the rear loading doors.
Go 242 B-5	Dual controls and improved rudder controls.
Go 242 C-1	Adopted for waterborne landings by fitting floats under wings and fuselage.

Gliding speed was up to 180 mph; normal towing speed up to 150 mph down to 120 mph. A total of some 1,530 gliders was made, and the glider saw operational service.

Gotha Go 244

Motorised version of the Go 242 glider designated the Go 244 B-1, B2, B4, and B5, adapted Go 242 B glider fitted with two 700 hp Gnome Rhône air-cooled radial engines. One hundred and seventy-four conversions are believed to have been made. Cruising speed about 155 mph with a range of 450 miles. Maximum load 5,950 lb.

Gotha Go 345 (Project)

Projected assault glider which could be fitted with two small jet engines under the wings. No production gliders were made and only one prototype Go 345 B was assembled.

Description, Go 345 A: Assault glider. High wing monoplane with a 69 ft wingspan. Wings and tailplane of plywood-covered wooden construction with fabric-covered control surfaces. Fuselage 42 ft 7 in long of fabric-covered welded steel tubing. Two top-hinged exit doors either side for rapid deployment of the eight troops and two pilots carried. Two wheeled take-off trolley, jettisonable after take-off. Extendable sprung landing skid for landing.

Go 345 B: Cargo glider. Specification as for the Go 345 A but without side doors – exit being via front nose section – including cockpit which lifted upwards in a manner similar to the Waco CG-4A Hadrian.

V

British Military Glider Forces History 1940–1957

O N 10 May 1940 Hitler unleashed his armies and invaded Belgium, Holland and Luxemburg in a Blitzkrieg (lightning war) attack spearheaded by glider-borne and parachute troops. Smashing their way forward in five main thrusts, the Germans won the first round of the Second World War in Europe. By 17 June 1940 most of the British forces, together with a number of French troops, had been evacuated to Britain, which now stood alone against the Germans.

But even in those dark days there were far-sighted men planning for a return to mainland Europe. On 5 June, before the cross-channel evacuation was completed, Lieutenant-Colonel Dudley Clarke, a General Staff officer and Military Assistant to Sir John Dill, Chief of the Imperial General Staff, conceived the idea of forming special forces to attack the enemy by all means possible, including raiding across the North Sea and the English Channel. The same day Sir John Dill broached the idea to the Prime Minister, who wholeheartedly gave his blessing and support, subject to the demands of war on British forces.

Accordingly, on 7 June, Section MO9 was formed at the British War Office under the command of Brigadier Lund, Deputy Director of Military Operations. Five days later, Lieutenant-General Sir Alan Bourne, Adjutant, Royal Marines, was placed in command of operations against the enemy. Working with enthusiasm and speed, he planned and mounted a small raid on the French coast on the night of 23/24 June by the new force, who were to be known as Commandos, a name chosen for them by Clarke, Lund and Dill.

MO9 decided to form ten Commandos, each of ten men, and volunteers were solicited from the British armed forces – in the face of some resistance from certain quarters, for commanding officers were reluctant to lose their best men to some unknown unit.

On 22 June, Prime Minister Churchill sent a memo to the Chief of Staff:

We ought to have a Corps of at least 5,000 parachute troops. I hear that something is being done to form such a Corps but only I believe on a small scale. Advantage must be taken of the summer to train these Forces who can none the less play their part meanwhile as shock troops in Home Defence. Pray let me have a Note from the War Office on the subject.

Two days later Major John Rock, Royal Engineers, was called to the War Office in London and placed in charge of British airborne forces, but without any specific brief whatsoever. No instructions were given to him as to training, weapons, mode of transport or objectives, probably because at that dark time no one knew what was going to happen – except that Britain would never surrender. It was difficult to contemplate the liberation of Europe with the Germans poised to invade Britain across the English Channel.

Major Rock was posted to RAF Ringway, three miles from Altrincham, Cheshire, (now Manchester Airport) to train and organize British airborne forces. RAF Ringway had been selected and re-named the RAF Central Landing School with Group Captain L.G. Harvey as Station Commander, as it was considered ideal for training purposes. Major Rock, with Squadron Leader Louis Strange, DSO MC DFC and Wing Commander Sir Nigel Normal CBE, began planning and training.

On 19 September 1940 a Glider Training Squadron was formed with Tiger Moth aircraft as tugs and Kirby Kite ex-civil gliders. Two sections for glider training were formed, which later became No. 1 Glider Flying School and the Airborne Forces Experimental Establishment.

At this time there were no British military gliders and an appeal went out to owners of civil gliders to loan or donate them to the embryo gliding school. The appeal was well answered, and a mass of civil gliders arrived at Ringway, where they were soon in use as trainers for glider pilots. Winch-launching was used when there were no tug aircraft available.

On 26 October 1940 the first British glider and tug demonstration was carried out, using two ex-civil sailplanes towed by two Avro 504 tugs. Since there were no British military gliders, the Ministry of Aircraft Production issued specification X10/40 for an assault and training glider capable of carrying eight troops and a pilot. General Aircraft Ltd (GAL) took up the specification and some four months later the prototype GAL 48 Hotspur Mark I flew successfully.

An initial order for 400 gliders was given but the Hotspur, when tested, did not come up to the original requirements as an assault glider and was relegated to a training role. A total of 1,012 Hotspurs were built in its three marks but it was never used operationally.

In anticipation of the forthcoming Hotspurs, Hawker Hector aircraft were allocated as tugs and the training unit moved to RAF Thame on 28 December 1940. On 21 February 1941 the first Hector tugs arrived but it was not until 6 April that the first Hotspur glider, serial number BV 125, arrived. It was in use on trials on the 9th. On the 26th an exercise was mounted for the Prime Minister, in which BV 125 and five Kirby Kite gliders, accompanied by six RAF paratroop-carrying converted Armstrong-Whitworth Whitley bombers flew past on a combined operation.

Discussion and argument still raged as to which service the men who would fly the gliders would belong – the RAF or the Army. Finally, it was decided that the glider pilots would belong to the Army but would be trained in flying by the RAF. The Royal Army Service Corps had the distinction of providing the first glider pilots to be trained for the Army. Lance-Corporal L. Morris, Lance-Corporal

Baker, Driver M. Cooper and Lance-Corporal H.J. Harrison were the pioneers.

On 20 May 1941 the Germans attacked and captured the island of Crete with gliderborne troops and paratroops, but suffered such appalling losses that Hitler forbade any more airborne assaults by German forces. The British however had no such thoughts and in November 1941 a full-scale training programme for 400 army glider pilots began which required a much larger training establishment. On 1 December the Glider Training Unit was divided to become Nos. 1 & 2 Glider Training Schools. Later Nos. 3, 4 and 5 were formed, together with Nos. 101 and 102 (Glider) Operational Training Units and a Glider Pilots Instructors School.

The 31st Independent Brigade Group had been reformed on 10 October as the 1st Air Landing Brigade, to incorporate the 1st Royal Ulster Rifles, 2nd Oxfordshire and Buckinghamshire, 2nd South Stafford and the 1st Border Regiments. On the 29th Major-General F.A.M. (Boy) Browning was appointed General Officer Commanding (GOC), Airborne Forces, with a small staff working from offices in London. The 1st Air Landing Brigade was to be part of the British 1st Airborne Division.

The headquarters of the 1st Airborne Division was established on 1 November in London and on 10 December Brigadier G.F. Hopkinson assumed command of the 1st Air Landing Brigade Group.

As more than half of the airborne forces were to be carried by glider, volunteers were sought for the formation of the Glider Pilot Regiment (GPR), which was duly formed on 21 December. The now Lieutenant-Colonel Rock was appointed Commanding Officer of the 1st Battalion of the Glider Pilot Regiment, with Major (later Brigadier) George J.S. Chatterton as second in command. Major Chatterton had served in No. 1 Squadron, RAF, as a fighter pilot but after receiving injuries in an air crash in 1935, which took him off flying, he had transferred to the Queen's Royal Regiment of the Army.

The establishment of the Glider Pilot Regiment was to be two battalions of six companies of sergeant pilots, who, apart from being glider pilots, also had to be trained fighting soldiers who would fight as soldiers on the ground after landing. Flying training on light aircraft was to be under the direction of the RAF at Elementary Flying Training Schools (EFTS), before glider pilot training began.

With the formation of the Glider Pilot Regiment, it was found that aircraft and air crews were needed for glider tug duties on an ever-increasing scale – so on 15 January 1942 the Army Cooperation Command of the RAF formed No. 38 Wing, under the command of the now Group Captain Sir Nigel Norman, specifically for airborne forces' training and operations. At first the wing only possessed eight aircrews, and it was some time before it reached its establishment of an EFTS, two Glider training schools, two Glider operational training units and one Glider exercise squadron – plus two units for paratroop training.

No. 38 Wing began to take shape: on 22 January 1942 No. 297 Squadron, RAF, was formed at RAF Netheravon, on Salisbury Plain, Wiltshire, from the Parachute Exercise Squadron, and received Whitley Mark 5s in February for paratroop dropping. The squadron moved to RAF Hurn near Bournemouth on 5 June.

No. 296 Squadron, RAF, which had been formed at RAF Ringway on 25

January 1942 from the Glider Exercise Squadron – using Hector and Hart aircraft as glider tugs – moved to RAF Netheravon on 1 February as 296 (Glider Exercise) Squadron. In June of that year the squadron received AW Whitleys as glider tugs. In July the squadron was divided into two flights, 296A and 296B, with 296A moving to RAF Hurn on 5 July – leaving 296B at Netheravon as the Glider Exercise Squadron.

Another airborne forces squadron, No. 295, was raised at RAF Netheravon on 3 August 1942, and began using Whitley bombers on leaflet-dropping sorties over France. By February 1943 the squadron had converted to Halifax bombers and on 1 May moved to RAF Holmesley South, near Christchurch, Hampshire. A Glider Pilot Regiment camp was established on the bleak Salisbury Plain at Tilshead, eleven miles north of Salisbury and adjacent to RAF Shrewton, opened in 1940 as a grass reserve landing grounding and satellite of Netheravon. It had been decided that the larger gliders would need two pilots; the 1st pilot, a staff sergeant; the 2nd pilot, a sergeant. The 1st pilot would fly the glider on take-off and landing; the 2nd while on tow and take over if the 1st were killed or injured. Military training commenced for the glider pilots and after three to four weeks the first pilots went to an RAF EFTS for eight weeks' flying training, usually on DH Tiger Moth aircraft, followed by eight weeks at a GTS on Hotspur gliders. On successful completion of the course a further four weeks was spent converting to the larger Horsa gliders which were beginning to come into service. The 2nd glider pilots had a shorter course of four weeks at an EFTS followed by three to four weeks' glider flying training. The 1st pilot would wear a flying brevet of a lion over a crown between two outstretched wings and the 2nd pilot a brevet with the letter G between two outstretched wings. The flying badges would be worn on the left breast over the top pocket of uniform.

Sadly, in October 1942 Lieutenant-Colonel Rock was killed as the result of a night flying accident in a Hotspur glider at Shrewton. The glider tow rope broke in flight and Colonel Rock tried to land in total darkness: the glider struck a pole and its ballast load of sandbags broke loose on impact crushing Colonel Rock and his co-pilot. Colonel Rock died of his injuries in a military hospital a few days later. With Rock dead, Chatterton took command of the 1st Battalion and handed over his command of the recently formed 2nd Battalion to Lieutenant-Colonel Iain Murray.

As the headquarters of 38 Wing, under the now Air Commodore Norman, was at RAF Netheravon, premises were required nearby in which the RAF and 1st Airborne Division planning staff could work side by side. The choice fell on Syrencot House, an old Georgian house which stood on its own grounds by the River Avon, and on the road from the military barracks at Bulford and the airfield at RAF Netheravon. Elements of RAF and Army Staff moved into the house, which was given the codename 'Broadmoor' but soon became known as 'the Madhouse' from the pace of work there and the fact that all the windows were barred and there was but one key for the building. (The house still stands – little changed – and is leased to a local firm of building contractors. A plaque was recently placed to the right of the front porch to commemorate its wartime use.)

On 19 November 1942 the first British gliderborne troops were used in an abortive attempt to destroy the Norsk plant at Vermork in German-occupied Norway. It was known that heavy water was being produced there for German atomic bomb research. Two Halifaxes of 38 Wing towing two Horsa gliders carrying men of the Royal Engineers took off from RAF Skitten, near Wick in northern Scotland, and flew to Norway. The two Horsas and one Halifax crashed in Norway in bad weather killing most of the occupants. Those who survived were later murdered by the Germans under Hitler's infamous order that all Commando forces be killed on capture.

The 6th Airborne Division was formed at Syrencot House on 3 May 1943 under Major-General Richard Gale. The prefix 6th had been chosen to fool the Germans into thinking there were six British airborne divisions, when in fact there were only two.

Coming into use and still highly secret was a homing device known as Eureka/Rebecca. This was designed to pin-point DZs and LZs for paratroop, glider and supply operations. Invented by the British Telephone Research Establishment (TRE) the beacon was in use by the end of 1942. The ground Eureka (old Greek for 'I have found it') set was contained in its packing case, measuring 30 in × 15 in × 10 in and weighing 100 lb. The device consisted of a five-foot long aerial mounted on a seven-foot high tripod with the set underneath. Operation was simple. The set was unpacked, tripod and aerial erected and the set switched on to emit eight watts of power. The airborne Rebecca sent out a coded signal on 214 megacycles to which the Eureka replied on 219 megacycles. Direction and distance was then shown on the airborne set which pin-pointed the LZ. As the device was top-secret an explosive charge was built into the Eureka so that it could be quickly destroyed if in danger of being captured. The charge was fitted in the base and operated by a small plunger, which was pulled out, then depressed to fire the explosive.

With the Germans beaten in North Africa, plans were made for the invasion of Sicily early in July. The 1st Air Landing Brigade, under Brigadier F.H.W. Hicks, comprising the 1st Battalion, Border Regiment, commanded by Lieutenant-Colonel G.V. Britten and the 2nd Battalion, South Staffords, commanded by Lieutenant-Colonel W.D.H. McCardie, embarked for Tunisia to assault Sicily by glider in the first large-scale operation by the British.

An immediate problem arose as to the availability of gliders to carry the air landing troops from North Africa to Sicily. The United States had begun to transport their Waco CG-4A gliders to North Africa but these were too small to carry a jeep and a gun. Each glider could carry either a jeep or a gun, so two gliders would have to be used. No. 38 Wing attempted to solve this problem by flying out the larger Horsa gliders towed by Halifax aircraft the 1,400 miles from England to North Africa. This solution, Operation 'Beggar' (or as it is sometimes called, 'Turkey Buzzard') was the brainchild of Group Captain Tom Cooper and Squadron Leader A.M.B. Wilkinson, and was carried out by 295 Squadron. The first Horsa reached North Africa on 28 June 1943, only twelve days before the Sicily D-Day.

Unfortunately, Air Commodore Sir Nigel Norman, Air Officer Commanding 38 Wing, was killed in an air crash on 20 May whilst en route from England to

North Africa. So ended the career of one of the pioneers of the British air landing forces. His place as Air Officer Commanding 38 Wing was taken by Air Commodore W.H. Primrose CBE, DFC.

In spite of the arrival of Horsa gliders in North Africa, there were still not enough gliders to air lift the 1st Air Landing Brigade to battle, and the US Waco CG-4A glider had to be used in large numbers, towed by USAAF aircraft, whose crews had very little glider-towing training and no combat experience. Nevertheless, the operation, codenamed 'Ladbrooke', went ahead as an Anglo-American venture and at 18:48 on 9 July 1943 the first combinations began to take off from Tunisia for Sicily.

Adverse weather conditions prevailed en route to Sicily, and owing to the inexperience of the tug pilots the gliders had to release too far offshore; many of the gliders fell in the sea. Only one Horsa, piloted by Staff Sergeant Galpin of the Glider Pilot Regiment, landed on its LZ, with two other Horsas landing nearby who were able to join the battle. The glider troops captured their objective, the vital Ponte Grande bridge, with a small force. Although the enemy retook the bridge, it was again taken by the British seaborne forces an hour later.

Operation 'Fustian', on 13 July, was not long in following – the objective being to capture another vital bridge in Sicily and allow the ground armies to push northwards. A small gliderborne force was to carry the guns of the Royal Artillery in Horsa and Waco CG-4As and the main force of paratroops would be carried in Dakota aircraft of the USAAF. Unfortunately, as the Allied aircraft flew over the Allied naval forces, they were mistaken for enemy aircraft and the ships opened up with heavy anti-aircraft fire, causing damage and casualties to the aircraft and gliders. Again very few gliders reached their LZs although a Horsa piloted by Sergeant White, of the Glider Pilot Regiment, managed to land one hundred yards from the bridge objective. A bitter fire fight ensued round the bridge which was taken, lost, then retaken finally on 16 July by the Durham Light Infantry of the ground armies.

In spite of the heavy losses in men and gliders – the Glider Pilot Regiment alone lost fifty-seven pilots – the potential of the glider was still appreciated and the hard-won experience was incorporated in future glider operations. Plans were being laid for the invasion of France, in which the glider forces would play a crucial role.

The large tank-carrying Hamilcar glider was now coming into service and the 6th Airborne Reconnaissance Regiment, Royal Armoured Corps, was formed at Larkhill on 14 January 1944. For the first time in history tanks would be gliderborne to the battlefield, as part of the 6th Airborne Division.

'Voodoo' was the name under which a flight took place in June 1943 that has never been equalled. This was made by an RCAF C-47 aircraft towing a Waco CG-4A glider loaded with supplies over the North Atlantic from Canada to Britain, the 3,500-mile flight being made in stages via Greenland and Iceland.

In August and September 1943 38 Wing carried out further long-range glider towing flights: Operation 'Elaborate' in which Horsas were towed from England to North Africa. Again the RAF and the Glider Pilot Regiment lost men and aircraft due to enemy action and weather conditions.

By October 1943, 38 Wing had expanded so much that is was reformed as a group, with Air Vice Marshal L.N. Hollinghurst in command; working alongside 6th Airborne Division it laid plans for the invasion of France. No. 46 Group, RAF, was formed on 1 January 1944, under Air Commodore L. Darvall, as an airborne forces transport group and equipped with American supplied C-47 Dakotas.

During the spring of 1944 training and exercises were carried out, each exercise getting larger. Mass daylight glider landings were practised, and seventy-four gliders landed in twelve minutes on the north and south airfields of Netheravon. Night-glider landing exercises were less successful, with a high rate of accidents. There is very little level surface at RAF Netheravon, as I remember only too well; it is up and down hill in all directions.

The planning staff for the invasion of France decided to land the seaborne forces on the beaches of Normandy. To protect their left flank 6th Airborne Division was to drop and land during the early hours of D-Day, 6 June 1944. The gliderborne troops were to play a vital role in the airborne operation – 'Tonga'. Two *coup de main* gliderborne units were to take the River Orne and the Caen Canal bridges – Operation 'Deadstick' – and another gliderborne unit the coastal gun battery at Merville with 9th Paratroop Battalion. Other gliders were to land with support equipment for the lightly armed paratroops attacking the Merville Battery. Later on the morning of D-Day another wave of gliders, including four large Hamilcars, were to deliver heavy equipment for the 6th Airborne Division on previously prepared landing strips cleared of obstructions by the paratroops. That was Operation 'Tonga' and in the evening of D-Day Operation 'Mallard' was to take place—7,500 troops of the 6th Air Landing Brigade would be brought in in 256 gliders, including thirty Hamilcars carrying tanks – the first to be air-lifted to battle by gliders in military history.

Both 'Tonga' and 'Mallard' were carried out gallantly and successfully, but at a cost in men and aircraft. Casualties were heavy but not as bad as had been forecast.

In Burma, the legendary Major-General Orde Wingate was fighting the Japanese with troops air-landed behind enemy lines. Beginning in February 1944, Wingate's forces, using US CG-4A Hadrian gliders towed by aircraft of the 1st Air Commando of the USAAF, were landed behind the Japanese lines. Fifty-one gliders landed in remote jungle LZs over a period of time with troops who cleared landing strips for Dakota aircraft to land with more men and equipment. Some of the gliders were snatched off the LZs, but many were abandoned where they landed. By 15 March a strong fighting force had been established behind enemy lines in difficult terrain for airborne operations. Unluckily Wingate himself was killed in an air crash on the 24th, but the campaign continued and by the end of April the main objectives had been achieved by the use of air-landed troops and equipment. For the first time in history, US Sikorsky YR-4 helicopters were used during the operations with success: the shape of things to come in later wars.

In Europe, glider operations were mounted in Yugoslavia, France and Greece. Operation 'Bunghole' involved pilots of the Glider Pilot Regiment flying CG-4A gliders towed by USAAF tugs, carrying a Russian Military Mission to confer with

Marshal Tito, the Yugoslavian resistance leader at his HQ in that country.

Another small but effective operation was 'Dingson', early in August 1944, when ten Waco CG-4A Hadrian gliders towed by the RAF, carried French SAS troops to Brittany to wreak havoc among the Germans and turncoat Russians serving with the German Army, before the arrival of US ground forces.

Striking at a supposed soft underbelly of the enemy in the south of France on 15 August 1944, in Operation 'Dragoon' US and British troops in Hadrian and Horsa gliders landed behind the invasion beaches in support of the seaborne forces.

By August 1944, however, the German army was retreating to the borders of Germany pursued by the Allied armies. Sixteen airborne forces operations were planned but abandoned by the Allies due to the speed of their advance. To 'bounce the Rhine' Field Marshal Montgomery went for a daring plan whereby airborne forces would be landed across the river barriers of the Maas, Waal and Lower Rhine for the ground forces to pass through them, outflank the Siegfried Line and push into Germany. The British 1st Airborne Division was given the task of taking and holding a road bridge over the Lower Rhine. This bridge was the furthest away from the Allied front line and the airborne troops would be in an exposed position till the arrival of the ground forces. The bridge was at Arnhem. Such was the scale of the operation, code-named 'Market', that the RAF was unable to lift all the airborne troops and supplies in one lift. Three air lifts had to be made to carry the 10,000 troops to battle. An armada of 692 tugs and gliders would lift the 1st Air Landing Brigade and divisional troops in three daylight landings on three successive days.

On the mornings of 17, 18 and 19 September 1944 a total of 692 gliders were towed off from bases in England. 621 gliders reached their landing zones, an almost 90 per cent success rate in the largest glider landing so far of the Second World War.

In spite of a bitter and hard fought battle by the valiant troops of 1st Airborne Division against heavy odds, the position became untenable and the gallant remnants of the division were forced to withdraw. The word Arnhem, a name few had heard of, now went round the world. On the night of 25/26 September, the survivors came back across the Rhine. They had fought on for almost ten days instead of an expected two. Their comrades of the Royal Air Force had striven to resupply them and had taken heavy losses without flinching.

With 229 dead, the Glider Pilot Regiment had lost a quarter of the glider pilots that flew in the operation, and many more had been injured; and so 1,500 officer and NCO pilots from the RAF were posted to the strength of the regiment and found themselves flying gliders instead of powered aircraft.

On 9 October 1944 the pilots of the Glider Pilot Regiment ferried Horsa gliders from England to Italy in Operation 'Molten'. Towed by the RAF, thirty-two set out and twenty-seven arrived safely in Italy via France. A week later, on the 16th, twenty Dakota aircraft towed twenty gliders onto the airfield at Megara, Greece, with men and supplies for the paratroops who had dropped there on the 12th.

During the winter of 1944 plans were made for the largest Allied airborne operation yet mounted. Operation 'Varsity' would land the 1st Allied Airborne Army over the River Rhine in a single lift. This would be the first tactical air landing of the war, but this time the airborne troops would be within the covering range of Allied artillery from the beginning of the assault. The hard lessons of Arnhem had been taken to heart and the 6th Airborne Division would not be out on a limb without artillery support.

The airborne troops' task was to land, take and hold ground, whilst behind them the ground forces would cross the River Rhine, pass through the Airborne Division and punch into the heart of Germany.

Before the assault, the Allied air forces pounded the German positions with success aided by the artillery of the land armies poised to attack across the Rhine. With the Germans reeling from the artillery, bomber and fighter-bomber bombardment, Operation 'Varsity' began on the morning of 24 March 1945. From eleven airfields in England an aerial fleet of 386 Horsa and forty-eight Hamilcar gliders were towed off by aircraft of 38 and 46 Groups, carrying the 6th Air Landing Brigade and the divisional troops of the 6th Airborne Division. On the Continent another aerial armada was taking off with the troops of the US 17th Airborne Division. Yet another fleet carried the parachute troops of the 6th Airborne Division.

Both air fleets rendezvoused over the Field of Waterloo in the greatest air armada ever seen in the history of warfare, and flew relentlessly into battle. At 13:00 that day the first of the gliders began to land in the murk and fog of war. Of the British 434 gliders which had been lifted off, 402 (92.63 per cent) landed successfully. But only eighty-eight were undamaged; of the rest, all were hit by flak and small arms fire from the defenders.

On landing, the troops went into battle and seized their objectives and by 10:00 the next day the advancing ground forces had linked up with their airborne comrades. Operation 'Varsity' had been a conspicious success. Yet despite the careful planning and the preliminary bombardment, over 1,000 casualties were sustained that first day. The Glider Pilots suffered 101 dead, of whom fifty-one were from the Royal Air Force – many of whom had gone into battle proudly wearing the red beret of the airborne forces. But the sacrifice had not been in vain – the way ahead into Germany lay clear and a few weeks later on 8 May 1945 the enemy surrendered in Europe.

In the war against the Japanese in the Far East, which was still being waged, the 44th Indian Division was formed, and planning and training went ahead to use gliders to transport them to battle. It had been found that the wooden construction of Horsas was unsuitable for the climate and preference was given to the American steel-framed Waco CG-4A Hadrian. However, the Japanese surrendered to the power of the atomic bomb in August 1945, and World War II came to a close.

With the end of the war, gliderborne troops and glider pilots were no longer needed and units began to be run down. By 1948 only two operational Horsa squadrons were left, at Waterbeach and Netheravon. One Hamilcar squadron remained at Fairford and glider training was concentrated at RAF Upper Heyford as No. 1 Parachute and Glider Training School. The RAF airborne squadrons were also run down: 46 Group was disbanded in March 1950, and 38 Group in February 1951.

By 1950 the Glider Pilot Regiment was reduced to a single squadron. It continued to fly Horsas, but the writing was on the wall for the glider pilots, and helicopters began to take over. On 31 August 1957 the Glider Pilot Regiment was disbanded. Next day the Army Air Corps began life. Gliderborne forces had lasted but a short time in military history: from the dark days of 1940, through the long years of trial and error, to the epic Operation 'Varsity' in 1945, then a slow decline to a redundant end in 1957.

The human cost of the glider was high: a total of 551 British glider pilots lost their lives between 1942 and 1945; their number included fifty-five pilots from the Royal Air Force and two from the Royal Australian Air Force. They are commemorated by a memorial window in a quiet part of Salisbury Cathedral, Wiltshire, where there is a memorial book containing the names of all who died in the glider force. At the foot of the memorial window is their epitaph: 'See that ye hold fast the heritage that we leave you – Yea, and teach your children that never in the coming centuries may their hearts fail or their hands grow weak.'

The names of all those other gallant men who went to war in gliders and did not return are recorded on war memorials in towns, cities, and villages the length and breadth of Great Britain. 'He who would true valour see let him come hither.'

VI

British Military Glider Operations

Operation 'Freshman'

The Germans occupied Norway in April 1940, mainly by airborne assault, and took control of the Norsk Hydro Electric Company's heavy water plant at Vermork. Heavy water (deuterium oxide D_2O) was needed by German scientists for their atomic research programme to produce an atomic bomb.

For the Allies, engaged on their own research, the need to destroy the heavy water installation at Vermork was vital and urgent, and it was decided in September 1942 to make plans for a gliderborne attack on the plant by volunteer specialist troops. Operation 'Freshman', as it was called, was to be the first British gliderborne operation of World War Two.

The plan was for two gliders towed by four-engined tug aircraft to carry a small force to a landing zone (LZ) some distance from the plant. The LZ would be pinpointed by the Norwegian Resistance, using the secret Eureka beacons responding to the Rebecca receivers in the tug aircraft. Each glider would carry fifteen men trained to identify and destroy the heavy water stock and installation at the plant. Escape was to be in plain clothes via Sweden, some ninety-three miles away. The 1st Airborne Division would supply the troops and 38 Wing, RAF, the aircraft, which would take off from the nearest British airfield to Norway. Combined Operations HQ together with Special Operations Executive and Military Intelligence co-operated in the Planning.

The men selected for the operation were volunteers from the Royal Engineers 9th (Airborne) Field Company and the 261st Field Park Company under the command of Lieutenant-Colonel H.C.A. Henniker. The then Group Captain Sir Nigel Norman, 38 Wing, RAF, whose HQ was at Syrencot House, Brigmerston, Wiltshire, together with staff of 1st Airborne Division, also based at Syrencot House, was responsible for providing and training the aircraft and aircrews.

In view of the distance to be covered towing a Horsa glider, Halifax aircraft were decided on, and Halifax crews from 138 and 161 Squadrons, RAF Tempsford, Bedfordshire, were detached to RAF Netheravon, Wiltshire, for a quick Horsa glider towing course. Norman chose three Halifax crews and three Horsa gliders for the operation – two of each were to be used – the third combination being spare aircraft. The nearest RAF airfield to Norway was RAF Skitten, near

Caithness, Scotland, an operational airfield used by RAF Coastal Command and some 400 miles from the target LZ.

On 19 November 1942, after delays due to bad weather conditions and unserviceable aircraft – all was ready and the decision was made to go although available weather data on the LZ was unsatisfactory. At 17:40 Halifax 'A-Able' piloted by Squadron Leader A.M.B. Wilkinson, with his commanding officer Group Captain Tom B. Cooper, as second pilot, took off from Skitten towing a Mark I Horsa glider serial number DP 349, piloted by Staff Sergeant Malcolm F. Strathdee and Sergeant Peter Doig, both of the Glider Pilot Regiment. The fifteen Royal Engineers on board were: OC Lieutenant David A. Methven (aged 20), 2 i/c Lance-Sergeant Frederick Healy (29), Corporal James D. Cairncross (22), Lance-Corporals Trevor L. Masters (25) and Wallis M. Jackson (21), Sappers James F. Blackburn (28), Frank Bonner (25), Robert Norman (22), Eric J. Smith (24), John W. Walsh (21), Thomas W. White (23) and William Jaques (30), and Drivers Peter P. Farrell (26), George Simkins (30), and John G.V. Hunter (22).

The other Halifax tug, 'B' for 'Baker', – serial number W7801 – was piloted by Flight-Lieutenant Arthur R. Parkinson, RCAF, aged 26, with RAF aircrew: Flight-Lieutenant Arthur E. Thomas (32) and Flying Officer Arnold T.H. Haward (28), navigators; Pilot Officer Gerard W. Sewell de Gency (20), 2nd pilot; Flight Sergeant Albert Buckton (23), wireless operator/air gunner; Flight Sergeant George M. Edwards (24), air gunner; and Flight Sergeant James Falconer (20), flight engineer.

The Horsa it towed, serial number HS 114, piloted by Pilot Officer Norman A. Davies, RAAF, and Pilot Officer Herbert J. Fraser, RAAF, both aged 28, carried these fifteen Royal Engineers: OC Lieutenant Alex C. Allen (24), 2i/c Lance-Sergeant George Knowles (28), Corporal John G.L. Thomas (23), Lance Corporals Frederick W. Bray (29) and Alexander Campbell (24), Drivers Ernest W. Bailey (31), John T.V. Belfield (26) and Ernest Pendlebury (25), Sappers Howell Bevan (22), Thomas W. Faulkener (22), Charles H. Grundy (22), Herbert J. Legate, Leslie Smallman, James M. Stephen and Gerard S. Williams (18).

Both combinations set course independently for Egersund on the Norwegian coast, the plan being for them to cross the coast at 10,000 feet to avoid detection by the Germans and for the gliders to be released at that height. The operation was timed so that the gliders did not approach the coast in daylight and for there to be sufficient moonlight for the gliders to land assisted by the Eureka beacons.

An area of 700 yards of level ground at Mossvatnet Lake was to be the LZ, marked by lights and a Eureka beacon. Each glider carried a roll of butter muslin to help the men it landed to conceal it, to keep undetected by the Germans for as long as possible.

At 23:41 the Operations Room at Wick, Scotland, received a radio signal from Halifax 'B' (Flight Lieutenant Parkinson) asking for a course to return to base. Radio direction finding (RDF) gave 'Baker's' position as over the North Sea at latitude 58 degrees 16 minutes north and longitude 00 degrees 17 minutes west. At 23:55 Wick received a radio signal from Halifax 'A' (S/Ldr Wilkinson) stating that their glider had been released in the sea, but RDF readings gave its position as over the mountains of southern Norway. The glider had been released near the coast many miles from the LZ. At 01:51, 20 November, Halifax 'Able' returned to Skitten. Group Captain Cooper reported that 'Able' had successfully crossed the North Sea but the Rebecca receiver in the Halifax had gone unserviceable, reducing navigation to map-reading only. Thick cloud was met some forty miles north of Vemork and the combination could not get out of it. The Halifax was by then on reserve tanks, which were quickly being used up looking for the LZ. Severe icing was encountered, causing both Halifax and glider to lose height over the dangerous montains of Norway. Near Stavanger the iced-up tow rope broke and the Horsa DP 349 had to make a crash-landing on the snow-covered mountains at Fylgjedal. 'Able' had just enough fuel to return to base. The failure of the mission was blamed on the Rebecca receiver going unserviceable and incorrect maps of the Norwegian area.

No further radio messages were received from Halifax 'Baker' and search and rescue plans were put into operation for the daylight hours of 20 November. At 11:05 on the 20th information was received from a Major Barstow of Combined Operations HQ, London, to the effect that agents in Norway had reported aerial activity during the night but no ground activity. All Army and RAF personnel left Skitten on the 20th and returned to Netheravon, and the operation, its result unknown was deemed a failure.

After this abortive mission, the Vermork plant was attacked by the Norwegian Resistance and partially damaged. Then the USAAF bombed the plant, again without complete success. On 20 February 1944, however, whilst the Germans were transporting a stock of heavy water by ferry over Lake Tinn, the ferry was blown up by the Norwegian Resistance and the heavy water cargo was lost to the Germans.

With the end of the war in 1945 enquiries were started by the British as to the fate of the aircrew of Halifax 'Baker' and the troops in the two gliders. It was ascertained that the Horsa glider DP 349 which had been towed by Halifax 'Able' had crash-landed on mountains at Fylgjdal, near Lysefjord, Rogoland Province, killing pilots Strathdee and Doig, and occupants Methven, Healey, Norman, Jaques, Simkins, and Hunter. Corporal Cairncross, Lance-Corporal Masters, Sapper John Smith, and Driver Farrell had been taken prisoner by the Germans and either poisoned or shot by a Dr Seeling, an SD Warrant Officer Hoffmann, a CID Inspector Peterson, a Private Feurlein and other Germans, on 23/24 November 1942, and their bodies thrown into the sea between Usken/Kuits island and never found. The other five, Lance-Corporal Jackson, Sappers Bonner, Blackburn, Welsh and White, had also been taken prisoner and sent to Grini Concentration Camp, Norway, but were later shot by the Germans in Trandum, Norway, on 18 January 1943, without trial and in obedience to Hitler's infamous *Kommandobefel* (Commando Order) of 18 October 1942, which ordered that all Commandos were to be executed immediately without trial. The remains of the soldiers were exhumed in 1945 and laid to rest in Westre Cemetery, Oslo.

The other Horsa glider, HS 114, in the hands of Pilot Officers Davies and Fraser, and carrying Lieutenant Allen's party of Royal Engineers, had crashed in the mountains north of Helleland. Three had died. The others had been taken prisoner by the Germans and executed after a few hours, again without trial. Their bodies had been thrown stripped into an unmarked grave in the sand. In 1945 the remains were recovered and given a proper burial at Eiganes Cemetery Stavanger, Rogoland, Norway.

Halifax 'Baker' crashed into a mountain at Hestadfjell, Helleland, Rogoland Province, Norway, at 22:45 on 19 November 1942, killing all on board. The bodies were buried roughly by the Germans in a marsh, then dug up the following spring of 1943 and reinterred in herring boxes by local people until the arrival of British troops in 1945. They now lie together at Helleland Cemetery, by the church.

Printed in every German soldier's paybook were 'ten commandments', the first of which read: 'The German soldier will observe the rules of chivalrous warfare. Cruelties and senseless destruction are below this standard'. No. 3 read: 'No enemy who has surrendered will be killed, including partisans and spies – they will be punished by the Courts. Prisoners of war will not be ill-treated.'

The enquiries that led to those responsible for the murder of the four men from Horsa DP 349 being traced resulted in a trial at which Seeling, Hoffmann and Feurlein were found guilty. Seeling and Hoffmann were later executed and Feurlein was handed over to the Russians to answer for atrocities against their troops and was no doubt executed.

For the four gallant soldiers of the 9th (Airborne) Field Company, Corps of Royal Engineers, Corporal James D. Cairncross, Driver Peter P. Farrell, Lance-Corporal Trevor L. Masters and Sapper Eric J. Smith, who have no known grave, a memorial was erected in Eiganes Churchyard, Stavanger, and unveiled on the 8 March 1985. Their sacrifice is also commemorated on the Brookwood Memorial, Surrey, England, 'Lest we Forget'.

Operation 'Beggar' (Turkey Buzzard)

At the end of April 1943, 295 Squadron, of 38 Wing, RAF, was instructed to ferry forty Horsa gliders from England to North Africa for use by air landing forces in the invasion of Sicily. The distance to be flown was 1,350 miles from RAF Portreath, Cornwall, England, to the US base at Salé, near Rabat, in North Africa; then another 1,000 miles over Africa to Tunisia. During the first part of the flight, over the open sea, the combinations would be liable to interception by German aircraft operating out of French bases. The RAF would not be able to provide escorts for much of the journey. There were no alternative landing airfields, so it was England to North Africa in one flight, for the combinations were not allowed to land at Gibraltar. Operation 'Beggar', or 'Turkey Buzzard' – the ferrying of Horsa gliders from England to North Africa between 1 June and 7 July 1943 by 295 Squadron, RAF, and the Glider Pilot Regiment – was the response.

Such an operation had never before been carried out by the RAF or the Glider Pilot Regiment. Aircraft had to be provided, modified and crewed up. RAF aircrew had to be converted to Halifax aircraft and trained in towing Horsa gliders long distances and dropping paratroops as the aircraft might be needed to do both tasks. Ten of the Halifaxes were to be left in North Africa for use on operations there.

At this time, 295 Squadron was based at RAF Netheravon, Wiltshire, with one flight of Mark V Halifaxes (A Flight) and two flights of Whitleys. As Netheravon was a grass airfield with no permanent flarepath, A Flight moved on 13 May 1943 to RAF Holmesley South, Hampshire, with thirteen Halifax aircraft under the command of its flight commander, Squadron Leader A.M.B. Wilkinson, and with the squadron commander, Wing Commander MacNamara. Squadron Leader Wilkinson was the only fully converted Halifax pilot on the squadron, with two others, Flight-Lieutenant Briggs and Flying Officer Tomkins, partly converted. Nine more pilots, Flying Officers Bewick, Blackburn, Collins, Cleaver, Muirhead, Smith, Sizmur and Warrant Officer McCrodden were converted, and three more during May – Flying Officers Horne, Norman and Shannon – while Flying Officer Grant was loaned from RAE Farnborough.

Ten Halifaxes, working in relays, would be required to tow the Horsas to North Africa. But to allow for going unserviceable, seventeen aircraft had to be modified and endurance-tested. Extra fuel tanks were installed in the bomb bays and all excess weight removed. Endurance tests of 1,350 miles were carried out lasting ten flying hours.

In order to reduce the drag of the glider, the Horsa's tricycle undercarriage would be jettisoned by parachute after take-off and the glider would land on its skids in North Africa. A spare undercarriage would be carried, and fitted after landing in North Africa – for the next 1,000-mile leg of the haul to Tunisia. Because of the considerable physical effort required to fly the Horsa on tow, it was decided to use three glider pilots, each doing an hour as 1st pilot, then an hour as 2nd pilot, followed by an hour's rest.

The final British departure airfield was RAF Portreath, near Redruth, Cornwall, where the main runway, running east to west, ended at the top of 295-foot cliffs overlooking the sea. The Whitleys of 295 Squadron were to tow the gliders from Netheravon to Portreath to avoid strain on the Halifaxes, which were flown there.

On 1 June the first combination took off but because of bad weather was forced to return to Portreath after six and a half hours' flying time. On 3 June four combinations took off at first light on a bright clear morning. Two reached Salé that afternoon. Another had to return to base due to bad weather and one had to ditch in the sea some 200 miles north-west of Cap Finisterre when the tow rope broke. The Halifax tug, piloted by Flying Officer Sizmur, returned to Portreath after sending out a rescue message on W/T.

The Horsa, flown by Major Alistair Cooper, Staff Sergeant Dennis Hall and Staff Sergeant Anthony Antopoulos, came down in the sea at 10:00 hours and quickly filled with water. The three pilots escaped through the roof hatch with their dinghy, which they inflated and scrambled into. The wooden Horsa remained awash with the tail and the top of the fuselage visible. At 22:00 hours that day the three pilots were picked up by a frigate of the Royal Navy. The Horsa, still afloat, was destroyed by the warship to leave no trace.

The three glider pilots were landed in Northern Ireland by the Navy then flown by 295 Squadron back to Netheravon – all returned to the ferrying operation. Major Cooper later lost his life in Operation 'Ladbrooke' in Sicily. On 14 June Staff

Sergeants Hall, Antopoulos and Conway were piloting a Horsa on tow over the Bay of Biscay when the combination was attacked by two German Focke-Wulf Condor long-range bombers, 100 miles north-west of Cap Finisterre. The Halifax tug, piloted by Warrant Officer McCroden, was shot down after a fierce gun battle and the Horsa was forced to cast off and ditch in the sea. The three glider pilots took to their dinghy but it was eleven days before they were picked up by a Spanish ship.

By 16 June eighteen gliders had been ferried to Salé and by the 30th twenty-five. Two more were delivered by 7 July, bringing the total to twenty-seven. On 27 June, a Halifax piloted by Flying Officer Horne took off with a Horsa on tow and was never heard from again; it was thought to have been shot down over the Bay of Biscay by German aircraft.

On 30 June 295 Squadron moved from Holmesley South to Hurn, near Bournemouth, which had better facilities as a repair base. Portreath was still the final take-off base.

Having reached Salé the combinations were faced with the next 1,000-mile leg of their journey to Tunisia. The first stage of this leg was a 400-mile flight from Salé to Froha, then another final leg of 600 miles to Sousse, the operational bases for the Sicily operation. This last 1,000 miles was over inhospitable mountains and desert, which caused severe turbulence to the combinations and overheating of the tug's engines. Two gliders had to force-land on this leg but one was recovered in time for the Sicily operation. The first gliders reached airstrip 'E' at Kairouan twelve days before the Sicily assault. Thirty gliders had been lifted off from England; three had ditched in the sea but twenty-seven had reached North Africa.

Apart from the two Halifaxes and one Horsa lost en route between England and Africa with their crews, several Halifaxes had been lost during training. One, flown by Flying Officers Collins and Smith, had crashed, killing the entire crew. On 19 May Flying Officer Blackburn had been killed whilst flying, and Flying Officer Tomkins's Halifax had crashed into a hill in Somerset, killing four of the crew.

The Glider Pilot Regiment lost seven men during the operation: Sergeants E.W. Hall, A. Higgins, J.E. Harrison, H. Norris and M.A.C. Chandler; Staff Sergeants F. Wheale and D.S. Casseldean.

Staff Sergeant (later Lieutenant) Bill Chambers' account of his part in Operation 'Beggar'.

The first flights took place on 1 June 1943 from RAF Portreath, Cornwall, which was on top of the cliffs 295 feet above sea level. Portreath airfield was unusual in that it had four runways instead of the usual three – QDMs (magnetic bearings) 194, 283, 336 and 242. We used 283 as it had the longest runway of 1,800 yards.

The Horsas on 'Beggar' took spare undercarriages with them; they landed on skids on the sand at Rabat Salé as the undercarriages used for take-off in England were then jettisoned. The spare undercarriages were fitted in an hour so that the glider was ready for a normal take-off for Sousse. Combination would assemble on the runway at Portreath between 02:30 and 03:00 ready for take-off at the first glimmer of daylight. Sometimes we had an escort of four Beaufighters or Mosquitoes nearly to Finisterre, but not always – it depended on availability.

If you were standing on the tarmac watching the take-offs, it was not unusual for both tug and glider to disappear from view below the cliff edge, and there was an agonising wait before they reappeared half-way to the next headland, where they would jettison the Horsa's undercarriage.

My first flight was in Horsa LG 574 with co-pilots Lieutenant Robin Walchi and Sergeant Owen; the Halifax tug skipper was Flying Officer Muir with a New Zealander, Freddie Schultz, as his 2nd pilot. We had to return from Finisterre having failed to get through heavy cloud up to 10,000 feet without the towing Halifax running out of fuel.

On 6 June we tried again in the same Horsa, but nearing Finisterre the tug developed a serious leak in the bomb-bay fuel tanks – Fuel was spraying back over our Horsa so we had to return; the whole trip took six and a half hours of flying.

At Portreath Group Captain Tom Cooper was waiting on the runway; he took off his jacket, donned overalls, and helped the fitters to repair the leak. Two hours later we lifted off again and after nine hours and twenty minutes of flying time we reached Rabat Salé.

I returned to Portreath on 14 June in a Halifax flown by Squadron Leader A.M.B. Wilkinson and on 5 July did the last 'Beggar' trip with co-pilots Owen and Ashton in Horsa LG 181 towed by a Halifax flown by Flying Officer Grant. The next day, as we were now the only crew at Rabat Salé, the same combination took off and set course for Sousse to take part in the Sicily operation. Incidentally, when we had arrived at Rabat all stores, arms, etc, had gone on to Sousse, so we were in battledress – rather hot wear for Africa in July!

We had to climb to 10,000 feet to clear the mountains en route for Sousse and it was very bumpy indeed. Owing to severe overheating two of the tug's engines failed so we had to cast off and force-land in the desert about 150 miles south of Algiers. The Halifax tug also had to force-land in the desert. When we landed, the desert was bare, but within one minute forty Arabs appeared from nowhere. When they were about a hundred yards away, I held up my hand and they stopped – thank goodness, as we only had a sheath knife between us; their leader came forward and I spoke to him in French, which I speak reasonably fluently, assuring him that we were friendly. Luckily they were too and after spending some two or three days with them (we slept in the Horsa) they lent us their two horses – real Arab steeds with wooden saddles – and a guide who, with Sergeant Owen and myself mounted on the horses, ran about eight miles to a French village, where he found the Halifax crew – all uninjured – already settled in with an ex-French Air Force officer and his family. As the only French-speaking member of either crew I arranged for a truck to pick up the other glider pilot back at the downed Horsa and we all consolidated at the village. We managed to get a signal through to Algiers and two days later a Hudson aircraft from Maison Blanche collected us. The Halifax and Horsa were left in the desert for collection later. Flying Officer Grant got us kitted out with RAF KD (khaki drill tropical kit), thank goodness, but when we did eventually manage to reach Sousse the Sicily operation was over!

Operation 'Elaborate'

After 'Beggar', more Horsa gliders had to be towed from England to North Africa by 295 Squadron and the Glider Pilot Regiment, as Operation 'Elaborate', between 15 August and 23 September 1943. The same take-off airfield – RAF Portreath – was used and the same flight route, the objective being to ferry thirty-five Horsas for use in the Middle East and Mediterranean theatre of operations.

Of the five combinations that took off from Portreath at the start of the operation on August 15, four reached Salé successfully. The fifth, DP 288 flown by pilots Johnson, Attwood and Brown, ditched in the sea. Another combination took off next day but the Horsa, DP 329 flown by pilots Saunders, Jackson and Wedge, also had to ditch in the sea.

On 17 August Horsa DP 647 was successfully towed to North Africa by Flying Officer Sizmur, with glider pilots Davis, Gabbot and Lewis at the controls of the Horsa. Two combinations took off on 21 August: Horsa LG 895 piloted by pilots Coombes, Halton and Jenks, and Horsa LG 947 flown by pilots Telfer, Humphreys and Vincent, both making Salé successfully.

On the 23rd four combinations took off from Portreath but one had to return to base and one, piloted by pilots Wright, Ridings and Robinson, had to land in Portugal. The two other combinations duly arrived at Salé. Three combinations took off on 3 September: two made the journey successfully, but the third Horsa, LH 209 flown by pilots Johnson, Attwood and Saunders, had to ditch.

Two more combinations lifted off on 7 September, one completing the long haul to Salé; the other, Horsa DP 824 flown by pilots Shuttleworth, Gabbot and Garnett, crashed. Four more took off on 15 September; three reached Salé, making a total of fifteen gliders successfully delivered. The other Horsa – LJ 209 – piloted by Staff Sergeants Channel, James and Thomson had to land in Portugal. At 07:40 hours on 18 September the twenty-third tow took off – Halifax DG 396 flown by Flying Officer Norman towing Horsa HS 102 flown by Lieutenant Prout and Sergeants Hill and Flynn. At 11:00 hours, flying at 1,000 feet in cloud and rain, the combination was attacked by twelve German Ju 88 aircraft flying in a three by four formation. Four of the 88s circled while the other eight attacked the combination.

Lieutenant Prout ordered Sergeant Flynn to cast off tow to free the tug to defend itself. The Horsa ditched, landing across the line of the waves, and the three glider pilots got into their dinghy, which was fired on by the Germans. The air gunners in the Halifax tug engaged the 88s and the rear gunner, Sergeant John Grant, succeeded in shooting down one of them, for which he was later awarded the Distinguished Flying Medal.

The Halifax tug – shot full of holes – managed to reach Salé, and the three glider pilots were picked up six hours later by HMS *Crane*. The last two tows took off on 23 September: Halifax DG 384 flown by Flying Officer Sizmur, towing Horsa HF 109 flown by Sergeants Baker, Barron and Sargent. For some unknown reason the Horsa ditched off the coast of Portugal and the three glider pilots were lost. Mystery exists as to the cause of the cast-off as the Halifax tug returned to Portreath successfully. The other take-off on the 23rd was aborted and the combination returned to base. With that, the operation ended. It had cost the lives of three glider pilots of the Glider Pilot Regiment.

Of the twenty-five combinations which took off from Portreath, fifteen had reached North Africa, no mean achievement: one was shot down, two landed in Portugal, four ditched, two returned to base and one crashed.

Next stop Portugal! Staff Sergeant Len Wright, DFM, recalls Operation 'Elaborate':

Date:	23rd August 1943
Horsa No:	LH 122. Take-off 08:02 BST
Horsa Crew:	Sergeants L. Wright, L. Ridings, C. Robinson
Halifax No.	DK 198
Halifax Crew:	Flying Officer Clapperton, Pilot Officer Archibold, Flight Sergeant Robinson, Sergeant Burness

We took off from Portreath at about 8 a.m. on 23 August. We had been there a few days waiting for weather. The Horsa had been collected from Netheravon and we had flown to Portreath behind a Whitley. The undercarriage was dropped on the Scilly Isles after the usual hair-raising take-off when it seemed doubtful if the combination would ever get off the deck. We seemed to be carrying a really heavy load with spare u/c, a number of large air-bottles and goodness knows what other spares that had been put aboard the Horsa. We wondered if the ground crew had loaded up with any thought of C of G and trim but they hadn't made a bad job of things because the glider handled quite well.

After the tail gunner had tested his guns and we had done the usual trip below the Halifax slipstream to test the low tow position, everyone settled down; we got our anti-glare goggles on and got down to sea level. The weather was good, the inter-com was working and all seemed set for a pleasant trip as we set out over the Bay of Biscay.

We had a set routine for flying; we each did one hour flying, one hour 2nd pilot and one hour in the back. We usually managed three rounds of 'duties' and when it got really warm the one in the back usually managed to get on his tropical kit.

We must have been flying about five hours; we were up to about 3,000 feet since the tug pilot had said we were clear of the fighters and out of their range, when I noticed smoke pouring from the starboard inner engine. I was flying at the time and immediately told the tug pilot, who said they would try and cope. Soon flames appeared. I saw the prop had been feathered then it stopped altogether. It was obvious we were in trouble, we were losing height and the tug pilot ordered us to get rid of all we could out of the glider; they would do the same in the Halifax and there was just a chance we would make it to Gibraltar.

Robbie and Les set to work with a will, and everything that was detachable went out of the door. I remember seeing an air bottle dropping below, very near to a tramp steamer. He would think he was being bombed. The glider was like a bucking bronco as the weight was disturbed, and I was soon bathed in sweat and so wet my hands kept slipping off the wheel. When all was got rid of and the Horsa was just a shell the port inner on the Halifax started to smoke. We had a quick committee meeting and decided we would pull off and give the tug a chance to get to Gib.

We could see the coast in the distance; we told the pilot what we had decided, he agreed and said he would get us as near to the coast as possible. When we got well below 1,000 feet I pulled off and landed half in the sea and half on the beach, the tug did a circuit above us, we waved and he set off for Gibraltar. I believe he made it. The tide was going out and we were soon high and dry on the very soft sand. We were just having a brew when I looked up and saw thousands (it seemed) of natives racing towards us. They stopped about thirty yards from us in a big circle, then retreated another twenty yards when Les pulled the flaps up. One chap stepped forward, he appeared to be a student and told us we were in Portugal and invited us to the village. We had been briefed to get in touch with the Army if we were in trouble, so we thought there may be someone in the village who might help. We collected our kit and started across the sands. It was really hot; it must have been about 2 p.m. when we arrived. We were led to a biggish wooden hut and sat down at a table; the rest of the village seemed to crowd into the room and soon one of the women brought in a terrific-sized plate with about two dozen fried eggs on it. They were really greasy! but we ate most of them, thinking it may be impolite to refuse.

We noticed, whilst we were eating, one small very dark, evil-looking chap was having a big argument with our student friend. Then the friend told us this little horror was very pro-German and had told the police we had landed and where we were. About an hour later three large black police cars arrived in the village, all our kit was confiscated, in spite of our protests, and we were bundled into the cars, one to each car with a policeman as escort. My policeman didn't have much to say. I tried to find out where we had landed and where we were going in my best schoolboy French but he stayed dumb.

By this time I was beginning to feel rather ill (probably the fried eggs and strong wine we had been given at the village) and the toilet was becoming a bit of a necessity. However, the cars travelled on, it was quite dark and eventually we came to a very large hotel in a brilliantly lighted town and the cars stopped at the bottom of a large flight of stone stairs, a rather wonderful staircase and lined either side with crowds of people all in evening dress. To put it mildly we were staggered! What with the lights (we were used to the black-out) and these people, obviously very well-off, friendly and all dying to shake hands; then they began to applaud as we walked up the stairs. Then the manager (or someone) lead us to a table set for three and we were left to get on with a meal which was being served. We were gasping for a cup of tea but no one seemed to understand and we were being plied with red wine. We managed to locate a toilet, settled down at our table to see what would happen next, then a procession of young girls came down the restaurant in pairs, each had a gift of some sort on a tray and the first one had a bottle of whisky with a union jack stuck in it. All the gifts were heaped up on the table, mostly sweets and fruit, then the leader gave us a menu card with their names on it and a 'V' drawn with a message, 'Good luck to the British Aviators'. I can remember this so well because I still have the menu.

All the people in the room were now giving the V-sign and saying 'Churchill' over and over again. We were having a helluva time, especially since we had opened the whisky. I could see Les Ridings was beginning to get too happy and began to dread what was going to happen. There was the usual discussion going on at the police-table near us; it was surrounded by 'civies' all shouting at once, then a policeman came to us, one we had never seen before, and he appeared to be a senior officer of some sort. He could speak a little English, and between his English and my French I discovered we were going to spend the night at this hotel. From what I could make out, this decision had been forced on them by the people staying there, who were wealthy French refugees sheltering in Portugal from the Germans, and the police did not want to cause any trouble. By this time the hotel was absolutely full and we had given the victory sign so often we began to feel like royalty. This senior policeman made us promise not to leave the hotel, gave us another bottle of whisky, locked us in a bedroom and put a guard on the door. It was a rather large bedroom suite, three beds, bathroom, the lot – film star treatment.

We got cracking on the two bottles of whisky and were soon very merry. Les decided he wanted to thank the locals for their hospitality; he couldn't get through the locked bedroom door but found the large bedroom window opened out on to a balcony. There were crowds of people below and Les made a wonderful speech in his best Burnley accent and the crowd cheered like mad. The outcome was the chief of police came in, playing hell. I had to pacify him; he locked the bedroom window and left us another bottle of whisky. Les filled his pipe with his Balkan Soubranie and proceeded to smoke and drink. He soon passed out. Robbie and I put him to bed then passed out ourselves.

The next morning, all suffering from very bad headaches, we were wakened very early and stuck in a local bus with a plain clothes policeman as a guard. The bus was full of fat old ladies carrying chickens and obviously on their way to some market. After a nightmare journey we arrived in Lisbon and went into the British Consulate via the back door. We had an interview with the Military Attaché, who seemed to know all about us and said he had been instructed to get us back to the UK as soon as possible. He went on to explain the Germans knew we had landed and had demanded we be interned, so he was sending us out of the way until he could get things organised for our return. After taking us to a shop to get civilian clothes and have photographs taken for passports, we went by train to a border town called Elvas. We were accompanied by a horrid individual who spent the whole journey spitting into a pocket flask and trying to get out of us what we had been flying, where we had been heading and just what we were going to do when we got there!

Our internment was not too unpleasant, but very boring. We were billeted in a small hotel and the manageress looked after us very well. Now and again I tried to get through on the phone to the Embassy for information but nothing was forthcoming. We spent most of the evenings visiting the open air cinema, luckily the films were all English or American. One night we were even invited to a dance, but none of the local ladies would take a chance. Another time we borrowed bicycles and cycled into Spain but it was too hot and we were threatened with prison if we went too far into Spain. The only restriction on us was we had to report to the police station every day at midday. Elvas was a Portuguese Military Base and we were not too popular, probably because we paid higher prices for the half-warm American beer. The manageress of the hotel loaned us some money; I hope she got it back after we left!

Another glider crew arrived just before we left and an American Liberator crew, both lots waiting to go back to UK. According to records, Charlie Channell, Bert Thornton and James were another crew who force-landed in Portugal. I never saw them and I can't remember the names of the glider crew who did share our hotel.

Eventually word came for Les, Robbie and me to get to Lisbon. A guide put us on the train, came with us and booked us into another hotel in Lisbon. We were there about three days before getting places on a plane to England. Once we were put on the plane, then taken off to make room for more important personnel. That plane, flying during daylight, was shot down, and from then all flights were made during the night. We were told later that the film actor Leslie Howard was on the plane that was shot down. We landed at Lyneham and after a few run-ins with the Military Police because we were wearing half-civies and half uniform and a lot of help from the RTO, we got back to Fargo for de-briefing.

I remember whilst we were interned in Elvas, we got news Italy had 'packed in' and were under the impression the war was just about over. During my absence my mother got a letter from Lieutenant Frank Davies, written from Hurn, dated 31 August '43 telling her that although I had been posted missing, not to worry I was OK. There was also a letter from AAC records on a later date telling her I was in Portugal, owing to an accident! Later in September another letter from records saying that I was back in UK. I also have a cutting from some national daily quoting a message from Reuters saying 'a four-engined Halifax bomber with a glider on tow was flying over the Portuguese coast, seventy-five miles north of Lisbon when the connecting cable broke and the glider force-landed, says German radio.'

Operation 'Voodoo'

In the summer of 1943 the first transatlantic towed glider flight was made from Canada to Britain. An 'air bridge' from Canada to Britain had been established since 10 November 1940, when seven Lockheed Hudson aircraft, flown mainly by civilian air crews, had made the 2,200-mile flight from Gander, Newfoundland, to RAF Aldergrove, Northern Ireland, in ten and a half hours. Flying the lead aircraft was British Overseas Airways Corporation Captain D.C.T. Bennett – Group Captain 'Pathfinder' Bennett as he later became in the RAF.

Under the Lend-Lease Act passed by the American Government and signed by President Roosevelt on 11 March 1941, the US was beginning to supply aircraft to the RAF by flying them to Canada for onward delivery to Britain by RAF Ferry Command, which had been formed on 20 July 1941, under the command of Air Chief Marshal Sir Frederick Bowhill.

The Canadian Government had built a large new airfield at Dorval, Canada, ten miles from Montreal, which became the receiving airfield for lend-lease aircraft from the US en route to Britain. Another large airfield was built at Goose Bay, Labrador, 820 miles north-east of Gander, which had three 7,000 ft runways. These airfields made it possible for medium-range aircraft to cross the Atlantic with a refuelling stop in Iceland. The US had also built an airfield in

Greenland, Bluie West One, as a refuelling stop between Labrador and Iceland. By the summer of 1942 a firm air bridge had been established over the North Atlantic and on 11 March 1943 RAF Ferry Command became RAF Transport Command still under the command of ACM Bowhill.

During the hard Canadian winter of 1942, the RAF and the RCAF decided to explore the feasibility of towing gliders across the North Atlantic from North America to Britain, a distance of 3,500 miles. Chosen to carry out the experimental flight were Flight-Lieutenant W.S. Longhurst, (tug captain) who was a Canadian pilot serving with the RAF, and Flight-Lieutenant C.W.H. Thompson, (co-pilot) a New Zealander also serving with the RAF. The glider pilots were Squadron Leader (later Wing Commander) R.G. Seys, RAF 1st pilot, and Squadron Leader F.M. Gobeil, RCAF, 2nd pilot.

Using RCAF Dorval as a base, flying trials were made to select a suitable tug aircraft and glider. The combination chosen was a Douglas C-47 Dakota as the tug aircraft and an American Waco CG-4A Hadrian as the glider. Flying locally at first, the trials soon extended to Gander and Goose airfields with the glider fully loaded with one and a half tons of freight weight. This triangular route flight set up a record for a freight-carrying glider of 820 miles on one leg of the flight – the previous American-held record had been 670 miles. The longest trial flight was 1,177 miles non-stop at an average speed of 150 miles per hour, which took eight hours. This flight gave the information and experience required for the transatlantic tow.

Trials completed, the take-off date for the operation was set for 23 June 1943. The C-47 Dakota 11, serial number FD 900, made by the Douglas Aircraft Corporation, California, carried the normal safety equipment for a transatlantic flight but was also fitted with long-range extra fuel tanks which could be jettisoned without damage to the towed glider. The other crew members of the tug were Flying Officer K. Turner, engineer, Mr H.G. Wightman, radio officer, and Pilot Officer R.H. Wormington, flight engineer.

A Waco CG-4A Hadrian glider, serial number FR 579 and nicknamed 'Voodoo', made in Connecticut by a firm of piano makers, Pratt Read and Company, was to be the glider for this the first transatlantic flight by a towed glider. The steel-tubed and fabric-covered fuselage of the Hadrian was fitted with flotation bags to keep it afloat and give the crew time to get out in case of ditching. A special knife was carried to enable the two-man crew to cut their way out of the fabric-covered hull if necessary. Full survival gear including an inflatable rubber dinghy was also carried. A 3360 lb freight load of medical supplies, engine and radio parts which, if the flight was successful, were to be sent on to Russia was carried. The nylon tow rope made by the Plymouth Cordage Company, Massachusetts, was designed to take a pull of 20,000 lb.

At 16:25 gmt on 23 June 1943 the C-47 tug towed the Hadrian glider off from RCAF Dorval and set course against a strong headwind for Goose Bay. Climbing slowly, the combination reached a height of 9,000 feet, searching for clear weather above the clouds. An altitude of 13,000 feet was reached but there was no clear break in the cumulus clouds. The cloud cover rendered the towing aircraft invisible to the glider pilots and they had to rely on the attitude of the tow rope to their glider to judge their towing position relative to the tug. Six hours into the flight the combination ran into bad weather – thunderstorms, ice and snow – and were forced down to 1,500 feet. An hour later they were landing at Goose Bay, touching down at 23:25 on the 23rd. Flight time had been seven hours.

On 27 June the combination was airborne again heading for Bluie West One; the weather was reasonably good and they made the airfield $6\frac{1}{4}$ hours later. Total flying time so far had been $13\frac{1}{4}$ hours. Three days later, on 30 June, the combination took off from Bluie West One at 13:22 gmt for the long and dangerous haul to Iceland in favourable weather conditions. The two pilots alternated at the control column as the Hadrian had to be flown at all times. Contact between the tug and glider was by radio – but as the glider radio was powered by batteries with no means of recharging them – the glider crew left the radio off most of the time. If they wished to speak to the tug crew, all they had to do was switch on and transmit – but if the tug crew wished to speak to the glider crew the tug pilot had to waggle his aircraft's wings as a signal for the glider pilot to switch on his set.

The combination landed safely in Iceland at 20:37 on 30 June, with a flight time of $7\frac{1}{4}$ hours for the leg and making a flying time of $20\frac{1}{2}$ hours so far. No major problems had occurred although the nylon tow rope had to be re-spliced and the steel towing coupling had to be straightened and welded – due to damage received when the rope was dropped by the tug after releasing the glider.

The final leg of the flight began less than nine hours later, at 05:30 on 1 July, when the combination took off for Britain in good weather. 850 miles over the sea lay ahead and the crews of both tug and glider were suffering from lack of sleep as good flying weather came before that. After $7\frac{3}{4}$ hours of flying the combination broke cloud at Prestwick, Scotland, at 13:15, right on their estimated time of arrival. The tug released the Hadrian over the airfield and the glider pilot made a smooth landing on the grass, to be followed two minutes later by the tug aircraft.

So ended a pioneering towed glider flight of 28 hrs 15 mins duration, the first towed glider flight over the Atlantic. Part of the tow rope used by the combination can be seen on display at the Army Museum of Flying, Middle Wallop, Hampshire, England, together with the signatures of both tug and glider crews.

On Monday, 11 October 1943 Squadron Leader Seys visited the Waco Plant at Troy, Ohio, in the United States to tell the workforce about his crossing of the Atlantic in one of their gliders. This is what he recalls:

We encountered very bad weather during the early stages of the flight. The turbulence was shocking. The glider was thrown about all over the sky – the tug made some pretty dirty lurches too. I had taken over the controls in anticipation of this bad weather before we began to go down through the clouds, and for the next three hours we took a terrific beating.

We passed through three belts of thunderstorms, with snow and ice so thick at times I lost sight of the tow plane and had only 50 to 100 feet of tow rope before me by which to judge its position relative to the tug. If I allowed the glider to get too low, the tow plane would have been pulled into a steep climb enough to stall it. Had this happened I would have had no alternative but to cut loose and make a forced landing, because a dive resulting from a stall by a tug probably would have resulted in pulling off the wings of the glider through exceeding its designed maximum speed.

We got through, however, and made the first stage, to an east coast field, with a smooth landing, only about twenty minutes late. I might say we were dead tired and after sleeping for five hours my shoulders and legs seemed to be a mass of aches from fighting the rough weather we had gone through. An Atlantic glider crossing had never been done before and, although we had made many experiments, the sensations were new to me. To be candid, I was more than somewhat frightened at the prospect of the tremendous haul before us. This was soon banished by the thrill of getting away according to plan.

The next take-off was again smooth but slow. We had an hour and a half of rough weather, flying under clouds before we were able to climb through them and reach smooth air above 6,000 feet. By this time the Atlantic, with ice fields and occasional towering icebergs, was visible below. I began to wonder whether, if it was necessary to make a forced landing in the sea, we would be able to land on the icebergs and stay long enough to be picked up. I felt they were much more solid than our rubber dinghy, which did not seem at all inviting. I am a bad sailor.

Snatches in a tow rope can be minimized greatly by a skilled glider pilot, but the tug pilot can do little about it. For instance, on seeing the tow rope getting slack the idea is to dive a little just as the tow plane begins to go ahead so that the glider gets up speed at the same time and the snatch is reduced.

Another of the difficulties was the noise. The air rushes past the glider with the sound of a train over rails – an odd rhythmic beat which does not cease until the glider drops below 70 knots just before landing. Squadron Leader Gobiel (my co-pilot) and I did not talk much to each other during the flight – we couldn't. Another strain was watching the tow rope so closely. The effects are hypnotic. In fair weather the average trick at the controls was two hours – if there was no horizon, one hour. But in bad weather a spell may last three. Concentration is imperative – even when the co-pilot takes over, the tension does not leave you. You seem to be flying the glider all the time – whoever is at the controls.

So glider flying is not just sitting in the cockpit and being towed. It is something similar to being towed in a car by a rope from another car – except that the one behind has no brakes and the only way that the pilot can slow down to avoid running over the tug or letting the tow rope get slack, which makes a frightful snatch, is to weave about and thereby lose a little more distance than the towing vehicle. In smooth air everything is delightful. But in bad weather you might as well be in a churn. Crossing the Atlantic we were forced below the clouds again about six hours from the North American continent and for some time we flew less than 1,000 feet above the waves. The weather was closing in, however, and we had to climb and get over the top. At 9,500 feet we still had not reached to top and it was snowing hard. I was at the controls and pretty busy. Gobeil said afterwards he was absolutely frozen wiping the snow which came in through joints in the cockpit. We were wearing the same clothing with US Army parka and woollens and I had on the red skull cap made from my wife's hat which I wear for luck, but I was working so hard that I kept warm.

After an hour of this we get into the clear again and had about six hours at 9,000 feet flying between two layers of cloud, where of course we could see neither sun nor sea. About thirteen hours from North America we hit another bad patch but it only lasted for half an hour, and from there it was plain sailing at 6,000 feet, with a layer of cloud covering the sea and the sun shining down on us. I had taken along a bunch of bananas for the family but they got frostbitten, as did our sandwiches, which almost broke our teeth when we tried to eat them. Finally, twenty-eight flying hours from Montreal we sighted the coast of Britain – after four false alarms which turned out to be low clouds on the horizon. I was never more glad to see the earth under me and upon receiving the signal from the tow plane to cast off – I did not argue. After a couple of circuits over the landing field we touched down smoothly.

Gobeil and I shook hands very solemnly as the machine came to rest. We were very tired and it was quite an effort to submit to the usual interrogation and attend to the unloading of the glider before she was wheeled away and put to bed in the hangar. I called the glider 'Voodoo' because its manner of flight (without visible means of support) recalled to mind the famous Indian rope trick.

(*Reprinted by courtesy of the Waco Historical Society Troy, Ohio, USA*)

The Invasion of Sicily. One: Operation 'Ladbrooke'

During December 1942, while the Allied forces were still fighting in Tunisia, studies were underway for planning the next step: the invasion of Europe. In January 1943 the Casablanca Conference was held, and President Roosevelt and Prime Minister Churchill, with their military advisers, decided that Sicily should be the next move prior to the invasion of Italy.

The Allied Forces Supreme Commander, General Eisenhower, designated the British General Harold L. Alexander, as Deputy Commander and Air Commodore R.M. Foster, RAF, to head his Air Staff. Their task was to plan the invasion of Sicily, codenamed 'Husky', and for this purpose a headquarters, to be known as Allied Force Headquarters (AFHQ Force 141), was set up in Algiers.

On 2 February 1943 AFHQ issued its first directive on 'Husky'; the next day planning began in earnest and by 12 February AFHQ was able to give its first assessment of the planned invasion. Various plans were then drawn up and discussed by the army commanders without result, so on 2 May General Eisenhower held a conference at Algiers to resolve the final plan. D-Day was set for the night of 9/10 July 1943, when there was a quarter moon which set at 00:30 on 10 July.

The British 8th Army would land from the sea on beaches of the Gulf of Noto south of Syracuse, and on both sides of the Pachino Peninsula. The US 7th Army would land from the sea on a seventy-mile-long beach front along the Gulf of Gela, from Licata to Scoglitti, on the left flank of the British.

On 21 May AFHQ allocated two airborne divisions for the invasion: the British 1st Airborne Division (General Hopkinson) and the US 82nd Airborne Division under Gerneral Ridgeway. The 82nd's mission was to be a paratroop drop during the night of 3,405 men five miles inland from the port of Gela, followed by another paratroop drop by the remainder of the 82nd later.

On 23 May General Montgomery and General Hopkinson decided that glider

forces would be landed at night before the main seaborne assault. The theory was
that a glider landing would give the airborne troops the firepower they needed to
mount an attack on their objective. Paratroops on their own would be dispersed
on their DZs and lightly armed. The British airborne forces expert, Group Captain Tom B. Cooper, RAF, objected to a night glider assault as he considered the
tug and glider crews did not have enough experience or training in a night attack.
He was overruled.

On 13 May German resistance in Tunisia had ceased. The US had begun to
ship 500 Waco CG-4A gliders from America to North Africa and the RAF was
delivering thirty-six Horsa gliders (Operation 'Beggar') from England to North
Africa. All were to be used in the forthcoming invasion.

By the end of May the final assault plan had been decided on: the British airborne landing, codenamed 'Ladbrooke', would be by the 1st Air Landing Brigade
of the 1st Airborne Division on three LZs south of the town of Syracuse. A force
of over 1,500 men would be involved: their objective the Ponte Grande bridge
over a canal, one and a half miles south-west of Syracuse. The 'Ladbrooke' gliderborne force would consist of:

1st Air Landing Brigade	CO, Brigadier P.H.W. Hicks.
2nd Battalion South Staffordshire Regiment	CO, Lt-Colonel W.D.H. McCardie.
1st Battalion Border Regiment	CO, Lt-Colonel G.V. Britten.
9th Field Company, Royal Engineers	
181st Airborne Field Ambulance	CO, Lt-Colonel G. Warwick.
1st Battalion Glider Pilot Regiment (reinforced by nineteen US glider pilots)	CO, Lt-Colonel G.J.S. Chatterton.

As well as the troops with their personal weapons, the gliders would carry seven
jeeps, six 6-pounder guns, ten 3-inch mortars. Each Horsa glider would carry men
of the South Staffords. The Waco gliders' load would vary according to the equipment carried; the maximum was eighteen troops, the minimum four troops and a
jeep. D-Day had been fixed for the night of 9/10 July with take-off times from
18:40 on the 9th onwards. By 3 June eighteen airstrips in the Kairouan area of
Tunisia had been allocated to the glider towing and paratroop forces. These
airstrips, newly constructed by the Allies, were 6,000-ft long by 300-ft wide dirt
strips, which raised clouds of dust on take-off. The pilots of the gliders were hard-
pressed to see their tow planes on take-off.

The US 51st Wings and two squadrons of 38 Wing, RAF, had been allocated
six air strips near Goubrine. No names were given to these dirt strips, merely letters, A, B, C, D, E and F. The US 52nd Wing had the other twelve airstrips close
to Kairouan to carry the 82nd Airborne on their missions.

On 29 May, 51st Wing began training its pilots on gliders. Gliders had been in
short supply, only Waco CG-4As being available in small numbers. But by 13
June 346 Wacos had been delivered, more than enough for training and the operation. The British Glider Pilot Regiment were to pilot the Wacos, reinforced by

nineteen US glider pilots who had volunteered for the mission. The British glider pilots had began training on the Wacos in May at Oran as they were unfamiliar with the US glider. Training continued until 27 June when the two squadrons of the Glider Pilot Regiment were towed with their gliders from Oran to Tunisia. On this 600-mile flight, one glider was lost, killing all on board when the tail fell off and it crashed.

The 1st Air Landing Brigade and the glider pilots were now established in base camps near the Kairouan airstrips. The glider pilots named their camp Fargo 2; Fargo 1 was their base camp in England.

Much difficulty was experienced in glider serviceability, which cut back on training but on the evening of 9 July, 109 Dakota, 28 Albermarle and 7 Halifax aircraft were ready to lift off 136 Waco and 8 Horsa gliders for Operation 'Ladbrooke'.

At 18:42 on 9 July the first combinations began to lift off and set course at 500 feet for the RV over the Kuriate Islands off the east coast of Tunisia. They continued to lift off at one minute intervals until 20:20; the Americans flew in echelons of four, the British independently in stream.

Six RAF Albemarles of 296 Squadron had to abort the mission for various reasons. One C-47 had to force-land shortly after take-off when the jeep in its glider broke loose, leaving 137 combinations heading for the RV. Circling over the RV, the armada formed into a stream and headed for Malta 200 miles to the east. The Halifaxes towing Horsas flew at 145 mph at 500 feet, with the Albemarles flying at 125 mph at 350 feet. The C-47s flew at 120 mph at 250 feet. The low height flown was to avoid enemy radar detection and some combinations flew so low that they were lashed with sea spray.

The first combination reached the turning point at Delimara Point on the south-east coast of Malta at 21:22, then turned north-east for the seventy-mile leg to Cape Passero, the south-east tip of Sicily. But this time the wind speed was about 45 mph from the north-west making difficult flying conditions for the combinations. However the wind moderated to about 30 mph as the force approached Sicily but the quarter moon gave insufficient light to locate the LZs.

Two C-47/Waco combinations turned back over the sea and returned, unable to locate their LZs. One Waco glider was accidently released en route and one Horsa broke its tow rope. The planned LZs were LZ3, a mile west of the Ponte Grande bridge, for the Horsas, with the Wacos landing on two LZs two to three miles south of the bridge. LZ2 was close to the sea shore and LZ1 a mile inland from LZ2.

At 22:10 the first seven releases were made near Cap Murro di Porca undetected by the enemy. The release point was 300 yards south-east of the shore line nearest to LZs 1 and 2. The plan had been for the Horsas to be released at an altitude of 5,000 feet and land on LZ3 and the Wacos to be released at 1,800 feet for LZ1 and 1400 feet for LZ2

As this first wave was released the enemy became alerted and opened up with anti-aircraft fire. Searchlights began to sweep the sky and this combination of flak and lights upset the tug pilots. Smoke from the flak drifted over the release area, making it impossible for the tug pilots to locate their release point. A confused

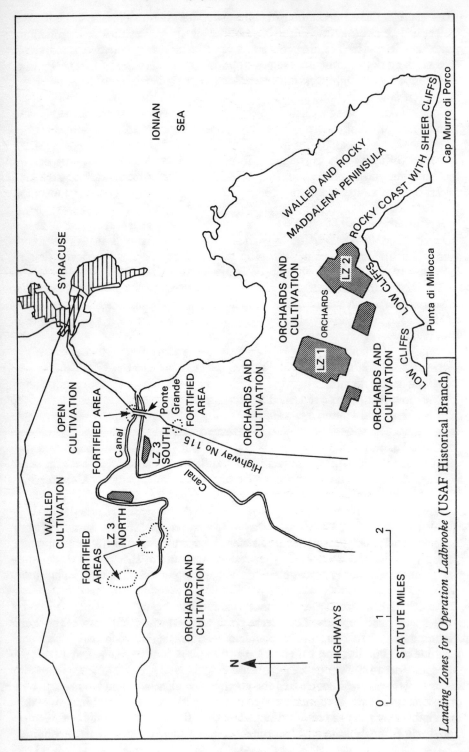

Landing Zones for Operation Ladbrooke (USAF Historical Branch)

situation developed with the air full of powered aircraft and gliders.

After releasing their gliders, the tugs dropped their tow ropes and turned south for Malta, then on to Tunisia; the first tug returned to base at 00:15. Although five crews lost their way, all 137 tug aircraft returned safely.

Back on Sicily chaos reigned. At least sixty-nine Wacos landed in the sea, drowning 207 men. Forty-nine Wacos and five Horsas landed on Sicily. Seven Wacos and three Horsas were missing, believed crashed in the sea with all aboard lost. Survivors of the ditched gliders later complained that they had been forced to release too far off shore. Later casualty figures were reckoned at 605, of whom 326 were missing, probably drowned.

The glider pilots, through being disorientated by the confusion and released too far off shore, could not reach their intended LZs. Only two Wacos landed on LZ1, one on LZ2 and only one Horsa on LZ3. Two more Horsas managed to land within a mile of LZ3.

Horsa glider No. 133, piloted by Staff Sergeants Galpin, DFM and Brown of the Glider Pilot Regiment, and towed by a Halifax piloted by Flight Lieutenant T. Grant, DSO, made a perfect landing on LZ3. Another Horsa piloted by Captain J.W.C. Denholm, Glider Pilot Regiment, and carrying part of C Company, 2nd South Staffords under Major George Ballinger, crashed into the canal bank only 400 yards from the Ponte Grande bridge, killing all but one of the occupants.

The occupants of Staff Sergeant Galpin's Horsa, a platoon of the 2nd South Staffords under Lieutenant Withers, immediately attacked the bridge and captured it.

One of the platoon, a former miner Private Curnock, RAMC, helped to remove the enemy demolition charges from the bridge. During the night the bridge party were reinforced by some thirty men of the 1st Border Regiment under Lieutenant Welch and some more men from the South Staffords. The senior officer now present, Lieutenant-Colonel A.G. Walch, OBE, took command with Major Beasley, Royal Engineers, as second in command. By morning eight officers and sixty-five men were holding the bridge. At 07:30 they were joined by more of the scattered troops including a US glider pilot, Flight Officer Samuel Fine, from the Waco glider LZ.

Captain A.F. Bouchier Giles, DFC, and Staff Sergeant Miller, pilots of another Horsa which had landed some distance away, also arrived with a six-pounder gun and four men of the Border Regiment. Captain Bouchier Giles was placed in command of the glider pilots, who now included Lieutenant A. Dale, and told to hold the south bank of the canal near the bridge.

At 08:00 the enemy counter-attacked and the men of the RAMC armed with captured Italian weapons took part in the defence. Casualties began to mount and about 09:00 Major Beasley was killed by a burst of machine gun fire which also killed one of the glider pilots. Constant attacks were made by the enemy until the bridge party was reduced to only fifteen unwounded men. At 15:30 with their ammunition gone they were overrun by the enemy and the bridge lost. But before the enemy had a chance to demolish the bridge the seaborne Royal Scots Fusiliers arrived and, counter-attacking, recaptured the bridge at 16:15. The enemy had held it for a mere forty-five minutes, but had had no explosives to carry out a demolition.

The 1st Air Landing Brigade later received this message from General Montgomery.

> For those responsible for this particular Operation [Labrooke], I am filled with admiration. Others who by their initiative fought isolated actions in various parts of the battlefield, have played no small part in this most successful landing action. Had it not been for the skill and gallantry of the Air Landing Brigade the Port of Syracuse would not have fallen until very much later.

Montgomery later said that the taking of the Ponte Grande bridge saved his forces seven days. The operation was costly but many important lessons were learned. The gliders had been released too far offshore (possibly due to misjudgement in the darkness and confusion) and at too low an altitude for the glider pilots to reach their LZs.

Men of the 2nd South Staffords earned three Military Crosses and five Military Medals during the operation. Lieutenant Withers was recommended for the DSO but was awarded the Military Cross specifically for the taking of the bridge. The South Staffordshire Regiment hold the unique distinction of being the first British regiment to go to battle by land, sea and air. Both the South Staffords and the 1st Battalion of the Border Regiment share the distinction of being the first British Regiments to be carried to battle in gliders.

In recognition of this, King George VI granted them the distinction of wearing an embroidered glider badge at the top of the sleeve of No. 1 Dress and battledress to commemorate the part played by them on the night of 9/10 July 1943, the first occasion in which British glider troops took part in a major tactical operation.

The Border Regiment suffered 250 casualties and the 2nd South Staffords 350, many of whom perished in the sea. Eighty-eight British and 13 US glider pilots were missing, presumed drowned.

Staff Sergeants Dennis Galpin and Nigel Brown: their part in the Sicily Operation, described by Staff Sergeant Galpin:

After several weeks at Salé and Froha helping with the ferrying of gliders from the UK Nigel Brown and myself eventually arrived at 'E' Strip, Kairouan, some forty-eight hours before the Sicily operation was due to begin. We were pleased to find that a glider and load had been allocated to us. The next forty-eight hours were taken up with briefing as well as studying photographs of our objective, the Ponte Grande, just outside Syracusa. As the landing was to be made at night we were given night maps which proved invaluable in our case because they showed the shape of the coast as well as the river and canal running inland from the bridge.

Eight Horsas, each carrying a platoon of the South Staffs Regiment, together with supporting arms, were allocated a landing zone right next to the objective. At the briefing we were told that we would be released at 5,000 feet one mile out to sea from Cap Moro de Poro, then should fly some five or six miles to the bridge using a predetermined compass course. This was ideal and would give us ample height to reach the objective – but our Intelligence rather underestimated the strength of the ground defences around the harbour at Syracusa.

Right from the take-off our tug seemed to be in some trouble, but we set course for Malta. However after flying for a few minutes and having reached 200 feet I heard over the intercom that we would be obliged to return to 'E' Strip due to engine trouble. Fortunately, just before I was preparing to cast off and land back at 'E' Strip, I heard that all was well again and once more we headed for Malta. Owing to the delay we were well behind the mainstream although we could see a few Wacos some way ahead of us.

The flight to Malta passed without any more trouble except that, near the island, the airspeed built up well over the maximum for a Horsa but once again the trouble was rectified and we proceeded on our way.

Approaching Sicily I heard over the intercom that our tug pilot was going to give us an extra 1,000 feet, making a casting off height of 6,000 feet, and would take us a little nearer the coast to allow for an anticipated increased wind from offshore.

On the instructions from the tug we cast off and turned on to our predetermined course for Syracusa but at first could not make out exactly where we were. However I was able to make out the shape of the coast line and after flying for a few minutes realised I had flown over the objective and was over Syracusa itself. On turning back I soon saw our objective, standing out exactly as depicted on the night map. I had too much height at 2,000 feet and the ground defences got on to us by searchlight and flak so I had to head out to sea to lose height then came in towards the bridge flying fairly low and fast. Just as we crossed the coast a searchlight beam showed the bridge and landing zone for a few seconds and I immediately pulled the nose up, applied full flap and landed. Although a ditch broke our nose wheel and caused damage to the floor of the cockpit, it did help to enable us to stop.

Our load of men of the South Staffordshires offloaded rapidly and took the nearby bridge.

My observations at the time were that the following points were of interest in planning future night operations.

1. The night maps were excellent and essential.

2. Remote releases were possible (provided the RAF did the towing) but the casting off point must be accurate as it was in my case.

3. Intercom through the rope was essential to enable the glider pilots to know what is going on at all times.

4. Landing right on top of the objective is the best recipe for success.

Staff Sergeant D. Galpin was awarded the Distinguished Flying Medal for his part in the Operation. His was the only Horsa to land on the LZ.

The Invasion of Sicily. Two: Operation 'Fustian'

The second airborne operation by British forces in the overall scheme of the invasion of Sicily. Code-named 'Fustian', the plan was to air-drop and land troops to take the vital Prima Sole bridge over the River Simeto, five miles south of Catania,

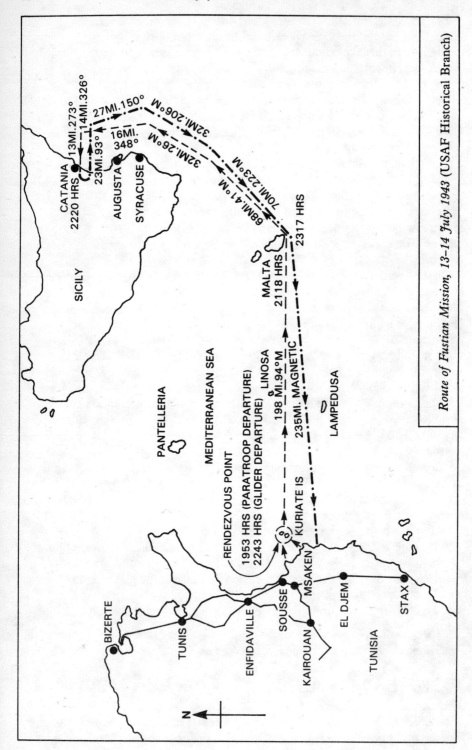

Route of Fustian Mission, 13–14 July 1943 (USAF Historical Branch)

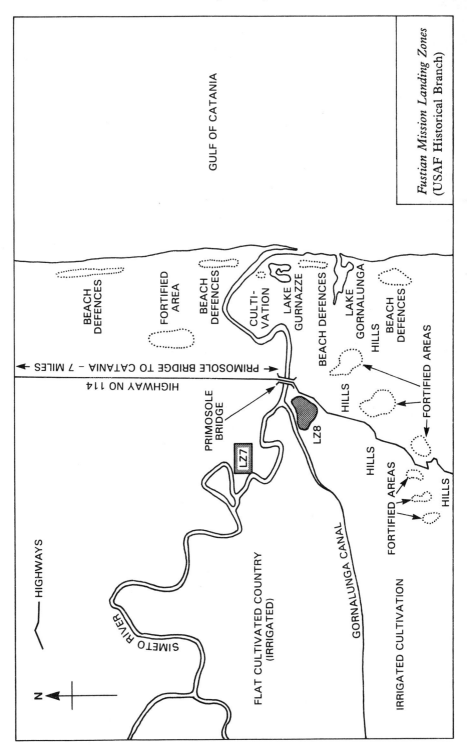

Fustian Mission Landing Zones
(USAF Historical Branch)

on the east coast of Sicily. This would allow the British 2nd Army to punch through into the Catanian Plain northwards towards Messina.

'Fustian' was to be a combined paratroop and gliderborne operation by the British 1st Parachute Brigade under Brigadier Lathbury, together with men from the Royal Engineers 1st Parachute Squadron and the Royal Army Medical Corps 16th Parachute Field Ambulance: a total of 1,856 men carried by 116 aircraft.

After the paratroops had landed, 8 Waco CG-4A gliders and 11 Horsa gliders towed by 12 Albemarles of 296 Squadron and 7 Halifaxes of 295 Squadron, ..AF, carrying 77 Royal Artillery gunners with ten six-pounder guns and 18 vei .cles, would land on two LZs (LZs 7 and 8) to the south and north-west of the Prima Sole bridge.

The dirt airstrips A, B, C, D, E and F near Kairouan, Tunisia, were to be used as take-off airfields for the operation with the aerial RV again over the Kuriate Islands off the Tunisian coast. The flight path was east to Malta, then north-west to Sicily. A similar route to that taken by the aircraft on Operation 'Ladbrooke' but the run in to Sicily was designed to keep the aircraft ten miles off the east coast of Sicily to avoid Allied naval forces off this coast.

At 19:20 on 12 July 1943, the US 51st Troop Carrier Wing began to take off from airstrips A, B, C, and D and head for the RV over the Kuriate Islands. At 22:00 38 Wing began to tow off the nineteen gliders. Two Waco and one Horsa gliders had to abort the mission, leaving sixteen to set course for the RV.

At 19:35 the paratroop aircraft left the RV and made for Malta, though one C47 and one Albemarle had to return to base with engine trouble. One Horsa was accidentally released over the sea, leaving fifteen gliders to carry on. The Dakotas flew at 140 mph with the glider towing Albemarles at 125 mph and the Halifaxes at 145 mph; all were in loose streams of two to eleven aircraft spaced at thirty-second intervals.

The naval commanders of Allied naval forces lying off the eastern coast of Sicily had been informed of the 'Fustian' route and time schedule, as there was a five-mile no-go area for aircraft off the invasion coast of Sicily. All the pilots engaged had been instructed to keep clear of the no-go zone. As the airborne force approached Cap Passero, however, some Allied ships opened fire on them. Some of the aircraft, thought to be at least thirty-three, had flown off course into the no-go area. Between Syracuse and Catania enemy anti-aircraft fire was encountered. (Later enquiries revealed that some thirty aircraft had been fired on by Allied naval ships in the area between eight and twenty three miles off the invasion coast.)

Two aircraft were shot down by Allied naval ships and a further nine had to turn back due to damage and injuries. Another six aircraft turned back to base the pilots later saying that they had been so instructed by their squadron commander. The remainder flew on towards their DZs and LZs in a hail of flak. Nine paratroop carrying aircraft were shot down but most managed to drop their troops. Four of the nine managed to ditch in the sea. Three glider towing aircraft went missing believed shot down. Fourteen aircraft in total were shot down, another thirty-four were damaged by flak and one was damaged by striking the cable of a barrage balloon.

Owing to the flak the paratroops were dropped over a wide area; some were dropped near the Mount Etna volcano twenty miles from their DZ. Dropping began at 22:15 but it was 01:00 before General Lathbury had collected some 100 men to take the bridge. On their arrival at the bridge they found a fifty-strong party of 1st Parachute Batallion under Captain Rann had taken the northern end of the bridge at 02:15. By 04:30 the bridge was in British hands.

Whilst the battle for the bridge was in progress, the gliders began to arrive over the area seeking their two LZs which were now clearly visible in the light of the intense enemy flak. Major A. Cooper, AFC, the veteran of Operation 'Beggar', together with the Royal Artillery commander, Lieutenant-Colonel C. Crawford and his staff aboard his glider, saw his tow plane hit by flak when they were at 500 feet. Major Cooper, unable to control his glider, crashed into the river bed losing his life together with Colonel Crawford and all his staff.

Only four Horsa glider units contributed to the bridge battle. One, piloted by Staff Sergeant White, landed on LZ8 and the gun and jeep on board were off-loaded and later brought into action. Another Horsa was landed on the highway beside LZ8 and one landed half a mile west of the LZ. The troops aboard were able to get two jeeps and three 6-pounder guns into action. Lieutenant Thomas landed his Horsa in a ravine seven miles away but managed to get his load, a jeep and gun into action next day at the bridge. Captain Barrie, one of the four who had landed his Horsa successfully, fought with his men for three days and was later awarded the DFC. Surviving Sicily, he lost his life at Arnhem. Of the fifteen gliders which had approached Sicily, four were missing probably shot down by flak. Three made fatal crash-landings and four landed among the enemy and most of the troops were taken prisoner. Only the four Horsas previously mentioned were of effective use in the battle.

Dawn broke next day with about 250 troops defending the bridge, armed with but two mortars and three of the gliderborne anti-tank guns. At noon the enemy attacked in strength and the British had to retire from the intact bridge due to lack of ammunition and back-up forces. At dawn on 16 July British forces counter-attacked and finally took the bridge.

The price paid by the Glider Pilot Regiment was high: both 'Ladbrooke' and 'Fustian' had cost the regiment 57 pilots.

The Royal Air Force lost the veteran of Operation 'Freshman', Squadron Leader A. Wilkinson, whose aircraft failed to return to base.

The combined casualty list of 38 Wing and the US 51st Wing for 'Fustian' was 1 known dead and 35 missing in action, with 14 wounded. A post mortem on the operation was dismal although the objectives had been achieved. Many lessons were learned and put to use later during the war.

Operation 'Bunghole'

Foreword by Captain Cornelius Turner, Commanding Officer

The object of Bunghole was to deliver to Tito in his mountain enclave 100 miles inside Yugoslavia a Russian general staff, led by a Marshal Korneyev, of thirty senior staff officers. They could have been delivered by parachute but preferred to take their chance in gliders. For the sake of accuracy of navigation all agreed that daylight was essential, provided that suitable escort protection was available. We decided against Horsas as no one was sure they could clear the 7,000 feet Dinaric Alps across our path. So on a bright February morning with unlimited visibility we took off from Bari on our 250-mile flight to a 4,000 ft forest clearing landing beyond the teeth of the mountain range, course due north.

The operation was under the direction of a cloak and dagger outfit called Force 133 who cheered us up no end by handing me on take-off six self-destruct morphia tubes, one per pilot, just in case. According to our briefing they had arranged for 25 Spitfires to cover the flight to the target, 25 Mustangs or Thunderbolts over it, and 50 Flying Fortresses doing a diversion raid on Zagreb.

After an uneventful flight (no wonder!) we plopped down side by side into three feet of snow, almost on top of the signal fires. It had been a remarkable piece of dead reckoning on the part of Colonel Duden's C-47s over terrain featureless but for the contours. We came out at the end of March when the snow had thawed sufficiently for a C-47 to land on our mountainside and, with some difficulty, took off again.

Operation 'Bunghole'
The first daylight glider landing of World War II took place on German-occupied Yugoslavia on 19 February 1944, where Waco CG-4A Hadrian gliders were flown in by the 1st Independent Squadron of the British Glider Pilot Regiment.

When the 1st Airborne Division returned to the United Kingdom in October 1943, they left behind parts of the division which were later designated the 2nd Parachute Brigade Group with supporting air landing units and a glider pilot squadron which became the 1st Independent Glider Squadron of the Glider Pilot Regiment. All of these units came under the direct command of the Commander Mediterranean Forces, Caserta. The Parachute Brigade, battle experienced from action in North Africa and Sicily, became spearhead ground forces of 8th Army on the Italian Front right flank.

The glider pilots, already veterans of the Sicily landings, went into further training at Comiso, Sicily, with the USAAF 64th Troop Carrier Group of the 51st Wing of the North African Troop Carrier Command, using Dakota C-47s as tug aircraft. The Americans gave their wholehearted support to the training, with unstinted use of all their airfields and aircraft facilities. The 64th TCG had been unique during the Sicily operation that on their paratroop drops they were the only group to keep whole formation.

The Pathfinder Company of the 2nd Parachute Brigade Group, under Captain Peter Baker, was a vital part of this training and cooperation, using their Eureka Beacons and landing aids. Together, glider pilots, tug crews and pathfinders reached standards of competence hitherto unknown. Using Horsa and Waco gliders, experimental training was carried out on loads, heights, limits, navigation by night and day and landing with and without landing aids.

At one time whilst flying with Captain Turner in a glider the legendary Popski of 'Popski's Private Army' (a well-known irregular force) explained how he could capture Rome with his troops carried in 400 gliders.

The United States was still delivering crated Waco CG-4A Hadrian gliders to Casablanca, where after assembly, they were flown by the Independent Squadron from Tunis to Sicily towed by C-47s of the USAAF. The strained relations between the USAAF and the British forces had improved since the debacle of Sicily.

At first, the British War Office via the intelligence unit Force 133 in Cairo, had instructed the Independent Squadron to carry out the operation to Tito HQ at Drvar using Horsa gliders. As there were no Horsas available in Sicily at this time, the glider pilots were therefore flown by the USAAF to the dirt airstrips near Kairouan in Tunisia, which had been used for the Sicily operation, to recover some Horsas left there after the Sicily operation. For six months in all weathers, the Horsas had been abandoned there without servicing. As they had no RAF airframe riggers to service and inspect the gliders, the pilots had to make their own inspection and pre-flight checks. Trusting to the strength of the Horsas, the glider pilots were towed back the 250 miles to Sicily, then immediately on to Bari in Italy. On arriving at Bari, however, the C-47 tug pilots expressed doubts that the Horsas could be towed over the 8,000 feet high Dinaric Alps of Yugoslavia, so three of the smaller Waco Hadrians were substituted. The Russian Military Mission of about thirty senior officers, led by Marshal Korneyev, took part in the loaded flying trials.

As it was winter in Yugoslavia with the mountains covered in deep snow, navigation would be too difficult for a night operation, so it was decided to carry out the operation in daylight. A diversionary raid by fifty Flying Fortresses of the 15th USAAF would be made on Zagreb and a fighter escort of twenty-five Spitfires would cover the combinations' flight path to the target. Another USAAF long range fighter escort of Mustangs and Thunderbolts would cover the actual landing which was in a valley called Medenapolu, two miles north of the small town of Bosan Petrovac, in the Dinaric Alps, some 100 miles from the Yugoslavian coast and 250 miles north-east of Bari.

The three glider crews chosen for the operation, now named 'Bunghole', were Hadrian glider No. 1, Captain C. Turner, i/c and Staff Sergeant Newman; Hadrian glider No. 2, Staff Sergeant A. McCulloch and Staff Sergeant Hill; Hadrian glider No. 3, Staff Sergeant W. Morrison and Staff Sergeant McMillen. The three towing C-47s of the USAAF 64th Troop Carrier Group, commanded by Lieutenant Colonel Duden, had as navigators men from the Dominion air forces, making the operation inter-Allied indeed.

At 11:00 on 19 February 1944, the three combinations took off from Bari in bright clear weather. The Russian mission split up between the three Hadrians – with Marshal Korneyev sitting on two large cases which were part of his baggage and deemed important. A dour Russian colonel sat behind Captain Turner clutching a sub-machine gun in his lap.

Climbing to 8,000 feet in a bitterly cold cloudless sky, the three combinations set course for the fighter rendezvous then north-eastwards towards their target. Scraping over the mountains, they neared their target after an uneventful flight, apart fom severe turbulence. Checking their position relative to their intended LZ, the three tugs with their gliders turned about and the glider pilots knew they had arrived.

Captain Turner, in the lead glider, cast off his tow and the other two Hadrians followed suit. Circling, the glider pilots saw the lighted straw fires that marked their 4,000 feet above sea level LZ. All three glided in and landed side by side in the three-foot deep snow almost on top of the signal fires. The deep snow had a braking effect on the Hadrians' landing run, reducing it to twenty feet after the gliders had gone nose down in the soft snow, then dropping back onto an even keel. They had arrived right on target, thanks to the USAAF tug pilots and navigators.

Warmly greeted by the welcoming partisans, the glider pilots and the Russians were taken by sleigh to the nearby town of Petrovac. The Russian Marshal's two crates went with him and when opened proved to contain bottles of vodka and tins of caviar.

The glider pilots had to stay with the partisans for a month, waiting for the spring to thaw the snow so that an aircraft could land on the LZ and bring them out. The Germans, who had assembled the 500th SS Parachute Mountain Battalion equipped with gliders at Bihac, were also waiting for the thaw to attack Tito and his partisans.

A month after the glider pilots had landed, two C-47s from Bari managed to land on the LZ which was still covered in nine inches of snow. Leaving again was not so easy, for all uneccessary weight had to be removed before the Dakota could take off in the dark and head back to Italy.

Another month later on 25 May, the Germans attacked Tito's headquarters at Drvar and other partisan strongholds, including the LZ used by the British glider pilots. Tito and the British and Russian military missions were able to escape to the mountains and in June were evacuated from Kupresko Polje by a Russian C-47 stationed at Bari, which was under the control of the Allied Balkan Air Force.

Operation 'Tonga'

The air lift by 38 and 46 Groups, Royal Air Force, of the 6th Airborne Division on the night of 5/6 June 1944, to Normandy to secure the Allied left flank in the opening of the invasion of France.

Airborne forces' objective and tasks

1. To secure and hold two bridges over the River Orne and the Caen Canal. Operation 'Coup de Main' or 'Deadstick'.
2. To neutralise a coastal battery at Merville.
3. To secure a base including above bridgeheads east of the River Orne.
4. To prevent enemy reinforcements moving towards the British left flank from the south-east.

The airborne forces landings would be divided into four phases:

Phase I

Six Horsa gliders would land on LZs 'X' and 'Y' and take the Orne and Caen Canal bridges, without landing aids.

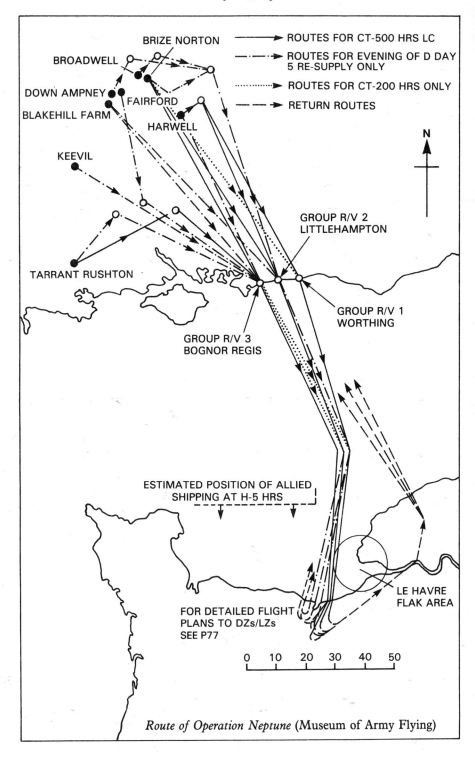

BRIZE NORTON

ROUTES FOR CT-500 HRS LC

ROUTES FOR EVENING OF D DAY
5 RE-SUPPLY ONLY

BROADWELL

ROUTES FOR CT-200 HRS ONLY

DOWN AMPNEY

RETURN ROUTES

FAIRFORD

BLAKEHILL FARM

N

HARWELL

KEEVIL

GROUP R/V 2
LITTLEHAMPTON

GROUP R/V 1
WORTHING

TARRANT RUSHTON

GROUP R/V 3
BOGNOR REGIS

ESTIMATED POSITION OF ALLIED
SHIPPING AT H-5 HRS

LE HAVRE
FLAK AREA

FOR DETAILED FLIGHT
PLANS TO DZs/LZs
SEE P77

0   10   20   30   40   50

Route of Operation Neptune (Museum of Army Flying)

Six aircraft would drop pathfinder paratroops on DZs 'N'. 'K' and 'V' to mark them and establish landing aids for paratroops.

Twenty-one aircraft would drop the advance parties of paratroops on DZs 'N', 'K' and 'V'.

Phase II

Eleven Horsa gliders carrying support equipment for the Merville Battery assault would land on DZ 'V'.

Six Horsa gliders carrying support equipment for paratroops would land on DZ 'K'.239 aircraft would drop paratroops and containers on DZs 'N', 'K' and 'V'.

Phase III

Three Horsa gliders would land on the Merville Battery as previously dropped ground forces attacked.

Sixty-eight Horsa and four Hamilcar gliders would land on DZ/LZ 'N' with Divisional Headquarters and support equipment.

Special Eureka and light beacons would be placed at points of departure for aircraft on the south coast of England for them to RV on.

Group RV 1: Worthing, Light flashing 'V', Eureka 'CA'
Group RV 2: Littlehampton, Light flashing 'K', Eureka 'DC'
Group RV 3: Bognor, Light flashing 'N', Eureka 'ED'

Return flights for all aircraft would be over Littlehampton at 3,000 feet. All aircraft would be marked with three white and two black stripes on the wings and fuselage to identify them to Allied sea, air and ground forces.

Phase IV

Operation 'Mallard', on the evening of D-Day: the air lifting of the 6th Air Landing Brigade and Divisional Troops.

At 22:49 on the evening of 5 June 1944, the seven Horsa gliders of E Squadron, Glider Pilot Regiment, were towed off from RAF Down Ampney by Dakota tugs of 271 Squadron and set course for LZ 'V' with close support equipment for the 9th Battalion, Parachute Regiment, who were to attack the Merville Battery.

A minute later from RAF Blakehill Farm six Horsa gliders of F Squadron carrying equipment for paratroops on LZ 'K' were lifted off by Dakotas of 233 Squadron. The 'Coup de main' platoons lifted off in six Horsas of C Squadron, towed by Halifaxes of 298 and 644 Squadrons, at 22:56 from RAF Tarrant Rushton. Four Horsa gliders of A Squadron also carrying equipment for the 9th Battalion assault on Merville Battery, were airborne at 23:10 en route for LZ 'V' towed by Albemarle aircraft of 295 Squadron from Harwell.

At 02:30 hours the three Merville Battery assault Horsa gliders lifted off from RAF Brize Norton, towed by Albemarle tugs from 297 Squadron, to land on the battery. Twenty-six gliders comprising the first wave were airborne and flying into history as the spearhead of the invasion of France.

Meanwhile at RAF Harwell, six Albemarle aircraft of 295 and 570 Squadrons had loaded with the Pathfinder paratroops of the 22nd Independent Parachute

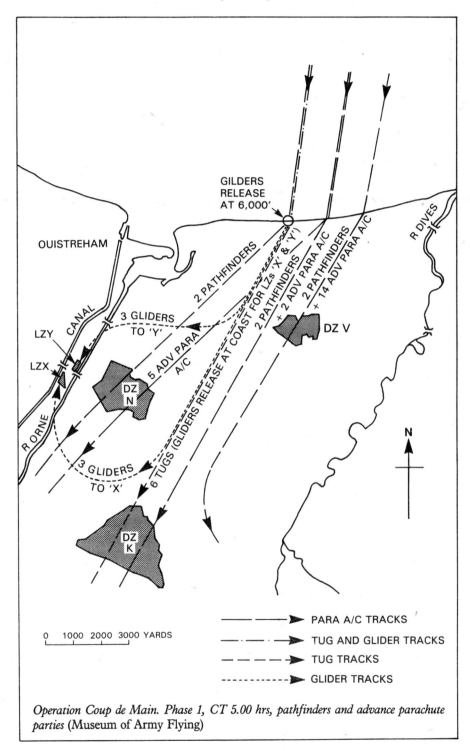

Operation Coup de Main. Phase 1, CT 5.00 hrs, pathfinders and advance parachute parties (Museum of Army Flying)

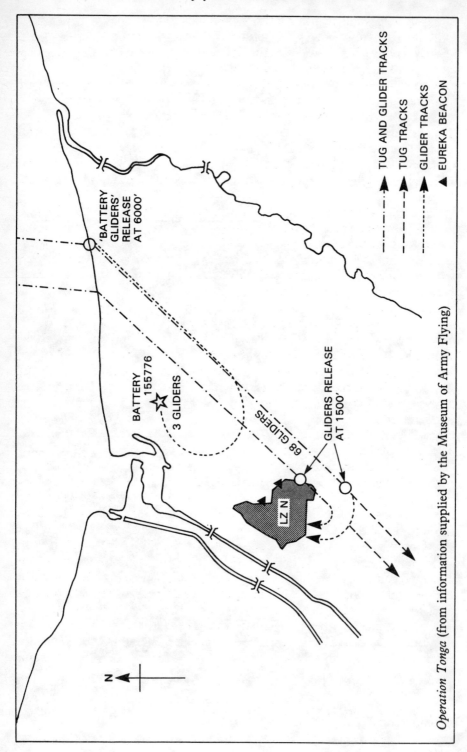

Operation Tonga (from information supplied by the Museum of Army Flying)

Company who would mark LZ/DZs 'V', 'K' and 'N' with lights and beacons. At 23:03 the first Albemarle, serial number V 1740, piloted by Squadron Leader Merrick, and, with Air Vice Marshal Hollinhurst and ten Pathfinder paratroops aboard, took off, followed by the other five aircraft, and made for the LZs. Another fourteen Albemarles of 295 and 570 Squadrons followed with the advance party of 3rd Parachute Brigade to drop in the wake of the Pathfinders.

The Phase I group of Horsa gliders were now coming up to their LZs. The Coup de Main platoons in their six gliders made successful landings. Give of the six landed on their intended LZs 'X' and 'Y' without landing aids in the darkness, a brilliant feat of flying skill. The other glider landed eight miles away, owing to being mistowed, but went into action and successfully fought their way to the bridges.

The eleven Horsas of A and E Squadrons, carrying the Merville Battery's paratroops equipment and guns, were unable to locate LZ/DZ 'V' owing to dust and smoke – the fog of war – raised by RAF bombing and had to land as best they could south of their intended LZ. Seven glider pilots were killed in the landings and most gliders suffered damage due to colliding with anti-glider poles – Rommel's asparagus as they were known. Their cargoes did not reach the Merville assault paratroops who attacked without it.

The six gliders of F Squadron encountered bad weather conditions over the Channel. Low cloud plus the fog of war obscured LZ 'K' and only two gliders reached it; the others landed as best they could in the adverse conditions. Nevertheless the glider pilots fought as infantry with skill and courage in the fire fights developing all over the Orne area. The Germans became more and more confused by the spread of the glider and paratroop landings and had no overall picture of the situation.

The Merville Battery gliders were now reduced to two, the tow rope of one having broken over England and the glider had to land at Odiham. The other two combinations carried on in bad weather conditions and the fog of war caused by the RAF bombing. The attacking paratroops had no means of contact with the two gliders whose pilots were now on their own flying skills on their intended landing. Both combinations were towed round the area of the battery four times, vainly trying to locate their target. Nevertheless both gliders cast off their tow ropes, Staff Sergeant Bone in one glider thought the village of Merville was the battery but by then he was down to 500 feet. Realising his error, he banked the Horsa and managed to land a mile from the objective. The other glider, piloted by Staff Sergeant Kerr, came in, but he knew he could not manage to land on the target so streamed his arrester parachute and landed only 50 yards away in an orchard. No sooner had they landed than they were engaging the Germans, a platoon who were rushing to strengthen the battery garrison. Outnumbered, the glider troops fought for several hours. The gallant troops of the 9th Parachute Battalion took the battery at heavy cost.

Operation 'Tonga' was being carried out successfully, albeit not quite according to plan; but the bridges and the battery had been taken. On LZ/DZ 'N' the parachute engineers of 5th Parachute Brigade were clearing four landing strips for the incoming sixty-eight Horsa and Hamilcar gliders. Rommel's asparagus was

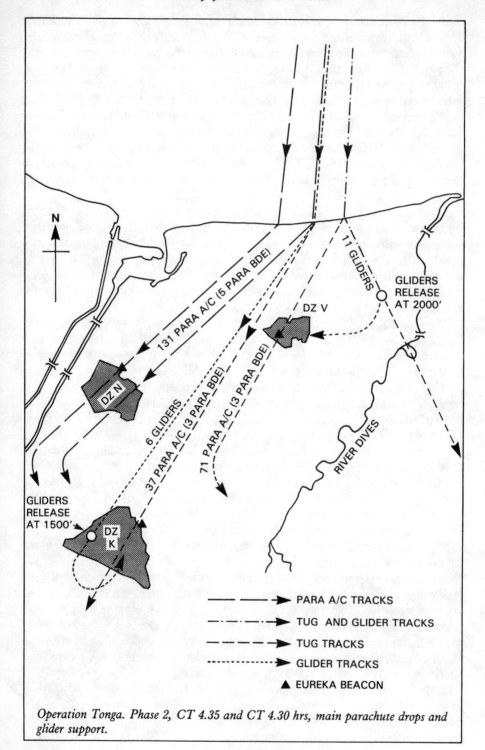

Operation Tonga. Phase 2, CT 4.35 and CT 4.30 hrs, main parachute drops and glider support.

being blown up by explosive charges and four landing strips were made. Each strip was 1,000 yards long, three were 60 yards wide for the Horsas and one 90 yards wide for the Hamilcars carrying heavy equipment. The way was clear for the main glider force to land although fire fights were still raging over the area.

Back in England seventy-two more gliders were lined up ready to be towed off. These would form the bulk of the 'Tonga' glider force; led by Lieutenant-Colonel Ian Murray they would land on LZ/DZ 'N' at 03:00. 'A' Squadron, Glider Pilot Regiment, would pilot twenty-one Horsas towed by 295 Squadron and 570 Squadron, RAF, from Harwell; B Squadron, Glider Pilot Regiment, would pilot seventeen Horsas from Brize Norton, towed by 296 and 297 Squadrons, RAF; D Squadron, Glider Pilot Regiment, would pilot thirty Horsas and four Hamilcars from Tarrant Rushton, towed by 298 and 644 Squadrons, RAF.

At 01:28 Wing Commander B.R. McNamara took off from Harwell in Albemarle V 1749 towing a Horsa glider piloted by Major S.C. Griffiths, DFC, with Major-General Gale and part of 6th Airborne Divisional HQ aboard and set course in low cloud and rain for Normandy, followed at intervals by twenty other combinations till all were airborne by 01:44. At the other airfields the gliders were being towed off and the seventy-two strong fleet made for the RV point on the English coast still flying in bad weather conditions.

Over Worthing two gliders had to cast off due to the tug aircraft becoming unserviceable, and had to return to England to be followed by another three shortly afterwards. As the gliders made landfall on the Normandy coast the enemy opened up with anti-aircraft fire and three gliders were hit. One Hamilcar, piloted by Staff Sergeants Dent and Rodgers, broke its tow rope over Bognor and landed at Ford. Another Hamilcar, piloted by Staff Sergeant Ridings, broke its tow rope one mile from LZ 'N' but landed safely. The other two Hamilcars reached the LZ. Twenty-five gliders were hit by enemy flak.

Fifty-seven Horsas reached LZ 'N'; weather conditions had moderated over the Channel but a belt of low stratus cloud with rain lay over the French coast and a strong cross wind was blowing across the LZ making landings difficult on the flarepaths. The glider pilots had to check (fly at an angle to the wind) their gliders onto the LZ but there were collisions on the landing strips. They had difficulty in offloading the gliders, owing to the damage they had suffered.

HQ 6th Airborne Division was established near the LZ and fifty-two glider pilots took up defensive positions around it, under the command of Major Griffiths, and were immediately engaged by the enemy. The gliders were, however, quickly unloaded of their jeeps and guns by troops of 6th Airborne Division.

Other glider pilots who had landed away from their LZs made their way on foot towards them. Major John Lyne, CO of D Squadron, with six men from his glider took three days to reach Divisional HQ at Ranville, covering many miles on foot through enemy-held ground and fighting two actions with German troops en route.

With the evening of 6 June came another fleet of gliders carrying troops of Operation 'Mallard'. Operation 'Tonga' had been a success; all the set tasks had been accomplished. Of the 196 glider pilots who had taken off from England, 34 gave their lives (17 per cent). Forty-nine gliders in all successfully landed on their

Air Movements Chart: Operation Tonga

Airborne Unit	RAF Unit	Aircraft	Gpr Unit	Glider	Chalk Nos	Airfield	Take-off	Remarks & load
4th A/L A/T Bty, RA 1st Canadian Para Battalion 3rd Para HQ.	271 Sqdn 46 Grp	Dakota	E Sqdn	Horsa	261–267 (7)	Down Ampney	22:49	LZ V 20 troops 7 jeeps 4 trailers 2 × 6 Pdr guns 4 motor cycles
8th Para Batt 224th Para Field Ambulance	233 Sqdn 46 Grp	Dakota	F Sqdn	Horsa	218–223 (6)	Blakehill Farm	22:50	LZ K 6 jeeps 6 trailers 8 motor cycles 12 bicycles
2nd Ox & Bucks 249 Coy RE I/C Major Howard	298 Sqdn	Halifax	C Sqdn	Horsa	91–93 (3)	Tarrant Rushton	22:56	Caen & Orne Bridges
	644 Sqdn 38 Grp	Halifax	C Sqdn	Horsa	93–96 (3)	Tarrant Rushton	22:56	Coup de Main Party
224 Field Ambulance	295 Sqdn	Albemarle	A Sqdn	Horsa	66–69 (4)	Harwell	23:10	LZ V rope broke (1)
9th Para Battalion	570 Sqdn 38 Grp	Albemarle	A Sqdn	Horsa		Harwell	23:15	LZ V ditched (2) short of coast
9th Para Battalion	297 Sqdn 38 Grp	Albemarle	B Sqdn	Horsa	27. 28. 28a	Brize Norton	02:30	Merville Battery Assault: two landed

Main Force

Airborne Unit	RAF Unit	Aircraft	Gpr Unit	Glider	Chalk Nos	Airfield	Take-off	Remarks & load
5th Para Brigade	296 Sqdn 297 Sqdn 38 Grp	Albermarle Albemarle	B Sqdn B Sqdn	Horsa Horsa	29–36 (8) 37–45 (9)	Brize Norton	01:41 01:10	LZ N LZ N
Gen Gale + HQ 6th 5th Para Brigade	295 Sqdn 570 Sqdn 38 Grp	Albemarle Albemarle	A Sqdn A Sqdn	Horsa Horsa	70–80 (11) 81–90 (10)	Harwell Harwell	01:28 01:28	LZ N LZ N
4th A/L A/T Bty Div HQ 3 Para Brigade	298 Sqdn 644 Sqdn 38 Grp	Halifax Halifax	D Sqdn D Sqdn	Horsa Horsa	97–111 (15) 112–126 (15)	Tarrant Rushton Tarrant Rushton	01:30 01:30	LZ N LZ N
4 × 17-pdr Guns	298 Sqdn 644 Sqdn 38 Grp	Halifax Halifax	D Sqdn D Sqdn	Hamilcar Hamilcar	500–501 (2) 503–503 (2)	Tarrant Rushton Tarrant Rushton	02:10 02:10	LZ N LZ N
Totals:				94 Horsas 4 Hamilcars 98 Gliders				

LZs. A total of 364 aircraft and 98 gliders had been involved. 4,512 paratroops were carried of which 4,310 were dropped (95.5 per cent); 59 gliders landed on their LZs (60.20%), carrying 493 troops, 44 jeeps, 55 motor cycles, 15 six-pounder guns, 2 seventeen-pounder guns and one bulldozer. The Royal Air Force lost 7 aircraft.

Forces involved in Operation 'Tonga'

6th Airborne Division
Divisional HQ
CRA: CO, Norris
CRE: CO, Lowman
Signals: CO, Tew
RASC: CO, Lovegrove
ADMS: CO, McEwan
ADOS: CO, Fielding
REME: CO, Powditch
SCF: CO, Hales
Recce: CO, Stuart

3rd Parachute Brigade
Brigadier S.J.L. Hill, DSO, MC
8th Parachute Battalion: CO, Pearson
9th Parachute Battalion: CO, Otway
1st Canadian Battalion: CO, Bradbrooke
211th Air Landing Battery, RA
3rd Anti-Tank Battery, RA
3rd Parachute Squadron, RE
224th Parachute Field Ambulance, RAMC

5th Parachute Brigade
Brigadier J.H.N. Poett, DSO
7th Parachute Battalion: CO, Pine Coffin
12th Parachute Battalion: CO, Johnston
13th Parachute Battalion: CO, Luard
212th Air Landing Light Battery, RA
4th Air Landing Anti Tank Battery, RA
591st Parachute Squadron, RE
225th Parachute Field Ambulance, RAMC

22nd Independent Parachute Company, Pathfinders.

Glider Pilot Regiment: CO, Colonel G.J.S. Chatterton, DSO
CO, No. 1 Wing: Lt-Colonel I.A. Murray
'A' Squadron: CO, Major H.T. Bartlett
'B' Squadron: CO, Major T.I.J. Toler
'D' Squadron: CO, Major J.F. Lyne
CO, No. 2 Wing: Lt-Colonel J.W. Place

'C' Squadron: CO, Major J.A. Dale
'E' Squadron: CO, Major B.H.P. Jackson
'F' Squadron: CO, Major F.S.A. Murray

Royal Air Force, Transport Groups
38 Group

295 Squadron	Albemarle,	Harwell, Berkshire
296 Squadron	Albemarle,	Brize Norton, Oxfordshire
297 Squadron	Albemarle,	Brize Norton, Oxfordshire
298 Squadron	Halifax,	Tarrant Rushton, Dorset
570 Squadron	Albemarle,	Harwell, Berkshire
644 Squadron	Halifax,	Tarrant Rushton, Dorset

46 Group

233 Squadron	Dakota	Blakehill Farm, Wiltshire
271 Squadron	Dakota	Down Ampney, Wiltshire

Supplying 13 Dakotas, 45 Albemarles and 40 Halifaxes to tow 98 gliders.

Glider Pilot Squadrons

A Squadron	Harwell	50 pilots
B Squadron	Brize Norton	40 pilots
C Squadron	Tarrant Rushton	12 pilots
D Squadron	Tarrant Rushton	68 pilots
E Squadron	Down Ampney	14 pilots
F Squadron	Blakehill Farm	12 pilots

Six squadrons, supplying 196 glider pilots.

Operation 'Coup de Main'

The gliderborne assault to capture intact the River Orne and the Caen Canal bridges in Normandy, France, during the early hours of D-Day before the main landings.

Foreword by Major John Howard, DSO, Commanding Officer, 'Coup de Main'

It was obvious at the outset to everyone involved, that the success of the bridges 'Coup de Main' operation, primarily depended upon the ability of the glider pilots to land the party near enough to the bridges to achieve full surprise. In the event five of the six gliders did exactly that! Four of them crash-landed their Horsas on the precise spots on the ground, where I had hopefully indicated during my briefing that they should finish up.

As soon as we first met our twelve glider pilots at Tarrant Rushton airfield about D-4, we all had complete confidence in their ability to do the job. Their manner and determined outlook was inspiring for us all.

Air Chief Marshal Sir Trafford Leigh-Mallory, commanding the Allied air forces on D-Day, praised the glider landings as the finest feat of piloting in World War II.

I am happy to say, that today I still have contact with all but one of the the survivors of that group of superb glider pilots.

Operation Coup de Main

The object of the operation was to seize the two bridges, over the Orne and the Caen Canal, intact and provide access over them between the main seaborne landings on Sword Beach by the British 2nd Army and the airborne troops of 6th Airborne Division, dropping and landing east of the canal and river to protect the left flank of the main force.

The task of taking the two bridges fell to the 2nd Battalion, Oxfordshire and Buckinghamshire Light Infantry, (Ox and Bucks). Under the command of Major John Howard, DSO, D Company and two platoons from B Company of the regiment were selected and began training for the operation in April 1944.

D Company was part of the 6th Air Landing Brigade commanded by Brigadier the Honourable Hugh Kindersley, DSO, MC, which in turn was part of the 6th Airborne Division commanded by Major General Richard Gale, OBE, MC. The division was further composed of the 3rd Parachute Brigade, commanded by Brigadier J.S. Hill, DSO, MC, and the 5th Parachute Brigade commanded by Brigadier Nigel Poett, DSO, MC (later KCB).

On 2 May 1944, Major Howard went to the Planning HQ of 6th Airborne Division at Syrencot House, where he was given his orders for the capture of the two bridges by Brigadier Poett. The orders were marked TOP SECRET and BIGOT, the latter meaning that Major Howard was now one of a select number who had access to D-Day Planning, but could not reveal any details except to others similarly classified. The popular name for the classification was 'Bigoted'

Major Howard's orders were to seize the two bridges and hold them until reinforced by the 7th Battalion, Parachute Regiment, commanded by Lieutenant-Colonel Pine Coffin, DSO, MC and part of 5th Parachute Brigade who would drop near Ranville about 1,000 yards from the bridges at 00:50. 3rd Parachute Brigade would drop at Le Mesil to the south-east at the same time. The airborne forces would hold the ground until reinforced by the 3rd British Infantry Division which was part of the seaborne assault force.

Major Howard's 'Coup de Main' force was to consist of: D Company plus two platoons of B Company, 2nd Battalion, Ox and Bucks, six platoons in all; a detachment of thirty Sappers of 249 Airborne Field Company, Royal Engineers, under the command of Captain Jock Neilson; six Horsa gliders, piloted by pilots of the Glider Pilot Regiment and towed by six aircraft of 38 Group, Royal Air Force. Gliders were to be used in preference to paratroops for six gliders could land 171 men almost at the same time and place instead of widely dispersed as paratroops would be. Silence, surprise and speed were to be the essence of the operation.

On 28 May, Major Howard and his men moved to RAF Tarrant Rushton, Dorset near the Channel coast, where they joined with the RAF glider tug pilots of 298 and 644 Squadrons, whose motto, 'Silent we Strike', seemed extremely apt. Together with the glider pilots of C Squadron, Glider Pilot Regiment, training began for the operation.

Major Howard divided his force between the six gliders, then into two groups of three gliders, one group to attack each bridge. All of the force were now informed of their task as they were confined to a secure section of Tarrant Rushton and out of contact with the outside world. All involved had a specific task allotted and each man familiarised himself with his part in the operation. Every platoon had to be prepared to do any of the tasks according to the order in which they reached the bridges.

Two landing zones (LZs) had been selected close to the two Normandy bridges and code-named 'X' and 'Y'. LZ 'X' was a triangular field south-east of the canal bridge and gave landing access right up to the actual bridge. LZ 'Y' was a rectangular field north-west of the River Orne Bridge and also gave landing access almost to that bridge. Both of these small fields had been considered too small by the Germans for gliders to land, but work was just beginning to erect anti-glider poles, Rommel's 'asparagus'. However, by 3 June the poles had not yet been erected.

The German garrison at the bridges was expected to be about fifty men, mainly drafted from several German occupied countries but led by tough and experienced German NCOs well armed with machine guns and machine pistols. Their other defensive weapons were four light anti-aircraft guns, an anti-aircraft machine gun, six light machine guns and two anti-tank guns. The main body of German troops in the area was a battalion of the 736th Grenadier Regiment and a unit with twelve tanks. It was expected that both bridges had been prepared for demolition by the Germans to deny their use of the Allies.

On 5 June, Major Howard's men completed their final preparations at RAF Tarrant Rushton. All the Horsa gliders were heavily overloaded at about 7300 lb each; it had been intended for each glider to carry a canvas assault boat weighing 180 lb but this was reduced to four of the Horsas carrying one boat each. The boats were for use as troop ferries in case the bridges were blown by the Germans. The training, carried out under the name 'Deadstick', was over; 'Coup-de-Main' was ready to go.

Each Horsa glider was allocated and marked with a chalk number. Nos. 91, 92 and 93 comprised the group that was to assault the canal bridge; 94, 95 and 96 were to take the River Orne bridge some 400 yards to the east.

Canal Bridge Force: LZ 'X'

Horsa 91, serial number PF 800. Towed by Halifax LL 355, piloted by Wing Commander Duder. Glider Pilots: Staff Sergeant Jim Wallwork, DFM and Staff Sergeant John Ainsworth, MM. Troops: 'A-Able' platoon, i/c Major John Howard, DSO. Lieutenant Den Brotheridge and 29 troops.

Horsa 92: towed by Halifax L 335, piloted by Warrant Officer Bain. Glider Pilots: Staff Sergeants Oliver Boland and Phillip Hobb. Troops: 28. 'B-Baker' platoon i/c Lieutenant David Wood with Captain Jock Neilson, Royal Engineers, i/c Sappers (30 strong).

Horsa 93: Glider Pilots: Staff Sergeants Geoff Barkway, (DFM) and Peter Boyle. Troops: 'C-Charlie' platoon, i/c Lieutenant Sandy Smith, MC.

River Orne Bridge Force

Horsa 94: Glider Pilots: Staff Sergeants Lofty Lawrence and Shorty Shorter. Troops: 'D-Dog' platoon i/c Captain Brian Priday; 2 i/c Major Howard and Lieutenant Tony Hooper, MC.

Horsa 95: towed by Halifax LL 406 piloted by Warrant Officer Berry; Glider Pilots: Staff Sergeants Stan Pearson, DFM and Len Guthrie, Croix de G. Troops: 28. 'E-Easy' platoon. i/c Lieutenant Tod Sweeney, MC.

Horsa 96: Glider Pilots: Staff Sergeants Roy Howard, DFM and Fred Baacke, Croix de G. Troops: 'F-Fox' platoon i/c Lieutenant Dennis Fox, MC.

At 22:56 on 5 June 1944, the first Horsa glider was towed off from RAF Tarrant Rushton, by Halifax aircraft, followed at one minute intervals by the other five gliders till the last was airborne at 23:01. Three Horsas were towed by 298 Squadron and three by 644 Squadron.

Flying at 7,000 feet over the Channel, the two groups set course for Normandy and crossed the French coast at 00:07. Casting off their tow at 6,000 feet, the two groups prepared to land. The Halifax tugs continued on to bomb a cement factory at Caen as a diversion and to conceal the purpose of their mission. Silently gliding over Normandy, the gliders descended on their landing zones.

The Canal Bridge Horsas landed unseen on LZ 'X', and unheard apart from a bridge sentry, Private Wilhelm Furtener, who thought it was a crashing RAF aircraft. The lead glider, number 91, using the arrester parachute in the tail of his Horsa to slow his landing run, finally came to rest forty-seven yards from the Canal bridge and entangled in the barbed wire defences. The time was 00:16. The very first fighting men to land on D-Day had arrived by glider, flown in brilliantly by Staff Sergeant Jim Wallwork.

The other two gliders, Numbers 92 and 93, glided in behind Wallwork's Horsa. Staff Sergeant Olly Boland used his arrester parachute to slow his landing run. Horsa 93 made a heavy landing in which the pilot, Staff Sergeant Geoff Barkway, lost an arm. The platoon commander, Lieutenant Sandy Smith, was thrown forward out of the glider's nose onto the ground. Six men were trapped inside the badly damaged Horsa and one drowned in a pond in which the glider partly lay. This was the only fatal casualty of the landings.

All three of the Horsas landing on LZ 'X' landed on their skids in a very small bumpy field, the pilots displaying a masterful degree of flying skill in the dark without landing aids.

Horsa number 96, piloted by Staff Sergeant Roy Howard and Staff Sergeant Fred Baacke, had released at 6,000 feet over the French coast, as had Horsa 95, piloted by Staff Sergeants Stan Pearson and Len Guthrie. Both of the crews had a difficult flight on their hands. They had to navigate various courses whilst on a flap angle of 45 degrees and dropping at 2,000 feet per minute. The River Orne bridge gliders had only about half the distance to fly as had the Canal bridge gliders but had released at the same height. This required gliders 95 and 96 to put on full flap immediately on cast-off to lose height quickly.

Staff Sergeant Roy Howard came in just over a line of trees; he streamed his arrester parachute in the tail of his glider and landed close to the River Orne bridge.

Horsa number 95, piloted by Staff Sergeant Stan Pearson, came in behind Roy Howard's glider and landed 400 yards from the river bridge. Staff Sergeant Lawrence's Horsa had been mistowed by its tug and landed eight miles west of LZ 'Y' near two bridges at Periers-en-Auge which resembled the canal and river bridges. The troops therein fought their way to their intended LZ to rejoin their comrades.

The troops from the three Horsas on LZ 'X' rushed the Canal bridge under fire from its defenders. Lieutenant Den Brotheridge, on the western end of the bridge, was hit and died about an hour later. A fierce firefight broke out which lasted some fifteen minutes and ended with the bridge under the control of Major Howard's troops. Many of the defenders ran away, one to his Headquarters to alert his commanding officer that the Allies had arrived and taken the Canal bridge.

At the River Orne bridge, the two platoons under Lieutenants Fox and Sweeney swiftly seized their objective in a determined attack. Consolidating their position, the radio operator, Lance-Corporal Ted Tappenden, gave the pre-arranged code signal for success, 'Ham and Jam', to Major Howard at the Canal bridge with great gusto. The speed with which the bridge was taken was due to the superb flying skill of the glider pilots, landing at night without landing aids, right on target.

At about 07:00 reinforcements from the air-dropped 7th Battalion Parachute Regiment arrived, and the bridge parties came under the command of their CO. A defensive perimeter was formed west of the two bridges.

The Germans mounted several attacks with the 8th Heavy Grenadier Battalion which were repelled. As the pressure of the attacks increased the situation became tense until at 13:30 the same day, the troops holding the bridges heard the sound of bagpipes and knew the seaborne force was coming. A few minutes later the defenders saw the green berets of the 1st Special Service Commando, led by the Lord Lovat, with his piper Bob Millin playing 'The Black Bear' on his pipes. The Commando passed over bridges, sustaining casualties in the process, to reinforce 6th Airborne Division east of the River Orne.

The Canal bridge is now known as Pegasus bridge having been so decreed by the French Government and the road renamed 'Esplanade Major John Howard' both in honour to the men who liberated it. The cost to the 2nd Ox and Bucks was 2 men killed and 14 wounded out of a force of 171 men.

The exploits of the 'Coup-de-Main' gliderborne assault force is now part of British military history and the bridges a much visited tourist attraction. As Major Howard rightly states, the operation could not have been a success without the superb flying skill of the glider pilots of the Glider Pilot Regiment.

The Taking of the River Orne Bridge

Staff Sergeant Roy A. Howard, DFM, *recalls his part in the taking of the River Orne Bridge shortly after midnight on 6 June 1944. The then 21-year-old Staff Sergeant Howard was the first pilot of the Horsa which successfully landed close to its target, the River Orne bridge, with Lieutenant Fox and his men. Staff Sergeant Howard had passed out from Heavy Glider Conversion Unit with above average ratings which resulted in his being selected as one of the Coup-de-Main (Deadstick) glider pilots. The success of the operation depended entirely on the skill of the pilots of the Glider Pilot Regiment.*

Staff Sergeant Howard recalls:

I was lucky enough to be teamed up with Squadron Leader Emblem as my tug pilot. He was Commanding Officer of 297 Squadron and as such, all his crew, including of course his navigator, were all leaders in their various fields. During training, Staff Sergeant Fred Baacke, who was nine years my senior, was my second pilot. During training we were to do a night landing of thirty gliders at Netheravon. I was by far the most junior person in the combination, yet when the message came from the tug, 'Down you go, this is it', I replied, 'I am sorry, but you have got the wrong airfield. We have been circling Upavon, not Netheravon.' (Upavon is several miles north east of Netheravon.) 'Steer 180 degrees and I will go when I am ready.' As a result, the exercise was a success but what I did not know at the time was that our own squadron commander, Major Toler, DFC, was also in the tug so I had a very good audience. It was a matter of luck really. There followed more successful exercises and on 21 April 1944, Fred and I were told that we were to start some special training. Apart from gathering that it had something to do with D-Day, we did not otherwise have the slightest idea at that stage of what we were ultimately to be required to do.

The training started in daylight with a 6,000 ft tow from Brize Norton to Netheravon where a very small area had been marked out with white tape. 'We want you to get in there', we were told. This went quite well and we repeated it several times until it was decided that out Albemarle tugs did not have sufficient power for the 6,000 ft climb with full load and we were transferred to Tarrant Rushton and to Halifax II tugs.

For the next phase a formation of trees close to the east side of Netheravon airfield had been selected and two small fields side by side were created. Each day the six chosen glider crews, three from B Squadron and three from C Squadron, were towed from Tarrant on the same height and course to simulate the operation's requirements of which we still knew nothing. Three gliders would land in each of these two very small fields. RAF ground crews were there each day to somehow get the Horsas back onto Netheravon airfield and service them. This meant that we could only do one landing each day.

The operation required that the three gliders which were to attack the River Orne bridge had to shed their 6,000 feet as quickly as possible, wheras the three gliders attacking the Canal bridge were to carry out a longer and more orthodox approach. Our three gliders had only about half the distance to fly although from the same height of 6,000 feet. In order to lose so much unwanted height in sufficient time we had to apply full flap as soon as we released. This would make navigation extremely difficult but it had been decided by those formulating this brilliant and audacious plan that the height was necessary to deceive the Germans into thinking it was a bombing raid. As soon as we cast off, the Halifax tugs were to continue on to bomb Caen.

By this time we were training at night. At first with a few lights on the ground but as our landings became more precise these were removed and we were told to do spot landings in these small fields with no lights or aids of any kind. At first I thought that it could not be done, but after one or two hairy missions we found that it could.

On 28 May we met our load of Major Howard and his Ox and Bucks Light Infantry, in my case Lieutenant Fox and his men. There followed the most intensive briefing on the military side of the operation greatly aided by an elaborate sand table (now on view at the Airborne Forces Museum at Aldershot). This showed every detail of the terrain with all the trees and of course the river and canal with their bridges. We did not know where it actually was until we were told about two days before D-Day.

At 21:00 on 5 June we assembled on the runway and loaded our troops under Lieutenant Fox. As No. 6 glider Fred and I were last off and we staggered into the air with a very heavy load at approximately 22:35 (double British Summer Time). Later I was to suspect that every man probably took a few more hand grenades and rounds of ammunition etc because the weight proved to be greater than we had allowed for.

We crossed the coast near Worthing and set a direct course for Normandy. About three miles from the French coast the tug navigator gave us a compass check and told us we were on course. Because of the very steep angle of descent of a Horsa with full flap applied (about 45 degrees) our standard P4 compass which would have become inoperative, had been supplemented with a gyro direction indicator (GDI) for we were required to do what had never been done before, nor to the best of my knowledge was ever required again in the subsequent airborne landings of Arnhem and the Rhine, namely to navigate various courses on a 45 degree angle of descent dropping at a rate of 2,000 feet per minute.

'Good luck cast off when you like,' came the tug navigator's message through the wire in the tow rope. Whether I liked it or not was at this stage academic. The culmination of all my training and indeed of the short twenty-one years of my life had reached a point of no return and I immediately cast off at the 6,000 feet which we had practised more times that I care to remember. I reduced speed and applied full flap but to my horror I found that I could not get the speed below 90 mph even with the stick fully back. That extra weight was going to ruin all our calculations. I turned my head to the right towards the door between the cockpit and my load and shouted, 'Mr Fox, sir, two men from the front to the back quickly!' This corrected our trim and the Horsa was under proper control again. What a load there was behind me!

It seemed so crowded behind that to this day I wonder whether in addition to extra stores and ammunition, a few more men had slipped in unobserved at the last minute before take-off.

As well as the gyro compass, Fred had been supplied with a special light strapped to his hand so as not to spoil my night vision, which in the next few precious minutes, was going to be so vital for all of us. So far we had seen nothing, not even the coast line where we had released. Suddenly, bright as day, we were illuminated by a German parachute flare. Thankfully we entered a cloud and when we emerged all was dark again but we were falling like a spent rocket and steering a course at the same time of 212 degrees to be held for 90 seconds as Fred checked the map and his stop watch. This covered the first two miles and we turned again onto 268 degrees which we held for 2 mins 30 secs covering a further 3.3 miles.

Still not seeing anything of the ground, but continuing our half way to the vertical dive with only the hiss of the slipstream to be heard among all the now silent men, we turned on our third course of 212 degrees for the final run-in.

We were now at 1,200 feet and there below us the canal and river lay like silver, instantly recognisable. Orchards and woods lay as darker patches on a dark and foreign soil. 'It's all right now, Fred I can see where we are,' I said, as I thought that it all looked so exactly like the sand table that I had the strange feeling that I had been there before.

I took off the flaps for a moment to slow our headlong descent and to ensure we had sufficient height. I put them on again as we shot towards the line of trees over which I had to pass, not by as much as fifty feet or we should overshoot and be crushed by the weight as we hit the embankment which I knew was at the end of the field. I had to just miss and scrape over the treetops as we deployed the parachute brake specially fitted to the rear of the glider in order to shorten our landing run to the minimum. Up with the nose and the heavy rumble of the main wheels as we touched down a few minutes after midnight close to the River bridge. 'You are in the right place, sir,' I shouted to Lieutenant Fox, who seemed both surprised and happy at the same time – as with a drumming and crash of army boots along the floor of the glider – he and his men disappeared into the night to shoot up the Germans guarding the bridge.

It was up to Fred and me to unload the rest of the stores, but now we received a shock as we climbed out through the door of the glider into the field. Apart from a herd of cows which had panicked in front of us as we landed, we were quite alone. Alone in occupied France, separated from our load. Alone in front of the whole invasion force which was not to land on the beaches six miles away until daybreak and ahead of the earliest parachute drop by one hour. Where were the other two gliders? We had been No. 6 and should have been third to land on our field.

It was only much later that we learned that No. 5 had undershot by some 400 yards, whilst No. 4, due to its tug navigator's error, was ten miles away with its load busy capturing a bridge on the wrong river. But realising the error they were later to orientate themselves and fight their way through the night to liaise at our bridge. An astonishing feat of skill and determination in itself.

At 01:00 we saw paratroops dropping in the Bois de Bavent area and shortly afterwards a force of gliders followed. The night was full of noise and alarms and I was glad when dawn came. Soon afterwards the naval and aerial bombardment preceding the seaborne landing began. The volume of noise was past anything in my experience and as the barrage lifted and came nearer we prayed that someone knew when to stop it.

At 13:00 we heard a hunting horn and Lord Lovat appeared, complete with walking stick and Piper, leading his Commando over our bridges, ignoring the fact that a sniper was methodically knocking out one in twelve of his men. This same sniper had already taken out a man who was standing between Fred and me earlier in the day.

At 21:00 the main glider force came into the Ranville area. Our task was complete and we decided to go home. Our orders were to return to UK as soon as practicable in order to be ready to fly in a further load if necessary. We took our leave of Major Howard who, with the other three gliders, had successfully landed on the Canal bridge.

We walked along the road to Ouistreham snatching as much fitful sleep in a field of cabbages as the 15-inch shells that HMS *Warspite* was pumping into Le Harve would allow.

As we arrived at the beach early on D + 1, a Ju 88 was shot down, crashing some thirty yards from us; it continued to explode and burn for some time. Later Colonel Murray and the glider pilots from the main landing force arrived. We all waded out to infantry landing craft and arrived back at Newhaven at 06:30 on 8 June.

So ends Roy Howard's story. Seldom in military history can so much skill, bravery and planning have been brought to such a successful conclusion by so few. To land an engineless aircraft weighing some seven tons, heavily loaded, in the dark, alongside a bridge in a foreign land guarded by hostile troops must surely have been one of the most daunting, well nigh impossible tasks which men in time of war have ever been asked to do. These men of the Glider Pilot Regiment together with the troops they carried were truly the spearhead of the whole invasion. Seldom can Distinguished Flying Medals have been more richly deserved.

The Assault on Merville Battery

In December 1943, Lieutenant-Colonel T.H.B. Otway, Royal Ulster Rifles, attached and commanding 9th Parachute Battalion, received orders from General Gale to plan for the assault and elimination of a German gun battery near Merville (Map Reference 155776), some one and a half miles from the Normandy coast of France.

The gun battery was believed to consist of four 150-mm calibre guns capable of firing on Sword Beach, the planned landing area of the British 3rd Division on D-Day. The four guns were thought to be in concrete emplacements with 6ft 6in thick walls and roofs. The roofs were also covered with 13 feet of earth. Surrounding the complex were minefields – one a hundred yards deep – and also barbed wire 15 ft deep and 5 ft high. A garrison of 130 men of the 176th Artillery Regiment manned the battery and had a 20-mm automatic cannon in the centre of the complex for defence against air and ground attack. Defensive trenches and foxholes gave the garrison overlapping fields of fire from machine guns over the open approaches. A huge anti-tank ditch had been dug in front of the battery on the seaward side.

It was a most difficult and deadly position to assault and eliminate. The RAF had attempted to do so by bombing it in March 1944, but although over 1,000 bombs had been dropped, only two had landed on target and they did not cause any damage to the well protected battery.

The assault plan decided on was for Colonel Otway and 600 paratroops of the 9th Parachute Battalion to drop on DZ 'V', a short distance away, early on the morning of D-Day and equipped with machine guns, mine detectors, flame throwers, and bridging ladders carried in eleven Horsa gliders which would also land on DZ 'V'; then move to and attack the battery.

At the same time as the paratroops attacked, three Horsa gliders, piloted by volunteers from the Glider Pilot Regiment, carrying fifty men from the 9th Battalion, Parachute Regiment, and eight Royal Engineer Sappers, would crash-land on the battery complex. The exact position was to be pin-pointed by the paratroops erecting a Eureka beacon and firing star shells to illuminate the area.

Just before the ground attack the RAF would bomb the battery with 100 Lancaster bombers for ten minutes. Three hours later another 100 bombers would bomb nearby Ouistreham to reduce another battery and flak positions. It was hoped that the bombing would stun the garrison and blow gaps through the minefields and barbed wire defences. The battery had to be taken by 05:15, as a fall-back plan was for the Royal Navy cruiser *Arethusa* to open fire on the batery position at that time unless otherwise ordered.

A mock up of the battery complex was constructed in record time at Newbury and assault training was carried out by the forces to be involved, day and night for several weeks.

On 25 May 1944, the 9th Battalion moved to RAF Broadwell, Oxfordshire, where on 30 May they were given their final briefing. The fourteen-strong Horsa glider force for the supply and assault landings assembled at three RAF airfields, with the three battery assault gliders at RAF Brize Norton and the eleven supply gliders at RAF Harwell and Down Ampney.

At 22:49 on Monday, 5 June 1944, seven Horsa gliders of E Squadron, Glider Pilot Regiment, were lifted off from Down Ampney, towed by Dakotas of 271 Squadron carrying the Merville assault troops' equipment. The last of the seven, which bore chalk numbers 261 to 267, was airborne at 22:54 heading for DZ 'V'.

The four Horsas of A Squadron Glider Pilot Regiment bearing chalk numbers 66 to 69 were lifted off from Harwell, towed by Albemarles of 295 Squadron, between 23:10 and 23:16 carrying more paratroops' equipment and also set course for DZ 'V'.

At 23:10 the Dakotas of 512 Squadron began to take off from Broadwell carrying the 9th Battalion. Led by the squadron commander, Wing Commander Coventry, thirty-two aircraft took off at intervals until 23:36 when all were airborne. Flying weather was bad, requiring instrument flying in almost continuous cloud cover and giving the paratroops and glider troops a bumpy ride. RV was made over Worthing, Bognor and Littlehampton on the south coast of England and course set for Normandy and into history.

The three Horsa gliders that were to land on the battery were towed off from Brize Norton between 02:30 and 02:31 by Albermarles of 297 Squadron. Horsa No. 27 was piloted by Staff Sergeant D.F. Kerr, with Sergeant Walker as second pilot and towed by an Albemarle flown by Flight-Lieutenant Thomson. Horsa No. 28 was piloted by Staff Sergeant S.G. Bone with Sergeant L.G. Dean as second pilot and towed by an Albemarle piloted by Pilot Officer Garnett. Horsa No. 28a was piloted by Staff Sergeant A. Baldwin, with Sergeant J. Michie as second pilot, and towed by an Albemarle flown by Flight Sergeant Richards. Unluckily, the tow rope of the glider broke and the wings were broken away for three or four feet right back to the main spar; fortunately the glider broke cloud over RAF Odiham which had its flare path lit and Staff Sergeant Baldwin with his load of 9th Battalion got down without difficulty. The two remaining gliders were towed on to Normandy in adverse weather conditions. Both Horsas were equipped with Rebecca sets to pick up the ground troops' Eureka beacon and tail arrester parachutes.

On the ground in Normandy only some 150 paratroops had assembled at their RV by 02:50 with the attack timed for 03:30. To make matters worse, the essential Eureka beacon had been destroyed by impact on landing which meant that the incoming gliders would have no landing aids and would have to depend on their own landing skills.

One hundred and nine Lancaster bombers dropped 382 tons of bombs, including some two-ton bombs, from 8,000 feet on what they thought was the battery but was in fact a nearby hamlet. The bombs missed the target completely and only narrowly missed the advance party of paratroops near the battery. Unfortunately for the incoming gliders, the bombs raised clouds of smoke and dust which drifted across the area, making map reading impossible on their run in. Nevertheless the pilots of the Horsas cast off their tow at 00:45 at 1,500 feet, with a patchy cloud base of 1,000 feet and a wind speed of 25 knots from 310 degrees. Struggling to fly in these adverse conditions, the gliders began landing south-east of DZ 'V' amid Rommel's asparagus, which caused damage and casualties to the incoming gliders. Seven glider pilots were killed and all the Horsas badly damaged. All the paratroops' support equipment was out of reach of Colonel Otway and his men.

Undaunted, Colonel Otway decided to attack with his depleted force, armed with but one machine gun and small arms. They had no mine detectors, mortars, 6-pounder guns, no Sappers or medical unit, apart from six RAMC medics. As the paratroops reached the outer defences of the battery, the alerted garrison opened up with machine guns, to which the paratroops answered with their one machine gun; the German machine guns were silenced by two parties of paratroopers.

Working their way through the defences the paratroopers began to sustain casualties. Regardless, two gaps were blown in the wire and the paratroopers stormed through, hurling grenades and firing their weapons in a valiant assault. Savage hand to hand fighting raged through the battery, but the superbly trained paratroopers swiftly gained control, with some Germans surrendering when they realised who it was they were up against. The Red Devils' reputation had gone before them.

As the ground attack began, the two remaining Horsa assault gliders appeared overhead, having flown the Channel in almost continuous cloud cover. Staff Sergeants Bone and Dean in glider 28, together with their paratroop load, had had a bumpy ride over the sea. The glider's parachute arrester gear had streamed over the Channel; the combination stalled and lost height but the jettison gear was operated, releasing the arrester parachute and flying control was regained. The arrester parachute drag had strained the glider's tail plane and the flying controls became sloppy; the starboard undercarriage had also been carried away.

German flak had opened up on both gliders as they crossed the French coast, wounding four troops in the glider piloted by Staff Sergeants Kerr and Walker.

Staff Sergeant Bone released tow at 1,800 feet; his tug Albemarle piloted by Pilot Officer Garnett had circled the area four times under fire trying to pin-point the battery without landing aids. Bone descended to 500 feet, thinking that the bombed village of Gonnerville was his target. Realising his error, Bone banked his Horsa and landed successfully a mile away from the battery at 04:24. In the circumstances and conditions, it was an outstanding feat of airmanship.

Horsa 27, flown by Staff Sergeant Kerr, had also been towed four times round the area trying to pin-point the battery. Casting off his tow at 1,200 feet, Kerr attempted to land on the battery; he could not quite manage it so he streamed his arrester parachute and landed at 04:24 in an orchard only fifty yards from his target. Again it was a marvellous feat of flying skill. No sooner had the troops emerged from the Horsa than they were in action against German troops rushing to reinforce the battery garrison. A fierce fire fight broke out which continued for four hours.

By 04:45 the battery was in British hands and the bloody fighting ceased. Only twenty-two Germans – all of them wounded – were left. The rest, about 100, were dead. The attackers' price was high: seventy men lay dead and wounded in the complex, all six RAMC soldiers included. Colonel Otway fired his 'success' signal to prevent the Royal Navy opening fire on the battery, which was acknowledged by an RAF aircraft observed waggling its wings and his signals officer, Lieutenant J. Loring, released a dishevelled homing pigeon to fly to England with news of their success. As Colonel Otway did not know for certain that his 'Success' signal was received by the Royal Navy ships, he withdrew his men for safety.

Later the same day the battery was recaptured by the German 736th Grenadier Regiment, and next day was again taken by 3rd Commando. It changed hands several times before finally being taken by British forces.

For their part in the Operation Staff Sergeants Bone and Kerr were awarded the Distinguished Flying Medal. From 7 to 13 June, when 9th Parachute Battalion was surrounded by the enemy in defensive positions at the Château St Côme, members of the Glider Pilot Regiment who had flown the Battalion and other units, fought with great bravery in an infantry role, alongside 9th Parachute Battalion.

The concrete emplacements of the Merville Battery are still in being and have become a tourist attraction. When the author visited the battery he spoke, somewhat in awe, to one of the surviving assault party, CSM 'Dusty' Miller, of 9th Battalion, and marvelled that anyone could survive crossing the open ground surrounding the battery under fire. Rightly, the Merville Battery assault had gone down in military history as an example of the valour and courage of the British airborne soldier.

Operation 'Mallard'

The air-lifting on the evening of D-Day of 6th Air Landing Brigade and Divisional Troops of 6th Airborne Division, as reinforcements for 6th Airborne Division holding the left flank of the invasion bridgehead, by 38 and 46 Groups of the Royal Air Force, and the Glider Pilot Regiment.

Between 18:40 and 19:35 on the evening of D-Day, 256 glider and tug combinations began to take off from seven airfields in southern England, carrying the troops of 6th Air Landing Brigade and Divisional troops of 6th Airborne Division, and including for the first time in history tanks of the Royal Armoured Corps 6th Airborne Division Reconnaissance Regiment.

One Horsa glider crashed on take-off and three other Horsas broke their tow ropes and had to land in England, leaving 222 Horsas and thirty Hamilcars to rendezvous at the exit points on the English coast. Weather conditions were good as the glider stream crossed the Channel and made for their two landing zones in Normandy. Three Horsas ditched in the Channel and one tug the remainder flying on into two streams: one stream for LZ 'W' passed north-west of Ouistreham; the other, for LZ 'N', over the mouth of the Caen Canal. Weather conditions were still good; visibility was ten to fifteen miles with little or no cloud over the LZs. Wind at the release height of 1,500 feet was 10 to 15 knots from 320 degrees.

At 20:51 the first of 142 gliders began to land on LZ 'N'; thirty-two minutes later all had landed successfully. All thirty Hamilcars landed safely and the first tanks in history had landed by air to battle. Their engines had been started whilst airborne and the moment the gliders came to rest they were driven out and into action regardless of any damage to the Hamilcars. The original plan to form an armoured group with the 12th Devons had to be abandoned as they were required elsewhere. Many of the nineteen tanks and six carriers became immobilised by discarded parachutes winding round the tank sprockets, an unforseen development which was resolved during the night by burning them off with blow lamps.

At dawn the Recce Regiment joined 8th Parachute Battalion in the Bois de Bavent and set up a series of observation posts overlooking the Troarn – Caen – Ranville and Escoville areas. Motorcycle patrols were sent deep into German-held territory and gained valuable information which resulted in very successful air strikes and naval bombardment from HMS *Mauritius* on German vehicle parks and armoured units.

Captain B. Murdoch of the Glider Pilot Regiment, who had flown his Horsa glider loaded with three gunners, a jeep and a six-pounder gun, safely onto the LZ, found himself acting as loader on the gun which went into action against Mark IV tanks of the 22nd Panzer Regiment which were fitted with long barrel 75-mm guns. When the gunlayer on Captain Murdoch's gun was killed, he took command and, with the remaining gunners, knocked out four tanks. The Germans, owing to tank losses, were unable to break through the British positions and halted their advance but the battle continued.

Meanwhile, on LZ 'W' 104 Horsa gliders began to land at 20:52. Considerable bunching occurred, and at one stage six combinations arrived line abreast. By 21:20 all were down. The leading glider landed in the wrong direction and the following majority followed suit. On both LZs, 246 gliders out of the 256 that had taken off landed successfully no mean achievement in the short period of landing time.

The 1st Battalion of the Royal Ulster Rifles were put down in the correct place at the right time and immediately grouped at their RV, a small village. At dawn C Company, led by Major Hynds, occupied the strategic feature of 'Hill 30', from which they gave covering fire with anti-tank and machine guns whilst the remainder of the Royal Ulster Rifles attacked and captured the village of Longueval.

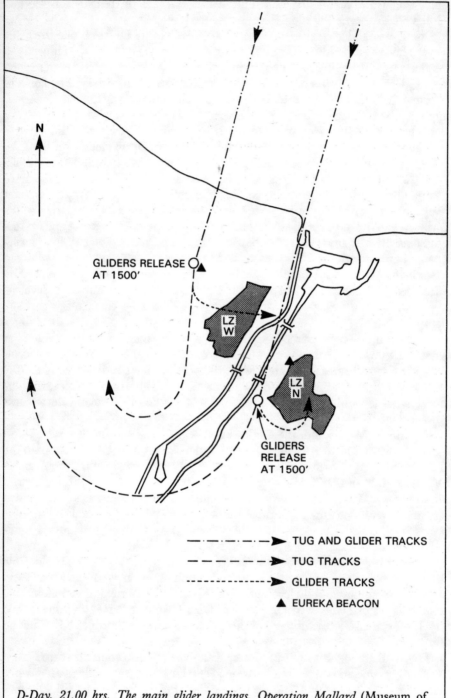

D-Day, 21.00 hrs. The main glider landings, Operation Mallard (Museum of Army Flying)

'C' Company on Hill 30 took heavy casualties from German mortar and self-propelled guns during the attack.

For two days the Royal Ulster Rifles were officially cut off when engaged in the capture of Longueval, in a position known to those outside as the 'Anzio Beach Head'; even the battalion regimental aid post, clearly marked with the Red Cross, came under fire, causing further wounds to already wounded men. It was not until 14 June that the battalion was relieved.

In the fighting that accompanied the German counter-attacks, the 195th Air Landing Field Ambulance, RAMC, established its Medical Dressing Station at Ranville complete with two operating theatres and carried out treatment on casualties despite shellfire which struck the station. The medics collected casualties from the regimental aid posts throughout the battle and brought them to the medical dressing station day and night. For ten weeks the MDS was the main and almost the only medical unit east of the River Orne. Over 2,500 casualties were treated and 400 surgical operations carried out with the Germans only a mile away.

'A' Company, 12th Devons

The 12th Battalion of the Devonshire Regiment was part of the 6th Air Landing Brigade, but on D-Day only A Company, under the command of Major J. Rogers, would be lifted to Normandy by glider; the remainder, commanded by the CO, Colonel G.R. Stevens, would land by sea.

'A' Company was to be part of a special force, Parkerforce, commanded by Colonel R.G. Parker, DSO, deputy brigade commander, consisting of the 6th Airborne Reconnaissance Regiment, a battery of the 53rd Light Regiment, RA, and one troop of the 3rd Air Landing Anti-tank Battery. Their task was to form a firm base with the artillery near Cagny so that the Recce Regiment could carry out reconnaissance south and south-east of the 6th Airborne Divisional area of operations.

Eight Horsa gliders had been allocated to the company; four would each carry a jeep, two trailers and six men of Company HQ, and the other four would each carry twenty-eight men and 300 lb of ammunition.

By 4 June the gliders had been loaded at Brize Norton and the company barracked at Faringdon. At 19:15 on D-Day the eight Horsas were towed off to Normandy. At 20:15 they flew over the seaborne elements of the 12th Devons who were due to land on 'Queen' beach at 10:00 the next day.

One Horsa had to ditch in the Channel eight miles off the French coast and six men were lost, listed as 'missing'. The remaining seven gliders were towed on to LZ 'W' landing at 21:30 without serious mishap amid anti-glider poles and minefields. The Horsas were widely dispersed and difficulty was found in removing the gliders' tails for off-loading; many were hacked off with axes and it was not until 23:00 that the company assembled.

The company moved to the Parkerforce assembly area south of Bréville, then at midnight reached Ranville but found it held by the Germans so a halt was made. At 03:00 next day Parkerforce was disbanded and 'A' Company was put under the command of 13th Parachute Battalion. At Ranville they engaged in clearing German snipers of which five were dealt with. At noon, the company occupied the village of Hérouvillette after clearing it of snipers and booby traps. Later that afternoon the 2nd Ox and Bucks, who had been in position at Escoville, were attacked and withdrew to the Devons' positions. A line was then taken up with the 2nd Ox and Bucks and the enemy held.

By 7 July the Devons who had been in the line in close contact and combat with the Germans for a month, handed over their positions to the 2nd Ox and Bucks and went into battalion reserve, a mere 1,200 yards from the German positions.

On 18 July the Devons were back in the line in action under 5th Parachute Brigade and continued in the line until 27 August. On 2 September they were withdrawn and embarked at the Mulberry port of Arromanches on the infantry landing ship *Princess Astrid* for Southampton. On 4 September they were back in barracks at Bulford, then given fourteen days' leave.

2nd Oxford and Buckinghamshire (52nd Light Infantry)

Taking off in their gliders from Harwell ˹ ᴉd Keevil, the 2nd Ox and Bucks began to land in France at 21:30. All the gliders carrying the regiment, except four, landed on or very near the LZ and casualties were small. After clearing the enemy out of Bénouville, the regiment assembled as scheduled accompanied by a battalion of the 3rd Infantry Division at the RV point just west of the River Orne, and moved out at 22:15 to the pre-arranged concentration point just east of the river.

Passing over Pegasus Bridge, the regiment reached Ranville château, where they set up a defensive perimeter in the grounds. There they were joined by the *Coup-de-Main* parties from the Canal and River bridges assault. Later Captain B. Priday and his men from 'Coup-de-Main' glider, which had been landed some miles away, rejoined the regiment.

C Company sent a fighting patrol into the small village of Hérouvillette but found it deserted of the enemy. At 04:30 the next day (7 June) the regiment moved off to Hérouvillette with C Company in the lead. Entering the village they found an injured glider pilot, who had been locked up by the Germans without food or water for twenty-four hours.

With the village secure and clear of the enemy, the regiment moved off at 08:30 to their prime objective, Escoville, which lay 1,000 yard to the south. Patrols from A and B Company were sent forward and reported German snipers in the village, but by 11:00 the Ox and Bucks were dug in to their defensive positions. Enemy resistance increased and the Regimental HQ could not reach its intended position – the château at Escoville.

At 15:00 that day German infantry supported by armoured fighting vehicles began to attack the regiment's positions and it became clear that Escoville could not be held without anti-tank guns. The commanding officer obtained permission to withdraw to Hérouvillette as the Escoville position was not a good one, being dominated by enemy-held high ground to the south and east.

During the regiment's withdrawal to better positions at Hérouvillette, A, B, and D Companies were heavily engaged in house to house and close quarter combat. C Company withdrew to a covering fire position forward of the village and the forward companies withdrew their positions. Elements of A and D Companies were cut off at Escoville but Major Edmunds led a counter-attack, which enabled

UK Air Movement Table: 'Mallard'

Load	RAF Unit	Aircraft	GPR Unit	Glider	Airfield	Take-off	LZ	Remarks
1st RUR & 195th Air Land Ambulance	48 Sqdn 46 Grp	C-47 Dakota	E Sqdn	Horsa (22)	Down Ampney	18:52–19:02	N	Down 21:03–21:09
	271 Sqdn 46 Grp	C-47 Dakota	E Sqdn	Horsa (15)	Down Ampney	18:40–18:50	N	21:06
	512 Sqdn 46 Grp	C-47 Dakota	F Sqdn	Horsa (18)	Broadwell	18:40–19:50	N	
	575 Sqdn 46 Grp	C-47 Dakota	F Sqdn	Horsa (19)	Broadwell	18:55–19:10	N	
33 jeeps 29 trailers 11 motor cycles	190 Sqdn 38 Grp	Stirling	C Sqdn & G Sqdn	Horsa (18)	Fairford	19:38–20:00	W	
211 A/L Bty RA 8 × 75mm guns	620 Sqdn 38 Grp	Stirling	C Sqdn & G Sqdn	Horsa (18)	Fairford	19:10–19:35	W	
716 Coy RASC Part HQ A.L. Bdge	296 Sqdn 38 Grp	Albemarle	B Sqdn	Horsa (20)	Brize Norton	19:08–19:46	N	Down 21:13–21:15
'A' Coy, 12th Devons	297 Sqdn 38 Grp	Albemarle	B Sqdn	Horsa (20)	Brize Norton	18:50–19:07	N	Down 21:12

UK Air Movement Table: 'Mallard' (continued)

Load	RAF Unit	Aircraft	GPR Unit	Glider	Airfield	Take-off	LZ	Remarks
2nd Ox & Bucks	196 Sqdn 38 Grp	Stirling	D Sqdn	Horsa (17)	Keevil	19:30–19:45	W	
	299 Sqdn 38 Grp	Stirling	D Sqdn	Horsa (16)	Keevil	19:03–19:26	W	
2nd Ox & Bucks	295 Sqdn 38 Grp	Albemarle	A Sqdn	Horsa (21)	Harwell	18:50–19:05	W	Down 20:52–20:55
	570 Sqdn 38 Grp	Albemarle	A Sqdn	Horsa (20)	Harwell	19:07–19:17	W	Down 20:52–20:55
3 men, 1 jeep, 1 gun	298 Sqdn 38 Grp	Halifax	C Sqdn	Horsa (1)	Tarrant Rushton	19:25	N	
5 tanks, 62 men, 12 trailers, 9 carriers, 16 motor cycles	298 Sqdn 38 Grp	Halifax	C Sqdn	Hamilcar (15)	Tarrant Rushton	19:35–19:50	N	Armoured Recce Regiment
3 men, 1 jeep, 1 × 6 pdr gun	644 Sqdn 38 Grp	Halifax	C Sqdn	Horsa (1)	Tarrant Rushton	19:25	N	Pilot of Horsa Capt Murdoch
15 tanks and 60 men	644 Sqdn 38 Grp	Halifax	C Sqdn	Hamilcar (15)	Tarrant Rushton	19:25–19:40	N	Armoured Recce Regiment
Totals:	14 Squadrons	74 C-47s 69 Stirlings 81 Albemarles 32 Halifaxes	7 GPR Squadrons	256 Gliders	7 Airfields		2 LZs	

the two companies to withdraw. The regiment then occupied defensive positions in Herouvillette, but had eighty-seven casualties in the withdrawal.

The 2nd Ox and Bucks remained in the line and fought their way to the River Seine. On 31 August orders were received to return to the United Kingdom. On 2 September the regiment embarked at Arromanches and on the 3rd arrived back at their base in Bulford, Wiltshire.

Operation 'Dingson'

The landing by Waco CG-4A Hadrian gliders of French SAS troops near Lorient France, on 5 August 1944, to carry out operations behind German lines.

By the beginning of August 1944, the US Army was advancing into the Brittany peninsula with their sights set on taking the ports of Lorient, Brest and St Nazaire, in order to bring in men and supplies direct from the US to France. Under their flamboyant leader General George S. Patton, their armoured divisions raced towards the ports bypassing any resistance.

Fighting in the peninsula were 20,000 armed men of the Maquis (FFI) under the command of a French officer, Albert M. Eon. On 3 August the BBC broadcast coded messages requesting the Maquis to increase their activity against the Germans by all means possible, short of open warfare.

In order to aid the Maquis and the US advance, the Allies decided to send in a small force of French SAS troops to attack strongpoints held mainly by Russians captured by the Germans and recruited into the German Army. As this was to be a small clandestine operation the smaller US Waco CG-4A Hadrian gliders were selected instead of the larger Horsas. Acccordingly fourteen Wacos were gathered at RAF Tarrant Rushton, Dorset, together with tug aircraft of 298 and 644 Squadrons, 38 Group, RAF.

Twenty-two glider pilots of the Glider Pilot Regiment, under the command of Captain 'Peggy' Clarke, were to fly the Wacos from Tarrant Rushton to a release point eight miles ENE of Lorient with their troops. Each Waco would carry a jeep and three men together with ammunition and equipment. The operation was set for 5 August 1944, and word was sent to the Maquis in Brittany to expect a force of gliders at 22:00.

At 20:05 hours (British Time) on the 5th, Halifax LL 326, piloted by Squadron Leader Norman, 644 Squadron, RAF, towed off the first of the Waco gliders from Tarrant Rushton, to be followed in rapid succession by four more Halifaxes, flown by Flying Officer Blake, Flight Lieutenant Egerton, Flying Officer Calverly, and Squadron Leader Rymills, each towing a Waco glider.

Four minutes later at 20:10 six Halifaxes of 298 Squadron, RAF flown by Flight Lieutenant Ensor, Flying Officer Lee, Flight Sergeant Cunliffe, Warrant Officers Smith and Bain, and Pilot Officer Doughill, towed off six more Wacos from Tarrant Rushton and streamed towards France. Almost at once the Waco towed by Flying Officer Lee went unserviceable and had to return to base at 20:50. The remaining five Wacos were towed on to France.

Each of the ten Wacos carried a jeep armed with a twin Vickers K machine gun fitted in front and a single machine gun at the rear. The French SAS crews of

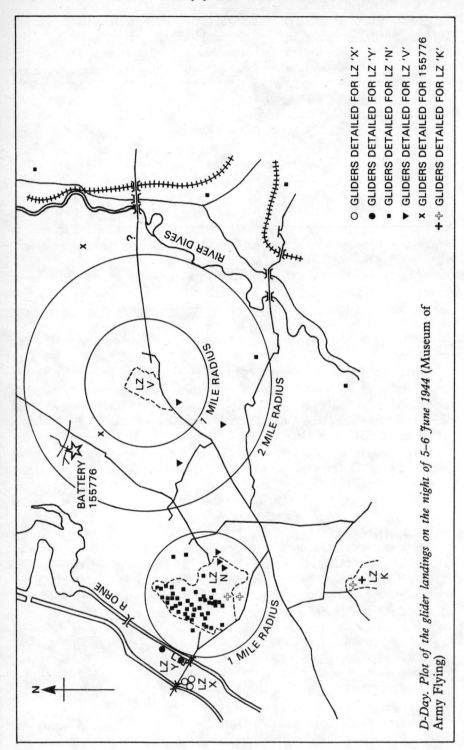

○ GLIDERS DETAILED FOR LZ 'X'

● GLIDERS DETAILED FOR LZ 'Y'

■ GLIDERS DETAILED FOR LZ 'N'

▼ GLIDERS DETAILED FOR LZ 'V'

✕ GLIDERS DETAILED FOR 155776

✚ ⊹ GLIDERS DETAILED FOR LZ 'K'

D-Day. Plot of the glider landings on the night of 5–6 June 1944 (Museum of Army Flying) three, a driver and two gunners, either sat strapped in the seat of the jeep or crouched behind it. All were armed to the teeth with pistols, knives and sub-machine guns.

As the first of the combinations arrived over the LZ at St Hélène, the Maquis set off purple marker flares to mark the landing area, and at 22:00 the Waco glider pilots began to cast off their tow lines at 1,000 feet. All but one landed safely; the Waco flown by Staff Sergeant Rossdale and Sergeant Newton crashed into trees in an orchard injuring both pilots. The Maquis spirited them away for medical treatment at once.

The French SAS troops unloaded their jeeps and supplies and armed to the teeth went off to attack the enemy in their armed jeeps. The glider pilots were taken to the Maquis HQ a short distance away and confined there as there was a 20,000 francs bounty on them by the Germans, dead or alive. The glider pilots stayed with the Maquis for a week and then, with the US armoured division rolling towards Aurai, they made contact there with the Americans.

Finally the glider pilots arrived at Rennes airfield where they managed to get a message to England requesting that they be evacuated. On 16 August they were picked up by a Dakota and flown to Netheravon. Twenty pilots had set out from Tarrant Rushton; eighteen came back to Netheravon. Rossdale and Newton had to stay behind in the care of the Maquis because of their injuries, but returned later. 'Dingson' had not cost the Glider Pilot Regiment any lives.

Operation 'Dragoon': 'Bluebird' Glider (British)

Mission

The invasion by Allied air and ground forces of the south of France on 15 August 1944.

The airborne assault, though largely by US Forces did contain a British element, landing by glider and parachute. As in Sicily it was found that the smaller capacity American Waco CG-4A Hadrian gliders could not carry the support equipment needed by the parachute troops. It required two Hadrians to carry a gun and jeep, and accordingly the much larger British Horsa gliders were needed.

The basic airborne assault plan was for teams of US and British Pathfinder paratroops to land during the early hours of 15 August, and mark the LZs for the landing of gliders and paratroops inland of the seaborne assault beaches. The airborne troops would seize and hold ground to prevent enemy reinforcements counter-attacking the Allied bridgehead and they would also harry the rear of the defenders.

Specially formed for the operation was the 1st Airborne Task Force under the command of Major General Robert T. Frederick, US Army. The British forces under his command were the 2nd Independent Parachute Brigade, under Brigadier C.H.V. Pritchard; Independent Squadron, Glider Pilot Regiment, under Major R. Coulthard; 64th Light Artillery Battery, Royal Artillery; 300th Air Landing Anti Tank Battery, Royal Artillery.

The artillery would be carried in forty Hadrian gliders and thirty-six Horsa gliders and would land on LZ 'O' which was about 400 yd square some three miles north of the village of Le Muy. The 1st Independent Parachute Platoon would drop at 03:30 as Pathfinders, to be followed at 04:10 by 2nd Parachute Brigade. The gliders would land at 'H'-hour, 08:00, the same time as the seaborne forces would assault the beaches. The take-off airfield for the gliders would be Tarquina airfield on the Italian coast north-west of Rome and the flight path would be the island of Elba, the northern part of Corsica, then landfall just east of Cannes on the French coast. The glider tugs would be C-47s of the USAAF Troop Carrier Command commanded by Brigadier General Paul L. Williams, and comprised the 75th, 76th, 77th and 78th Squadrons of the 435th Troop Carrier Group of the 53rd Troop Carrier Wing who would tow thirty-six Horsa gliders piloted by the Glider Pilot Regiment and forty Hadrian gliders piloted by US pilots. The Hadrians would be on double tow and the larger Horsas on single tow. This part of the operation would be codenamed 'Bluebird'. Before dawn on D-Day, Tuesday, 15 August 1944, the glider operation began. At 05:30 the first combinations began to lift off from Italy and headed for France via Elba and Corsica.

One glider was forced to return to base with unserviceable ailerons but the rest flew on in brilliant sunshine towards Corsica. One C-47 tug towing two Hadrians had to return to Italy with engine trouble.

Off the French coast Allied warships began bombarding the invasion beaches between St Raphael and Cavalaire at 07:30. The 'Bluebird' glider mission force flying over Corsica received a radio message from General Williams, instructing them to return to Italy as mist was blanketing the landing zones. The smaller Hadrians were to fly on to their LZs.

The leading Horsa combination turned over Corsica and the rest of the Horsas followed suit in radio silence; the pilots were unaware of the reason for returning to base. Two of the tugs developed engine trouble and had to cast off their Horsas but both gliders managed to land on Corsica.

The Hadrian gliders flew on to their LZ, but on reaching it found it shrouded in fog making it impossible to land. For an hour the combinations circled the area waiting for the sun to burn off the fog. At 09:26 the fog had thinned enough for the LZs to be seen and the Hadrians began to land. The LZ had been largely cleared of Rommel's asparagus and Germans by the paratroops and the gliders were able to land without fatality, although eight pilots were injured in heavy landings. The glider loads of guns and jeeps were quickly offloaded and soon in action against the enemy.

Meanwhile the Horsa wave was flying back to Italy, the troops aboard unaware of what was happening or where they were. As they cast off their tow and began landing some of the troops thought they were in France. In one Horsa the Royal Artillery gunners prepared to drive out with jeep and gun through the wooden tail of the glider without worrying about damaging the fuselage. In the nick of time they were stopped from rendering the Horsa to wreckage.

Tarquina airfield became a hive of industry with the tow planes having to be re-fuelled and the gliders re-marshalled for lift-off. By 14:30 the same day they began to lift off again for France. Within thirty minutes all were airborne. This time there was no recall instruction and at 17:45 the Horsa wave arrived over LZ 'O' casting off at 1,200 feet and landing in echelon of threes in fields and vineyards without enemy opposition.

The leading Horsa, flown by the squadron commander, Major Coulthard, missed the LZ and landed heavily, causing him serious injuries. His glider cargo was undamaged, however, and was unloaded at once, as were the cargoes of the other gliders: some thirty guns, jeeps, ammunition and gun crews. For the next three days the glider pilots were engaged defending the LZ against any possible counter-attack and distributing the re-supply loads dropped. Shortly afterwards they were withdrawn.

The Glider Pilot Regiment suffered one fatal casualty, Sergeant W. R. Jenner, who died from injuries received on landing and was later buried at Fréjus.

Operation 'Bluebird' was a success, with only light casualties to the British glider force. The Independent Glider Squadron had displayed great flying skill and in spite of a mid-operation aerial recall had re-mounted a classic gliderborne supply operation.

Operation 'Molten'

The ferrying of Horsa gliders from England to Italy on 9 October 1944, as glider reinforcements for future glider operations.

In August 1944, 38 Group, RAF and the Glider Pilot Regiment were instructed to ferry thirty-two Horsa gliders from RAF Fairford, Gloucestershire, to the Allied air base at Chiampino, Rome, Italy. Nos. 190 and 620 Squadrons, RAF, equipped with Stirling IV aircraft would tow the Horsas of 22 Heavy Glider Conversion Unit based at RAF Fairford and D Squadron Glider Pilot Regiment, under the command of Major J.F. Lyne, would pilot the gliders.

On 4 October 1944, Major Lyne and pilots of D Squadron reported to RAF Fairford to be briefed for the operation. The glider pilots tried to get themselves included in the RAF aircrews' briefing but were told that it was not necessary. They were merely given aerial photographs of Istres airfield, on the south coast of France which would be the first stop, and Chiampino airfield, the final destination.

From these photographs the glider pilot commander had to decide where to land his gliders. A rough flight plan of the route to Istres and Chiampino was also supplied. Apparently it had been decided that the glider pilots did not need detailed operational briefing, as they were on tow. It was also decided by the RAF that the glider crews would not be crewed up with particular RAF tug crews, so the glider pilots could not confer with their individual tug crews. Another jarring factor was that crew rations for the glider pilots would be carried in the tug aircraft and divided on landing in France. The normal first-class cooperation between the Royal Air Force and the glider pilots did not seem to be in evidence on this occasion.

At 10:00 on 9 October 1944, the first of thirty-two Horsa gliders were towed off from Fairford by Stirlings of 190 Squadron and set course for the south of France. At 16:00 the same day twenty-nine combinations arrived over Istres. One glider had to cast off tow in cloud over Swindon and two gliders lost their tow over

France; one landed near Toulouse, the other at Bayonne. Two of the Horsas suffered damage to their wing tips on landing but the other twenty-seven were undamaged.

The glider pilots marshalled their gliders into position ready for take-off the next day, after having flown them for six hours. Dirty and hungry, they were ready for a meal but found that the tug crews had not been told that the glider crews rations were included in theirs. The glider pilots were not happy. The US forces at Istres, displaying their usual generosity, came to the rescue and provided the glider pilots with food and drink.

By 06:00 the next day the glider pilots were back at work marshalling their Horsas for lift-off to Rome. The pilots had had to collect their cast-off tow ropes from where they had been dropped by the tugs, and lay them out on the runway between tug and glider; it was a heavy dirty job, as I well remember. By 10:00 twenty-seven Horsas were ready to go, but had to wait until their tugs were refuelled. At 12:00 the twenty-seven gliders began to be towed off for the last leg of the trip. The two damaged gliders with their crews were left behind to be repaired and later flown to Italy.

At 16:00 the first of the twenty-seven Horsas arrived at Chiampino and all were down by 16:30. Again the US forces were most helpful in collecting the cast-off tow ropes and providing meals.

No one at Chiampino seemed to know what to do with the gliders, for the US commanding officer had not received any instructions. The CO did advise that the gliders be guarded in case they disappeared via the local peasants as firewood, so the glider pilots now found themselves acting as guards on their gliders until it was arranged for the British 2nd Parachute Brigade to supply sentries.

The sixty glider pilots were now faced with the task of getting themselves back to England. It was only after much effort that C-47 Dakotas were secured to fly the pilots back, and it was not until 17 October that all were back at their home base.

Operation 'Molten' was a success: twenty-seven of the thirty-two gliders that lifted off on 9 October had been delivered intact to Italy the next day in a flight time of ten hours by the pilots of the Glider Pilot Regiment.

Operation 'Market'

The air landing of the British 1st Airborne Division at Arnhem, commencing on 17 September 1944.

In June 1944 General Eisenhower, Supreme Commander Allied Forces Europe, approved the formation of an Allied Airborne Army, with unified control of all Allied airborne troops. On 16 July 1944, Lieutenant-General Lewis H. Brereton, USAAF, was placed in command and on 2 August received official notice of his appointment. The British airborne commander, Lieutenant General F.A.M. Browning, was appointed Deputy Commander on 4 August and on 16 August the airborne army was designated the 1st Allied Airborne Army, directly under Supreme Headquarters Allied Expeditionary Forces (SHAEF). All Allied air-

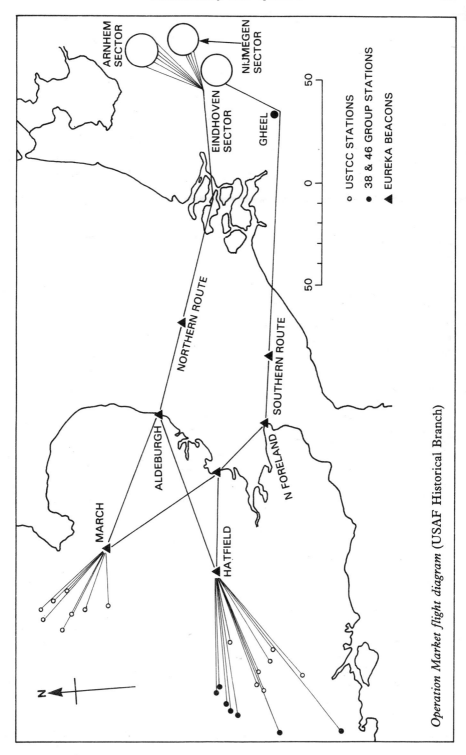

Operation Market flight diagram (USAF Historical Branch)

ARNHEM SECTOR

NIJMEGEN SECTOR

EINDHOVEN SECTOR

GHEEL

NORTHERN ROUTE

SOUTHERN ROUTE

ALDEBURGH

N FORELAND

MARCH

HATFIELD

○ USTCC STATIONS

● 38 & 46 GROUP STATIONS

▲ EUREKA BEACONS

N

borne forces came under its control, and it also had operational control of all British and American troop, supply and tug aircraft. Command of the new army was exercised through HQ 1st Airborne Corps under General Browning for British forces and 18th Airborne Corps under US General Matthew Ridgeway for US forces.

By August 1944, Allied forces, having fought their way from Normandy, were in pursuit of the retreating German armies falling back towards Germany. Ahead of the Allies was the formidable Siegfried Line, a chain of static defences, to which the retreating Germans could occupy and hold.

The aggressive US General George S. Patton, with his 3rd Army, was spearheading a rapid drive east and General Miles Dempsey's British 2nd Army was advancing east through Belgium. But both armies were outrunning their chain of supply which stretched back 200 miles. Petrol, essential for a rapid advance, was in short supply.

The question arose as to which army thrust should receive priority, General Patton with his plan to smash through the Siegfried Line with his armour, or General Montgomery who wanted to attack through Holland and outflank the Siegfried Line, then push into Germany. The prize was Berlin and a quick end to the war in Europe.

During August Montgomery proposed to General Eisenhower that the British 21st Army Group and the US 12th Army Group be launched northwards through Belgium and Holland, to take the port of Antwerp, then wheel right and turn the Siegfried Line. Eisenhower accepted Montgomery's plan, and by 4 September Montgomery's forces had driven through Belgium and Holland taking Brussels and Antwerp. But by 8 September German resistance had stiffened and the advance came to a halt on the Meuse Escaut and Albert Canals.

On the morning of 10 September, Montgomery conferred with Eisenhower and obtained permission to use the 1st Allied Airborne Army. Code-named 'Market' the bold plan was to lay a carpet of US airborne troops from Eindhoven to Nijmegen by paratroop and glider landings, to take and hold bridges over canals and rivers for the ground forces to advance over. The ground attack was code-named 'Garden'. British airborne troops would land by parachute and glider at Arnhem to take and hold the vital road bridge there. This bridge was the real prize but it was also the furthest away from Allied ground forces. When the Arnhem objectives had been taken, the British 52 (Lowland) Division would be air-lifted into Arnhem as reinforcements.

The proposed plan gave an airhead from ten to almost sixty miles behind German lines and relied on the ability of the British 2nd Army, spearheaded by armour, to punch along a single road through Eindhoven and Nijmegen to link up with British troops at Arnhem.

D-Day was set for 17 September and H-Hour 13:00 (one hour ahead of Greenwich Mean Time).

At 18:00 on 10 September, General Brereton held a conference at his HQ at Sunnyhill Park, Berkshire; General Browning was designated airborne forces commander for the operation and US General Paul L. Williams as air commander of troop, glider and supply aircraft. General Browning would fly into the airhead

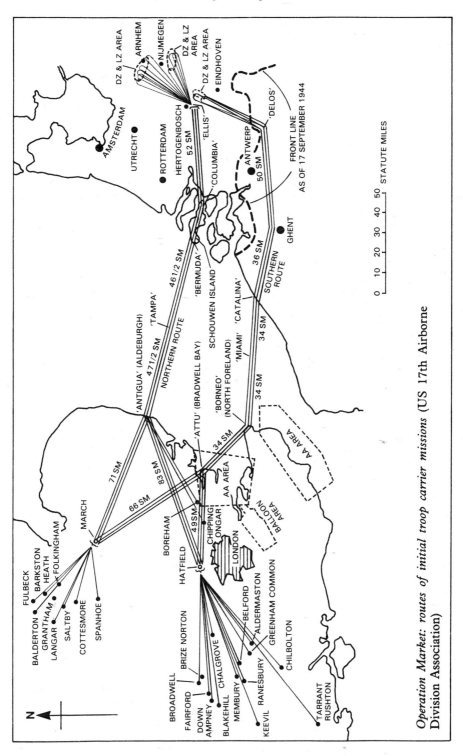

Operation Market: routes of initial troop carrier missions (US 17th Airborne Division Association)

by glider with a small staff to direct operations until contact was made with the advancing 2nd Army.

At 09:00 on 11 September another conference was held to select the routes to the airhead and the landing zones. Two routes were chosen: a northern route that ran from the English coast at Aldeburgh, Suffolk; then across the North Sea for ninety-five miles to the Schouwen Islands, then sixty miles to the Initial Point code-named 'Ellis', which was three miles south of Hertogenbosch, and thirty miles south west of the DZs and LZs at Arnhem. The southern route ran from Bradwell Bay, Essex, across the River Thames estuary to the North Foreland in Kent, then 159 miles to the Initial Point, code-named 'Delos' in Belgium on the Albert Canal, then thirty-one miles north-east to the Eindhoven DZs and LZs.

Three glider landing zones were chosen, S, Z and L. The 1st Air Landing Brigade would use LZ 'S', a mile long by half a mile wide, just north of the Amsterdam to Arnhem railway line and some five miles from the Arnhem bridge, the main objective. LZ 'Z' was north of the village of Heelsum and south of the railway line. LZ 'L' was half a mile east of LZ 'S' and was intended for use by the Polish Parachute Brigade and the US 878th Aviation Engineer Battalion who would land on D+2 to prepare landing strips to airland the 52nd (Lowland) Division.

General Brereton decided that the airborne operation should be carried out in daylight to reduce landing losses, though this increased the risk of losses from enemy fire; so both the RAF and USAAF were to attack and eliminate all known enemy flak positions before the airborne fleets were over the LZs.

Beginning on the night of D−1 and up to the morning of D-Day, 404 RAF and 872 USAAF aircraft dropped 4,191 tons of bombs along the intended routes of the troop carrier aircraft and around Arnhem, Ede and Nijmegen. 100 RAF aircraft made a diversionary raid on Walcheren Island to conceal the real airborne attack points. For the airborne operation the RAF had 812 Horsa and sixty-four Hamilcar gliders available to be towed by seventeen squadrons of 38 and 46 Groups, but with over 10,000 men to carry to the battlefield, it was impossible to transport all of them on the same day. Of necessity, therefore, the delivery operation had to be phased over three days.

First to land on D-Day would be the paratroop Pathfinders to mark the landing zones followed by the 1st Parachute Brigade and the 1st Air Landing Brigade plus half the Gunners, Engineers and Divisional troops. The remainder would follow next day on a second lift. A total of 8,969 troops plus 1,384 glider pilots would be involved overall.

The basic battle plan for the operation was for the 1st Parachute Brigade to drop and take the vital single span steel road bridge over the Lower Rhine at Arnhem, together with a pontoon bridge three-quarters of a mile east and a railway bridge $2\frac{1}{2}$ miles eastwards. By evening it was hoped that a half circle bridgehead would be held with the ends anchored on the banks of the Lower Rhine. When the remainder of 1st Airborne Division were air-landed on D+1 it was intended to enlarge the bridgehead.

The Polish Parachute Brigade would drop south of the Lower Rhine and land by glider on LZ 'L' to reinforce 1st Parachute Brigade. 1st Air Landing Brigade, less half of the 2nd Battalion South Staffords who would land in the second lift, would land on LZ 'S' north of the railway line and secure the LZs so that the second lift could come in safely. The King's Own Scottish Borderers (KOSB) would protect north of the LZs, the Border Regiment the south and west, and the South Staffords the east towards Arnhem.

The normal establishment of an Air Landing Battalion in 1944 was:

Battalion Headquarters

Four rifle companies each of four platoons.

HQ Company

Signals platoon, Pioneer platoon, Transport platoon and Administration platoon.

Support Company

Mortar Group. One platoon of six 3-inch mortars on handcarts. One platoon of six 3-inch mortars in jeeps.

Anti-tank Group. Two platoons each of four six-pounder guns.

Medium Machine Gun Group. Two platoons each of four MMGs.

Strength. Officers   44; 1st line reinforcements with battalion 14 =   58
          Other Ranks 796; "   "   "   "   "   180 = 976

Weapons:

Rifles, 493; sniper rifles, 32; 2-inch mortars, 17; 3-inch mortars, 12; Sten guns, 212; Pistols .38, 148; LMG .303, 67; MMG, 8; Piats, 23; 6-pounder guns, 8.

Transport:

Trade bicycles, 150; folding bicycles, 72; heavy motor cycles, 15; light motor cycles, 43; 15 cwt trucks, 8; 3 × 1-ton lorries, 8; jeeps, 43; trailers, 70; handcarts, 51; motor cars, 2.

D-Day, Sunday 17 September, dawned fair in England. At 10:10 the eighty-six Pathfinders of the 21st Independent Parachute Company under Major B.A. Wilson took off in twelve Stirlings of 620 and 190 Squadrons from RAF Fairford, Gloucestershire. Led by Squadron Leader Bunker in Stirling LJ 930, the Pathfinder Team set course for Holland and located LZ 'S' and DZ 'X' accurately. Arriving over the zones at 12:40, with only one aircraft fired on and damaged, the Pathfinders began to drop. Every one of the team was dropped on the correct zone without mishap and within fifteen minutes had set up the landing aids of Eureka beacons, coloured panels and smoke flares. Immediately behind the Pathfinders flew 143 troop aircraft, carrying 1st Parachute Brigade and 354 tug/glider combinations – together a vast fleet of 497 aircraft.

The gliders, 331 Horsas, fourteen Hamilcars and nine Hadrians (Waco CG-4As) carried troops of 1st Air Landing Brigade: 7th KOSB (the only Scottish troops in 1st Airborne Division), part of the South Staffordshire Regiment and the 1st Battalion of the Border Regiment; plus nine 17-pounder guns, five carriers and ninety troops carried in the fourteen Hamilcars.

Thirty-two Horsas and six Hadrians, containing 105 troops of 1st Airborne Corps HQ under General Browning, were towed by 38 Group to LZ 'N' near Nijmegan in the US area.

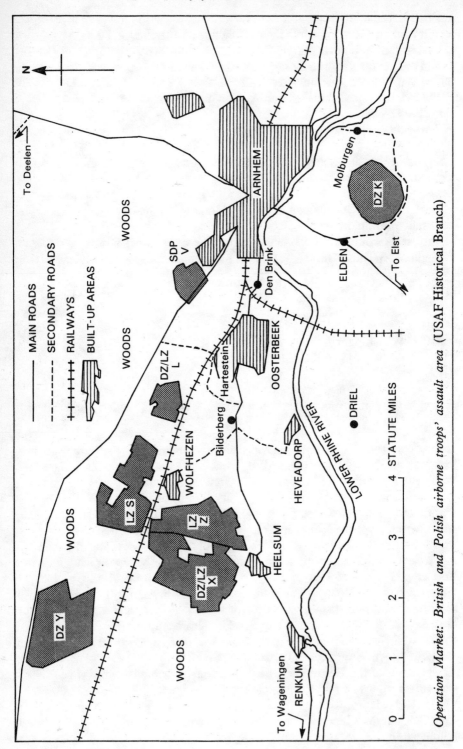

Operation Market: British and Polish airborne troops' assault area (USAF Historical Branch)

One Horsa had to force-land in England, one ditched in the sea and one broke its tow rope over Holland. The remaining thirty-five gliders landed near Groesbeek at 14:10. Twenty-eight managed to land on LZ 'N'. By 15:30 1st Airborne Corps HQ was functioning, but was unable to make radio contact with 1st Airborne Division. Radio contact was established with HQ in England and 2nd Army but General Browning had no information about the situation at Arnhem until 08:00 on 19 September.

The Arnhem bound fleet of paratroop and glider towing aircraft began to lose gliders; twenty-three broke tow ropes over England. Flying in cloud at 2,500 feet the glider stream lost another glider over the sea and seven more over Holland. One combination tug had to return to base with engine trouble and three other tugs with engine trouble had to release their gliders. Everyone in the downed gliders was either rescued by the Air Sea Rescue Service or landed safely. In total, thirty-nine gliders failed to reach the LZs.

Very little flak was encountered en route to the LZs, but on reaching the Arnhem area the glider stream came under small arms fire which damaged six tugs. Arriving over the LZs at 13:25, the glider pilots began to cast off their tow ropes, and landed in a light and variable breeze. 132 gliders landed on or near the LZ 'S' and 116 landed on LZ 'Z' with another twenty-seven very near.

The 7th KOSB, under Lieutenant-Colonel R. Payton Reid, landed at 13:30 amid slight small arms fire. One of their gliders crashed into a tree killing the pilot; this was the only fatal casualty on their LZ. Several gliders made heavy landings on the soft ground which forced the undercarriages up through the bottom of the fuselage. To the sound of the bagpipes playing 'Blue Bonnets over the Border' the battalion assembled; 740 all ranks, including forty officers, answered roll call and at 15:00 the battalion moved off to their positions in defence of the LZs to the north.

Encountering a German armoured car, A Company dealt with it but the other companies took up their positions without opposition, capturing several Germans including a female member of the Luftwaffe. The 181st Air Landing Field Ambulance, RAMC, under Lieutenant-Colonel A.T. Marrable and Major S.M. Frazer, landed in their gliders between 13:15 and 14:00 with ten officers and 104 other ranks. By 16:00 they had established a dressing station at Wolfhezen $2\frac{1}{2}$ miles north-west of Oosterbeek.

All the Hamilcar gliders managed to land, but two overturned killing the pilots and two 17-pounder guns were lost. One of the Hamilcars, piloted by Staff Sergeant Jenks and Staff Sergeant Rathband, was landed near a mental hospital at Wolfhezen and the two glider pilots stayed with the 17-pounder gun and crew they had carried and took part in the action that followed.

The 1st Parachute Brigade (1st, 2nd and 3rd Parachute Battalions plus a parachute squadron of Royal Engineers) moved off their DZ at once to seize the bridges at Arnhem. 'A' Company, 2nd Battalion, reached the railway bridge but it was blown up by the enemy. The Battalion then fought on to Arnhem and seized the northern end of the road bridge – the great prize – and held it in spite of the odds against them.

The first lift of the South Staffords, consisting of Battalion HQ, B and D Companies, with a platoon each of mortars and machine guns, went well and all except two gliders landed. One glider came down in enemy-occupied territory and the other, with B Company's commanding officer Major Cain, came down in Kent. The Staffords landed under machine gun fire from the enemy and had nine casualties; but they silenced the opposition, taking twenty prisoners, then dug in and spent a quiet night – apart from the noise of battle at Arnhem.

On landing, the 1st Battalion of the Border Regiment moved off with the KOSB to take up positions to defend the landing zones for the second lift due in next day. The battalion occupied all its objectives without German resistance but came under enemy mortar fire during the night.

At dawn on 18 September, Lieutenant-Colonel Frost's paratroops at the Arnhem road bridge numbered some 550 men. They had been reinforced piecemeal during the night by Battalion HQ, B Company and troops from other units. The 3rd Parachute Battalion had followed behind Colonel Frost's troops but were heavily engaged by the enemy and came to a halt.

1st Parachute Battalion had fought their way towards the Arnhem bridge but came to an enforced halt against strong German forces north of the railway station. The German 9th and 10th Panzer Divisions had moved into the Arnhem area to refit, but although this was known to British Intelligence it was not given credence. Also in the Arnhem area was the German Field Marshal Walter Model, Commanding Officer Army Group B, and at fifty-four years of age the youngest field marshal in the Wehrmacht, who had his HQ at Oosterbeek a mere three miles from the landing zones. When Model saw the British airborne forces descending, he ordered his Panzer divisions into action at Arnhem, so that the British were faced with numerically superior and more heavily armed forces from the start. On the evening of 17 September, the Germans had found a copy of the Allied operational battle plan in a crashed glider, but this was ignored as a plant by the German High Command.

D+1 saw Colonel Frost and his men still fighting hard at the Arnhem bridge. 1st and 3rd Parachute Battalions were still trying to fight their way forward but could only make a few hundred yards' progress against strong German positions. Casualties began to mount, and the 1st and 3rd were reduced to about 100 able-bodied paratroops each.

The commander of 1st Air Landing Brigade, Brigadier Hicks, ordered Colonel McCardie and his South Staffords to get through to Arnhem Bridge. Moving off at 10:30, the South Staffords came under German air attack from fighters and ground attack from snipers. They reached Oosterbeek, but the troops came under machine gun and sniper fire from high ground towards Mariedaal. D Company dealt with the snipers and remained in position to cover the remainder of the South Staffords, who reached the outskirts of Arnhem where they joined 1st Parachute Battalion under Lieutenant-Colonel Dobie – who had but seventy men left. Rather than risk the small force in street fighting in the dark, the advance was halted. At 11:23 on D+1, USAAF aircraft of the 314th and 315th Troop Carrier Groups took off from England with 2,119 paratroops of the 4th Parachute Brigade plus 51 tons of supplies for DZ 'Y'. Arriving over the DZ at 14:06, the paratroops, jumping from 800 to 1,000 feet, made a good drop under fire. Twenty aircraft of the USAAF were damaged and six were lost. Of the six lost, five managed to drop their paratroops, but the sixth went down killing all on board.

Low cloud and rain prevailed over the English take-off airfields, but at 10:45 the first of the gliderborne reinforcements lifted off. By 12:15 279 Horsa and fifteen Hamilcar gliders were airborne and in stream to LZs X and S with the second lift of 1st Air Landing Brigade. The combinations had to fly in eight-tenths cloud with a base of 2,000 feet, which caused seven gliders to break their tow ropes over England and two over the North Sea.

Streaming over Holland with the Germans alerted, heavy flak was encountered and thirty of the tugs and several gliders were damaged. One tug was shot down but the glider released and came down near Arnhem. Thirteen gliders released over Holland and one over Belgium, because of German flak.

Seventy-three gliders were intended for LZ 'S' and sixty-seven landed on or very near the zone. 223 gliders were due on LZ 'X' and 189 landed on or near the zone. Another fourteen gliders landed in the vicinity of the zones. Of the 294 which had been towed off, 270 had landed.

All the gliders carrying the 2nd South Staffords under Major J.C. Commings, the second in command, landed safely, including Captain R.H. Cain, whose glider had broken its tow rope over Kent the previous day. By 15:30 all the gliders were down, some coming under attack by the Germans. One platoon of C Company had to fight under Lieutenant D.K. Edwards to secure the load from a glider and became detached from the main body of South Staffords.

Major Commings and his men moved off towards Arnhem with 'A' Company in the lead and fought their way to the outskirts of Arnhem where they linked up with the 11th Parachute Battalion at 05:30. Neither the Staffords nor the paratroops could get further than near the St Elizabeth Hospital, some distance from the all-important bridge at Arnhem.

After heavy fighting and much confusion as to what was happening overall, the Border Regiment and 7th KOSB succeeded in reaching their objectives west and south west of Arnhem, but they were running out of ammunition and had sustained many casualties. By nightfall on the 18th, 1st Airborne Division had moved to positions near Hartenstein, two miles west of Arnhem.

The glider pilots who had brought the division to battle now engaged the enemy as soldiers on the ground. The first lift pilots had ringed the LZs and fought off the enemy, despite casualties. When reinforced by glider pilots from the second lift, they fought with the 7th KOSB and the South Staffords and later formed the defence perimeter of Divisional HQ at Hertenstein.

On D+2, 19 September, the South Staffords, followed by the 11th Parachute Battalion, attacked at dawn along the road to Arnhem. A, B and D Companies of the Staffords moved off at 04:30 and at 05:00 D Company reached the St Elizabeth Hospital, but had suffered forty per cent casualties and called on the 11th Parachute Battalion for assistance.

At 08:00 strong enemy counter-attacks began to develop and by 10:50 the situation became serious, and the Staffords had to withdraw to the St Elizabeth Hospital until the 11th's paratroops attacked.

A strong German attack with Tiger tanks overran the Staffords' positions and the commanding officer and the second in command were wounded and taken prisoner. Captain (Acting Major) Cain took command and ordered a withdrawal to form a defensive perimeter around Oosterbeek. This position became known as the Station Oosterbeek defence.

German Tiger tanks launched a vicious attack from the river direction, but the 6-pounder guns of the Staffords knocked out five. Lance-Sergeant John Daniel Baskeyfield, in command of a gun section, held his fire until the tanks were within 100 yards. Opening fire, he took out two Tiger tanks and a self-propelled gun. He was badly wounded in the leg, and the rest of his gun crew killed or wounded. Refusing to be evacuated, Baskeyfield stayed by his gun, alone. At 14:30 the enemy attacked again, and Sergeant Baskeyfield stopped the Germans in their tracks. His gun was put out of action by the enemy, but he managed to drag himself to another gun of his section, the crew of which had been killed, and opened fire, knocking out a self-propelled gun. As he prepared to fire another round, he was killed. He was awarded a posthumous Victoria Cross.

In England bad weather prevented the airlift of the Polish Parachute Brigade by the 114 aircraft of the USAAF 52nd Troop Carrier Wing to DZ 'K' south of the Arnhem Bridge. There the Germans began to reduce Colonel Frost's 2nd Parachute Battalion, or what was left of them, by vicious tank attack but the paratroops still held out.

From seven airfields in England the third and final lift of gliders began at 12:08. 43 Horsa and one Hamilcar gliders lifted off with Polish troops, RASC, Jeeps, trailers and machine guns. Thirty-five Horsas were scheduled to land on LZ 'L' with the Poles and eight for LZ 'X' plus one for LZ 'S' which had been left over from the second lift. Once airborne, the small force almost immediately lost four Horsas over England, three with tow rope breakage, and one with a shifted load. Two more Horsas ditched at sea and five more broke tow over Belgium. The Hamilcar had to force-land at Ghent.

Heavy flak was encountered over the Arnhem area as the small fleet approached at 16:00, for there was no fighter escort due to an error of timing. One glider was shot down, and one was damaged and had to cast off. Twenty-eight Horsas were released over LZ 'L' and landed in the middle of a battle. Heavy casualties were taken. Two gliders landed on LZ 'X' and one is thought to have landed on LZ 'S'. Most of the Polish troops reported at roll call, but they had lost many men. B Company of 7th KOSB helped the Poles to remove their vehicles from the Horsas.

Also scheduled for 19 September was a re-supply drop by 38 and 46 Groups of the Royal Air Force. The intended drop zone, SDP 'V', was in enemy hands and frantic efforts were made by the ground forces to inform the aircraft pilots of this but to no avail. The 100 Stirlings of 38 Group and sixty-three Dakotas of 46 Group headed for the original SDP 'V' and, crossing enemy positions at 1,000 feet, came under an intense hail of German flak that set several aircraft on fire. The Royal Air Force pilots, determined to aid the ground forces, flew on into the flak. One pilot, Flight Lieutenant D.S.A. Lord, DFC, of 271 Squadron, 46 Group, out of Down Ampney, who was flying a Dakota had his starboard wing hit twice by flak and the engine caught fire. The crew were uninjured, and the drop zone was coming up three minutes' flying time away. With his starboard wing engine blazing, Flight Lieutenant Lord let down to 900 feet and his aircraft became a prime target for the German gunners. Ignoring this fire, Lord dropped all but two of his supply containers, then, determined to drop the last two, went round again. For eight minutes his aircraft was under fire. Finally he ordered his crew to bale out, but did not do so himself. He stayed at the controls as his aircraft crashed in flames. So died a gallant pilot of the Royal Air Force who was awarded a Victoria Cross for valour in the face of the enemy.

One hundred and forty-five aircraft dropped their loads on SDP 'V', but thirteen were lost and ninety-seven damaged by enemy flak. 388 tons of supplies were dropped, but only 21 tons reached British ground forces; the rest fell into German hands. Despite the odds the Royal Air Force continued to try and support the ground troops but only 7.4 % of the supplies reached 1st Airborne Division. The two RAF groups lost fifty-five aircraft and had 320 damaged by flak. At times the pilots came down to 300 feet to drop their loads and their air gunners engaged the enemy at what was for them point-blank range.

By 19 September, 1st Airborne Division were short of ammunition, food and water and held an area of less than two miles square between Oosterbeek and Hartenstein. Now there was no hope of linking up with 2nd Parachute Battalion at the Arnhem bridge who still fought on doggedly outnumbered.

Another Victoria Cross was won by Captain L.E. Queripel of the 10th Parachute Battalion, who carried a wounded sergeant to safety under heavy enemy fire. Although wounded in the face himself, Captain Queripel continued to lead his men from the front. Alone, he attacked a German machine gun post and wiped out the machine gunners. Later he was wounded again, but still covered the withdrawal of his men. When last seen he was attacking the Germans with grenades and his pistol.

The divisional commander decided to form a perimeter around the village of Oosterbeek, and hold out until relieved by 2nd Army. The western side of the perimeter was held by what was left of the 1st Battalion Border Regiment, some Polish troops, Royal Engineers and a detachment of the Glider Pilot Regiment, all commanded by Brigadier Hicks. The eastern side was defended by men of the Glider Pilot Regiment, some Borderers, Recce Squadron, 21st Independent Parachute Company, and elements of the RASC plus paratroops from the 10th and 156th Parachute Battalions. Also 'Lonsdale Force' under Major R. Lonsdale, DSO, MC, which comprised 1st, 3rd and 11th Parachute Battalions, 2nd South Staffords, all under Brigadier John Hackett.

The south-east corner was held by the South Staffords with about 150 men under Captain (Acting Major) Cain. Three other parties of the South Staffords were with the Border Regiment and the Pioneer Platoon defended Divisional HQ.

By 20 September, D + 3, 7th KOSB strength was down to 270 men, the remnants of three rifle companies plus a Support Company and Battalion HQ Staff. Nonetheless they fought on aggressively; Lieutenant Hannah and Corporal Watson, using an anti-tank gun, engaged and knocked out a 56-ton tiger tank.

CSM R.F. Tilley of the Glider Pilot Regiment found himself the ranking officer in a party of 7th KOSB when all the officers were either dead or wounded, and fought with such gallantry that he was awarded the Distinguished Conduct Medal. Corporal John Moir of 1st Airlanding Brigade Provost Section went into a bayonet charge with five men from the Borderers; only he and two of the men returned. Sergeant Austin Roberts, also of the Provost Section, was last seen, one arm blown away, charging the Germans with a Bren gun under the remaining arm, firing till he was killed.

At Arnhem bridge, Colonel Frost was badly wounded and command of the small band of defenders passed to Major C.F.J. Gough, MC, commander of the Recce Squadron. Incessantly raked by enemy fire and suffering mounting casualties, the gallant defenders fought on, now reduced to 116 men. Finally, they were forced to make their last stand under the bridge. Here Lieutenant J.H. Grayburn led a series of counter-attacks, and for his gallantry there and during the whole battle, was awarded a Victoria Cross which he did not live to receive.

By 20 September 1st Airborne Division in their perimeter of defence at Oosterbeek, were still fighting hard. Brigadier Hackett was wounded and his command passed to Lieutenant-Colonel Ian Murray of the No. 1 Wing, Glider Pilot Regiment. HQ under Major-General Urquhart was at the Hartenstein Hotel which was almost in the centre of the perimeter.

At his position north of Oosterbeek Church, Captain (Acting Major) Cain and his South Staffords were repeatedly attacked by German tanks and self-propelled guns. Single-handed, Cain attacked a Tiger tank and knocked it out with a Piat. A self-propelled gun became a serious threat and Cain fired fifty projectiles at it, knocking it out, but in so doing was concussed himself by a Piat projectile which exploded as it left the muzzle of his Piat. Refusing to leave his command he fought on and when all the Piat ammunition was gone, used a 2-inch mortar fired at a low angle against the Germans. For his valour and command in battle Cain, too, was awarded the Victoria Cross. The 2nd South Staffords had now earned two Victoria Crosses in one battle, the only battalion to do so in WWII.

By 21 September the situation was going badly for 1st Airborne Division. The tanks of the Guards Armoured Brigade had been stopped by enemy anti-tank guns three miles north of Nijmegen and could go no further. The road was the only route to Arnhem; the fields on either side were marshy and impassable for armour.

On the afternoon of the 21st, the 52nd Wing of the USAAF 9th Troop Carrier Command took off in impossible weather conditions over England. Cloud extended from 150 to 9,000 feet but the pilots of the 315th and 314th Troop Carrier Groups somehow managed to get airborne with 1,511 Polish paratroops and 100 tons of supplies and made for Arnhem. Meeting heavy German flak, the two groups dropped 998 troops and 69 tons of supplies on fields at Driel, south of the Rhine and almost opposite Oosterbeek. That evening 750 paratroops managed to assemble and by 21:00 had reached the banks of the Rhine, where they found the Germans in position opposite and were unable to cross. On the night of the 23rd, 250 Polish paratroops tried to cross the river but only 150 managed to get through to 1st Airborne Division.

On the night of 24 September, 250 troops of the 5th Battalion Dorset Regiment made a gallant attempt to reach 1st Airborne Division but only elements of four companies made the other side of the Rhine. Led by Lieutenant-Colonel Tilley, the Dorsets strove towards their beleaguered comrades of 1st Airborne. Colonel Tilley led a bayonet charge and was last seen engaging the Germans and shouting encouragment to his men. He was not seen again. Some of the Dorsets and Poles managed to fight their way through to 1st Airborne but their numbers were too small to affect the outcome of the battle.

Just before dusk on the 24th, the glider pilots were forced out of a house they were holding by heavy German shellfire and took up positions behind KOSB; both regiments continued to resist the German attacks with rifle, machine gun and mortar fire. The 2nd Army Artillery now at Nijmegen had the range of Arnhem and 1st Airborne did not hesitate to call down its fire on their own positions when in serious straits.

Montgomery saw that it was impossible to hold a bridgehead over the Rhine and on the morning of 25 September ordered that all his airborne army withdraw south of the river; the odds against them were too heavy. Accordingly at 22:00 on the night of 25/26 September the remnants of the airborne army began to withdraw. The glider pilots of the Glider Pilot Regiment were stationed along the withdrawal route to guide the exhausted airborne soldiers to the river bank. The weather, for once, was in favour of 1st Airborne; rain and high wind covered the withdrawal of 1,741 men of 1st Airborne, plus 422 glider pilots, 75 Dorsets and 160 Polish paratroops.

Many more airborne soldiers hid and evaded capture by the Germans and during the next few weeks, assisted by the Dutch people, managed to reach Allied lines. Some 6,200 soldiers were taken prisoner and some died en route to the German prison camps. Many were wounded and suffered from lack of attention by their captors. 1,500 British and Polish soldiers lost their lives during the battle of Arnhem but it is estimated that the airborne army had killed over 7,000 of the enemy. When the soldiers of 1st Airborne Division finally reached the German POW camps they were greeted with awe; senior German officers, resplendent in Wagnerian red cloaks, wanted to be photographed with 1st Airborne but were ignored.

A roll call of the 2nd South Staffordshire Regiment revealed that only six officers and 133 other ranks returned from the battle. Forty-seven officers and 820 other ranks had set out. However, later elements of B Company, who had been missing in battle rejoined the Regiment.

A mere thirteen soldiers of the Airborne Provost Company returned to England; others including the Provost Marshal Major O.P. Haig although wounded, managed to get out. The Glider Pilot Regiment suffered 229 glider pilots killed and 469 taken prisoner. The total of 698 men lost to the regiment was shattering.

The roll call held by the 7th King's Own Scottish Borderers at Nijmegen showed that 4 officers, 2 sergeants, 12 corporals and 58 lance-corporals and private soldiers returned. 740 men of all ranks had landed at Arnhem on 17 September; 76 returned. Royal Air Force casualties were 294 officers and men lost.

Montgomery's offensive did not outflank the Siegfried Line and it was four

UK Air Movements Table: Operation Market
1st Lift, 17 September 1944

Load	RAF Unit	Aircraft	GPR Unit	Glider	Airfield	First take-off	LZ	Gliders landed & remarks
7th KOSB 1st Abn Provost Coy 542 troops 19 jeeps 4 × 6 pdr guns	48 Sqdn, 46 Grp	C-47 Dakota	E Squadron	Horsa (23)	Down Ampney	09:57	S	19 landed 292 troops
	271 Sqdn, 46 Grp	C-47 Dakota	E Squadron	Horsa (24)	Down Ampney	09:40	S	19 landed
	437 Sqdn, 46 Grp (RCAF)	C-47 Dakota	E Squadron	Horsa (2)	Down Ampney	10:03	S	1 landed
1st ALB 130 Troops 17 Jeeps	190 Sqdn, 38 Grp	Stirling	D Squadron	Horsa (19)	Fairford	10:25	Z	18 landed
	620 Sqdn, 38 Grp	Stirling	D Squadron	Horsa (19)	Fairford	10:45	Z	16 landed
1st Abn LT Regt RA Royal Engineers 1 Para Brigade	196 Sqdn, 38 Grp	Stirling	D Squadron	Horsa (25)	Keevil	10:40	Z	21 landed
	299 Sqdn, 38 Grp	Stirling	D Squadron	Horsa (25)	Keevil	10:15	Z	21 landed Double Hills Crash
7th KOSB	233 Sqdn, 46 Grp	C-47 Dakota	F Squadron	Horsa (22)	Blakehill Farm	09:56	S	21 landed
308 troops 1st Border Regt	437 Sqdn, 46 Grp (RCAF)	C-47 Dakota	F Squadron	Horsa (12)	Blakehill Farm	10:03	S	12 landed

Load	RAF Unit	Aircraft	GPR Unit	Glider	Airfield	First take-off	LZ	Gliders landed & remarks
1st Airborne Corps HQ	295 Sqdn, 38 Grp	Stirling	A Squadron	Horsa (25)	Harwell	11:20	N	22 landed 154 men
1st A/L Lt Reg RA	570 Sqdn, 38 Grp	Stirling	A Squadron	Horsa (20)	Harwell	11:08	Z & N	
1st A/L A/Tk Bty & HQ 1st Airborne Co.	296 Sqdn, 38 Grp	Albemarle	B Squadron	Horsa (21)	Manston	10:55	Z & S	
	296 Sqdn, 38 Grp	Albemarle	B Squadron	Hadrian (7)	Manston	11:00	N	
2nd South Staffs	297 Sqdn, 38 Grp	Albemarle	B Squadron	Horsa (24)	Manston	10:40	N	26 landed
	297 Sqdn, 38 Grp	Albemarle	Hampstead Norris	Hadrian (3)	Manston		N	
	ORTU	Albemarle		Horsa (2)	Manston			
4 × 17-pdr guns 6 carriers, 45 men Recce Regt.	298 Sqdn, 38 Grp	Halifax	C Squadron	Hamilcar (7)	Tarrant Rushton	10:20	N	7 landed
4 × 17-pdr guns, 2 carriers 42 men	298 Sqdn, 38 Grp	Halifax	C Squadron	Horsa (13)	Tarrant Rushton	10:20	N	7 landed
	644 Sqdn, 38 Grp	Halifax	C Squadron	Hamilcar (6)	Tarrant Rushton	10:20	N	7 landed
	644 Sqdn, 38 Grp	Halifax	C Squadron	Horsa (15)	Tarrant Rushton	10:20		
544 troops of 1st Border Regt	512 Sqdn, 46 Grp	C-47 Dakota	G Squadron	Horsa (22)	Broadwell	10:00	S	22 landed
	575 Sqdn, 46 Grp	C-47 Dakota	G Squadron	Horsa (24)	Broadwell	09:45	S	19 landed
Totals:	16 Squadrons plus 2 aircraft from Operational Refresher Training Unit.	129 Dakotas 133 Stirlings 56 Albemarles 41 Halifaxes ——— 359 Tugs		336 Horsas 13 Hamilcars 10 Hadrians ——— 359 Gliders				

Operation Market
2nd Lift, 18 September 1944

Reinforcements	RAF Unit	Aircraft	GPR Unit	Glider	Airfield	Take-off	LZ	Gliders down
132 troops, 17 jeeps, 22 trailers	48 Sqdn	C-47 Dakota	E Sqdn	Horsa (25)	Down Ampney	11:00	S	24 landed
	271 Sqdn	C-47 Dakota	E Sqdn	Horsa (24)	Down Ampney	11:13	S	24 landed
92 troops, 18 jeeps, 7 scout cars, 4 guns	190 Sqdn	Stirling	D Sqdn	Horsa (21)	Fairford	11:52	X	17 landed
	620 Sqdn	Stirling	D Sqdn	Horsa (22)	Fairford	11:25	X	21 landed
	196 Sqdn	Stirling	D Sqdn	Horsa (22)	Keevil	11:50	Z	19 landed
	299 Sqdn	Stirling	D Sqdn	Horsa (22)	Keevil	11:25	Z	21 landed
84 troops, 15 jeeps, 8 × 6-Pdr guns.	233 Sqdn	C-47 Dakota	F Sqdn	Horsa (17)	Blakehill Farm	10:45	X	16 landed
21 troops, 4 × 6 Pdrs, 2 jeeps.	437 Sqdn (RCAF)	C-47 Dakota	F Sqdn	Horsa (6)	Blakehill Farm	10:45	X	All landed
RAF stores, 6 men HQ AEAG 250 Coy RASC	295 Sqdn	Stirling	A Sqdn	Horsa (3)	Harwell	12:15	X	2 landed
	570 Sqdn	Stirling	A Sqdn	Horsa (10)	Harwell	12:07	X	9 landed
	296 Sqdn	Albemarle	B Sqdn	Horsa (20)	Manston	11:46	X	18 landed
	297 Sqdn	Albemarle	B Sqdn	Horsa (22)	Manston	11:40	X	22 landed
	298 Sqdn	Halifax	C Sqdn	Hamilcar (8)	Tarrant Rushton	11:22	X	All landed
	298 Sqdn	Halifax	C Sqdn	Horsa (8)	Tarrant Rushton			All landed
	644 Sqdn	Halifax	C Sqdn	Hamilcar (7)	Tarrant Rushton	11:25	X	5 landed
	644 Sqdn	Halifax	C Sqdn	Horsa (8)	Tarrant Rushton			8 landed
1st Border Regt 235 troops of 2nd South Staffs.	512 Sqdn	C-47 Dakota	G Sqdn	Horsa (24)	Broadwell	10:45	S	All landed
	575 Sqdn	C-47 Dakota	G Sqdn	Horsa (25)	Broadwell	10:47	X	24 landed
Totals:		121 Dakotas 100 Stirlings 42 Albemarles 31 Halifaxes 294 Aircraft		279 Horsas 15 Hamilcars 294 Gliders				

Operation Market
3rd Lift, 19 September 1944

Reinforcements	RAF Unit	Aircraft	GPR Squadron	Glider	Airfield	First take-off	LZ	Gliders landed
6 troops, 2 jeeps, 3 trailers	190 Sqdn	Stirling	D Squadron	Horsa (2)	Fairford	12:30	X	1 landed
6 troops, 1 jeep, 1 m-gun	620 Sqdn	Stirling LK 509 F/Lt. Jack	D Squadron	Horsa (1)	Fairford	12:30	X	
Polish troops 19 troops, 9 jeeps, 5 trailers	196 Sqdn	Stirling	D Squadron	Horsa (9)	Keevil	12:10	L	5 landed
	299 Sqdn	Stirling	D Squadron	Horsa (7)	Keevil	12:13	L	6 landed
6 troops, 1 jeep & trailer, 1 m-gun	233 Sqdn	C-47 Dakota KE 448 F/Lt. Cody	F Squadron	Horsa (1)	Blake Hill Farm	11:38	X	Landed
Polish troops	296 Sqdn	Albemarle P 1851 F/Lt. Scott	B Squadron S/S Proctor & McCulloch	Horsa (1)	Manston	13:20	-	Returned to Manston. Glider load shifted
Polish troops	298 Sqdn	Halifax	C Squadron	Horsa (10)	Tarrant Rushton	12:08	L	9 landed
Polish troops	644 Sqdn	Halifax F/O Blake	C Squadron	Hamilcar (1)	Tarrant Rushton	12:15	L	Force-landed Ghent
	644 Sqdn	Halifax	C Squadron	Horsa (10)	Tarrant Rushton	12:07	L	8 landed 1 shot down

Operation Market
3rd Lift, 19 September 1944 (continued)

Reinforcements	RAF Unit	Aircraft	GPR Squadron	Glider	Airfield	First take-off	LZ	Gliders landed
Admin 4 Troop 250 Coy RASC 1 jeep & 2 trailers	570 Sqdn	Stirling V8L-LK 199 F/Lt. Brierly	A Squadron	Horsa (1)	Harwell	12:50	–	Glider released at Eindhoven
17 troops KOSB & 2 trailers	48 Sqdn	C-47 Dakota F/Lt. Whitfield	E Squadron S/S Melrose & Sgt MacDonald	Horsa (1)	Down Ampney	13:00	S	Glider No. 272 left over from 1st lift
Totals:		2 Dakotas 20 Stirlings 1 Albemarle 21 Halifaxes 44 Aircraft		43 Horsas 1 Hamilcar 44 Gliders				

Grand Totals: All Lifts

Aircraft		Glider		Grand Total: Gliders and Tugs
252 Dakotas 253 Stirlings 99 Albemarles 93 Halifaxes	697 Tug Aircraft	658 Horsas 29 Hamilcars 10 Hadrians	697 Gliders	1,394

months before the Canadian 1st Army attacked from Nijmegen. In hindsight it would be easy to list the reasons that, apparently, the British part of 'Market' failed. Montgomery in a message to General Urquhart said:

> In the annals of the British Army there are many glorious deeds. In our Army we have always drawn great strength and inspiration from past traditions and endeavoured to live up to the high standards of those who have gone before. But there can be few episodes more glorious than the epic of Arnhem and those who follow after will find it hard to live up to the standard you have set. So long as we have in our armies of the British Empire, officers and men who will do as you have done, then we can indeed look forward with complete confidence to the future.
>
> In years to come it will be a great thing for a man to say – I fought at Arnhem.
>
> B.L. Montgomery

There was no failure of 1st Airborne Division at Arnhem.

Order of Battle
1st Airborne Division, Operation 'Market', Arnhem, 17-26 September 1944.
General Officer Commanding: Major-General R.E. Urquhart, DSO.

Divisional HQ
CRA: Loder Symonds
CRE: Myers
Signals: Stephenson
CRASC: St.J. Packe
ADMS: Warrack
ADOS: Mobbs
Adj REME: Ewens
SCF: Harlow
Pro: Haig

1st Airlanding Brigade
Brigadier P.H.W. Hicks
1st Battalion Border Regiment: Hadden
7th Battalion KOSB: Payton Reid
2nd Battalion South Staffs: McCardie
1 A/L Lt Bty RA: Walker
181 Para Fd Amb: Marrable

4th Parachute Brigade
Brigadier J.W. Hackett, MBE, MC
156th Para Battalion: des Voeux
10th Para Battalion: Smyth
11th Para Battalion: Lea
2nd A/L Lt Bty RA: Linton
2nd A/L A Tk Bty RA: Haynes
4th Para Sqn RE: Perkins
133rd Para Fd Amb: Alford.

1st Parachute Brigade
Brigadier C.W. Lathbury, DSO, MBE
1st Para Battalion: Dobie
2nd Para Battalion: Frost
3rd Para Battalion: Fitch
3rd A/L Bty RA: Mumford
1st A/L A-Tk Bty RA: Arnold
1st Para Sqn RE: Murray
16th Para Fd Amb: Townsend

Divisional Troops
No. 1 Wing, Glider Pilot Regt: Murray.
1st Light Regt RA: Thompson
9th Field Coy RE
250th Lt Coy RASC
Ord Fd Pks (Det)
89th Fd Security Sec

No. 2 Wing Glider Pilot Regt: Place
No. 1 FOU
21st Independent Para Coy
93rd Coy RASC (Det)
REME Workshops
Div Provost Coy

Polish 1st Parachute Brigade
Major-General S. Sosabowski

Arnhem Diary
Major T.I.J. Toler, DFC, TD, Commanding Officer, B Squadron, Glider Pilot Regiment, recalls the Battle of Arnhem:

Friday, September 15th: I go over to Harwell in the morning and get all the information for the operation from Brian Bottomly. He is pretty apathetic also not expecting it to come off. It is Operation Market and much the same as Comet [a pre-Arnhem rehearsal airborne exercise] – only this time the whole airborne army is to be in operation. The American 82nd and 101st Airborne Divisions landing at Grave and Nijmegen to hold the bridges and the British Airborne Division to land at Arnhem to capture and hold the bridge there – this for thirty-six hours until the British 2nd Army, who were just then north of Eindhoven, could link up with us. Corps HQ were landing in the Groesbeek area south of Nijmegen and were being protected by A Squadron. Apart from this, all the British glider pilots would be at Arnhem. Flak is likely to be heavy but will be dealt with by our fighters. D-Day is likely to be Sunday, September 17th.

I return to Harwell, tie up our positions on the LZ with Colonel Place at Broadwell, put Jimmy in the picture and leave him for another night to pick up any last minute information on the morrow and get a plane which leaves at four o'clock. Arrived at Manston we have a quiet night in preparation for the morrow.

Saturday, September 16th: I start to get out the brief while Heinkel works out the flight plan. It is fairly easy being so similar to Comet and the briefing material and orders are for once fairly complete. Our military plan is in general to remain with our loads until the situation stabilises sufficiently for the glider pilots to be drawn into a central area. There is one rather doubtful point. I am to take approximately twenty crews or one flight who land on the first lift straight to Nijmegen to assist in the defence of Corps HQ. This is all very well but it is through twelve miles of enemy territory. I don't think it is on and say so in no uncertain terms. Major Royle agrees and we decide to remain with the unit until Division HQ is established and then to see how the land lies and whether it is possible to get to Corps – how little we knew of what was to turn out.

Briefing was in the afternoon and once again by evening all was ready. Robert Irvine arrived to replace Mick Powell who is still out of action. Jimmy arrived with the latest gen which was nothing fresh, and Colonel McCardie arrived later, full of confidence that it would come off. We have heard that before. However, as the evening went on no cancellation came through and we went to bed with the feeling that it might come off.

Take-off was to be at a reasonable hour – 1040 hours – so we had time the following morning for final briefing and last minute adjustments. A Tiger Moth has arrived for my personal use as the communications aircraft I had asked for. I have a feeling this operation will come off. I shall not get the chance of using my Tiger.

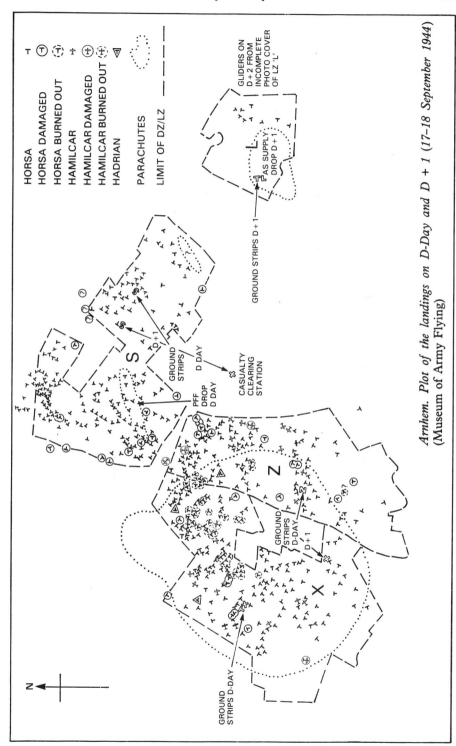

Arnhem. Plot of the landings on D-Day and D + 1 (17–18 September 1944)
(Museum of Army Flying)

Sunday, September 17th: The great day dawns. It is a lovely day, fine and clear with the sun shining with an autumn brightness. Take-off is at 10:40 hours. I drive down to the tow path and chat with Jimmy and Dusty who are flying together. Staff Sergeant Baldwin is No. 2 I tell him jokingly to keep in formation on the landing. As it turns out – he does. Terry Miller, who is on the second lift, says, 'Have you seen the latest flak map? The LZ is thick with light and heavy.' 'What a help you are,' replies Jimmy. 'Well think of the line you can shoot when you come back and there wasn't any there at all,' from Terry in cold comfort.

It is ten minutes before take-off. I climb into the glider, see that the passengers are strapped in, that all my own kit is stowed where I can get it, and do my cockpit check for the tenth time. John is on the tow path — I wave to him and to thousands of others. My tug 'V' Victor taxies out – the rope is connected and the intercom fixed as well as the elastic to the 'Angle of Dangle'. I call up the Wingco, the lights go from amber to green and we are away gathering speed along the runway. My nose wheel starts a most monumental judder. I heave back on the stick and at last she responds and the weight comes off the nose. Then I ease forward again or I shall become airborne too soon, perhaps stall, and make it even more difficult for the the tug to become airborne. At last we are off, a trifle nose heavy but nothing to worry about.

It is a little bumpy on the forming-up course. We meet a squadron of Spits and Tiffys outward-bound which sends our morale sky high. We come back over Ramsgate and looking down at the drome I see nothing on the runway so all must be off. Baldwin is formating on me. At times his tug pilot comes a little too close for comfort. As we head out to sea we pass behind a formation of Dakotas flying on a course almost 90 degrees to ours. My glider hits their slipstream – a most awful bump. I feel certain we must have hit something solid. I'm sure this is the end; however as I gingerly try the controls and find them normal, my confidence returns. Flying over the North Sea is very steady and after a short time we sight the rest of the force, stretching as far as the eye can see; little specks in the sky each of which contain at the very least a dozen men and in many cases as much as thirty, and guns, jeeps and weapons of all kinds.

At last we sight the Dutch coast. There is a bank of cloud which may prove troublesome and what are those black smudges in the sky way over in the front? It is flak and it may be for us before very long. This is where the morale pills would come in – if we had any! The land over which we are flying is flooded as we were told it would be. Little red roofed houses sticking up through a mass of dirty, yellowish water. Typhoons and Spits are now appearing. A house is burning below us – probably a flak position. A Dakota bursts into flames on our port. After a second, which seems like ages, the troops bale out followed by two white 'chutes which must be the crew. A second later the machine dives into the flood water and disappears.

A glider towed by a Dakota breaks away on our starboard and goes down to make a forced landing. Cannot see where it lands as I am too busy with map reading, coping with the slipstream of preceding combinations, and cloud which we go into for a couple of minutes. Shackleton, my co-pilot is invaluable – I have the greatest confidence in him and while he is flying and fighting the slipstreams,

I can concentrate everything I have on reading the map and checking where we are. We are nearing the target RV. I can see the three rivers. We are running over the bends in them as we arranged. Bang on. I can see the bend in the Lek which is our last pinpoint. There is a lot of smoke coming up from the woods surrounding the LZ – our bombers must have been busy, good. I see the release point and the LZ.

Up into the high tow – a shout of thanks to the tug pilot over the intercom and we are off. Speed back to 90 – half flap – almost up to the LZ, full flap and nose down. The stick is fully forward and still the speed keeps at 80. Terrific juddering as if we were stalling but we are dropping fast and going straight for the LZ. I aim a little short of some trees and pull up over them to get rid of some surplus speed that has built up. The landing is OK and well short of the overshoot boundary. I take off flap to run on. Half way across the LZ we run into soft plough and this pulls us up more rapidly than I expected – but it does not matter. We come to rest and undoing my straps I follow Shackleton out and lie panting on the ground hugging my Sten gun.

There appears to be no opposition – it is a lovely day and the sun is shining. Gliders are all around us and the field is surrounded by trees. I go to the rear of the glider where Shackleton has already cut the control cables preparatory to removing the tail. I start to slacken the bolts – the bottom one sticks and I am sweating before it is eventually removed. The tail drops off with a crash and is pulled to one side. The load does not wait to get out the troughs but drive the jeep and trailer straight out, nearly causing a disaster as there is three foot drop to the ground.

Colonel McCardie asks me where we are. I study the map and the ground and find that we are in the correct field not fifty yards from the RV. We now make a dash for the hedge in case there are any Bosche lurking to pick us off as we leave the glider. At Reigers Camp – the RV – we meet Boy Wilson of the Independent Parachute Company, very cheerful. 'Did you see our markings and the coloured smoke?' he shouts. 'Yes, OK,' I reply. Apparently there were a few Jerries round the DZ when they landed and shots were fired, but they gave up as soon as the Independents opened up on them. We see them now – a disconsolate lot and the first enemy prisoners we are to meet.

It is altogether too quiet, ominously so. We start to dig in, rather too enthusiastically, as I have blistered my hands in a very short time. Some more gliders are coming in; a Hamilcar goes very close overhead, the air a little distance away is thick with paratroops. Enemy flak opens up. In our inexperience we think it is directed at us and dig in all the harder.

Everything quietens down once again. We eat our sandwiches and rest. I check up on Angus's Flight. Hooper and Hooker are wounded, they were unlucky enough to land within a few yards of an enemy MG which opened up killing some of their load and wounding them before it was liquidated. Jummy and Dusty, Geary and Bristow are missing. The Dutch people in the farm seem pleased to see us. The farm appears prosperous and the farm implements in first class condition. We might be on a farm in Cheshire on an exercise except that the barn contains tobacco leaves laid out to dry.

Shackleton and I improve our trench by putting on some top cover on the advice of the South Stafford's sergeant-major. During the night I try to sleep but it is not easy with the excitement. I take an hour and a half's spell on watch. There is spasmodic rifle and MG fire from all round but no bullets come our way. It seems mainly in the direction of Arnhem which is five or six miles away. We see some of our Spitfires in the evening and during the night our bombers go over.

Monday, September 18th: All is quiet, the weather clear and sunny, and we have a complete wash and shave at the tap in the farm house. My shirt is full of sand from the trench. Breakfast is porridge, meat tablets and biscuits from our 24-hour ration packs. Everyone is strolling about and it is just like an exercise, only we see the Padre burying one of our men who has died in the night. Perhaps after all it is the real thing. Lockwood and Chadwick turn up with a Bren-carrier which they have salvaged from a Hamilcar. (Two Hamilcars have turned over in the soft ground and both pilots killed.) A Horsa in our area has crashed through a line of trees but the fuselage is still intact. We arrange parties to salvage what we can from the surrounding gliders.

Colonel McCardie tells us that the General has been captured and Brigadier Hicks is now commanding the division. The South Staffords are to move to the area of Division HQ, which is south of Wolfhezen, with a view to supporting 1st Para Bde on the bridge at Arnhem. I decide to keeps my Glider Pilots with the Staffords as this seems the best way of eventually contacting Division HQ.

When the time comes to move off the problem of carrying our rucksacks is almost impossible. The carrier comes in very useful and a jeep which pulls three trailers and one handcart which is unbelievable unless you see it. We move off at the rear of the column and cross the railway at Wolfhezen, which has been bombed heavily. The Dutch people wave to us and seem quite at home. We see two German snipers who have been captured in their camouflaged suits. I meet Colonel Place and Peter Jackson for a moment.

Jeeps and 17-pounder gun towing vehicles now meet us, pick us up and rush us down the road to speed our advance. We hear aircraft overhead – I think they are Thunderbolts; Eardley RE doubts it. He is right! they are FW 190s and Me 109s strafing the LZ. There has been a battle on this road which is through the forest. We see the first dead German and shortly afterwards a dead paratrooper. Baker and others are salvaging motorcycles as we mean to be mobile. Collect German rifles and ammo and machine gun for future use. Some Dutch people present us with fruit which is very welcome as it is hot and thirsty.

McCardie tells us that we are held up by MG positions on railway and may have to attack. For the present my glider pilots are to act as rearguard, so there is no hope of getting to Division HQ yet.

We now come out into the main Utrecht–Arnhem road where at the cross roads is a staff car with two dead Germans hanging out of it. Move cautiously along the road which is ominously deserted of civilians. Column stops. Everyone is a little jumpy. We meet a party of 1st Para Bn at the next crossroads who have had a rough time. Spasmodic rifle fire ahead. McCardie sends for me and I roar along the road on the pillion of a motor cycle which he has sent to fetch me. I meet Major Timothy who commands a Coy of 1st Para and agree to come under his command. We wait in the woods around a building which is later to become our MDS; it is now three o'clock in the afternoon and still no sign of the second lift which was due at ten this morning. Everyone is very anxious. The noise of aircraft and flak opening up gives us hope. Later we hear a report that gliders have been seen. This cheers everyone up. A Dutch woman in the house opposite holds up the Stars and Stripes and the Union Jack. There is more firing, probably our own, and I move down the street with the 'O' group. It is quite fantastic. Our weapons at the ready looking for snipers at every turn, and the streets with civilians moving about quite normally, and shops as if it were a street in Manchester or Liverpool. We move into a house which has been the local Gestapo HQ, very comfortably furnished and well stocked with food. I take a tin of asparagus. There is continual firing and sniper hunts and a bullet comes through the window. I meet Captain Dickinson of the Light Regiment.

We now have orders to move down towards the railway. I have at last contacted Angus Low and his flight and we move off at the rear of Major Timothy's men as usual. It must be between five and six o'clock and everyone is feeling a little tired. More fruit from the Dutch is very welcome. A Dutchman produces a Bren and ammo, two stens, a rifle, grenades and more ammunition for which we are very thankful. The advance is very slow and heavy rifle and machine gun fire is coming from the woods north of the railway on our left.

I do a small reconnaissance to the right and see that the railway bridge over the river has been blown. I rest near the railway station with Timothy and eat the tin of asparagus which is not very filling.

We move on to a house which overlooks the road into Arnhem. It is getting dark and everyone is tired. The firing in the direction of Arnhem is increasing and now includes mortars, shells and lots of tracers and is altogether a very good reproduction of the 'infernal regions'. Timothy and I go down the road to recce and meet a squadron leader in charge of a radar section. He looks rather out of place in a blue uniform in this rather unhealthy place. His tug – a Stirling – was shot down south of the river. They force-landed successfully and got across the river by the simple expedient of going to the ferry and asking to be taken across on payment of the usual fare! He is trying to join Division HQ; so am I trying to do the same. I suggest he stays with my pilots until an opportunity arises when we can go and try and locate it. It doesn't look at the moment as if the opportunity will arise. All civilians are in air raid shelters and one woman is in hysterics.

For want of other orders we decide to stay the night in this area. I fix positions and give the order to dig in and arrange to park the transport (we have now acquired a jeep which the Sgt-Major and Baker have made out of two). A house down the road is set on fire by a shell, flares up and lights the whole area.

In the dark Arnhem is looking like Dante's Inferno. We are very tired. The Dutch in the house are very helpful and we start to get some food. Alas, we have hardly started when an order comes from McCardie that we are to advance and put in an attack with Timothy – when and where is not stated. We rouse the men and start on the road again towards Arnhem, from which direction the firing has not diminished.

Shackleton and I go with Timothy's 'O' group. The darkness helps and the firing seems to be going over our heads. The pace is very slow and we stop in a street with houses on one side and a high wall on the other. Here we lie down on the pavement and in spite of the smell of drains, and the tracer bullets from the enemy position on the hill behind the houses continually passing over our heads, and mortars dropping unpleasantly close, we drop off to sleep spasmodically from sheer exhaustion. I also hear what I presume must be the enemy rocket projectors going off with a devilish hissing sound followed by an almighty crump.

I lose Angus for a while. He is looking for transport with our rucksacks. One thing is certain we could never have carried them ourselves. The Sgt-Major is near me. It must be two o'clock in the morning when Timothy arrives and directs me to a certain house which is the Staffords' temporary headquarters. There is a lot of wrecked transport on the road, both German and British. The house is dark save for a single candle in the front parlour which might be the same as any house in any British suburb. The furniture is all there as the owners have left it and yet this house is in the middle of a battle. The only evidence for this at present being a hole in the window blind where a bullet came through a little while before. Round the candle are McCardie, looking a lot older than when I saw him a few hours before, Lt-Col Dobie, commanding 1st Parachute Battalion, Major Buchanan and the Adjutant and Intelligence Officer of the Staffords.

The atmosphere is tense and dramatic. Lt-Col Frost, commanding the 2nd Para Bn reduced to eighty men, is holding the bridge at Arnhem only a mile or so away and must be relieved.

The bridge to hold, which is the object of the whole operation. The divisional commander has decided that it is impossible to hold the bridge without taking the high ground behind us which dominates the bridge. This he has so far failed to do. He has not heard from Frost and assumes he has been wiped out, so he has ordered a stop. McCardie knows Frost is still there as he is in wireless touch with him and knows his plight. He decides he cannot let him down. We all go out and McCardie and Dobie make the decision to advance to the bridge at all costs, turning like Nelson a blind eye to the divisional commander's orders.

The Staffords are to advance along the road into the town past the St Elizabeth Hospital, which is just down the road from us, and press on to the bridge in spite of a 20mm gun firing directly down one of the streets we have to pass. The 1st Parachute Bn is to advance along the river bank which is known to be strongly held. Zero is 03:45 hours. Fortunately before this time a message comes through from Division upholding McCardie's decision having contacted Frost.

McCardie now calls me and tells me that my pilots will not advance to the bridge with him but will return to Division HQ as was originally intended. I must admit I was very thankful, but feel I am deserting some very brave men on a forlorn hope. I wish the Colonel God Speed and retrace my steps along the road to find Angus and the flight.

Our troubles are not over by any means. Angus and I try to find the jeep on which are the flight's rucksacks. We must have inspected every vehicle on the road without success and expecting to be fired on at any moment. We decide as it is approaching dawn and the road we had to pass was under enemy observation and fire, we must sacrifice our stores and get moving. Setting off with the squadron leader who has lost his men, we retrace our steps along the road. Firing is still very heavy and we can see the rifle flashes on the hill. I cannot imagine how they can miss us in the light of all the fires going on around.

Some way down the road I meet Major Cain (later to get a VC), leading the remainder of the Staffords. He should have been here on the first day but force-landed and Geary, his pilot, brought him over today. I told him where he was and where McCardie was and the plan for the advance.

After we have passed the station and crossed the railway, we are going up the road we traversed earlier in the evening, when a burst of tracer comes straight down the road. Thank God we are marching at the side. Tracer is also coming over us from the embankment on our left. I decide it is no place for us and decide on a detour. Do we move quickly! It is rapidly getting light but we get away safely. As it is comparatively quiet we lie up in the garden of a house until it is light. No casualties so far.

Tuesday, September 19th: As it gets light, the people in the neighbouring houses wake up and bring us water and fruit. A Dutchman with an orange armband tries to help and shows me where there is a German sniper. We move off our Bren carrier leading and everyone keeps a wary eye open for snipers which fortunately do not appear. Eventually we got back onto the main road from Utrecht where we were yesterday. It is a fine morning and the sun is shining. We have no difficulty in finding Division HQ which is in the hotel in Hartestein. I report to Colonel Murray who seems glad to see me. All seems to be going well here and he tells me that I can rest my men in a house in the hotel grounds. This we proceed to do by breaking down the door. There is blood in the kitchen and a filthy smell and a cannon shell hole in the shutters. One of our troops has been killed here.

The rest of the house is in good order. Geary and Bristow who came over in the second lift bringing Major Cain, join us. We take off our boots and I have a general clean up, cook some food – porridge, meat and tea from the 24-hour pack which is still going strong after 72 hours! Someone makes a very good stew and we have some bottled fruit from the cellar.

Angus is with me. John Neale, my second in command who was in charge of my squadron's second lift, appears and reports all well with the second lift and no casualties. Says he is off to join Major Linton with the Light Regt to whom he is attached, and 'to keep away from Wing HQ'. That is the last time I ever see him. I get a little sleep. There is rifle fire, mortaring or shelling going on in the distance. Aircraft overhead. It is the first resupply – Stirlings and Dakotas. The flak is fairly heavy. A Dakota is hit and bursts into flames. We do not know that the dropping zone is in enemy hands. An enemy aircraft tries to machine gun us.

The owners of the house return in the afternoon and start collecting this and that. A canary has disappeared; we search for it and eventually find it. It is agreed that we keep half the food in the cellar. Language is the great difficulty but Angus makes a hit with the daughter who is young and attractive. We might almost think the battle was over!

Our comparative peace is rudely shaken by Major Royle and the Colonel who say we have to take up defensive positions round the hotel at once. I go off on a recce with Shackleton and meet Brigadier Hicks and Colonel Murray and am told to hold the area of a small house south-east of Divisional HQ. Unfortunately it is rather close to a hospital. The occupants of the house are still in residence. I advise them to move and order the flight to proceed to 'dig in' in the garden. We are rather isolated but fairly well sighted for fire except to our immediate front.

I share a slit trench in very sandy soil with Shackleton. It is just about big enough for one and we entwine our legs together in a most intimate fashion. Cramp is inevitable and every time we move brings a cascade of sand on top of us. Sleep is impossible but comes spasmodically all the same – rather as an animal, I should imagine, as one wakes automatically at every noise or movement and then drops off again. Murray and Royle come round after dark to see that all is well and sentries posted. A mad woman walks down the road past our position and away into the darkness singing an unintelligible song in a high pitched monotonous voice without any intermission until she is out of earshot. It is as if she is afraid to stop singing at the peril of her life. Most eerie, particularly as the sounds of the battle have stopped at this moment and there is a background of silence.

After she is gone a gun keeps firing close to our position. I hope it is ours but hardly care as it keeps sleep ever further away.

Wednesday, September 20th: A fine day again but somewhat cloudy. Water is no longer available in the taps so we shall have to conserve our resources. I am feeling very tired. It is an effort to do anything. I make some porridge and some tea in the kitchen of the house. Some shells fall about fifteen paces from our position. Move to cellar where I clean sten magazines which are jammed with sand. My sten is jammed with sand. Sand is everywhere – pistols, grenades, equipment all have to be cleaned. Terry Miller, one of the flight commanders on the second lift, arrives looking very tired and asks for the loan of our jeep to go down to his men who, he says, are all in good heart and with the Light Regt at the church at Oosterbeek. He goes off in the jeep and I do not see him again until he is repatriated after being in a German prison camp.

Brian Bottomly, the regiment's intelligence officer, arrives and reports that the 2nd Army will link up tomorrow; the supplies we saw yesterday have gone a bit astray and the bridge is still held. He is very cheerful and stands out in the open in spite of the occasional shell or bomb. He tells me we are to move to new positions round the gardens about 100 yards behind us where we shall not be so isolated. Later Bill Barrie and Tony Murray appear, the latter very white and shaken as he has had heavy casualties by mortaring.

During the morning the Sgt-Major has been snooping around and has returned with a beautiful BMW coupé which had belonged to the local German Gestapo. It was a lovely car and we felt that it would be ideal to drive into Arnhem when we eventually took it, which we were still confident could not be long delayed as was the advent of the 2nd Army. He had also acquired a trailer for our jeep so that our transport section was now very well set up.

Angus, the Sgt-Major, and myself then went to recce the new positions which were surrounding the tennis court of the hotel, in a vegetable garden and down a line of trees. Maurice Priest was on my left and the right, although somewhat open was ostensibly protected by the 1st Air Landing Brigade who were in a wood opposite this flank. I took up my HQ in the cellar of the pavilion.

During the afternoon the flight dug in. Tiny Maddon came over and said that there were some snipers in a house opposite our position. We organized fire from everything we had including the Piat. It was most impressive and satisfied the urge to hit out at something but I doubt if the sniper was really there. I heard that Major Royle had been killed and later Bill Barrie. We are lucky not to have had casualties so far. There is another supply drop in the evening. The flak is heavier but we are powerless to do anything. These chaps are marvellous but again much of the drop goes astray. I clean my sten gun yet again and sleep in a slit trench by myself this time.

Thursday, September 21st: It is again quite a pleasant morning and enemy activity does not seem so much or perhaps it is that we are getting used to it. The flight is fairly well dug in and the transport stowed away in the garden between a hedge and a row of runner beans. I am sitting in my cellar cleaning my sten for the umteenth time when there is a loud explosion outside. Looking out I find a mortar bomb has landed three feet from the entrance and the fin is still there. On picking it up I see it is made in Paris. I keep it for a souvenir.

Later on there is a whining, whistling noise and a series of sharp explosions – very loud and close. A moment later as I dash up the steps of the cellar I see Angus staggering towards me, exclaiming, 'Andrews is killed'. Sgt Andrews was his second pilot and both of them had been in their slit trench which was three or four paces from the pavilion, when a mortar bomb had landed actually on the lip of the trench, killing Andrews instantly and wounding Angus in the hand. How he escaped is a miracle, as he told me afterwards that he was on top of Andrews when the bomb fell. We got him down to the cellar and I quickly went round the flight to find that we had several casualties as the whole position had been plastered by a multiple mortar or 'Moaning Minnie'. Sgt Ragget had been killed in his slit trench by blast alone. McCarthy, who was in the trench with him, was only slightly wounded. There were two other pilots wounded by shrapnel. Sgt-Major was indefatigable and with his jeep and trailer driven by Sgt Caunter got all the wounded to the hospital. Meanwhile I urged everyone to dig deeper and deeper and to put on top cover to their trenches because it was lack of this which had caused our casualties. It was an expensive lesson but only experience can teach. I dug in with Shackleton and I think fear of annihilation made us dig with an energy I found surprising.

Water was short and the day was hot and our mouths were full of sand. We ripped doors off the pavilion to make roofs to the trenches and by degrees our position became more tenable. None too soon for we had to endure many more 'Moaning Minnies' that morning. Fortunately for us they increased the range slightly and they mostly went over us but for our nervous tension it was just the same.

Friday, September 22nd: Much the same as the previous day, heavy shelling followed by comparative quiet. During one of the quieter times we heard a loudspeaker from the direction of the enemy saying they had captured Colonel McCardie (who was in my glider) and that it was pointless for us to hold out. We replied with a burst of Bren fire in the direction of the voice which stopped.

Saturday, 23rd September: Rained in the morning. Heavy mortaring and shelling. I am going round the positions when I hear one of the shells coming – we are learning to judge them pretty well now. Just as I reckoned it was about to land I make a dive for the nearest slit trench. I must have timed it a fraction late as I have a vivid memory of seeing the burst which hit our jeep as I was upside down completing my dive below ground. Later Shackleton and I were in our pit when the shells really got our range. The concussion in the pit was appalling. I did not feel any happier when 'Shack' said, 'This is it, sir – I think we've had it.' I didn't like to let him know I entirely shared his view. I know I was as frightened at that time as ever I have been and felt certain death was only a second or two away. The top of the pit was blown in, my sten gun blown in the air and we were covered with earth. The pit was no longer any protection and as there was a couple of seconds lull, both Shack and I, without saying a word jumped out of our pit and ran the three yards to Sgt Geary's trench which was still intact. I remember again as I dropped in head first saying politely to the occupants, 'You don't mind if we join you do you?' I was certainly surprised to be still alive.

Sunday, September 24th: Looking at the remains of our weapon pit of yesterday, we see an unexploded shell lying just on the lip of it. If that had gone off I should not have been writing this. We get the Sappers to blow it up which they do with great glee. My shaving kit which I had left above ground as I was starting to shave when yesterday's bombardment started, has gone for a Burton. I am so tired for once I don't care. During one of the shellings during the day I am sharing a slit trench with the Sgt-Major. I am lying on top of him and being pretty tall, I can't get all my legs in. The top of one boot is protruding. After the bombardment I notice a piece of shrapnel has taken a neat piece out of the toe of the boot, but missed the foot. During the afternoon I am told to go to wing HQ which is in the Hartenstein Hotel, only 100 yards from our position. Here I am told that as Brigadier Hackett has been wounded and taken prisoner, Colonel Murray is to take over his Brigade and I am to take over command of the Glider Pilot Wing.

Around the hotel there was a great deal of sniping and I was warned not to go across the entrance as the sniper was shooting at anything that moved. It seemed so quiet I could hardly believe that so I put my steel helmet on the end of a stick and moved it about by the entrance. To my great astonishment immediately there was a loud crack as the sniper fired at it and the bullet embedded itself in the doorway.

Very heavy mortaring and shelling at the HQ that afternoon and an attack was expected at any minute but it never came. I spend the night at the HQ – I remember we had to take the clothes out of the wardrobe to keep warm. They were very nice coats and dresses and it seemed a shame to make such a mess of them, but their owners would probably never see them again.

Monday, September 25th: Very tired finding it difficult to concentrate and thinking is an effort. At 1200 hours we hear from Colonel Murray that orders for withdrawal across the river have been given. It is to start at 20:45 up until then Colonel Murray has had the Pegasus Divisional Flag ready for when the 2nd Army arrived. It never did so now we put it away. I am unshaven and in my present state probably could not have cared less. Colonel Murray is wonderful; he very tactfully suggests that if we are getting out tonight we don't want the rest of the Army to think we are tramps and offers to lend me his razor and a minute bit of lather which he has conserved over many shaves. I manage to get the worst off and it is amazing how much better I felt both mentally and physically. Colonel Murray was probably suffering more than I of fatigue and physical exhaustion but his example and leadership was better than mine. He was a Grenadier Guardsman and it counts for something one cannot explain.

As the evening draws near a feeling of relief overcomes everyone; we feel we have not acquitted ourselves too badly and it is time to get out. Whether we shall live to see the withdrawal is another matter. The Glider Pilots are to act as guides down to the river where the Canadians are to be waiting to ferry us over in boats. 2nd Army will put on a hell of a bombardment to cover us and tracer across the river to mark our crossing places. We are to muffle our boots and fade away very quietly.

As the time approaches it is very quiet and we set out through the dark woods down towards the river. We have to cross a ditch which I go into up to my middle – the faithful Shackleton who was still with me tells me afterwards that it was a sewer and I stunk like a polecat but I certainly don't remember it. As we approached the river there were scores of men lying on the field next to the water's edge. Then the enemy started to mortar. There was no cover and we just hugged the earth. I remember feeling something hot above my neck but thought no more about it. (When I got to the hospital at Nijmegen the next day I found a piece of shrapnel had gone through the neck of my airborne smock, the neck of my shirt, and had torn my string vest. I still have the smock and the shirt as a souvenir of how close I was to death to this day.)

As nothing seemed to be happening after this I went down to the water's edge. Boats were being loaded and I think I helped Shackleton who had been wounded to get into one.

The next thing I remember was seeing a boat loaded with men hit by something and start to sink. It seemed the men could not swim and were drowning. I think this simply made me go into the water although I could not get to any of them. However once in the water I was immediately out of my depth. (I have since been back to the spot and the water is very deep and swift flowing.) Although I am a fairly strong swimmer I should probably not have been able to swim the river under those conditions had it not been for another lucky break. We had been issued with an inflatable rubber ring for use if we had to ditch when flying the gliders. Discussing this with my second in command John Neale when we were issued with them some weeks before, I remember him saying, 'I am going to keep mine with me during an operation – it is not much weight and would be a fine thing to help one cross a river in full equipment.' Remembering this I had kept mine under my smock and just before getting to the river had blown it up. It now saved my life because I was easily able to keep afloat and swim where I liked. My troubles were not over. I was swimming slowly wondering whether I should strike out across the swift flowing river which was like a picture out of Dante's Inferno – tracers ripping across where the troops were marking the crossing, flashes of guns and shells bursting all around and mortar bombs dropping in the water.

I wondered for a minute whether I should be safer totally submerged but remembered a vivid picture of fishes coming to the surface stunned by an exploding grenade. However I decided to risk it and went right under for as long as I could hold my breath while the mortars dropped in the water around. It seemed to work – I felt no great concussion. When I came to the surface I was just by a loaded boat with an outboard motor, so hanging onto the side I let it pull me to the other side. Before going into the water I had had time to take off my boots which in the approved fashion I hung round my neck. Unfortunately the boots had not catered for someone being towed and when I arrived at the other side and climbed up the bank I found my boots had disappeared!

I was certainly glad to see the friendly faces on the opposite bank, the first friendly troops we had seen other than those who had come by air when we landed eight days ago. They quickly hustled us off the bank and told us to get going along the road. I had never realised how difficult it was to march any distance without boots or shoes. I don't know how far it was but it was damned painful and I was glad to arrive at a medical aid post where we were given a delightful cup of hot cocoa with rum! As I still had my revolver and a couple of grenades with me I had to give these up which seemed a shame. The revolver, automatic I think it was, had come with me a long way. However I was too tired to care very much.

Tuesday, September 26th: My memory of this is not very clear. We were eventually taken to Nijmegen to a hospital. At some time we were in an ambulance and the driver had obviously lost his way. We felt it would be pretty ironical if he drove us back into enemy territory which we knew was not far away. However after a council of war we decided on a direction which fortunately was the right one. However we eventually got to an airfield whose name I cannot remember and we were flown home in a Dakota. So ended for me and others the Arnhem operation.

Megara, Greece, 1944

By September 1944, the continued occupation of Greece by the Germans had become untenable. In Italy Allied forces were advancing northwards and the Russians were on the Hungarian frontier smashing towards the Balkans. Both these advances would eventually cut off German forces in Greece and Yugoslavia, so they began to withdraw, although fanatical units still held on to several islands in the Aegean, in obedience to Hitler's no surrender order.

With the partial withdrawal of the Germans from Southern Greece, a power vacuum developed with the various left and right wing political factions seeking to fill it. The British, therefore, wished to install the exiled Greek Government in Athens as soon as was possible to stabilize the situation. On 23 September British air and seaborne forces captured the airfield at Araxos in the Peloponnese, preparatory to re-entering Athens. By 10 October the airfield at Megara, twenty miles west of Athens, had also been seized although it was still within range of German guns.

The British commander, General Wilson, decided to launch an operation to take Athens by using air and seaborne troops. The operation, code-named 'Manna', would require the British 2nd Parachute Brigade to drop on the airfield at Megara carried in C-47s of the US 51st Troop Carrier Wing. The paratroops' guns and ammunition would be flown in after the drop in Waco CG-4A Hadrian gliders piloted by pilots of the Independent Squadron Glider Pilot Regiment stationed at Bari, Italy.

On 13 October, commencing at 05:00, the seaborne troops would sail from Alexandria. Other troops would sail from Naples and Taranto in Italy, including the Greek Government in an infantry landing ship, the *Prince David*.

On 12 October, a company of the British 4th Parachute Battalion was dropped over Megara airfield in a strong wind which caused many casualties. To add to the difficulties the Germans managed to shell the landing zone, causing more casualties.

On 13 October the 1st Independent Squadron, led by Captain Cornelius Turner, was towed off in Waco CG-4A Hadrians by the USAAF from Tarquina. Captain Turner was somewhat put off by his load, 4,000 lb marked 'High Explosive'. It was Friday the 13th! At first all went well but on nearing Corinth violent storms blew up and the combinations had to return to Bari. Weather conditions got worse and the main paratroop drop had to be delayed till 14 October.

On 15 October the weather improved: forty four C-47s of the 51st Troop Carrier Wing, USAAF, took off again from Bari to Megara; twenty-four carried supplies and twenty towed Waco Hadrians loaded with either a jeep or gun and six troops. One carried a small bulldozer for airfield repair. The glider pilots of the 1st Independent Squadron had to use Hadrians as there were no Horsas available. They had been expended on Operation 'Bluebird' in the south of France in August.

The British glider pilots mostly managed to make good landings in spite of the bomb and shell craters on Megara. These were soon filled in using the flown-in bulldozer. The glider loads were quickly off-loaded and in the hands of the paratroopers.

The main British seaborne force landed in the Piraeus at 06:30 on 16 October and two days later in Athens, the Greek Government under Prime Minister Papandreou was installed.

Operation 'Manna' was a success, marred only by the casualties to the paratroops dropping in a strong wind on Megara. The Hadrian gliders remained at Megara for a month until civil war broke out among the Greeks; then they were used to evacuate the 1st Independent Squadron glider pilots back to Tarquina.

Operation 'Varsity'

The first Allied airborne tactical operation of World War II on 24 March 1945.

The hard lessons of Operation 'Market' at Arnhem now well and truly learned, the Planning Staff determined that Operation 'Varsity' should be tactically

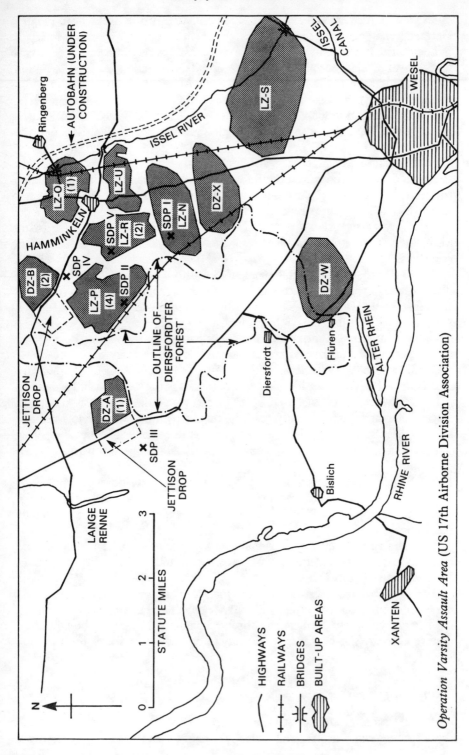

Operation Varsity Assault Area (US 17th Airborne Division Association)

different. The 18th Airborne Corps of the 1st Allied Airborne Army was to carry out the operation and consisted of the British 6th Airborne Division and the US 17th Airborne Division. The 18th Corps was commanded by General Matthew B. Ridgeway, with General Richard Gale as his Deputy. 17th Airborne Division was commanded by Major-General William M. Miley and 6th Airborne Division by Major-General Eric L. Bols.

The two airborne divisions were to be dropped and landed over the River Rhine four hours after the start of the ground assault across the river by the US 9th and the British 2nd Armies. The re-supply of the airborne troops was to be made six hours after their landing and not at a later date as at Arnhem. It was intended to land by glider and parachute 21,680 troops in a single air lift. The logistics of the plan were staggering, as a grand total of 1,585 paratroop and glider towing aircraft with 1,340 troop-carrying gliders were to be used to transport the airborne troops.

Their tasks were to take, clear and hold the Diersfordter Forest on high ground overlooking the Rhine north-east of the small town of Wesel; to secure the bridges over the River Issel north of Wesel; and to make contact with the advancing ground forces attacking across the Rhine.

Brigadier Chatterton, commandant of the Glider Pilot Regiment, had in consultation with the Royal Air Force and 6th Airborne Division, evolved a method of tactical glider landing in which specific targets were chosen for specific glider-carried troops. These gliders were to land as near as possible to their intended targets, not to spread out en masse. Airborne troops were at their most vulnerable during the run-in, landing and forming-up after landing. The tactical landing gave a concentration of men and reduced the chance of enemy fire disrupting the attack before it began.

The first stage of the operation was the bombing by aircraft of the RAF Bomber Command and the US 8th Air Force of all lines of communication and transport to the Ruhr, to prevent the German 15th Army and the 5th Panzer Army, some twenty-one divisions in all, moving towards the Rhine and counter-attacking in strength. Railways in the Ruhr were attacked by the RAF and the US 8th and 9th Air Forces plus the RAF's 2nd Group of 2nd Tactical Air Force. German troop concentrations and anti aircraft guns were heavily attacked on 22 March by seven squadrons of 83 Group, 2nd Tactical Air Force.

At 15:30 on 23 March, seventy-seven Lancaster bombers of the RAF Bomber Command pounded the town of Wesel, which was the objective of 1st Commando Brigade attacking across the Rhine. As soon as the bomber attack ended, the guns of 2nd Army commenced firing and continued all day pouring shells into the German positions. At 22:35 the same day the RAF again bombed Wesel, with 212 bombers of Nos. 5 and 8 Groups, Bomber Command, dropping 1,100 tons of bombs on the town. Immediately afterwards 1st Commando Brigade and the 51st Highland Brigade attacked across the Rhine and stormed into what was left of Wesel.

During the night Mosquito aircraft of No. 2 Group, 2nd Tactical Air Force, attacked German transport in front of the advancing ground forces, dropping 31 tons of bombs on German positions and causing heavy damage. A pall of smoke and dust arose from the battered town of Wesel and, carried by the westerly wind,

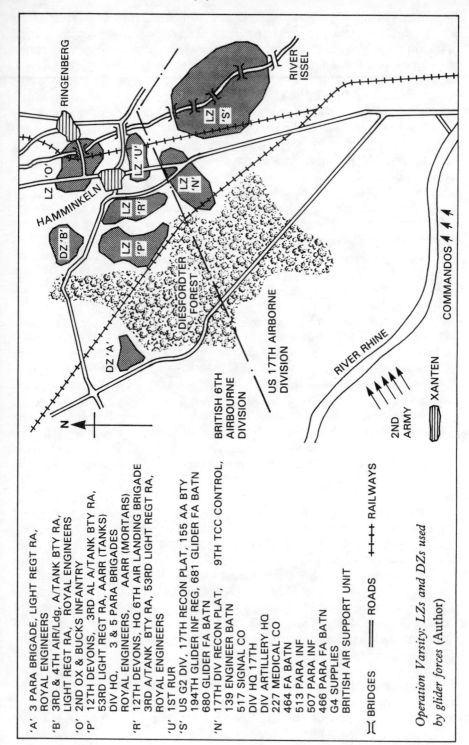

'A' 3 PARA BRIGADE, LIGHT REGT RA,
     ROYAL ENGINEERS
'B' 3RD & 4TH AIR/Ldg, A/TANK BTY RA,
     LIGHT REGT RA, ROYAL ENGINEERS
'O' 2ND OX & BUCKS INFANTRY
'P' 12TH DEVONS, 3RD AL A/TANK BTY RA,
     53RD LIGHT REGT RA, AARR (TANKS)
     DIV HQ,   3 & 5 PARA BRIGADES
     ROYAL ENGINEERS,   AARR (MORTARS)
'R' 12TH DEVONS, HQ 6TH AIR LANDING BRIGADE
     3RD A/TANK BTY RA, 53RD LIGHT REGT RA,
     ROYAL ENGINEERS
'U' 1ST RUR
'S' US G2 DIV, 17TH RECON PLAT, 155 AA BTY
     194TH GLIDER INF REG, 681 GLIDER FA BATN
     680 GLIDER FA BATN
'N' 17TH DIV RECON PLAT,   9TH TCC CONTROL,
     139 ENGINEER BATN
     517 SIGNAL CO
     DIV HQ 17TH
     DIV ARTILLERY HQ
     227 MEDICAL CO
     464 FA BATN
     513 PARA INF
     507 PARA INF
     466 PARA FA BATN
     G4 SUPPLIES
     BRITISH AIR SUPPORT UNIT

)(BRIDGES   ═ ROADS   +++ RAILWAYS

*Operation Varsity: LZs and DZs used
by glider forces (Author)*

began to obscure the intended LZs and DZs of the airborne armies.

At 06:00 on 24 March 1945, the 1st Allied Airborne Army began to take off 6th Airborne Division from airfields in England and the US 17th Airborne Division from airfields on the Continent. The van of the British and American paratroops were scheduled to drop at 10:00 and the first British gliders to land at 10:21 with the last glider landing at 11:00; the first US gliders landed at 10:36 and the last at 12:43.

The British air fleet formed over Essex with the paratroop-carrying aircraft leading in an eighteen-minute time length stream. The glider combinations followed in a 39-minute time length stream. The armada crossed the English coast at Hawkinge, Kent, and set course for Cap Gris Nez on the French coast. The paratroop aircraft were flying at 1,500 feet above sea level, and the glider stream at 2,500 feet, at ground speeds of 115 (C-47–Horsa) mph to 145 (Stirling–Horsa) mph.

The US air fleet formed over three areas in France and set course for Belgium; the paratroop aircraft led with a thirty-minute time length stream and flying at 1,500 feet; the glider combinations with a 2 hr 6 min time length stream at the same height, with ground speeds of 146 (C-46 Commando) and 140 (C-47 Dakota) and 110 (C-47-CG-4A) miles per hour.

Of the 440 British gliders that lifted off, four had to abort almost at once due to tow ropes breaking or tug engine failure. Crossing the Channel two gliders fell into the sea and nineteen more suffered tow rope breaks over France. This was put down to severe air turbulence caused by the slipstream of the aircraft stream.

The two air fleets met south of Brussels over the historic field of Waterloo and flew side by side, in a mighty armada, the last ninety-two miles to the final RVs, code-named 'Yalta North' and 'Yalta South', before peeling off to their respective US and British LZs and DZs.

As the airborne army was approaching the battlefield, Typhoon fighter bombers of the RAF were attacking German anti-aircraft batteries on the battlefield with rockets, cluster bombs and cannon fire but, owing to the fog of war, were unable ot pin-point the German defences. With the airborne troops arriving seven minutes before their ETA, the RAF were forced to break off their attack to allow the landings to begin, but several squadrons remained over the battlefield all day to give air cover and provide cab-rank attacks. (These were attacks on specific targets requested by the army on radio telephone to the aircraft.)

As the airborne troops began to descend, the Germans opened fire with small arms and light anti-aircraft guns causing casualties and damage. Of the British gliders that reached their LZs, only eighty-eight landed undamaged. Thirty-seven were burned out but did reach their LZ.

The 'Varsity' battle plan called for the 6th Air Landing Brigade to seize the bridges over the River Issel near Hamminkeln and Ringenberg. The 3rd and 5th Parachute Brigades would drop on the northern flank and hold off enemy counter-attacks. The divisional troops would land in the centre and the US troops would land further south and take the other bridges over the River Issel.

Fifteen Horsa gliders of 'F' Squadron, Glider Pilot Regiment, commanded by Squadron Leader Reynolds, carried the Coup-de-Main to take the Hamminkeln

Air Movements Chart: Operation Varsity

Troop Unit	RAF Groups & Squadrons	Glider	Chalk Nos	Airfield	LZ	Down	Remarks
2nd Ox & Bucks	46 Grp Dakota	Horsa	1-8	Gosfield	O	10:21	Coup de Main. Bridges 15 gliders Major A.J Dyball. 3 MkII Horsas
1st RUR	46 Grp Dakota 271,512,575	Horsa	9-15	Gosfield	U	10:21	
2nd Ox & Bucks	46 Grp Dakota 271,512,575	Horsa	16-30 (30)	Gosfield	O	10:21	9 MkII Horsas
2nd Ox & Bucks	46 Grp Dakota 48,233,437 RCAF	Horsa	31-63 (33)	Birch	O	10:24	15 MkII Horsas
2nd Ox & Bucks	46 Grp Dakota	Horsa	64-72	Gosfield	O	10:27	14 MkII Horsas
1st RUR	46 Grp Dakota 271,512,575	Horsa	73-93 (30)	Gosfield	U	10:27	
1st RUR	46 Grp Dakota 48,233,437 RCAF	Horsa	94-120 (27)	Birch	U	10:30	15 MkII Horsas
1st RUR	38 Grp Stirlings	Horsa	121-131	Rivenhall	U	10:33	4 MkII Horsas
12th Devons	38 Grp Stirlings	Horsa	132-146	Rivenhall	R	10:33	10 MkII Horsas
12th Devons	38 Grp Stirlings 295,570	Horsa	147-152 (32)	Rivenhall	P	10:33	4 MkII Horsas
HQ 6th A/L Bge	38 Grp Halifax	Horsa	153-167	Earls Colne	R	10:36	
3rd A/Tk Bty	38 Grp Halifax	Horsa	168-172	Earls Colne	R	10:36	
53rd Lt. Reg RA	38 Grp Halifax	Horsa	173-175	Earls Colne	R	10:36	
195th Field Amb.	38 Grp Halifax 296,297	Horsa	176-182 (30)	Earls Colne	R	10:36	23 MkII Horsas
12th Devons	38 Grp Stirling 190,620	Horsa	183-206 (14)	Great Dunmow	R	10:39	11 MkII Horsas
12th Devons	38 Grp Stirling ORTU	Horsa	207-226 (20)	Matching	R	10:42	11 MkII Horsas
4th Air Landing A/Tk Bty RA	38 Grp Halifax 298,644	Horsa	227-238 (12)	Woodbridge	B	10:45	12 MkII Horsas

Troop Unit	RAF Groups & Squadrons	Glider	Chalk Nos	Airfield	LZ	Down	Remarks
3rd A/L A/Tk Bty RA	38 Grp Halifax	Hamilcar	239–244	Woodbridge	R	10:46	48 Hamilcars landing at three minute intervals.
3rd A/L A/Tk Bty RA	38 Grp Halifax	Hamilcar	245–246	Woodbridge	P		
3rd A/L A/Tk Bty RA	38 Grp Halifax	Hamilcar	247–254	Woodbridge	B		
53rd Lt Reg RA	38 Grp Halifax	Hamilcar	255–258	Woodbridge	P		
AAR Regt	38 Grp Halifax	Hamilcar	259–266	Woodbridge	P		
Divisional HQ	38 Grp Halifax	Hamilcar	267–278	Woodbridge	P		
3 Para Brigade	38 Grp Halifax	Hamilcar	279–281	Woodbridge	A		
5th Para Brigade	38 Grp Halifax	Hamilcar	282–284	Woodbridge	B		
Royal Engineers	38 Grp Halifax 298,644	Hamilcar	285–286	Woodbridge	P		
53 Lt Reg RA	38 Grp Stirling 196,299	Horsa	287–314 (28)	Shepherds Grove	P	10:48	15 MkII Horsas
Divisional HQ	38 Grp Stirling 295,570	Horsa	315–342 (28)	Rivenhall	P	10:51	20 MkII Horsas
53rd Lt Reg RA	38 Grp Halifax 296,297	Horsa	343–372 (30)	Earls Colne	P	10:54	20 MkII Horsas
4th A/L A/Tk Bty	38 Grp Stirling 190,620	Horsa	373–378 (6)	Great Dunmow	B	10:57	5 MkII Horsas
3rd A/L A/Tk Bty	38 Grp Stirling	Horsa	379–384	Great Dunmow	A	10:57	5
3rd A/L A/Tk Bty	38 Grp Stirling	Horsa	385–393	Great Dunmow	P		8
53rd Lt Reg. RA	38 Grp Stirling	Horsa	394–402	Great Dunmow	P		8
AARR Mortars	38 Grp Stirling 190,620	Horsa	403–408 (30)	Great Dunmow	P		6 27 MkII Horsas
3 Para Brigade	38 Grp Stirling	Horsa	409–420	Shepherds Grove	A	11:00	8
Light Reg RA	38 Grp Stirling	Horsa	421	Shepherds Grove	A		1
Royal Engineers	38 Grp Stirling	Horsa	422–423	Shepherds Grove	A		2
5 Para Brigade	38 Grp Stirling	Horsa	424–435	Shepherds Grove	B		8
Light Reg RA	38 Grp Stirling	Horsa	436–438	Shepherds Grove	B		3
Royal Engineers	38 Grp Stirling 196,299	Horsa	439–440 (32)	Shepherds Grove	B		2 24 MkII Horsas
Totals:	120 Dakotas 120 Halifaxes 200 Stirlings 440 Aircraft	48 Hamilcars 392 Horsas 440 Gliders		8 Airfields	6 LZ		

and Ringenberg bridges. Eight carried the 2nd Ox and Bucks. and seven the 1st Royal Ulster Rifles. These were to land as near as possible to the bridges and take them intact. This placed them in the van of the assault and the first to land.

At 10:25 the Horsa glider carrying Major A.J. Dyball, OC D Company, 1st Royal Ulster Rifles, landed 150 yards from the bridge. The landing was a heavy one and some of the troops were thrown out of the glider. They immediately came under enemy fire and the wireless operator was killed. No. 22 Platoon of the Royal Ulster Rifles landed nearby and went into action clearing houses near the river bridge. The Germans were still holding the bridge, but they were seen to run away as the troops from the Royal Ulster Rifles, a small number of glider pilots, a few men from the 2nd Ox & Bucks and some Royal Engineers went into the attack capturing the bridge killing twenty Germans and capturing twenty-five.

By 14:30 the fighting had died down but the Royal Ulster Rifles suffered sixteen officers and 243 other ranks casualties.

At Hamminkeln the 12th Devons attacked, took it and prevented a flank attack from the west. The other gliderborne 'Coup-de-Main' parties of the 2nd Ox & Bucks landed on the west side of their target bridge and took it by 12:00. The RAF glider pilots joined in the attack and acquitted themselves well. Some went into battle wearing the red beret. Squadron Leader Reynolds, who was carrying the CO of the Ox and Bucks. in his glider, landed near an enemy flak battery with his second pilot firing a machine gun from the Horsa cockpit as they were landing. The flak battery was taken, but came under fire from other enemy gun pits, so Flying Officer Bailey, RAF, fired an anti-tank projectile at the troublesome gun pit and knocked it out. As was later said, the RAF glider pilots with but three weeks' military training fought well on the ground as soldiers. Fifty-one RAF glider pilots were killed in action.

The 6th Airborne Armoured Recce Regiment were carried into battle in Hamilcars and Horsas. Twelve Locust tanks and a 4.2-in mortar troop were flown in under flak attack when airborne and on landing. Only 50 per cent of each survived but they gave a good account of themselves; one tank though immobilised is reported to have killed over 100 Germans.

The 195th Field Ambulance, RAMC, landed in their gliders at 10:30 in flak north-west of Hamminkeln and immediately went to aid the wounded. Two of the medics, Privates P.M. Lenton and T. Downey, engaged in rescuing wounded troops from wrecked gliders. Private Lenton was awarded the Military Medal and Private Downey was Mentioned in Dispatches for their conduct on the field. Corporal F.G. Topham, Royal Canadian Army Medical Corps, was awarded the Victoria Cross for his conduct in rescuing wounded troops under fire although wounded himself. RAMC records showed 3,000 casualties dealt with by the corps.

The 6th Air Landing Brigade Divisional Signals established their communications without delay, and the brigade command network was in use within twenty-five minutes. The unit lost three officers and sixty-three men killed in action but by late evening had established divisional headquarters in Kopenhof Farm.

By 14:30 most enemy resistance had crumbled; German morale had been shattered by the preliminary bombardment and the sight of the overwhelming might of the Allied airborne army. Isolated pockets of resistance still lingered, but at 15:00 hours the same day contact was made with the ground armies advancing from across the Rhine. Operation 'Varsity' had ended, the greatest and most successful tactical air landing of the war. The largest army ever to take to the air to do battle had achieved its objectives, and the way ahead to Germany lay open.

The cost in lives, however, was heavy. The Glider Pilot Regiment lost 101 men, including the Royal Air Force pilots who died wearing their red berets. All had fought their way into history flying in their fragile wooden gliders then fighting on the ground. The Royal Air Force lost 43 men killed, 153 wounded and 163 were missing.

Geoff Yardley of B Company 2nd Ox and Bucks, relates his story of the landing.

This story is written in memory of those who died and with the hope that some of the very few survivors may read it and make contact. It is about a glider, two pilots and a platoon of well trained airborne soldiers of the British 6th Airborne Division. The time span is a few hours longer than the flight time from Gosfield/Birch to Hamminkeln, Germany, by when most of them will be dead. It starts back in March 1945, when the 6th Division left England en route for Germany. Halifax, Dakota and gliders took off in the darkness of the morning of the 24th, gathering in great numbers and set course for Brussels, then east to the area of Wesel just across the Rhine.

Once again the 52nd Light Infantry, better known as the 2nd Ox and Bucks, were leading the 6th Air Landing Brigade and right at the point of the flying sword were the gliders carrying B Company in numerical platoon order. First, 17 Platoon under Lt J. Cochran, MC, second, 18 Platoon under Lt R. Preston, third, 19 Platoon under Lt H. Clarke, MC, and so on. I flew in No. 2 glider as a member of Bob Preston's 18 Platoon piloted by Staff Sergeant Bill Rowland and Staff Sergeant Geoff Collins of E Squadron, the Glider Pilot Regiment, two names I was not to know until forty years later.

Some three hours' flying time passed uneventfully, as many such flights had been in the past, except that once again, in less than twelve months, this was for real. Darkness turned into a lovely morning, clear sky and the promise of good weather. Now and again the sight of the escort fighters gave the feeling of some security against attack by the Luftwaffe.

At last the River Rhine came into view. As we approached it at about 3,000 feet, the order was given to open the doors, one forward on the port side and one rear starboard. As I sat on the starboard side forward, I watched Ginger Belsham pull the forward door upwards and at that precise moment flak burst under the port wing banking the aircraft over to starboard and almost throwing Ginger out of the door, only to be pulled back by the platoon commander and sergeant. This took perhaps two seconds and allowed this man to live for another few minutes for he and 60 per cent of the platoon were soon to die. The dropping and landing zones were shrouded in smoke which must have made target identification very difficult for the pilots. The gentle jerk of the tow line being cast off was felt as the nose went down and the landing procedure began, with our arms linked in each other's and a silent prayer.

The enemy were waiting for us, with a prepared concentration of ack-ack guns and being the first gliders in our regiment we took the full weight of the defences, as historical records were later to show. We descended through the heavy barrage of flak, many lives being lost during these first few minutes, including one of the pilots, Geoff Collins, and Bill Rowland was wounded. One chap by the name of Shrewsbury, who sat opposite me got a burst of machine gun fire through the back; the bullets then passed between the heads of myself and Ted Tamplin who sat on my right – a gap of about 8 to 10 inches (luck number one).

With some of the controls damaged and no compressed air to operate the landing flaps we flew across the landing zone, over the railway and the River Issel to crash on into a wood at ground level. At a speed of over 70 knots, a fully loaded wooden glider the size of a heavy bomber becomes a pile of matchwood in about one second flat.

While all this was going on, No. 1 glider (17 Platoon) had also been badly hit by flak and was breaking up, spilling men and equipment out, finally to crash as we had done, except for them there were no survivors.

I was one of the lucky ones (luck number two), being the centre one of five men still sitting on one piece of seat with harness on. With the exception of a few cuts and bruises, we five were okay. I remember going over to Staff Sergeant Rowland, wounded by the flak and hurt in the crash and asking him silly questions like what speed we had been doing and what had happened to the brake parachute etc., a conversation he was to recall some forty years later. Several other chaps were alive but wounded, but most were dead including the platoon commander, sergeant and two corporals leaving a corporal, myself and another lance-corporal and some others unhurt.

The wounded were attended to by the platoon medic, Lance-Corporal Greenwood and Ted Noble, who did sterling work during the following few hours. During this time a recce patrol reported a tank at the west end of the next wood and large enemy troop concentrations in the area.

I took a compass bearing on artillery fire, assuming it was our own firing according to plan and established our position on the map (which I still have). From the information we had of the enemy strength and positions it was agreed that the best plan would be to try and link up with the nearest Allied unit which was the 1st Royal Ulster Rifles at their objective on one of the two bridges over the River Issel.

As the shortest distance between two points is a straight line, this meant we had to run like hell over some 1,000 yards of open ground to reach it. There were eight of us capable of doing this; one man, Ted Tamplin, had an injured ankle and offered to stay behind with the wounded, knowing he would probably be taken prisoner or maybe shot. He was taken but did escape some days later and rejoined the regiment. Bill Rowland recalls coming round and finding himself looking up at a German officer demanding whether they were English or American. Bill was convinced that had they been American they would have been shot – I wonder why? By the Grace of God they were allowed to live and were told they would be left to their own devices as they would be picked up by their own side. They were, some 48 hours later.

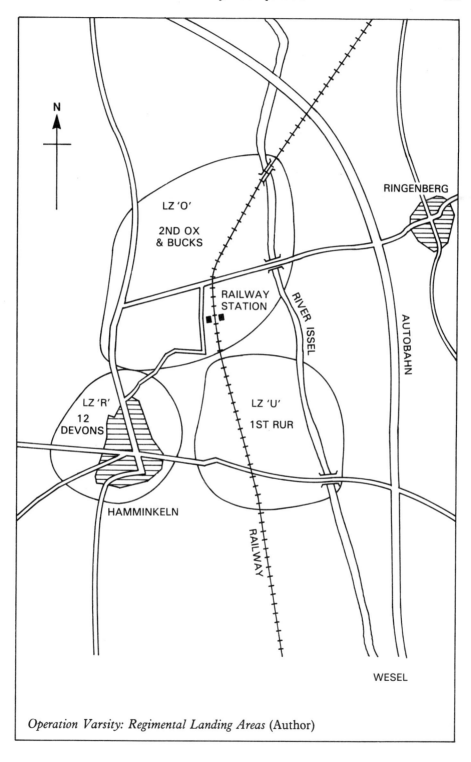

Operation Varsity: Regimental Landing Areas (Author)

The moment for our hasty departure was indicated by the sound of the enemy sweeping the wood from the other end and so, with the old saying in mind, 'He who fights and runs away (may) live to fight another day', we ran like bats out of hell. A line of bobbing red berets weaving across a large open field must have appeared easy targets to the enemy who opened up on us from all angles, but either we had been trained very well or a lot of Germans were bad shots as no one was hit.... or maybe we were lucky (luck number three).

Fortunately the Royal Ulster Rifles had taken the bridge, and a rich Irish voice shouting, 'Halt, who goes there?' was a most welcome sound. We crossed the bridge between burst of machine gun fire and reported to an officer with a request for stretcher-bearers and some help to go back for the wounded. This request was denied, coupled with an order to stay put (the significance of that order was not known until forty years later when I discovered that enemy fire was stonking the wood we had just left and a shell exploded by Bill Rowland taking off his arm and leg).

We rejoined our regiment the next day, March 25th, my twentieth birthday. As for the men I lived and nearly died with I never saw or heard of them again that is until the spring of 1985 when I managed to contact Ted Noble, Bill Rowland, Ted Tamplin and Captain Hugh Clarke, platoon commander of No. 3 glider and several others.

Order of Battle: Operation 'Varsity'
British Forces

6th Airborne Division, GOC, Major General E.L. Bols, DSO
6th Air Landing Brigade, CO, Brigadier R.H. Bellamy, DSO
2nd Battalion Oxfordshire & Buckinghamshire Light Infantry, CO, Lt-Colonel M. Darre Brown.
12th Battalion Devon Regiment, CO, Lt-Colonel P. Gleadell, DSO
1st Battalion Royal Ulster Rifles, CO, Lt-Colonel R.J.H. Carson
Royal Artillery Commander, CO, Brigadier C.K.T. Faithfull
3rd Anti-Tank Battery, RA
4th Anti-Tank Battery, RA
53 Light Regiment, RA
195th Field Ambulance, RAMC
249 Field Company, RE
HQ Staff 6th A/Ldg Brigade
6th Airborne Armoured Recce Regt, CO, Lt-Colonel Stewart
Glider Pilot Regiment, CO, Colonel G.J.S. Chatterton, DSO
1st Glider Wing, CO, Colonel I.A. Murray DSO
'A' Squadron CO, Major H.T. Bartlett. DFC.
'B' Squadron CO, Major T.I.J. Toler. DFC.
'C' Squadron CO, Major J.A. Dale, DFC.
'D' Squadron CO, Major J.F. Lyne. MC.
'E' Squadron CO, Major P.H. Jackson. DFC.
'F' Squadron CO, S/Ldr. V.H. Reynolds, RAF

'G' Squadron CO, Major R.S. Croot, TD
3rd Parachute Brigade CO, Brigadier S.J.L. Hill, DSO
5th Parachute Brigade CO, Brigadier J.H.N. Poett, DSO
Elements of 3 and 5 Parachute Brigades to be carried in twenty-five gliders.

Royal Air Force and United States Army Air Force
USAAF
9th Air Force, HQ, Sunninghill Park, Berkshire, England
9th Troop Carrier Command: HQ. Ascot, Berkshire, England

52nd Troop Carrier Wing
61st Troop Carrier Group. 14th, 15th, 53rd and 59th Squadrons
315th Troop Carrier Group. 34th, 43rd, 309th and 310th Squadrons
316th Troop Carrier Group. 36th, 37th, 44th and 45th Squadrons
Supplying 243 C-47 Dakota aircraft for paratroop dropping British 3rd and 5th
Parachute Brigades from: Boreham, Chipping Ongar and Wethersfield, Essex

Royal Air Force
38 (Airborne Forces) Group

190 Squadron	Stirling	Horsa glider tug	Great Dunmow
196 Squadron	Stirling	Horsa glider tug	Shepherds Grove
295 Squadron	Stirling	Horsa glider tug	Rivenhall
296 Squadron	Halifax	Horsa glider tug	Earls Colne
297 Squadron	Halifax	Horsa glider tug	Earls Colne
298 Squadron	Halifax	Hamilcar glider tug	Woodbridge
299 Squadron	Stirling	Horsa glider tug	Shepherds Grove
570 Squadron	Stirling	Horsa glider tug	Rivenhall
620 Squadron	Stirling	Horsa glider tug	Great Dunmow
644 Squadron	Halifax	Hamilcar glider tug	Woodbridge
ORTU	Stirling	Horsa glider tug	Matching

Supplying 120 Halifax and 200 Stirling aircraft to tow 48 Hamilcar and 273 Horsa gliders.

46 Group

48 Squadron	Dakota	Horsa glider tug	Birch
233 Squadron	Dakota	Horsa glider tug	Birch
271 Squadron	Dakota	Horsa glider tug	Gosfield
512 Squadron	Dakota	Horsa glider tug	Gosfield
575 Squadron	Dakota	Horsa glider tug	Gosfield

120 aircraft to tow 120 Horsa gliders.

Total aircraft:

	243	C-47 Dakota, USAAF, Paratroop dropping
	120	C-47 Dakota, RAF, Glider towing
	120	Halifax, RAF Glider towing,
	200	Stirling, RAF Glider towing
Total:	683	transport and towing aircraft

                    392 Horsa gliders
                     48 Hamilcar gliders
      Total: 440 gliders
      Total: *1,117 aircraft*

                    USAAF from Continental Bases
                    298 C-47 Dakota   Paratroop dropping.
                    610 C-47 Dakota   Glider towing.
      Total: 908 aircraft

                    906 Waco CG-4A Hadrian gliders (some on double tow)
      Total: 1,814 aircraft

Grand Total: *2,931 aircraft:*   1,585 paratroop and glider towing aircraft
                                      and 1,346 gliders.

VII

British Military Gliders

GAL 48 Hotspur Marks I and II

In June 1940, the British Ministry of Aircraft Production issued Specification X10/40 for a military assault glider capable of carrying eight men. The glider had to be capable of a high altitude tug release and a silent descending glide approach to its target. It had to be cheap and expendable and used for one mission only. These requirements seem to have been prompted by the successful use of the DFS 230 glider in the assault on Fort Eben Emael, Belgium, on 10 May, 1940. The specification called for a fully laden glide flight of 100 miles from a 20,000 ft cast-off.

General Aircraft Company of Feltham, Middlesex, England, took up the specification under their chief designer, F.F. Crocombe, and designated it the GAL 48 Hotspur glider Mark I. A first order of 400 was placed by the Ministry and three prototypes, serial numbers BV 134, 135 and 136, were built; the first one flew some four months later.

Description: Military Assault glider.
Mid-wing monoplane of all wooden construction, with normal aircraft flying control surfaces. 61 ft 10¾ in wing span with pointed wing tips and a wing area of 272 sq ft. Aspect ratio 12. Length 39 ft 3½ in. Height 10 ft 10 in. Weight loaded 3,598 lb unloaded 1,661 lb. Capacity, eight troops with light weapons seated in three compartments (two in tandem in the nose and six in cabins, in front and behind the wings, seated on benches). Two-wheel undercarriage on struts under each wing which could be jettisioned for rough landings when a long centre skid and a small tail skid took the landing impact. Removable fuselage lid for the troops to enter and exit over the sides. Towing hooks at front and rear (it was thought at one time that these gliders could be towed in train). A total of twenty-four Hotspur Mark Is were built.

BV 134–140	(7)	Slingsby*	BV 200	(1) Airspeed
BV 146–151	(6)	Slingsby		
BV 190–199	(10)	GAL		

* Slingsby Sailplanes Ltd, Kirkbymoorside, Yorkshire, England.

Trials of the Mark I showed that the Air Ministry specification could not be met, although when not carrying a load the Hotspur could be flown in free flight like a sailplane glider. BV 199 became the Mark II prototype as the War Office had changed its view in October 1940 on the role of gliders from their original concept. The new thinking was that the tug aircraft would cast off the glider at low altitude on the LZ and that the glider would land quickly with a steep approach This required a stronger glider: Specification X22/40 was issued and taken up by the General Aircraft Company who sub-contracted it to several furniture-makers, Harris Lebus, Lawrence Mulliners, Waring and Gillows.

Description: Hotspur Mark II
Wing span 45 ft 10 in square-tipped. Length 39 ft $8\frac{3}{4}$ in. Height 10 ft 10 in. Weight loaded 3,598 lb, unloaded 1,661 lb. Door fitted to port side for troop entry and exit. Cockpit cover hinged to right for access by 1st and 2nd pilots and fitted with air speed indicator, altimeter, compass, turn and bank indicator, and a cable operated tow rope release. A white identification letter was painted in the nose and training yellow and black livery under the wings and fuselage. A total of 987 Mark IIs were built:

BT 479–513 (35)	HH 109–153 (45)
BT 534–557 (24)	HH 167–198 (32)
BT 561–579 (19)	HH 223–268 (46)
BT 594–640 (47)	HH 284–333 (50)
BT 658–693 (36)	HH 346–388 (43)
BT 715–755 (41)	HH 401–431 (31)
BT 769–799 (31)	HH 448–493 (46)
BT 813–861 (49)	HH 517–566 (50)
BT 877–903 (27)	HH 579–623 (45)
BT 916–948 (33)	HH 636–674 (39)
BT 961–990 (30)	HH 688–732 (45)
BV 112–129 (18)	HH 751–800 (50)
	HH 821–853 (33)
	HH 878–919 (42)

In an effort to increase the load-carrying capacity of the Hotspur, an experimental prototype twin hull glider, serial number MP 486, was built in 1942.

Two Mark II Hotspur fuselages were joined together by a 12 ft wide centre wing section and a similar type tailplane. Two Mark II square-tipped wings were added to the outer side of each fuselage, giving a wing span total of 58 feet. This odd design gave a visual twin boom effect to the glider. The prototype MP 486 was flown from the left-hand cockpit and first flew in August 1942, towed by an RAF Whitley bomber. However, the glider later crashed and the project was abandoned.

British Government specification X23/40P put the Hotspur into production by General Aircraft Ltd and fifty-two Mark IIs were converted to Mark IIIs increasing the weight loaded to 3,653 lb, and unloaded 1,755 lb.

BT 540, 735, 823	HH 143, 330, 694, 781	HH 321, 536, 754, 835
BT 566, 747, 895	HH 175, 373, 698, 783	HH 261, 555, 767, 834
BT 602, 751, 917	HH 180, 518, 704, 784	HH 294, 564, 774, 839
BT 632, 777, 946	HH 190, 526, 723, 786	HH 323, 610, 775
BT 663, 784	HH 228, 529, 724, 789	HH 326, 691, 776

The main differences between the Mark II and III was that the glider was towed from the nose section, not the keel as on the Mark II. The tailplane was braced unlike the previous Mark. The second pilot had an instrument panel, flap lever and intercom. A welcome improvement was the fitting of a cable angle indicator, the famous 'Angle of Dangle' as it was known to all who flew and serviced the glider. The author well remembers the first time he heard this term used and thought it was some rude reference until otherwise informed. The CAI was an instrument dial which gave the glider pilot his position relative to the tow rope.

Twenty-two Hotspurs were transferred to the Royal Canadian Air Force:

HH 418, 558, 659	HH 521, 564
HH 419, 559, 667	HH 551, 579
HH 421, 560	HH 552, 580
HH 425, 561	HH 553, 646
HH 427, 562	HH 557, 647

The Hotspur glider was never used operationally, but was used widely in glider pilot training. A total of 1,012 was built and the Hotspur became the standard trainer for the Glider Pilot Regiment at Glider Training Schools.

Slingsby Type 18: Hengist I

British Government aircraft Specification X25/40 called for design for a military transport glider capable of carrying fifteen fully armed troops and two pilots. The well known firm of civilian glider makers, Slingsby Sailplanes Ltd, took up the specification and their designer, F.N. Slingsby, MM, AFRAeS, began the firm's design for the glider later to be named the Hengist. In January 1941 work began on the prototype and in October 1941 a confirmed order for eighteen gliders was placed. The first four were to be prototypes. Main delivery was planned for the summer of 1942.

A year later, in January 1942, the first of the four prototypes, serial number DG 570, was test-flown at RAF Dishforth, Yorkshire, by Group Captain H.J. Wilson; the tug was a Whitley bomber, serial number Z 6640. (Some three years later, on 7 November 1945, Group Captain Wilson captured the world's air speed record for Britain by flying a Gloster Meteor IV at a speed at 606.38 mph.)

The three other prototypes, serial numbers DG 571, DG 572, and D G573, were also built and the latter two were delivered to the Airborne Forces Experimental Establishment in January and February 1943. DG 571 crashed at Dishforth in 1943, owing, it was thought, to overloading. The remaining initial order of fourteen gliders went into production, with serial numbers DG 673 to DG 686, and delivery was completed by the summer of 1943.

The Hengist had been originally intended as a paratroop dropping glider and was equipped with a tail hook for towing another glider behind, so that a force of thirty men could be dropped at one time. But with the advent of larger transport and bomber aircraft that could carry and drop larger forces of paratroops, policy changed and the Hengist programme was concluded in 1943. All the produced gliders were put into storage and in 1946, scrapped there being no requirement for them.

Description: Slingsby Hengist Glider
High wing monoplane of all wooden construction built in sections. 59 ft 2 in long fuselage of rectangular wooden cross section with plywood skin. Constructed in two sections: forward section for the two pilots sitting side by side; rear section extending back to the trailing edge of the wing, which carried the load of fifteen troops seated on fifteen tip-up seats facing inwards on each side. Entry and exit were by two doors in the side of the fuselage, one forward on the starboard side and one aft on the port side. The rear section fuselage behind the wing was hinged to port to reduce travelling length when on ground transport.

Wings: Wooden construction with single main spar and plywood-skinned. 80 ft span with an area of 780 sq ft and a loading of 10.7 lb per square foot. Spoilers fitted to the upper surface of wing. Bellows type trailing edge flaps.

Tail Plane: All wooden construction with single fin, plywood covered.

Undercarriage: Two wheeled, jettisonable after take-off. Landing on a pneumatic skid under fuselage and another under the tailplane. Main skid incorporated a 20 ft long inflated bag to absorb landing stresses.

Speeds: Towing, 130 mph. Landing, 80–90 mph. Stalling, 48 mph.

Weights: All-up, 8,350 lb. Empty, 4,629 lb. Payload, 3,721 lb.

Airspeed Horsa: Marks I and II
In 1940 the British Ministry of Aircraft Production issued Specification X26/40 for a military troop-carrying glider capable of carrying twenty-five troops and two pilots. The specification was taken up by the British aircraft company Airspeed in December 1940, and design work carried out at Salisbury Hall, London Colney, Hertfordshire, England, under the direction of Airspeed's technical director Hessel Tiltman and designer A.E. Ellison.

The project was brilliantly conceived and carried out. Many small firms were involved in building part of the Horsa, as it was later named; they included furniture-makers, coach-builders and several small firms. The component parts were made into thirty main sections and delivered to RAF maintenance units for final assembly.

Two prototypes, serial numbers DG 597 and DG 603, were built at Fairey's Great West Road airfield (now part of London Airport) and DG 597 towed by a Whitley bomber made its first flight from there on 12 September 1941, a mere ten months from the design stage.

The Horsa was of almost all wood construction using spruce and plywood, laminated for greater strength. Every use was made of wood, including the three-spoked control column and wheel. The wings and tailplane were wooden-framed with plywood and doped fabric coverings. Mahogany and metal were used for the main spar anchorage points.

The Mark I Horsa was a high wing military glider capable of carrying twenty-five to twenty-eight equipped troops and two pilots. A wing span of 88 feet gave a wing area of 1,104 sq ft and an aspect ratio of 7. The fuselage was 67 ft in length. All up weight was 15,250 lb, with an unladen weight of 7,500 lb. A tricycle undercarriage was fitted with a castor nose wheel and the two main wheels mounted on a split axle. Strut shock absorbers on each of the main wheels each side of the wing roots. If required the undercarriage could be jettisoned after take-off and landing made on a central heavy duty skid fitted with a shock absorber. An arrester parachute could be fitted behind the tail to reduce the landing run.

Large two-piece flaps were fitted to the trailing edges of each wing with a maximum depression of 80 degrees enabling a steep angle of descent on landing. I well remember when flying a Horsa being amazed at the angle of descent followed by a shallow glide landing. Normal flying surfaces of rudder, aileron and elevators with trim tabs on rudder and elevators.

Three compressed air bottles housed in the large cockpit supplied pressure for the flaps, wheel brakes and the undercarriage jettison release. The wings were fitted with equipment container carrying points – four under each wing – which were released by two pull handles from inside the fuselage. One handle released four containers on each side. Sanitary arrangements consisted of a bottle for the pilots in the cockpit and a sanitary tube in the main cabin for the passengers. Troop seating was on plywood benches along each side of the main cabin plus five more individual seats front and rear.

The flying instruments were mounted on a central panel in the cockpit; left to right, air speed indicator, artificial horizon, rate of descent indicator. Below these were an altimeter and turn and bank indicator. Another small panel held the compressed air pressure gauge and the famous 'Angle of Dangle' cable angle indicator. An RAF aircraft compass completed the instrumentation.

Communication between the tug and glider was by an intercom line interwoven into the 350 ft long $3\frac{3}{4}$ in thick tow rope. This intercom line frequently broke down owing to the stresses of towing and the dropping of the tow rope on the ground after cast-off. During training flights the tow ropes were dropped by the tug on a DZ marked by a yellow cross. The recovery of the tow ropes was a dirty, tiring task, as I well remember having volunteered to assist on one occasion. A bifurcated yoke bridle tow rope was used at first, but this was later changed to a single tow line to the Horsa nose section.

Entry to the glider was by a large door on the port side which was lowered to form a sloping ramp. There was another small door on the starboard side. The Mark II Horsa had a hinged nose section, which gave direct access to the passenger cabin. Two hatches, one in the roof of the main cabin the other in the floor, were provided for defensive or offensive small arms fire.

It was at first considered that the glider could be used for paratroop dropping and two rails were provided over the doors for parachute static lines to be clipped onto. At one time in 1941 it was even thought that the Horsa could be used as a bomber. Horsa AS 52 Project converted a Mark I by cutting a bomb bay under the fuselage to enable a 12,000 lb armour-piercing bomb to be carried. The Ministry of Aircraft Production Specification X3/41 was for such a glider but although a prototype was flight tested in 1941 the idea was abandoned. Other ideas were to fit engines and rocket motors. Trials were made on the rocket-assisted take-off principle using Horsa DG 597 towed by a Whitley bomber but the project was not adopted.

With the need to offload equipment quickly on the battlefield after landing, experiments were carried out in removing the glider's tail section by means of a ring of Cordtex explosive inserted around the rear bulkhead. When fired, the explosive charge cut the fuselage neatly dropping it onto the ground. However, it was found that the explosive could damage the load carried, and in flight it was possible that enemy fire might set off the explosive with dire results for the glider and crew, and the practice was abandoned. Colonel Chatterton discovered that the tail section was held on by bolts and could be detached by unscrewing them with a spanner, so a spanner was included in the glider inventory for this purpose.

A total of 3,655 Horsa gliders was built: 695 at Christchurch and 2,960 by furniture-makers and other firms. The glider was used extensively by Allied forces on operations from 19 November 1942 (Operation 'Freshman') until the end of the war in Europe. Post-war training was carried out till the 1950s when the use of gliders was concluded.

GAL 49 and 50 Hamilcar

When the Ministry of Aircraft Production issued Specification X27/40 calling for designs for a tank or heavy cargo military glider, General Aircraft Ltd (GAL), took up the specification, and produced the heavy glider later named the Hamilcar.

Two prototypes, serials DP 206 and DP 210, were ordered in July 1941, together with another ten pre-production gliders for evaluation. A half scale model was built (serial number T 0227 (GAL 50)) which flew in the autumn of 1941 at Hounslow towed by a Whitley tug aircraft. The serial number was changed to DP 226 but the glider did not last long being written off in a heavy landing.

The prototype DP 206 (GAL 49) was built at GAL's base at Feltham, Middlesex, but the airfield was too small for test flying so the glider was taken by road to RAF Snaith, Yorkshire, an RAF bomber base with a 2,000 yd tarmac runway. Here it made its successful maiden flight on 27 March 1942.

The second prototype, DP 210, was built and further trials made at the Airborne Forces Experimental Establishment on its handling capabilities. In August 1942, DP 210 was delivered to RAF Newmarket and flight trials were carried out between 6 August and 9 September, most of which were successful. All ten pre-production Hamilcars, serial numbers DR 851 to 860, were built by GAL during the winter of 1942 and then delivered to various RAF units for flight trials and assembly instruction at maintenance units.

Owing to the size and weight of the Hamilcar, a suitable tug aircraft had to be found, and trials were carried out with Lancaster, Halifax and Stirling four-

Above *A DFS 230 with Afrika Korps emblem under cockpit.* (Bundesarchiv)
Below *A Messerschmitt Me 321 Gigant, with the front doors ajar and landing skids under the nose.* (Bundesarchiv)

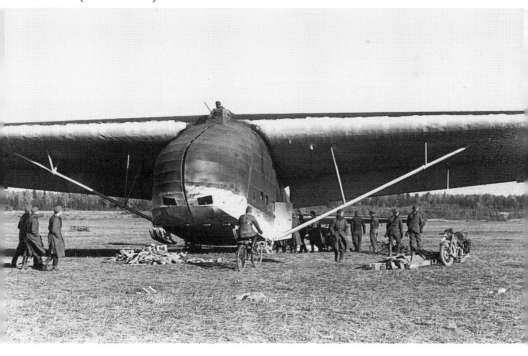

Above *A DFS 230 glider with a Ju 87, Italy 1943.* (Bundesarchiv)
Below *Hitler with the Iron Cross-decorated victors of Eben Emael. Left to right: Lt Delica, Lt Witzig, Capt Koch, Lt Zierach, Hitler, Lt Ringler, Lt Meissener, Lt Kiess, Lt Altman, and Lt Jager.* (Bundesarchiv)

Above *The German Mammut Ju 322 at the end of its one and only flight.* (Bundesarchiv)

Below *Gotha Go 242 in flight over Greece, towed by a Junkers Ju 52.* (Bundesarchiv)

Left *A German Gotha Go 242 on the Russian Front, 1943.* (Bundesarchiv)

Below left *The first group of pilots at the Glider Pilot Regimental Depot at Tilshed, Salisbury Plain. Major Chatteron is centre, first row.* (Middle Wallop AA Corps)

Right *Brigadier G.J.S. Chatterton, OBE, DSO, World War II Commandant, Glider Pilot Regiment.* (David Brook)

Below *12th Devons on training in a Horsa. Parachutes were not usually carried.* (Army Museum of Flying)

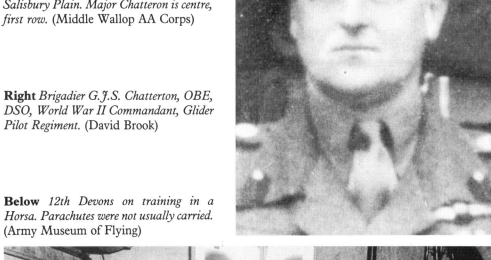

Above *Norsk Hydro Plant, Vermork, Norway, the target of Operation 'Freshman'.* (Army Museum of Flying)

Below left *An electrolysis cell from the Norsk Plant presented to the Royal Engineers Museum, Chatham, in 1982 by the Plant.* (Royal Engineers Museum)

Below right *Merville Battery, Normandy, before the Assault. The bomb craters are widely scattered.* (Air Ministry)

Above *Pegasus Bridge, Normandy 1944.* (Alan Whitcher, war photographer)

Below *Operation 'Voodoo' after landing at Prestwick, Scotland.* (Waco Historical Society)

Above *Glider pilots decorated by King George VI, December 1944. Left to right: Bruce Hobbs, DFM, Stan Pearson, DFM, W. Herbert, DFM, Jim Wallwork, DFM, and Tommy Moore, MM.* (Eagle)

Below *A light tank emerging from a Hamilcar glider. The glider's main role was to carry light tanks to the battlefield.* (Imperial War Museum)

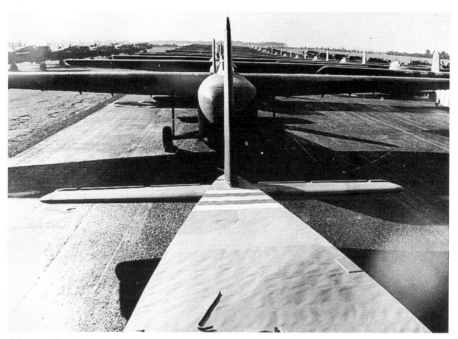

Above *Hamilcars lined up for D-Day at RAF Tarrant Rushton, 1944* (Army Museum of Flying)

Below En route *to Arnhem, taken from a towing aircraft of 570 Squadron, 1944.* (A. Burr)

Above left *Major Robert Henry Cain, VC, South Staffordshire Regiment.* (Staffordshire Regiment)

Above right *Lance-Sergeant John Daniel Baskeyfield, VC, South Staffordshire Regiment.* (Staffordshire Regiment)

Below *A Hotspur glider on rocket-assisted take-off trials.* (Air Britain, J. Halley)

Above *Hotspur Gliders in formation, 1942, No 2GTS.* (Army Museum of Flying)

Below *Hotspur glider, BV 136.* (Imperial War Museum)

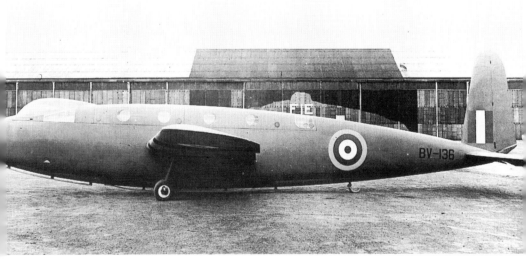

Above left *Major T.I.J. Toler, World War II commander, B Squadron, Glider Pilot Regiment, now President of the Glider Pilot Regimental Association.* (David Brook)

Above right *Interior of a Hengist glider, looking forward, 1942.* (Army Museum of Flying)

Right *Slingsby Hengist glider, Dishforth, Yorkshire, 1942.* (Army Museum of Flying)

Below *Hengist glider, 1942 — cockpit layout.* (Army Museum of Flying)

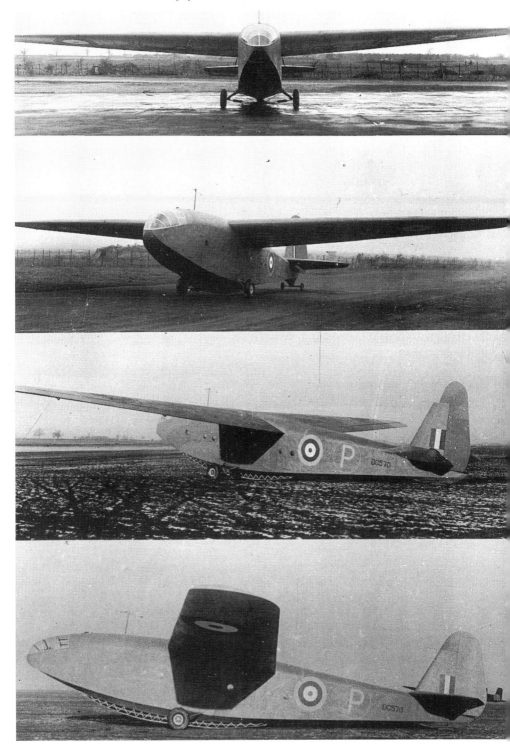

Above *Hamilcar X (Ten) powered glider.* (Air Britain, J. Halley)

Below *Instrument panel of the CG–4A Hadrian Mark I.* (Charles Case)

Above *Interior of a loaded Hamilcar.* (Army Museum of Flying)

Below *No 1 intake of the Glider Pilot Regiment.* (David Brook)

Above *Horsas on dispersal at RAF Rivenhall, 1945. Note the double-barred glider flying cross in the foreground indicating glider flying in progress.* (A. Burr)

Below *Man snatching using a USAF C.130 Hercules.* (Joe Dabney and Lockheed Aircraft)

Above left *Major-General Joseph Harper, World War II Commander 401st/327th Glider Infantry, 101st Airborne, US Army. At Bastogne the then Colonel Harper carried the US reply 'Nuts' to the German call for surrender.* (Major-General Harper)

Above right *An Airborne trooper of the US Army, cold and ragged but still smiling.* (Ron Driver, GPR)

Below *US glider troops boarding a CG-4A glider.* (US Army)

Above *'High Tow' CG–4A being towed off. The glider is airborne before the tug.* (US Army)

Below *General Anthony C. McAuliffe, 101st Airborne Division, US Army.* (Ron Driver, GPR)

Above left *Brigadier Ord Wingate in discussion with Colonel Phillip Cochrane of the 1st Air Commando, India & Burma, 1943.* (USAF)

Above right *Operation 'Market', September 1944 — C.47 tugs and Waco CG-4A gliders lined up for take-off.* (USAF)

Below *The US CG-10A which could carry 40 troops and had a 105-foot wing span. It was intended to produce 1,000 of the type for the invasion of Japan.* (USAF)

Above *A US XCG–17 glider converted from a C.47. Only one conversion was made, in 1944.* (USAF)

Below *A US Waco CG–15A glider on rigid tow by a C–47 which is also equipped with a snatch hook.* (J. Kessler/R. Semmler)

Above right *A Russian A–7 glider after landing during a partisan re-supply operation.* (Janac Milan)

Right *A Russian TS–25 glider. Six examples are thought to have been built.* (Flieger Revue)

Below right *The Russian IL 32 glider in 1948. The prototype was later rebuilt as the IL–34 powered glider.* (Flieger Revue)

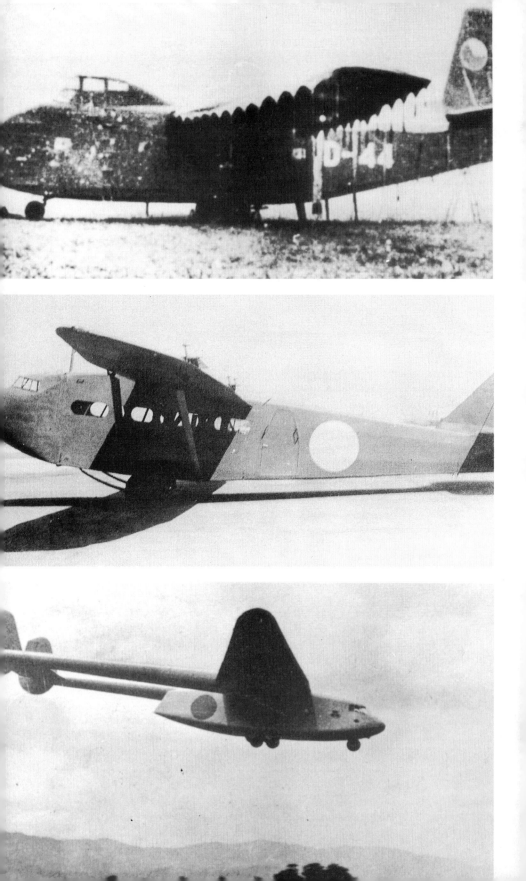

Above left *A YAK–14 in Czech colours as the NK–14. A winter photograph showing wings covered with sheeting.* (Flieger Revue)

Left *The Japanese KU–8–11 military glider.* (USAF)

Below left *The Japanese KU–7 'Crane' glider.* (USAF)

Above *The Argentine I. AE Manque (Vulture) glider.* (Daniel Hagedorn and Fabrica Militarde)

Below *A Chinese glider.* (USAF)

Above *Swedish AB Flygindustri FI-3 Glider. Five gliders were built but were not used in action.* (Sven Stridsberg)

Below *The author in Horsa BP 2124 at RAF Fairford, 1946.* (Author's collection)

engined bombers. It was found that a long take-off run was needed, which resulted in the tug's engine overheating, due to the drag weight of the Hamilcar, even without an operational load. Eventually it fell to the Halifax to tow the Hamilcar on operations.

In a bid to get the heavy Hamilcar off the ground more easily trials were carried out in January 1943, into the use of rocket-assisted take-off (RATO) for the glider. The Royal Aircraft Establishment at Farnborough, Hampshire, designed 25-inch diameter welded steel cylinders, each containing twenty-four 3-inch rockets which were fired in pairs at 1.2 second intervals to give a mean thrust of 2,000 lb for twenty-nine seconds. One rocket container was fitted under each wing well clear of the fuselage, giving a total thrust of 4,000 lb. Once the Hamilcar was airborne the containers were dropped by parachute to the ground.

Trials were conducted at RAF Hartford Bridge, Hampshire, when two rocket cylinders were fitted beneath the wings of Hamilcar DR 854 towed off by a Halifax. The glider pilot waited until the Hamilcar reached a speed of 70 mph, then fired the rockets until a height of 100 feet above the ground. At 300 feet he jettisoned the rocket containers to reduce weight and drag. The tests were successful, reducing the take-off run from 1,700 to 1,300 yards, but the experiment was not acted upon, as more powerful-engined tugs became available.

GAL built the first twenty-two gliders, comprising the two prototypes, ten pre-production and ten production gliders (serials HH 921 to 930). The bulk orders were manufactured as sub-assembly parts by the Birmingham Railway Carriage and Wagon Company, The Co-operative Wholesale Society and AC Motors Ltd. The sub-assembly parts were erected at RAF Lyneham, Wiltshire, and RAF North Luffenham, Rutland.

Description: Hamilcar Heavy Transport Military Glider.

High wing monoplane of wooden construction with plywood and fabric covering. Fuselage 68 ft, with interior dimensions of 27 ft long by 8 ft wide, and 6 ft 8 in high. Front loading door hinged to starboard operated manually from inside or outside, or by the driver of the vehicle being carried driving forward which actuated a push rod which opened the door automatically. Tandem twin pilot cockpit on top of fuselage reached from inside the fuselage by a fixed ladder and a hatch on top of the fuselage roof. Unladen weight was 18,000 lb and a military load of from 17,600 to 19,000 lb, depending on towing tug, could be carried. Typical load was a British Tetrarch tank weight 7 tons or the US Locust tank weighing 8 tons. The two wheel undercarriage could be collapsed for loading and unloading by releasing the pressure in the shock absorbers which allowed the front fuselage to rest on the ground on its four wooden skids. A rapid exit could be made from the nose door by the driver of the vehicle carried simply driving forward thereby operating the door opening push rods. An even more rapid exit could be made by the driver crashing through the wooden nose door and into action as happened to one Hamilcar on Operation 'Mallard'.

The Hamilcar had a 100 ft wing span of wooden construction, plywood-covered with fabric-covered flying control surfaces. Wing loading was 21 lb per square foot with a reported maximum of 34.3 lb per square foot, an extremely high figure. A towing speed of from 125 to 150 mph was usual depending on the tug used. The Hamilcar was used on Operations 'Tonga', 'Mallard', 'Market' and 'Varsity'.

'*Tonga*': Four towed off from RAF Tarrant Rushton by Halifaxes of Nos. 298 and 644 Squadrons. One returned to Dorset, owing to tow rope breakage and the other three landed on their LZ.

'*Mallard*': Thirty towed off by Halifaxes of Nos. 298 and 644 Squadrons. All made their LZs but one made a heavy landing and the tank carried was driven out from the wreckage and into action. Owing to difficulty in recovery from the LZs, all were written off.

'*Market*': Thirty towed off from Tarrant Rushton by Nos. 298 and 644 Squadrons. Fourteen were used on the first lift and all made the LZ. Fifteen went on the second day, but only one on the third day; and that had to land at Ghent as the tow rope broke. The third lift had originally been planned for ten to be landed.

'*Varsity*': Forty-eight were scheduled to be used, though records are not clear as to how many actually went. They landed at three per minute, having been towed off from RAF Woodbridge, Suffolk, by Nos. 298 and 644 Squadrons, who had moved base from Tarrant Rushton in early 1945 in order to reduce flying time to the LZ over the Rhine. All the Hamilcars used were struck off charge on 7 April 1945; it was a one way trip; the original airframe life was but ten hours with this in mind.

The 'Varsity' operation was the last time that Hamilcars were used and the remaining gliders were used for training. I flew in a Hamilcar from RAF Fairford in 1947 whilst serving in 38 Group, and found it a yawing and pitching experience but very interesting. The Hamilcar was not loaded and flew well in free flight with responsive controls but had a noisy and bumpy landing on the grass.

GAL 58 Hamilcar X

Specification X 4/44 called for a powered version of the Hamilcar for use in the Far Eastern theatre of operations; the idea was to assist the towing tug on take-off and reduce the strain on tow in tropical conditions. Designated the GAL 58 Hamilcar X, the prototype, LA 728, first flew in February 1945, at Feltham, after being converted by strengthening the wings to take two 965 hp Bristol Mercury engines and increasing the track of the landing gear. Apart from this the glider was unchanged. From May to August 1945, LA 728 was test-flown from Beaulieu by the AFEE. Fuel was carried in two 195 gal wing tanks with a balance cock in the front cockpit. Another 230 gal fuel tank could be fitted in the cargo hold. The all-up weight for testing was 32,000 lb. Take-off distance was 620 yards and a ferry range of 590 miles was estimated, longer with additional fuel tanks.

An order for 100 conversions was placed, but after twenty had been completed the war ended in August 1945, and the project was cancelled. The Hamilcar X was never used on operations.

Known conversions to Hamilcar X were: LA 728 and LA 704 prototypes; RR 948, 949, 953, 956, 986; RZ 413, 430 and 431; TK 722, 726, 735, 736, 737,

738, 741, 742, 743, 744, 746, 747. Total: 22

With the end of the war, there seemed no further use for the Hamilcar, but in August 1947, LA 728 was used at RAF Defford for testing airborne radar warning installations. The TRE fitted radar in the redesigned nose of the glider and successful tests were carried out. The tests were concluded in January 1948 and LA 728 was scrapped.

Waco CG-4A: Hadrian

The first Waco CG-4A glider to arrive in Britain was renamed the Hadrian and numbered FR 556. It had been towed over the Atlantic on Operation 'Voodoo' in July 1943. This was the first of 1,095 Hadrians supplied to the RAF; the remainder came in packing cases by sea convoy.

RAF records show the following Hadrians supplied:

Mark I

FR 556–580	(25)	FR559 and FR 560 lost at sea en route. FR580 sent to Canada.
NP 664	(1)	Test glider at AFEE, Sherburn in Elmet.
KK 569–789	(221)	
KK 792–968	(177)	
VJ 120–165	(46)	
VJ 198–222	(25)	
VJ 239–284	(46)	
VJ 313–349	(37)	
VJ 368–413	(46)	
VJ 735–781	(47)	
VJ 821–847	(27)	
VK 573–609	(37)	
VK 623–655	(33)	
VK 874–877	(3)	
Total	771	

Mark II

FR582–778	(198)	
KH871–922	(122)	Sent to India for use by 343 & 344 Wings, GPR.
KH994–997	(4)	Sent to Canada
Total	324	

Both Marks total 1095.

Taylorcraft 'H' Glider

During the Second World War the Taylorcraft Aeroplane (England) Company of Leicester produced a prototype training glider similar to the American Taylorcraft TG–6. Basically, the glider was a two-seat, light, powered aircraft with the single nose-positioned engine removed, and replaced with a glazed nose section containing a third seat.

Construction: Three-seat primary training glider which could be flown from any of the three seats. Wing span 36 ft, high wing monoplane, strut-braced with two laminated wooden main spars and pressed metal ribs covered with fabric. Tubular steel V strut-braced the wings to the lower fuselage longerons. Fabric covered ailerons with split trailing edge flaps.

Fuselage 24 ft welded steel tube with wooden stringers, fabric-covered. Tail section tubular metal framed with fixed trim tabs on rudder and elevators. Mass balanced rudder.

Undercarriage: Doughnut wheels attached to lower fuselage longerons. Skid under tailplane.

Only one prototype was built. Training aircraft livery with 'P' symbol on fuselage behind the RAF roundel. Upper surfaces dark green and earth-coloured; lower surfaces diagonal black stripes on a yellow background.

GAL 55: Training Glider

In response to the British Government's Specification TX 3/43 for a military training glider, General Aircraft Limited produced the GAL 55 a midwing glider with two seats and a wing span of 35 ft. Fuselage was 25 ft 6 in long with an all-up weight of 2,407 lb. Flaps and air brakes were fitted together with a tricycle undercarriage.

The Second World War ended before acceptance trials were carried out by the Airborne Forces Experimental Establishment at Beaulieu, Hampshire, on the prototype serial number NP 671. Under tow it was found that there was a tendency to yaw and then a 120 mph towing speed was reached the glider became unstable. In free flight the glider's flying controls were light and the flaps excellent. A speed of 165 mph was reached in a dive and a landing speed of 70 mph was obtained. The glider was found to be unsuitable for military use and the project was concluded.

Miles M 32: Project

British Government Specification X27/40 called for designs for a tank-carrying glider; the Miles Aircraft Company took up the specification with the Miles M 32 Project. Its design was a two-pilot high wing monoplane to carry twenty-five troops or 16 troops and a jeep or two guns. An upwards lifting door and downwards-dropping ramp was fitted in the nose, with the pilot's cockpit above, to allow direct loading and unloading. Two defensive machine gun positions were fitted, one on top of the fuselage behind the pilot's cockpit; the other in the fuselage floor behind the main cabin. The large square-tipped wings were V-braced to the bottom fuselage longerons and had nacelles to carry troop supply containers. For tow-off a jettisonable trolley was used, and a large skid used for landing. Two pusher detachable engines could be fitted for tow-off.

As the Hamilcar tank-carrying glider gave a larger payload and the Horsa glider a larger troop carrying capacity, the design was not proceeded with.

The Baynes Carrier Wing Glider

During 1941, the well-known designer L.E. Baynes drew up plans for a flying wing glider which could be attached to a tank to give it aerial mobility to battle. A military battle planners' dream, which was eventually realised on D-Day, when for the first time in history, tanks were flown by glider into action on the battlefield. To test the design a one-third scale glider was constructed by Slingsby Sailplanes Ltd, and air-tested at the Airborne Forces Experimental Unit at Sherburn-in-Elmet Yorkshire, by Flight Lieutenant R. Kronfeld, AFC, in August 1943.

In appearance the glider looked like a bat, as there was no tailplane fitted. Flying control was effected by vertical end plate fins and rudders on the end of each wing tip. 'Elevons', combined ailerons and elevators, were fitted to the wings. Attached to the underside of the wings were split-bellows type flaps. The single pilot's cockpit projected beneath the wing with a glazed cockpit cover above. For take-off a twin wheel trolley was fitted with a wooden skid for landing.

The glider performed well on air test, both on tow and in free flight, but the design was abandoned as the large tank-carrying Hamilcar was preferred. However the glider was used at the Royal Aircraft Establishment, Farnborough, for research into tail-less aircraft flight.

The Baynes Wing weighed 963 lb and had a 33 ft wing span. It reached an indicated air speed of 105 mph in a dive, stalled at 50 mph and landed at 55–65 mph. Level free flight speed was 90 mph. The small scale glider bore RAF markings and was finished in training livery of dark earth and green on top, and black and yellow underneath.

VIII

British Military Glider Training Units

THE first British military glider training unit was formed at RAF Ringway near Manchester, England, on 19 September 1940, and designated the Glider Training Squadron (GTS); it used Tiger Moth aircraft as tugs and Kirby Kite gliders as trainers.

On 28 December 1940, the Glider Training Squadron moved to RAF Thame, Oxfordshire, with five Tiger Moth aircraft for use as glider tugs. Hawker Hectors were then allocated and began to arrive in strength on 21 February 1941. The first British military glider, the Hotspur, was beginning to come off the production lines and on 6 April 1941, the squadron received its first Hotspur, serial number BV 125. On 26 April 1941, a demonstration excercise with the Hotspur and five Kirby Kite gliders was carried out for the Prime Minister, Winston Churchill.

As the Glider Pilot training programme was expanded to train 400 glider pilots, the Glider Training Squadron was divided to become No. 1 and 2 Glider Training Schools on 1 December 1941, and transferred from RAF Army Cooperation Command to Flying Training Command.

No. 1 Glider Training School
Airfields used: RAF Thame, 1 December 1941, (Reserve Landing Ground Kingston Bagpuize, Berkshire); RAF Croughton, 19 July 1942.

The school was disbanded on 23 March 1943, and all personnel were posted to No. 20 (Pilots) Advance Flying Unit. The school was reformed at RAF Kidlington, on 1st November 1944; posted to RAF Brize Norton 1 June 1945 (as part of No. 21 Heavy Glider Conversion Unit), and was disbanded on 19 June 1946.

No. 2 Glider Training School:
Formed from part of the Glider Training Squadron at RAF Thame, and moved to RAF Weston on the Green, Oxfordshire, on 8 December 1941, with a tug establishment of one Hawker Hind, sixteen Hawker Hectors and two DH Tiger Moths. Glider establishment was thirty Hotspurs divided into two flights, A and B. Personnel establishment was nine tug pilots and twelve glider pilot instructors. Students arrived every three weeks for a six-week course in glider pilot training. On 17 February 1942, the No. 1 Course

Two red balls hoisted on the mast one above the other and a double white cross displayed in the signal area indicate that glider flying is in progress.

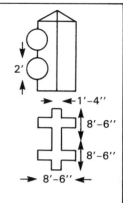

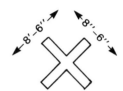

A single yellow cross is used to indicate the cable dropping area.

Red balls and yellow crosses (Author)

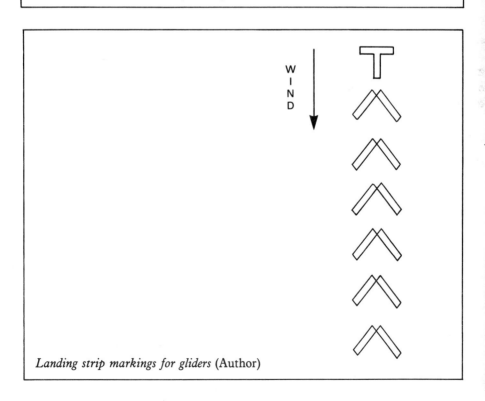

Landing strip markings for gliders (Author)

had finished training; also eight students from No. 1 GTS, having finished their glider pilot training, came for tug pilot training. On 23 March 1943, No. 2 GTS was absorbed into No. 20 (Pilots) Advanced Flying Unit.

No. 3 Glider Training School: Formed at RAF Stoke Orchard, Gloucestershire, on 21 July 1942, with an establishment of thirty-four tug aircraft (Miles Master II and Airspeed Oxfords) and forty-six Hotspur gliders. RAF Northleach, Gloucestershire, was taken over as a Reserve Landing Ground (rlg) on 2 November 1942. Detachments from the school were posted to RAF Aldermaston, Berkshire, in February 1943; other detachments went to RAF Wanborough, Wiltshire, in December 1943; RAF Zeals, Wiltshire, in October 1944 and RAF Culmhead, Somerset, in December 1944.

On 16 January 1945, No. 3 GTS was transferred to RAF Exeter, Devon, and by 1 February 1945 began receiving Albemarle aircraft as tugs and Horsa gliders. Total aircraft held on this date were 6 Albemarles, 7 Horsas, 61 Hotspurs, 7 Tiger Moths and 69 Miles Master IIs. On 24 July, most of the school moved to Wellesbourne Mountford, Warwickshire, and used RAF Gaydon, Warwick, as a satellite. The school was finally disbanded on 3 December 1947.

No. 4 Glider Training School: Formed at RAF Kidlington on 13 July 1942, by re-naming No. 101 (Glider) Operational Training Unit. Used Kingston Bagpuize as a satellite airfield in January 1943. On 6 April 1943, the school was disbanded and personnel posted to No. 20 (Pilots) Advanced Flying School.

No. 5 Glider Training School: Formed at RAF Kidlington on 30 June 1942, and moved to RAF Shobdon, Herefordshire, on 30 July 1942. Equipped at first with Westland Lysanders and Hotspur gliders. In August 1942, Miles Master IIs replaced the Lysanders as glider tugs. RAF Hockley Heath, Warwickshire, was used as a reserve landing ground during July 1944. The school disbanded on 30 November 1945.

No. 20 (Pilots) Advanced Flying Unit: Formed on 10 March 1943, at RAF Kidlington, and absorbed the personnel of Nos. 1, 2 and 4 GTS in late March and early April 1944. On 1st November 1944 the unit became No. 1 GTS.

No. 101 (Glider) Operational Training Unit: Formed at RAF Kidlington on 1 January 1942, using a reserve landing ground at RAF Barford St John, Oxfordshire. During June 1942, another RLG was used at RAF Kidlington, Oxfordshire. On 13 July 1942, the unit became No. 4 GTS at RAF Kidlington.

No. 102 (Glider) Operational Training Unit Formed at RAF Kidlington, on 10 February 1942, with training beginning on 27 February 1942, with Hawker Hinds and Audax tugs towing Hotspur gliders. In June 1942, Westland Lysanders replaced the Hind and Audax tugs. On 13 July 1942, the unit, together with No. 101 (Glider) Operational Training Units became No. 4 GTS; the Westland Lysanders were transferred to No. 5 GTS.

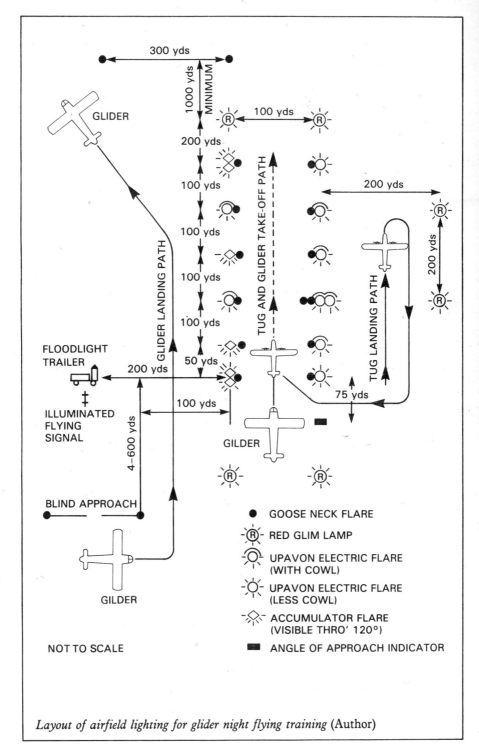

Layout of airfield lighting for glider night flying training (Author)

The Glider Instructors' School: Formed at RAF Thame for the purpose of teaching glider pilot instructors on 25 August 1942. The school was disbanded on 13 January 1943.

Glider Servicing & Conversion Units – 1944

1st Heavy Glider Servicing Unit	Hamilcar and Horsa	Netheravon
21st Heavy Glider Conversion Unit	Horsa	Brize Norton
22nd Heavy Glider Conversion Unit	Horsa and Hadrian	Keevil
23rd Heavy Glider Conversion Unit	Horsa and Hadrian	Peplow
No. 1 Glider Servicing Echelon	Horsa	Wethersfield
No. 2 Glider Servicing Echelon	Horsa	Wethersfield
No. 3 Glider Servicing Echelon	Horsa	Great Dunmow
No. 4 Glider Servicing Echelon	Horsa	Great Dunmow
No. 5 Glider Servicing Echelon	Horsa	Rivenhall
No. 6 Glider Servicing Echelon	Horsa	Rivenhall
No. 7 Glider Servicing Echelon	Horsa	Earls Colne
No. 8 Glider Servicing Echelon	Horsa	Earls Colne
No. 11 Glider Servicing Echelon	Horsa	Blakehill Farm
No. 12 Glider Servicing Echelon	Horsa	Netheravon
No. 13 Glider Servicing Echelon	Horsa	Netheravon
No. 14 Glider Servicing Echelon	Hamilcar	Tarrant Rushton
No. 15 Glider Servicing Echelon	Hamilcar	Tarrant Rushton
No. 16 Glider Servicing Echelon	Horsa	Blakehill Farm

IX

Glider Snatching

THE technique of a low flying aircraft snatching a stationary glider off the ground had its origins in pre-war America where a small aviation firm, All American Aviation, of Wilkington, Delaware, operated an air mail service. A small cable winch, fitted with brakes, was installed inside the fuselage of their light aircraft; the cable ran through guides to an external extended arm and was attached to a hook on the end of the arm. When the hook engaged a loop on a mail bag on the ground the bag was snatched into the air. The winch cable unwound to absorb the inertial energy of the mail bag weight, then the operator braked the winch and rewound it to retrieve the mail bag into the aircraft.

With the advent of the Second World War this technique was adapted to snatch heavier loads by increasing the size of the winch, so that gliders could be retrieved after landing on operations. A glider could be loaded with casualties and snatched off the ground from places where an aircraft could not land; the glider would then be available for another operation.

The All American Aviation Company produced their Model 40 winch which was successful and later their Model 80 which had been developed to snatch the Waco CG-4A military glider. Trials were carried out in the United States and Britain with good results. The evolved technique was for a 220 ft glider tow rope to be secured to the nose of the stationary glider on the ground with the other end of the cable attached to a triangular loop which was mounted on two 12 ft poles twenty feet apart. The snatching aircraft, usually a C-47 Dakota, flew in at about twenty feet above the ground at between 120 and 130 mph with its snatching hook extended on the external arm. The glider was placed diagonally to the track of the aircraft to avoid the arm striking the stationary glider. When, and if, the snatching hook engaged the triangular loop and took up the tow rope it was pulled away from the offset extended arm to avoid fouling it in flight. The winch cable was unwound by the weight of the glider and absorbed the snatching shock. The winch operator rewound the cable, which brought the tow rope to the aircraft's towing rope attachment point. A weak link was built into the towing cable and broke at a pre-determined strain, usually seven tons. An explosive cutter was also fitted on the winch to cut the cable in an emergency.

Depending on the terrain at the snatch point, a glider could be snatched off from an area of 600 to 700 feet long and the glider could be airborne in as little as 60 feet depending on its weight. Glider snatching was successfully employed in Europe to remove gliders from Normandy for use on other operations; thirty-nine British gliders were so recovered. Casualties loaded in gliders were also evacuated. In the Far East campaign, gliders were also snatched from cleared ground in the Chindit penetration.

In Britain, the RAF set up the Glider Pick-Up Flight at RAF Ibsley, Ringwood, where pilots of the Glider Pilot Regiment and the RAF were trained in the technique. Only C-47 Dakotas and Waco CG-4A gliders were used.

I took part in glider-snatching exercises at RAF Fairford and found it stimulating; to fly at 120 mph some twenty feet above the ground heading for two poles twenty feet apart, called for a high degree of airmanship on the part of my pilot.

Allied to glider snatching was the technique of snatching a man off the ground using the same type of equipment modified to allow for the weight difference between a man and a glider. Experiments were conducted in England in 1945 using a small All American Aviation Company winch fitted to an Avro Anson aircraft. Tests were carried out using dummies at first, then in May 1945, a successful live snatch was made with Lieutenant Lee Warner as the subject. Wing Commander Winfield and Squadron Leader Stewart of the RAF Medical Branch were also successfully snatched. Successful demonstrations were carried out at the Royal Aircraft Establishment, Farnborough, but with the war in Europe over the experiments came to an end.

In the United States interest was revived in the snatch technique for the US Space programme when tests were carried out using snatch equipment to recover space capsules ejected from orbiting space craft and parachuting to earth.

The USAF, using Lockheed JC-130B transport aircraft equipped with extended boom poles and winches, successfully recovered space capsules. A special satellite recovery unit was formed and based at Hickam Field, Hawaii, using adapted C-130B Hercules aircraft. The USAF Aerospace Rescue and Recovery Service (AARS) tested the Fulton surface to air recovery system (STAR) using a specially adapted Lockheed C-130B Hercules aircraft. The STAR system consists of a package, which can be dropped from the air to the rescue on land or water; it contains a helium-filled balloon which when inflated will air lift a 525 ft nylon lift rope attached to a body harness and protective suit. The person to be rescued dons the suit and harness, inflates the balloon, then sits on the ground or floats in the water. A yoke fitted to the nose of the C-130 engages the balloon-supported lift rope, with the aircraft flying at 144 mph. The lift rope is locked onto an inboard winch and reeled in lifting the person off the ground into the air, then into the Hercules. Two people or a 500 lb load can be recovered in one intercept.

On 3 May 1966, at Edwards AFB, California, Captain Gerald Lyvere was successfully snatched and winched 400 feet from the ground. Later the same day two men were snatched at the same time in one intercept. Two days later three men were snatched from the sea in an exercise off the California coast.

The 8th Special Operations Squadron of the 1st Special Operations Wing,

USAF, is responsible for training USAF aircrew world-wide; it operates out of Hurlburg AFB Florida, using the Lockheed MC-130 E Combat Talon Hercules aircraft.

Staff Sergeant Joe Michie looks back forty-three years to his course in glider snatching:

On 17 August 1945, I reported to RAF Ibsley which was three miles north of the small Hampshire town of Ringwood, for a three-day course on glider pick-up.

The Glider Pick-Up Flight, using Dakota aircraft modified for glider snatching and American-made Hadrian gliders, some of which still bore their USAAF serial numbers, had formed at RAF Ibsley shortly after the end of World War II, to train pilots of the Glider Pilot Regiment on glider pick-up technique. RAF Ibsley had been an 11 Group Fighter Command airfield during the war and lay in a flat part of the River Avon valley. It had three runways, QDMs 010, 050 and 320, with no flying obstructions. The main runway, 010, was 1,600 yards long with under-shoot and overshoot extending it to 3,600 yards.

On 18 August I commenced the course which consisted of eight pick-ups, four as pupil pilot and four as first pilot with light and heavy loads. My first pick-up was as pupil pilot on a Mark II Hadrian, serial number 533075, with Flying Officer Marande as my instructor.

The nylon tow rope was attached to the nose of the Hadrian and laid out to the two vertical 12 ft high poles twenty feet apart and ending in a loop suspended between the two poles. The snatching Dakota came thundering in at 125 mph. We could hear it but did not see it till it flashed by twenty feet above the deck. The second pilot had to sit with his hand on the tail trim control to trim back instantly on lift-off. The Dakota's snatch hook engaged the loop of the tow rope between the two poles and the glider shot forward as the tow rope was taken up. In a few seconds we were travelling at 150 mph and feeling the G force. The winch operator in the tug reeled in the tow rope and we were on normal tow flight. We were airborne in about sixty feet from rest.

Casting off our tow, we circled, pulled the Hadrian's nose up to lose speed, and came in to land; the glider had a short landing run, using the brakes and putting the nose skid down into the grass.

Flying Officer Marande and myself repeated the pick-up later the same day in the same glider. Both flights lasted ten minutes each; the course was designed to qualify glider pilots in snatch technique rather than on flying the glider itself.

The next day Flying Officer Marande and myself did another snatch in Hadrian KK559. Then it was my turn as first pilot in the left-hand seat; my regular second pilot was Sergeant O'Connor. My strongest memory is sitting there both hands gripping the wheel, sweating profusely in case the Dakota missed the tow loop, while the Dakota came in on the blind side. Instantly we were travelling forward and off the ground, with me shouting to the second pilot to trim back. Then in seconds we were on normal tow, followed minutes later by a flashy final side slip and landing.

On the third and final day of the course I was second pilot to Staff Sergeant East, who had come through Sicily, Normandy and Arnhem. We did a heavy pick-up in

Hadrian 341049 followed by my being first pilot on three more pick-ups. Sometimes the Dakota's snatching hook would miss the loop and as it thundered past you would sit there sweating blue lights.

On 23 August I was certified as having qualified as a Hadrian glider pilot on snatch pick-up, by the Commanding Officer of the Glider Pick-Up Flight, and this was entered in my flying log book.

Looking back I am surprised at how short the course was: just eight take-offs and forty minutes of flying in three days.

X

Royal Air Force Tug Squadrons

A total of sixteen squadrons were used during World War II to tow gliders on operations from the United Kingdom and Tunisia, including one RCAF squadron. These squadrons came from four sources as follows: seven formed as Airborne Support Squadrons, Nos. 295, 296, 297, 298, 299, 570 and 644; four formed as Transport Squadrons, Nos. 271, 437 (RCAF), 512 and 575; three transferred from Coastal Command, Nos. 48 and 233 (formerly Hudson squadrons); and two transferred from Bomber Command, Nos. 196 and 620.

The six squadrons of 46 Group (48, 233, 271, 437 (RCAF), 512 and 575) were formed and used as transport squadrons, but trained for airborne support duties as required.

No. 47 Squadron, 38 Group
First formed at Beverley on 1 March 1916, and began a long history of Army Co-operation at Khartoum in 1927 with DH 9A aircraft and continued in such co-operation until 1940. On 1 September 1946, No. 644 Squadron was re-numbered 47 Squadron and equipped with Halifax A7 and A9 aircraft and was engaged with airborne forces duties until September 1948.
Aircraft DH 9A, Halifax A7 and A9, Hastings C1 and C2.
Airfields Fairford 30 Sept 46, Dishforth 14 Sept 48.

No. 48 Squadron, 46 Group
Formed on 15 March 1916 at RAF Netheravon. In 1944 the squadron was transferred to Transport Command and equipped with Dakota aircraft. On 6 June 1944, D-Day, No. 48 provided thirty aircraft for para drops and carried out twenty-two glider towing sorties. In September 1944, the squadron successfully towed forty-nine gliders to Arnhem (Operation Market) but suffered heavy losses of one-third of its strength in re-supply sorties. The squadron took part in the Rhine Crossing (Operation 'Varsity') with twelve glider tugs, then went to India. It was disbanded in January 1946, but was reformed in February 1946. It later engaged in supply-dropping in Malaya. It was disbanded on 7 January 1976.
Aircraft Dakota III and IV and C4.
Airfields Bircham Newton, 21 Feb 44; Down Ampney, 24 Feb 44.

No. 190 Squadron, 38 Group

Originally formed at Newmarket on 24 October 1917 and disbanded in January 1919. Reformed on 1 March 1943, then disbanded again on 31 December 1943. Reformed at RAF Leicester East on 5 January 1944, as an airborne forces squadron equipped with Stirling aircraft and engaged in glider-towing exercises. On D-Day the squadron was engaged in Operation Tonga on para-dropping on the initial DZ, then towed eighteen gliders. At Arnhem the squadron flew forty missions towing gliders and lost eleven aircraft to enemy flak when on re-supply drops. Thirty Stirlings towed gliders on the Rhine Crossing in Operation 'Varsity'. The squadron was disbanded on 28 December 1945.

Aircraft   Short Stirling IV, Halifax III and VII.
Airfields Leicester East, 5 Jan 44; Fairford, 25 Mar 44; Great Dunmow, 14 Oct 44.

No. 196 Squadron, 38 Group

Formed at RAF Driffield on 7 November 1942 then transferred to airborne forces duties on 18 November, 1943. Engaged on glider towing and para-drop training with Stirling aircraft. On D-Day for Operation 'Tonga' the squadron's Stirlings carried paratroops to Normandy, followed later the same day towing seventeen gliders. At Arnhem on Operation 'Market', the squadron towed in fifty-three gliders during the assault. For Operation 'Varsity', thirty aircraft were employed towing gliders over the Rhine. The squadron was disbanded on 16 March 1946.

Aircraft   Short Stirling Mks III, IV and V.
Airfields Leicester East, 18 Sep 43; Tarrant Rushton, 7 Jan 44; Keevil, 14 Mar 44; Wethersfield 9 Oct 44; Shepherds Grove, 26 Jan 45.

No. 233 Squadron, 46 Group

First formed at Dover in August 1919. In February 1944, the squadron was equipped with Dakota aircraft and became an airborne forces squadron. On D-Day the squadron supplied thirty aircraft to tow six gliders and drop paratroops, followed later the same day by supply drops. Four aircraft were lost. Later it carried out casualty evacuation duties from Normandy. At Arnhem on Operation 'Market' the squadron lost three aircraft during its missions which included towing forty-one gliders. This was followed by thirty five re-supply sorties. During the Rhine Crossing operation twenty-four aircraft were used, all of which were glider tows.

Aircraft   Dakota III.
Airfields Bircham Newton, 1 Mar 44; Blakehill Farm, 5 Mar 44; Birch, 24 Mar 45.

No. 271 Squadron, 46 Group

Formed during September 1918 at Otranto, Italy, and disbanded on 9 December 1918. The squadron reformed on 1 May 1940 at Doncaster, and carried out transport duties. In January 1944, the squadron was re-equipped with Dakota aircraft although it still retained Handley Page Harrow I and II aircraft for casualty flights. In the same month it became an airborne forces unit and provided twenty-two glider tugs on D-Day for Operation 'Tonga'. The squadron's Harrow aircraft were used for casevac flights from the Normandy beachhead. During Operation 'Market' the squadron supplied forty-eight aircraft to tow gliders. For Operation 'Varsity' 271 towed twelve Horsa gliders into Germany. Seven of the squadron's Harrow aircraft were destroyed during a Luftwaffe attack at Evere airfield on New Year's Day, 1945. The squadron was re-numbered 77 Squadron on 1 December 1946.

Aircraft   Handley Page Harrow Mks I and II. Dakota I, II and IV.
Airfields Down Ampney, 29 Feb 44; Doncaster (Part), 29 Feb 44; Blakehill Farm, 31 May 44; Northolt, 20 Feb 45; Gosfield, 23 Mar 45; Croydon, 2 Apr 45; Odiham, 30 Aug 45; Broadwell, 5 Dec 46.

No. 295 Squadron, 38 Group

Formed at RAF Netheravon on 3 August 1942 as an airborne forces unit. Equipped at first with Whitley V aircraft. In February 1943 the squadron received Halifax V aircraft. In June 1943, the squadron was engaged in towing Horsa gliders from Netheravon/Portreath to North Africa (Operations 'Beggar' and 'Elaborate') until September 1943, for use in the invasion of Sicily. The squadron converted to Albemarle aircraft in October 1943 and engaged in supplying the Resistance in France whilst awaiting D-Day. One aircraft from each of 295 and 570 Squadrons were the first to drop troops in Normandy on D-Day. Later the same day 295 sent thirteen aircraft towing gliders to the LZs (Operation 'Tonga') Twenty more glider tugs were sent with troop reinforcements (Operation 'Mallard'). At Arnhem (Operation 'Market') the squadron towed twenty-five Horsa gliders in the first lift and three Horsas on the second lift. Three aircraft were lost on the re-supply missions. For Operation 'Varsity' the squadron towed thirty Horsa gliders over the Rhine. After the end of the war in Europe the squadron carried British troops to Norway to disarm the Germans there which was followed by other trooping duties until 14 January 1946, when the squadron was disbanded. Two weeks later on 1 February 1946, the squadron was again reformed and equipped with Halifax aircraft but was again disbanded on 31 March 1946. It again reformed at RAF Fairford with Halifaxes on 19 September 1947, (where I flew with it) as an airborne forces unit but was finally disbanded on 1 October 1948.

Aircraft   Whitley V; Halifax V; Albemarle I and II; Stirling IV; Halifax VIII; Halifax A9.
Airfields Netheravon, 3 Aug 42; Holmesley South, 1 May 43; Hurn, 30 Jun 43; Harwell, 14 Mar 44; Rivenhall, 7 Oct 44; Tarrant Rushton, 1 Feb 46; Fairford, 10 Sep 47.

No. 296 Squadron, 38 Group

Formed at RAF Ringway on 25 January 1942 from the Glider Exercise Unit. Moved to RAF Netheravon on 1 February 1942 on being equipped with Whitley aircraft. In July 1942, the squadron was divided into two parts, 296A and 296B Squadrons. 296A moved to RAF Hurn and became 296 Squadron and 296B was renamed the Glider Pilot Exercise Unit. In October 1942 the squadron began leaflet-dropping flights over France. In January 1943 the squadron began converting to Albemarle aircraft. These were flown to Froha in North Africa in June 1943, to take part in the invasion of Sicily (Operation 'Husky') and returned to England in October 1943, to RAF Stoney Cross and later to RAF Hurn a short distance away. On 14 March 1944 the squadron moved to RAF Brize Norton, and on D-Day for Operation 'Tonga' supplied three aircraft as Pathfinders and sent eight more towing Horsa gliders in the first wave of airborne troops. This was followed later the same day in Operation 'Mallard' by the squadron towing twenty Horsas. For Operation 'Market' the squadron towed in twenty-one Horsa and seven Hadrian gliders on the first lift, to be followed on the second lift by towing in twenty Horsas. No aircraft losses were incurred. During September 1944, the squadron converted to Halifax aircraft and took part in supply drops to the French Resistance. Operation 'Varsity' saw the squadron tow in thirty Horsa gliders from their base at Earl's Colne. When the war ended the squadron was employed in air trooping of British troops to Norway and Denmark and repatriating prisoners of war to England. The squadron was disbanded on 23 January 1946.

Aircraft Hawker Hector; Hawker Hart; Whitley V; Albemarle I, II, V and VI; Halifax V, III and VII.
Airfields Ringway, 25 Jan 42; Netheravon, 1 Feb 42; Hurn, 25 Jun 42; Andover, 25 Oct 42; Hurn, 19 Dec 42; Froha, 4 Jun 43; Goubrine, 24 Jun 43; Stoney Cross, 25 Jun 43; Hurn, 15 Oct 43; Brize Norton, 14 Mar 44; Earls Colne, 29 Sep 44.

No. 297 Squadron, 38 Group

Formed at RAF Netheravon on 22 January 1942 from the Parachute Exercise Squadron, and equipped with Whitley aircraft. Leaflet-dropping began in October 1942, and by February 1944, the squadron was equipped with Albemarle aircraft. The squadron towed twelve Horsa gliders to Normandy on Operation 'Tonga', including three for the Merville Battery Assault, of which two reached the target; the other Horsa broke its tow rope over Odiham. Twenty more Horsas were towed in Operation 'Mallard' on the evening of D-Day. During Operation 'Market' the squadron towed in twenty-four Horsa and two Hadrian gliders on the first lift and twenty-two Horsas on the second lift. In October 1944, the squadron converted to Halifax aircraft and provided thirty tugs to tow in Horsa gliders during the Varsity Operation. The squadron continued as an airborne force support unit until 15 November 1950 when it was disbanded.

Aircraft Whitley V; Albemarle I, II, V and VI; Halifax III, VII, V and A9.
Airfields Netheravon, 22 Jan 42; Hurn, 5 Jun 42; Thruxton, 25 Oct 42; Stoney Cross, 1 Sep 43; Brize Norton, 14 Mar 44; Earls Colne, 30 Sep 44; Tarrant Rushton, Mar 46; Fairford, 21 Aug 47; Dishforth, 17 Oct 48; Germany, 13 Dec 48; Topcliffe, 13 Dec 49.

No. 298 Squadron, 38 Group

Formed at RAF Thruxton on 24 August 1942 as an airborne forces squadron equipped with Whitley aircraft. Disbanded on 19 October 1942, it was reformed at Tarrant Rushton on 4 November 1943 from A flight of 295 squadron, and equipped with Halifax aircraft. On D-Day the squadron supplied six tugs to tow the Horsa gliders for Operation 'Deadstick', the taking of the Caen Canal and River Orne bridges in Normandy before the main assault. Two Hamilcar gliders were also towed in for Operation 'Tonga'. For Operation 'Mallard' the squadron towed in one Horsa and fifteen Hamilcar gliders. For the SAS Operation 'Dingson' the squadron towed six Hadrian gliders to Brittany. During Operation 'Market' 298 towed in fifteen Hamilcars and thirty-one Horsas in three lifts. For Operation 'Varsity' the squadron towed in six Horsas and twenty-four Hamilcars. The squadron was disbanded on 21 December 1946.

Aircraft   Whitley V; Halifax V, III and VII.
Airfields   Thruxton, 24 Aug 42; Tarrant Rushton, 4 Nov 43; Woodbridge, 21 Mar 45; Tarrant Rushton, 24 Mar 45.

No. 299 Squadron, 38 Group

Formed at RAF Stoney Cross on 4 November 1943 from a cadre provided by 297 Squadron, and equipped with Ventura aircraft which were soon replaced with Stirling aircraft in January 1944. In April 1944, the squadron began to drop supplies to French Resistance forces. For D-Day the squadron supplied twenty-four Stirlings to drop paratroops (Operation 'Tonga') and later for Operation 'Mallard' provided eighteen Horsa glider tugs, during which the squadron lost two aircraft. At Arnhem the squadron towed in fifty-four Horsa gliders during the three lifts. Seventy-two aircraft were used in re-supply drops and five aircraft were lost to enemy flak. During the Rhine Crossing the squadron supplied thirty tugs to tow in Horsa gliders without loss. In May 1945 the squadron air-trooped British troops to Norway. The squadron was disbanded on 15 February 1946.

Aircraft   Ventura I and II; Stirling IV.
Airfields   Stoney Cross, 4 Nov 43; Keevil, 15 Mar 44; Wethersfield, 9 Oct 44; Shepherds Grove, 25 Jan 45.

No. 512 Squadron, 46 Group

Formed at RAF Hendon on 18 June 1943, and equipped with Dakota aircraft. Until February 1944, the squadron carried out transport duties to North Africa and Gibraltar. It then began training with airborne forces and before D-Day carried out leaflet drops over France. Before dawn on D-Day the squadron carried out paratroop drops followed by towing eighteen Horsa gliders on Operation 'Mallard'. During the Arnhem Operation 512 towed twenty-two Horsa gliders in the first lift and twenty four on the second lift. This was followed by twenty-nine re-supply drops in which the squadron lost three aircraft. For the final Operation 'Varsity' the squadron towed twenty-four Horsas. The squadron was disbanded on 14 March 1946.

Aircraft   Dakota I and II.
Airfields Hendon, 18 Jun 43; Broadwell, 14 Feb 44; Evere, 31 Mar 45.

No. 570 Squadron, 38 Group

Formed at RAF Hurn on 15 November 1943, equipped with Albemarle aircraft as an airborne forces squadron. On D-Day 570 sent twelve tugs towing Horsa gliders in Operation 'Tonga'. Later the same day on Operation 'Mallard' the squadron provided twenty Albemarles to tow Horsas to Normandy. During July 1944, the squadron converted to Stirling aircraft and sent nineteen tugs towing Horsas to Arnhem in the first lift. For the second lift eleven Horsas were towed in. On the third and final lift the squadron towed in one Horsa. Eleven aircraft were lost during the re-supply missions which totalled fifty-nine. Thirty tugs towed Horsas for the final Operation 'Varsity'. Following the German surrender, the squadron engaged in air-trooping to Norway. On 8 January 1946, the squadron was disbanded.

Aircraft   Albemarle I, II and V; Stirling V.
Airfields Hurn, 15 Nov 43; Harwell, 14 Mar 44; Rivenhall, 7 Oct 44.

No. 575 Squadron, 46 Group

Formed at RAF Hendon on 11 January 1944, equipped with Dakota aircraft. For D-Day the squadron towed eighteen Horsa gliders on Operation 'Mallard' and twenty-one aircraft for paratroop-dropping. At Arnhem the squadron provided twenty-four Horsa tugs in the first lift and twenty-five Horsa tugs on the second lift. Thirty-eight re-supply sorties were then carried out. For Operation 'Varsity' 575 provided twenty-four Horsa tugs. After performing transport duties the squadron was disbanded on 15 August 1946.

Aircraft   Dakota IIIs.
Airfields Hendon, 1 Feb 44; Broadwell, 14 Feb 44; Gosfield, 24 Mar 45; Melbourne, 5 Aug 45; Blakehill Farm, 16 Nov 45; Bari, 1 Feb 46.

No. 620 Squadron, 38 Group

Formed at RAF Chedburgh on 17 June 1943 as a bomber unit equipped with Stirling aircraft. On 23 November 1943, it became an airborne forces squadron at Leicester East. During the early hours of D-Day the squadron sent twenty-three aircraft to drop paratroops. Later the same day on Operation 'Mallard', 620 sent eighteen Horsa tugs. At Arnhem, six aircraft were engaged in paratroop-dropping and nineteen towed Horsa gliders in the first lift. On the second lift, twenty-two Horsas were towed, and on the third lift one Horsa. During sixty-one re-supply sorties five Stirlings were lost. During the Rhine Crossing, 620 provided thirty Horsa glider tugs. The squadron was then engaged on air-trooping to Norway. In January 1946 the squadron moved to the Middle East (Aqir & Cairo) and acquired some Dakota aircraft. On 1 September 1946, the squadron was renumbered No. 113 Squadron.

Aircraft   Stirling I, III, and IV; Halifax VII and IX.

Airfields Chedburgh, 17 Jun 43; Leicester East, 23 Nov 43; Fairford 18 Mar 44; Great Dunmow, 17 Oct 44; Aqir, 1 Jan 46; Cairo, 3 Mar 46.

No. 644 Squadron, 38 Group

Formed at RAF Tarrant Rushton on 23 February 1944, from a cadre provided by 298 Squadron and was equipped with Halifax Aircraft as an airborne forces squadron. On the early morning of D-Day, 644 towed eighteen Horsa and two Hamilcar gliders on Operation 'Tonga', to be followed on Operation 'Mallard' by fifteen Hamilcar and one Horsa gliders. At Arnhem the squadron provided seven Hamilcar and thirteen Horsa tugs in the first lift, to be followed on the second lift by towing seven Hamilcar and nine Horsa gliders. On the third and final lift, 644 sent one Hamilcar and ten Horsa tugs. On the Rhine Crossing the squadron provided six Horsa and twenty-four Hamilcar tugs. After hostilities ended in Europe the squadron engaged in air-trooping to Norway and repatriating prisoners of war. 644 moved to Quastina, Egypt in November 1945 and was renumbered No. 47 Squadron on 1 September 1946.

Aircraft Halifax V, III and VII.
Airfields Tarrant Rushton, 25 Feb 44; Woodbridge, 24 Mar 45; Quastina, Nov 1945.

Indian Squadrons

Six airborne forces squadrons numbered 668 to 673 were formed in India during 1944 and 1945. Each squadron was to have an establishment of 80 Waco CG4A Hadrian gliders, as the wooden Horsa could not stand up to the climate, and ten light aircraft. Pilots were to be from the Royal Air Force and Glider Pilot Regiment. Two Wings were created with three squadrons in each.

343 Wing
668 Squadron: Formed Calcutta, 16 Nov 44. Disbanded 10 Nov 45.
669 Squadron: Formed Bikram, 16 Nov 44. Disbanded 10 Nov 45.
670 Squadron: Formed Fatehjang, 14 Dec 44. Disbanded 1 Jul 46.

344 Wing
671 Squadron: Formed Bikram, 1 Jan 45. Disbanded 25 Oct 45.
672 Squadron: Formed Bikram, 16 Nov 44. Disbanded 1 Jul 46.
673 Squadron: Formed Bikram, 27 Jan 45. Disbanded 25 Oct 45.

None of the six squadrons saw action.

XI

United States Military Glider Forces History

O N 2 July 1926, the US Army Air Corps was created as part of the US Army. On 1 March 1935, a separate headquarters for the corps, The General Headquarters, Air Force, was formed. This led to the US Army Air Forces being created on 20 June 1941; almost a year later, on 9 March 1942, the titles Army Air Corps and General Headquarters, Air Force were dropped and the name became the US Army Air Force. Later, owing to the expansion of the USAAF, sixteen Army Air Forces came into being. The title USAAF remained until 18 September 1947, when the United States Air Force was formed as a totally separate service. However, in 1948 the US Army again formed its own air branch known as the US Army Air Force for Army Operations.

The US Army had experimented with parachute troops in 1928 when three men and a machine gun were dropped onto Brooks Field, Texas. The experiment was successful but nothing came of it; the US army generals held to the idea that the way to use infantry troops in an airborne capacity was merely to carry them in transport aircraft to enhance their mobility. Aircraft were merely another means of transportation.

On 6 May 1939, the first steps were taken to establish an airborne forces structure within the US Army. At once dispute arose as to whose command the troops would be under, the Army Air Corps or the Army. As they would be fighting on the ground as infantry, the Army thought they should be under its control – again aircraft were only a means of transport. After much discussion the officers' of the US War Department General Staff decided that they should be under Army control.

A small experimental unit was formed under the command of the Commanding Officer of the US Infantry School, at Fort Benning, Georgia, on 25 June 1940. This led to the formation of the 1st Parachute Battalion on 16 September 1940, and on 10 March 1941, a Provisional Parachute Group HQ was created at Fort Benning. On 30 April 1941, a Parachute School was also established at Fort Benning. Growth and expansion followed, first into battalions then into regiments, by February 1942. By 30 July 1942, the 1st Parachute Infantry Brigade was in being. Lieutenant-Colonel William C. Lee had been put in command of the Provisional Parachute Group in July 1940, and later became the first commander of the shortly to be formed Airborne Command.

On 1 July 1941, the first US Army air landing force was created at Fort Kobbe, in the US Canal Zone, when the 550th Airborne Infantry Battalion was established, under the command of Lieutenant-Colonel Harris M. Melaskey.

On 21 March 1942, the US Airborne Command was formed at Fort Benning with Colonel Willam C. Lee in command, under the direction of US Army Ground Forces. The Airborne Command consisted at this time of a Headquarters, the 501st Parachute Infantry, the 503rd Parachute Infantry and the 88th (Glider) Infantry Airborne Battalion. On 9 April 1942, the command moved to Fort Bragg, North Carolina, then on 4 April 1943 to Camp Mackall, also in North Carolina. The Parachute School at Fort Benning was incorporated within the command in May 1942.

On 21 April 1942, another command was formed: the Army Air Force Air Transport Command would supply the aircraft to transport the airborne forces. In June 1942, it was renamed Troop Carrier Command (TCC) and, in July 1942, 1st Troop Carrier Command. Its task was to provide air transport for parachute, glider and airborne infantry troops together with their supplies and equipment.

At its inception Troop Carrier Command was supposed to have 600 transport aircraft and 2,000 gliders to carry out its tasks. It began with 56 transport aircraft. TCC established its HQ at Stout Field, Indiana, and began training. The newly constructed Laurinburg-Maxton Field, North Carolina, and Pope Field, at Fort Bragg were used in conjunction with Airborne Command.

The backbone aircraft at Troop Carrier Command was the Douglas DC3 modified for military use as the C-47 (called the Dakota by the British) and later, with more modifications, as the C-53 Skytrooper. During the summer of 1944, a larger aircraft, the Curtiss C-46 Commando, came into TCC service and saw combat. Other aircraft, such as the C-54 Skymaster, Fairchild C-82, B-24 Liberator, B-17 Flying Fortress and P-38 Lightning, were tested but not put into general use. Each TCC Command's table of organization was wing, group, then squadron. A wing had four or more groups and each group had an HQ, plus four squadrons of twelve aircraft each.

On 25 February 1941, General Henry 'Hap' Arnold, commanding officer of the US Army Air Corps, ordered a feasibility study on the use of gliders for US forces. His attention had been drawn to the possibilities of gliderborne troops by the German gliderborne assault on Fort Eben Emael, Belgium, in May 1940. At this time there were no military gliders in the United States or any glider pilots. Airborne troops consisted of parachute troops or other troops who could be landed by transport aircraft.

On 4 March 1941, General Arnold sent a memorandum to the US Army Air Corps at Wright Field, Dayton, Ohio, requesting flight design engineers based there to design gliders to carry twelve to fifteen troops with their equipment or a pay load of military supplies. Accordingly orders were put out to contract with civilian designers to design and produce military gliders. By May 1941, the Glider Branch at Wright Field had ordered ten gliders for evaluation and experimental tests. They pointed out to General Arnold, however, that men would have to be trained to fly them.

Twelve power-trained pilots were selected to take a thirty-hour glider flying course at the Elmira Soaring Corporation, Elmira, New York, and at the Lewis School of Aeronautics, Lockport, Illinois. On 1 June 1941, the twelve began their training on one-seater Franklin PS-2 gliders. After eight hours' instruction they graduated to Schweizer sailplane gliders to complete the three-week course. The far-sighted General Arnold realised that a proper military glider training programme had to be set up and detailed Brigadier General Carl Spaatz to prepare a plan for training 150 pilots as glider pilot instructors. By August General Arnold had received Spaatz's plan recommending that the 150 pilots be trained at Elmira, New York. After graduation they would be formed into a military glider training school to instruct military glider pilots.

Since there was no one in the US forces suitable to be in charge of the military gliding training programme, General Arnold selected a civilian, Lewis B. Baringer, a well known and expert civilian glider pilot. Baringer commenced his new duties on 15 October 1941, and in May 1942 was commissioned in the rank of major in the US Army Air Force.

With the entry of the United States into the Second World War the glider building and glider pilot training programmes expanded. A 1,000-strong glider pilot training programme began and as well as officers, other ranks were allowed to volunteer from the US forces. In May 1942 General Arnold called for volunteers for a 6,000-strong glider pilot training programme. This produced problems of supply and strenuous efforts were made to find volunteers, including recruiting from the civilian population.

On 28 June 1942, Staff Sergeant William T. Sampson was awarded the first pair of Glider Pilot wings in the US Army Air Force, at Washington Airport. The silver wings were the same as for powered flight except they had the letter G in the centre.

During the summer of 1942 the US Secretary of State, Cordell Hull, and the British Government Minister Viscount Halifax, met to discuss USAAF operations from airfields in the United Kingdom. On 3 September 1943, they agreed a reciprocal aid pact in which Britain would provide airfields for US forces. Owing to shortages of manpower in Britain it was agreed that US aviation construction engineers would build or convert the required airfields. More than 140 airfields were built or converted for the USAAF. Troop Carrier Command used seven, and the rest were used by the 8th and 9th Air Forces. The 12th and 15th Air Forces used some at first, but later moved to North Africa.

With the glider building and glider pilot training programmes getting into high gear, there remained the troops to be carried to battle in the gliders. Across the United States hundreds of thousands of volunteers were enlisting in the services and the US War Department decided to form two airborne divisions. Chosen for this honour was the famous 82nd Infantry Division, which had had an impressive record in the First World War in France. One of its regiments was the 325th Infantry Regiment which had been activated on 25 March 1942, at Camp Claibourne, Louisiana, under the command of Colonel Claudius M. Easley, who was the 325th's third CO since its original formation on 25 August 1917. In March 1942, Colonel Easley was made ADC to the 82nd and Colonel Harry

Leigh Lewis (Light Horse Harry) took command of the 325th. The commanding Officer of the 82nd Division was Major-General Omar N. Bradley with Brigadier-General Matthew B. Ridgeway as second-in-command. Both officers were destined for high command later in the war.

By August 1942, the 82nd had been shaped into a fighting division by General Bradley who, on the 15th, called the entire division together and announced that the 82nd would be split in two, and two airborne divisions formed: the 82nd and 101st. The structure of the two divisions would be two glider and one parachute regiments with artillery, signal, medical, engineer and transport complements. The strength of each division would be 8,825 men, less than the normal 14,000-strong US division, but highly trained and motivated. General Ridgeway became the 82nd divisional commander and had the 325th Glider Infantry Regiment (GIR), plus the 504th and 505th Parachute Regiments under his command. The 82nd retained its original shoulder patch, embroidered 'AA' (All American) but added the word 'Airborne' on top.

The 101st (The Screaming Eagles) was put under the command of Major-General William C. Lee, with the 327th Glider Infantry Regiment commanded by Colonel George S. Wear, and the 401st Glider Infantry Regiment commanded by Colonel Joseph H. Harper. The 101st's shoulder patch was a white eagle on a black shield with the word airborne on top. The eagle was 'Old Abe' the mascot of a regiment of the Iron Brigade during the US Civil War. The black shield represents the Iron Brigade itself.

Until November 1942, US glider pilots were appointed as staff sergeants, but from this date the rank was changed to flight officer (warrant officer) and the pilots had the opportunity of becoming commissioned officers. US glider pilots differed from other countries' glider pilots in that they were not officially trained as soldiers to fight on the ground after landing. Their basic task was to get the glider to the battlefield and unload it. Needless to say many pilots took part in combat with distinction. No extra pay was given to US glider pilots until mid-1944, unlike the paratroops who received fifty dollars a month more. This led to friction between the glider pilots and gliderborne infantry and the paratroops.

In October 1942, the 325th, 327th and the 401st Glider Infantry Regiments moved to Fort Bragg to begin training in airborne warfare. Early in 1943 glider flight training began at Laurinburg-Maxton Army Air Base, at Maxton, North Carolina, about fifty miles from Fort Bragg. Air experience followed on the Waco CG-4A gliders now coming into service; much use was made of steel helmets as no sick bags were issued. Many of the glider troops volunteered for the parachute regiments after flying in gliders; they thought parachuting was safer.

The third week in March 1943, the glider and parachute troops carried out an exercise at Pope Field, near Fort Bragg, witnessed by General George C. Marshall, Field Marshal Sir John Dill and Anthony Eden, the British Foreign Secretary. Shortly afterwards, on 11 April, the glider troops staged a second exercise for General Arnold.

On 15 April 1942, the US 17th Airborne Division was activated at Hoffman, North Carolina, with a strength of 8,505 men. The division sprang from the 101st Airborne Division at Fort Bragg. From the time of its activation the division was commanded by Major-General William M. Miley, and assigned to the US Air-borne Command. The shoulder patch was a gold-coloured claw on a black circular background with the word airborne in arc above. The divisional slogan was 'Thunder from Heaven'.

29 April 1943 saw the 82nd and the 325th Glider Infantry Regiment sail from New York to Casablanca in North Africa. Arriving on 10 May, they set up base camp together with the 319th and the 320th Glider Field Artillery, Engineers and Medical Units of the 307th Regiment. All were under the control of the US 5th Army, commanded by Lieutenant-General Mark W. Clark.

In May 1943, the British General Montgomery decided to use gliderborne troops for the assault on Sicily. Against the advice of the Royal Air Force, he decided to land them at night to seize the vital Ponte Grande bridge in a *Coup de Main* operation. In command of the British glider pilots was Colonel George Chatterton to whose unit forty-two US glider pilots were attached. The task of the US glider pilots was to act as instructors to the British Glider Pilot Regiment on the Waco CG-4A gliders then being delivered to North Africa.

On 6 June 1943, the US glider pilots were asked to volunteer to fly as second pilots on the Sicily operation code-named 'Ladbrooke'. Thirty of the US glider pilot instructors volunteered for the operation and were attached to the British Glider Pilot Regiment.

Before the Sicily operation, the Northwest African Air Force Troop Carrier Command (Provisional), under the command of Brigadier-General Paul L. Williams, had been created as air transport for the operation. It consisted of the US 51st and 52nd Troop Carrier Wings and 295 and 296 Squadrons, RAF.

On 9 July the glider forces lifted off from North Africa and headed for Sicily via Malta. Flying in bad weather, the 137 combinations approached Sicily to be met with heavy flak. Many gliders were released too far offshore to reach land far less their LZs and many crashed in the sea with heavy loss of life. Thirteen US glider pilots were drowned but several fought with the British forces on the ground. One, Flight Officer Samuel Fine, was wounded three times but took part in the coup-de-main capture of the Ponte Grande bridge in the best traditions of the British Glider Pilot Regiment to which he was attached. Uniquely, the surviving US glider pilots were made members of the British Glider Pilot Regiment and awarded the brevet flying badge of the regiment by Lieutenant-Colonel Chatter-ton. Flight Officer Fine was recommended for a US decoration but this was not approved by the USAAF.

The 82nd Division's glider troops had moved camp to near Kairouan, Tunisia, to be ready for the assault on Sicily, but on Friday, 9 July, they had to watch as the C-47s carrying the 82nd's paratroopers flew off to Sicily. The glider troops were told that they would follow as fast as the available air transport would allow. The glider troops were briefed to take off on 12 July for Sicily but the operation was cancelled and they stayed in reserve at Kairouan.

On 13 August, the US 13th Airborne Division was activated; it had been con-stituted in the Army of the United States on 9 January 1942. Under its first com-mander, Major-General George W. Griner, it contained the 189th and the 190th Glider Infantry Cadres. Later two more glider infantry regiments, the 88th and the 326th, were transferred to the 13th Airborne and the 189th and the 190th were inactivated and their troops posted to the 88th and 326th Regiments. At this time, December 1943, the 13th Division came under the command of General Eldridge G. Chapman. The 326th had been in the 82nd Division during the First World War in France where it had served with distinction.

By the end of 1943 the United States had eight glider infantry regiments: the 88th, 187th, 193rd, 325th, 326th and the 401st among its five airborne divisions – the 11th Airborne Division had been activated early in 1943.

In the United States the 101st Division was on the move together with the 327th and the 401st Glider Infantry Regiments. On 22 August they began to move out and sail to Europe. The 327th GIR arrived in Liverpool, England, on 15 September 1943. The 401st GIR were delayed by engine trouble on their troopship and remained at St John's, Newfoundland, for a month until another troopship landed them at Liverpool on 18 August 1943.

The landings at Salerno, Italy, on 8 September, by the Allies were strongly opposed by the Germans and at one time all Navy ships were on standby to evacuate the landed troops. Reinforcements were urgently needed and five battalions of the 82nd were sent into the beachhead. On 13 September the 325th GIR were loaded into landing craft and at 23:00 15 September landed on Salerno beach and dug in for the night. The glider troops had made their first combat landing by boat instead of glider.

Two days later they began to climb the 4,000 ft high Mount Angelo to reinforce the US Rangers who held it. After a six-hour climb they made the top and dug in. Early in the morning of 18 September the glidermen suffered their first casualties during a German artillery barrage. At 07:00 on 20 September the Germans attacked Mount Angelo but were driven back by the 325th's mortar, machine gun and rifle fire till at 13:30 the same day the attack died away. 'C' Company of the 325th cleared and occupied the island of Ischia in the Bay of Naples. In early October 1943, they moved into Naples on occupation duty.

Leaving Italy, the 325th arrived in Northern Ireland in December 1943, and in February 1944, moved to Scraptoft, Leicester, England, to prepare for the invasion of France.

As the US airborne divisions were moving to the United Kingdom, so did the US troop carrier forces required to carry them into combat on mainland Europe. In February 1944, the 9th Troop Carrier Command was activated under Brigadier-General Paul L. Williams with his headquarters at Ascot, Berkshire. The new command had three wings, the 50th, 52nd and 53rd, and came under the control of the US 9th Air Force at Sunninghill Park, Berkshire.

By the end of May 1944, the command had 1,000 crews and 1,176 aircraft. Each Troop Carrier Group had six pathfinder crews to carry the troops who would drop and mark the DZs and LZs prior to the main landings. A decision was made that the 82nd Airborne would train with the 52nd Wing and the 101st Airborne would train with the 50th and 53rd Wing.

On 14 August 1943, President Roosevelt and Prime Minister Churchill met in Canada to formulate plans for the furtherance of the war. High on the agenda was the future conduct of the war against the Japanese. As a result of the Conference,

South East Asia Command (SEAC) was formed under Lord Louis Mountbatten with the US Lieutenant-General Stillwell as deputy commander. It was also decided to form an air unit, at first known as 5318th Air Unit and code-named 'Project Nine', with US Colonel Phillip C. Cochran in command and Colonel John R. Allison as second-in-command.

A miniature air force was created of bombers, fighters, transports, gliders and six helicopters, some 393 aircraft in total with a 523 strong air and ground staff, to transport and aid the British Major-General Orde Wingate's Chindit forces in their behind the Japanese lines operations. In charge of the 100 glider pilots of the unit was Major William H. Taylor, with 175 gliders at his disposal. The 'Project Nine' unit was now know as 1st Air Commando and provided the only way that Wingate's troops could be supplied.

A seventy-strong US glider unit with twenty-seven gliders had arrived in Australia in February 1943, for use in the New Guinea campaign, and it was later reinforced with another fifty-two glider pilots and ground staff; however, they were never used operationally and the unit was deactivated.

On the night of 5/6 March 1944, 1st Air Commando went into action with twenty-six C-47s with CG-4A gliders on double tow. Lifting off from Silcher, India, they carried the Chindits to a LZ 165 miles behind the Japanese lines in Operation Thursday, flying at 8,000 feet over the Chin Hills for LZ 'Broadway'. It had been intended to use two LZs but aerial photographs showed one LZ, 'Piccadilly', obstructed by logs so at short notice all the gliders were routed to 'Broadway'. Both LZs were deep in the jungle held by the Japanese.

Two hours after take-off the first of the gliders began landing. Of the gliders lifted off from India, thirty-six arrived at 'Broadway'. Three carried bulldozers and these were soon at work clearing the LZ. Eight gliders broke tow and landed east of the Chindwin river in Allied territory, but nine landed in Japanese-occupied areas. During the first night of the operation 539 troops, 29,972 lb of supplies and three mules were landed. The troops who had been landed included the 900th Airborne Engineer Company, who cleared the LZ for the next wave of aircraft due in the next night.

Another LZ, 'Chowingree', also deep in the jungle was selected and twelve gliders were towed there to prepare a strip with a bulldozer they carried. Unluckily, the bulldozer was destroyed, when its carrying glider crashed on landing. Next day another bulldozer was delivered by glider and used to create an airstrip. Three days later the Japanese bombed the airstrip, but the Chindits were gone and the serviceable gliders had been snatched out from the LZ. By the end of six days, 9,052 troops, 1,183 mules, 175 ponies, and 500,000 lb of supplies had been landed.

The 1st Airborne Commando continued its operations until the end of August 1944, when the Japanese were in retreat with British forces pursuing them. Operation 'Thursday' had ended and 1st Air Commando had proved its worth in an unorthodox campaign successfully waged on the enemy by the use of gliders.

Early in 1944 the US War Department changed the table of organization for their airborne divisions and decreed that the 82nd Airborne would have three glider infantry battalions instead of two as at present. A decision was made to transfer the 2nd Battalion of the 401st Glider Infantry Regiment, from the 101st Airborne to the 82nd Airborne's 325th Glider Infantry Regiment to bring it to three battalion strength.

This meant that the commander of the 2nd Battalion, Colonel Joseph H. Harper, would lose his command and become a spare. Determined to be in on the Normandy landings, the 45-year-old colonel decided to land in Normandy by parachute. Not being a qualified parachutist, he had to learn how to do it. His basic training consisted of learning how to put a parachute harness on, jumping off a kitchen table four times and rolling on landing. A few days later he made a practice jump with the RAF, then received permission to accompany the 327th/401st Glider Infantry Regiment to France.

With the 82nd Airborne in camp round Leicester and the 101st spread around Berkshire and Wiltshire, preparations and training began for the Normandy landings. To the two US airborne divisions was given the mission of taking and holding the right flank of the invasion front and preventing the Germans reinforcing their beach defences.

The 82nd would drop and land near Ste Mère Eglise on the Cherbourg Peninsula and the 101st would do likewise to the south and east of the small town which stood on a crossroads. The primary task for the 82nd was to take and hold Ste Mère Eglise and to secure bridgeheads over the Merderet River west of the town. The mission of the 101st was to take and hold five bridges over the Douvre river and four causeways over marshland leading from the invasion beaches. The glider troops of the 327th Glider Infantry Regiment learned that owing to a shortage of glider pilots, only their thirty-strong anti-tank gun platoon would travel by glider; the rest of the 327th/401st would land by sea.

In March, 1944, the 101st's commander, General Lee, suffered a heart attack and his command was taken over by Major-General Maxwell Taylor, who had been artillery commander of the 82nd Division. Brigadier-General Donald F. Pratt was assistant divisional commander. By April 1944, the 9th Troop Carrier Command of the 9th Air Force had assembled on airfields in the south of England, having flown in from the United States and the Mediterranean theatre of operations. They comprised the 50th, 52nd and 53rd Troop Carrier Wings. These three wings were further composed of fifteen Troop Carrier Groups of four squadrons, each equipped with sixteen aircraft.

For the US airborne assault in the Cherbourg Peninsula six glider operations were scheduled. The 82nd would mount four, 'Detroit', 'Elmira', 'Galveston' and 'Hackensack'; and the 101st two, 'Chicago' and 'Keokuk'. 'Detroit', 'Elmira', 'Chicago' and 'Keokuk' would take place on D-Day, 6 June, and 'Galveston' and 'Hackensack' would land on D + 1, 7 June.

Three LZs, 'E', 'W' and 'O' had been chosen at Hiesville, Les Forges and six miles inland from the invasion beaches of 'Utah'. The 'Detroit' and 'Chicago' missions would fly in from the Atlantic side of the Cherbourg Peninsula, the other missions would come in from the Channel side over 'Utah' beachhead.

The flight plan route for the two airborne divisions was to RV over the English coastal town of Portland, Dorset (codenamed 'Flatbush') then fly south at 500 feet until they reached their second RV, a British submarine, codenamed 'Hoboken' which was stationed north-west of Guernsey. There they would turn left for the coast of France climbing to 1,500 feet over the coast out of flak range. Once over the coast they would descend to 500 feet for their final descent to their LZs. To make sure that they would not be fired on by Allied naval ships, all aircraft were painted with black and white stripes on wings and fuselage – a simple but effective idea to prevent the debacle which occurred at Sicily. As an insurance all naval ships were forbidden to fire their guns within the air corridors of the airborne divisions during their times of passing over the navy ships.

At 00:20 on 6 June over 1,000 paratroop carrying aircraft began to take off from England with the 82nd and the 101st Airborne Divisions. Preceded by Pathfinder aircraft whose paratroops would land and mark the LZs and DZs, the vast aerial fleet set course for the west coast of the peninsula. Reaching the French coast the Pathfinders found cloud covering their targets and failed to locate their LZs and DZs, and so they were unable to set up their homing beacons and landing lights. Nevertheless both airborne divisions dropped into darkness with the 101st leading. The commanders of both divisions found themselves alone on landing. Some of the paratroops landed twenty miles from their DZ, but gradually during the night the troops began to form themselves into fighting units. In spite of the scattered landings the airborne divisions gave a good account of themselves. The whole situation was confused owing to the scattered drop, but the Germans were just as confused by reports of paratroops landing all over the area.

Back in England the 434th Troop Carrier Group began to lift off fifty-two Waco CG-4A gliders from Aldermaston, Berkshire, at 01:19 in Operation 'Chicago' with troops of the 101st Airborne and headed for LZ 'E'. In the lead glider, named the 'Fighting Falcon', was Brigadier-General Donald F. Pratt, second in command of the 101st. Four miles into the flight the Waco carrying the 101st's command radio broke its tow rope and had to land in England; the rest of the gliders flew on to France. Over the Cherbourg Peninsula one combination was shot down by flak and several others were hit. One glider released eight miles south of its LZ but the other forty-nine made the LZ; the first began its cast-off at 03:54. The glider carrying General Pratt crashed into a hedgerow and the general was killed. Six Wacos managed to land on LZ 'E' in the dark, ten landed on another LZ 'W' instead of 'E'. The rest were scattered around the LZs. It was a magnificent result considering the situation on the ground.

The anti-tank gunners of the 327th GIR came under machine-gun fire and some had difficulty in unloading their guns from their gliders; one gun crew was unable to get its gun into action until daylight owing to German fire.

In England Operation 'Detroit' was under way; the gliders of the 82nd Airborne were lifted off from Ramsbury, Wiltshire, by the 437th Troop Carrier Group with arrival time at LZ 'O' being 04:10. Seven gliders broke tow in cloud over the French coast and another seven released too soon on the western side of the flooded Merderet river. However, twenty-three managed to land either on their LZ or very near it; most were within two miles. Their payloads of jeeps and guns were retrieved as soon as was possible in the conditions prevailing. Two gliders landed in the swamp lands of the river and their howitzer guns could not be retrieved.

By the afternoon of D-Day the 101st had assembled 2,500 of its troops from the scattered drops and was able to take the vital causeways leading from the invasion beaches of 'Utah'. The 82nd in a grim fire fight had taken Ste Mère Eglise and cut the Route 13 highway to Cherbourg. Some of its troops had been misdropped twenty five miles away from their DZ and many in the swamps of the Merderet.

At 06:30 the morning of D-Day the US 4th Infantry Division had begun landing on 'Utah' beach and by 08:00 the same day had made contact with the airborne troops. The glider troops of the 327th/401st GIR came in by sea, having left England on the afternoon of 5 June crammed aboard assault landing craft. At dawn they reached the French coast behind the first wave of assault troops. For some reason the bulk of the glider men had to stay on their landing craft till much later with the offshore invasion fleet under fire from the German shore batteries. It was not until the night of 7 June that all the troops of the 327th/401st were ashore and into action in a thrust towards St Côme du Mont. On D+4 the glider troops were the first to link up with the advancing US troops from the 'Omaha' beachhead to the east.

Meanwhile the 101st's second glider mission of D-Day began to lift off from Aldermaston. Operation 'Keokuk' would take place in daylight with the gliders lifting off at 18:30, and due on LZ 'E' at 21:00 on the evening of 6 June. Punctually at 18:30 the first of thirty-two Horsa gliders, loaded with jeeps and guns, were towed off by the 434th Troop Carrier Group and made for France. Flying in good weather conditions and with a strong fighter escort the gliders came in over 'Utah' beach and under fire cast off their tow ropes. Landing on LZ 'E' part of which was still under German fire, some of the glider crews were captured by the enemy.

The 82nd's 'Elmira' mission, tasked to reinforce the division with troops, jeeps and guns carried in seventy-six Horsa and Waco gliders destined for LZ 'W' was divided into two waves to avoid congestion on the landing zones. The first wave of twenty-six gliders were lifted off from Ramsbury at 18:48 towed by the 437th Troop Carrier Group; the second wave, 50-strong, at 19:07 from Greenham Common, towed by the 438th Troop Carrier Group.

Part of LZ 'W' was still under German control in spite of gallant efforts by the 82nd Division on the ground to clear it. General Ridgeway, the 82nd's Commander was at Ste Mère Eglise, but was minus his command radios, lost in glider crashes, so he could not warn the approaching glider wave that their intended LZ was under enemy fire. As the combinations began to arrive in daylight over the LZ they came under German fire, but two Horsas landed on the LZ and twelve others three-quarters of a mile away. Five glider pilots were killed and seventeen wounded; others were missing.

In July the glider troops of the 325th, 327th and the 401st were back from France and resting in England. On 8 September 1944, on the rolling greens of Scraptoft golf course, the 325th Glider Infantry Regiment were presented with a Presidential Unit Citation for gallantry and outstanding performance of duty during the assault on the coast of Normandy, 7 to 9 June 1944.

With the Allied Armies smashing out from Normandy and into the heart of France a decision was taken to invade the south of France by air and sea in Operation 'Dragoon'. On 11 July 1944, a new unit was formed: the 1st Airborne Task

Force under the command of Major-General Robert T. Frederick. The glider-borne part of the operation was composed of troops of the 550th Glider Infantry Battalion, which had come straight from the United States, a mortar battalion, anti-tank company and an airborne engineer company. Solely for the air lift another new unit, the Provisional Troop Carrier Air Division, was created to tow the gliders from Italy to France. 348 Waco CG-4A gliders were to air lift the troops to landing zones a few miles inland from Cannes on the French coast. On 15 August the operation commenced and was carried out with great success. By mid-day on 17 August the seaborne troops had driven inland and linked with the glider troops; by 9 September contact had been made with US forces fighting south from Normandy into the heartland of France.

On 2 August 1944, 1st Allied Airborne Army was formed with Lieutenant-General Lewis H. Brereton in command of all US airborne divisions together with the 9th Troop Carrier Command. In addition all British airborne troops and 38 and 46 Groups, RAF, came under Brereton's control. The deputy commander was the British Lieutenant-General F.A.M. Browning.

Eighteen airborne operations were planned but had to be cancelled due to the rapid advance of the ground armies. But in early September German resistance began to stiffen and slow the Allied advance. In an effort to shorten the war and outflank the Siegfried Line, the Allies decided to use 1st Allied Airborne Army by landing it behind the German lines in a line stretching from Eindhoven to Arnhem, to capture the vital bridges over the Maas, Waal and Lower Rhine. This operation, if successful, would enable the Allies to pour into Germany.

The British 1st Airborne Division would land at Arnhem to take and hold the road bridge, the furthest away. The 82nd would take and hold the Waal and Maal bridges and the 101st would capture and secure the road from Eindhoven to the 82nd's LZ at Nijmegan to allow the ground forces to advance and link up with the airborne troops at Arnhem.

In conference with General Montgomery, General Browning expressed his view that perhaps they were going 'a bridge too far'. This statement was to prove prophetical. On 10 September, General Brereton placed General Browning in command of all airborne troops for the operation code-named 'Market' with the ground attack code-named 'Garden'.

As there were not enough aircraft to drop and land the three airborne divisions at once, the operation had to be in lifts over three days. On 16 September the Allied air forces began to bomb the Germans in Holland using over 1,000 aircraft in an effort to destroy flak positions, so rendering the air landing forces an easier passage to the LZs.

At 10:25 on Sunday, 17 September, British and American Pathfinder aircraft took off from England to mark the landing zones. Twenty minutes later an immense fleet of aircraft – 1,545 paratroop planes, 451 tug and glider combinations guarded by over 1,000 fighter aircraft began to take off from airfields in the south of England.

All three airborne divisions landed with considerable accuracy but ran into strong German defensive forces. General James Gavin, now in command of the

82nd, had his advance stalled just short of the Nijmagen bridge. General Maxwell Taylor in command of the 101st was struggling to take the town of Eindhoven. At Arnhem the British 1st Airborne Division was fighting hard on the Arnhem bridge. The British link-up tank attack was meeting strong German resistance to its drive to the airborne forces.

Bad weather on the English airfields hampered the airlift of reinforcements to the battle, but at 11:20 on the 18th the 327th/401st GIR of the 101st managed to get off from Membury. The first echelon of 178 gliders arrived at Zon at 15:30 under the command of Colonel Joseph H. Harper, he who had learned to parachute jump from a kitchen table. In another glider was Brigadier-General Anthony C. McAuliffe, the divisional artillery commander. When Colonel Harper's glider was on its landing approach it came under small arms fire to which the colonel replied with his M1 carbine while still airborne.

The 82nd's reinforcements of 1,900 troops and sixty guns had been lifted off in their gliders at 11:09 and made for Holland coming under flak en route and on landing. On 19 September bad weather still prevailed over England but at 11:30 the first of 385 gliders lifted off from England carrying the 3rd Battalion of the 327th GIR and parts of the 327 and 907th Glider field artillery of the 101st Division a total of 2,300 troops and 68 howitzers. Flying in bad weather, seventeen crash landed in the Channel and another thirty-one broke their tow ropes over Belgium. Over Holland they were met by a hail of flak and small arms fire. Part of the last wave of gliders was recalled owing to bad visibility over the English Channel but on landing back at Membury two gliders collided with the loss of all on board. In spite of the flak and adverse weather, 1,340 troops and 40 howitzers reached the LZ.

On 20 September fog still shrouded the English airfields, grounding the paratroop and glider reinforcements, but by now the 82nd had taken the all-important Nijmagen bridge. The British tanks, however, could go no further owing to strong German defences and so could not reach the embattled British airborne division at Arnhem bridge. It was indeed a bridge too far.

D+6 saw the fog clear over England and the 82nd's glider troops, the 325th GIR, now commanded by Colonel Charles Billingslea owing to the illness of its former commander Colonel Lewis, was lifted off in their gliders. By this time the Germans were alert to the re-supply missions along the air corridor to Holland and every German who could handle a weapon was out firing at the passing glider stream.

The main body of 406 gliders carried 3,385 troops, mostly of the 325th GIR, though eighty-four Wacos carried artillery troops of the 101st Division who made a good landing on their divisional LZ. The remainder carried on towards the 82nd's LZ near Nijmagen. One glider, serial A 16, out of Fulbeck was hard hit. Out of forty gliders only eighteen reached the LZ; six gliders were missing, two had landed in England and fourteen were shot down twelve to thirty miles from their LZ. Many of the glider troops marched to their LZs after crash landing, including the CO Colonel Billingslea. On arriving at the LZ the 325th was given the task of clearing and holding the south and south-east border of the airhead perimeter and engaged the Germans in heavy fighting.

On the night of 25 September the aerial part of 'Market' ended but it was 13 November before the 82nd Division was relieved by Canadian troops, and 27 November before the 101st Division was relieved by the British from the still intense fighting. Both airborne divisions moved to Reims, France, to rest and reform, but still remained the Allied strategic reserve. The depleted divisions were reinforced by men from the US 13th Airborne Division to such an extent that the 13th was left with very few officers and no private soldiers.

Operation 'Market' had been the greatest Allied airborne operation yet mounted: 13,781 troops had been transported by glider together with 568 guns and 1927 vehicles. Casualties to US forces from D-Day to D + 30 on Operation 'Market' were:

82nd Airborne Division

Killed	Wounded	Missing	Total
336	1912	661	2909

101st Airborne Division

573	1987	378	2938

Total

909	3899	1039	5847

9th Troop Carrier Command
454 Casualties.

The US airborne forces had accomplished their tasks in hard fighting with success. The gallant British 1st Airborne Division at Arnhem had fought against the odds but in the end had been forced to retire with 7,384 casualties. The airborne troops had done more than had been asked of them in spite of bad weather over England preventing reinforcements arriving. The incomplete success of the operation was due to the failure of the ground forces, owing to strong German resistance – to link up in time. Late in September 1944, the 50th Wing of 9th Troop Carrier Command moved to France to be nearer any future operations and to avoid the bad weather of England.

On 26 August 1944, the US 17th Airborne Division, commanded by Major-General William W. Miley, arrived in England by sea from the United States and by 30 August were in base camp at Chiseldon, Wiltshire. Within the division were the 193rd and 194th Glider Infantry Regiments and the 680th and 681st Glider Field Artillery Battalions. On arrival the division engaged in training from RAF Ramsbury some few miles away.

With the cold European winter approaching fighting slowed but on 16 December the Germans launched a massive counter-attack with 200,000 troops and armour. The 82nd and 101st were rushed to the front, the 82nd to Werbomont and the 101st to Bastogne. The Germans punched sixty miles into the Allied front lines heading for Antwerp to split the Allied forces.

The 101st were surrounded at Bastogne but stood firm; the small Belgian town was a vital junction where seven roads and three railroads converged. The glider troops of 327th and the 401st Regiments held the village of Marvie, with the 82nd's Glider regiment, the 325th, pushing south from Werbomont and securing a line facing south towards Bastogne. Heavy fighting ensued with the German

22nd 'Das Reich' Panzers. As General Maxwell Taylor was in the United States, the 101st was under the command of General McAuliffe who, on the morning of 22 December, received a demand from the Germans to surrender his forces. Colonel Harper, CO of the 327th Glider Infantry personally took General McAuliffe's reply, 'NUTS' to the German envoy under a flag of truce. The Germans were unable to understand this American expression and asked Colonel Harper for clarification to which Harper, later to become a Major-General, elaborated. 'It is the same as go to hell.'

The Germans kept up the pressure on the 101st and on Christmas Day McAuliffe radioed to 8th Corps HQ requesting glider resupply to his encircled troops. Responding to the request, a Waco CG-4A with surgeons and medics was towed off by the 440th Troop Carrier Group from Etain, Belgium, and an hour later landed at Bastogne where the two surgical teams immediately went to work among the wounded.

At 15:00 on 26 December ten CG-4As were towed off from their base at Orleans some 260 miles away from Bastogne, loaded with supplies and medical staff. As the gliders approached Bastogne enemy flak opened up and killed seven passengers in the gliders. All the gliders made the LZ at Bastogne, most were hit by enemy fire but there was no casualties to the glider pilots. Shortly after the glider landings the US 4th Armoured Division broke through to Bastogne but the 101st Airborne still required ammunition and fuel, so on 27 December a fifty-strong CG-4A glider mission was mounted carrying fuel and ammunition. Fifteen gliders were shot down en route but fifty tons of supplies reached Bastogne.

Meanwhile, the 17th Airborne Division had moved to France from England and rushed up to the front to assist in stemming the German advance. The 17th took up positions to the left of the 101st on the morning of 4 January. The new and as yet untried 17th had ranged against them the crack Panzer Grenadiers commanded by Remer, former CO of Hitler's fanatical bodyguard. The Germans made a vicious attack to sever the Bastogne corridor by assaulting from the north-west but they were stopped in their tracks by the 17th Airborne. With only a ten-minute preliminary artillery bombardment, the 17th Airborne launched an attack with the 194th Glider Infantry Regiment, the 550th Airborne Infantry Battalion and the 513th Parachute Infantry Battalion. The 193rd Glider Infantry Regiment remained as tactical reserve.

In heavy snow the 17th fought on, suffering heavy casualties; the first three days saw the division take 1,000 casualties a day. By 7 January the division had taken its objectives and the enemy were in retreat. Fighting on bitterly cold snow-covered ground, the 17th Airborne Division had outfought Hitler's best Panzer troops and sent them reeling back.

On 18 January the 101st were pulled out from Bastogne after five weeks of continuous combat and moved to a quieter section of the front in Alsace. The 82nd withdrew to rest on 10 January to Pepinster, Belgium, to refit.

By the end of January the Germans had been pushed back to where they started. The Battle of Ardennes (the Bulge) was over but US forces had suffered 19,000 troops killed. The Germans had 110,000 killed or wounded and thousands more captured. With the Germans behind the River Rhine and using it as a natural defensive barrier the Allied advance was halted but a force of US troops managed to cross over the Remagen Bridge and establish a bridgehead on the eastern bank.

The methodical Montgomery decided to attack across the Rhine with ground and airborne troops preceded by a massive ground and air bombardment. The airborne assault, Operation 'Varsity', would land over the Rhine near Wesel after the assault across the river by ground forces. This would be the largest tactical air landing of the War but this time the airborne troops would be within covering range of Allied artillery firing from the west bank of the river.

As the 82nd and 101st Airborne Divisions had been badly mauled during the battle in the Ardennes, the 1st Allied Airborne Army would consist of the US 17th Airborne Division, commanded by Major-General Miley, and the British 6th Airborne Division, commanded by Major General Bols. Both divisions had acquitted themselves well, the 6th in Normandy and the 17th in the Ardennes. Within the 17th would be the 194th GIR, commanded by Colonel James R. Pierce.

The task of 17th Airborne was to seize, clear and secure the divisional area with priority to the high ground just east of Diersfordt and the bridges over the Issel river; to protect the right flank (south), establish contact with 1st Commando Brigade coming across the Rhine north-east of Wesel, with the British 15th Division and 6th Airborne Division. The 194th GIR was to land in the southern part of the 17th divisional zone, clear its area and attack north-east.

Taking and lifting off on the morning of 24 March 1945, from Continental airfields, the 17th was carried in a mighty fleet of 2,875 gliders, tugs and paratroop aircraft to begin landing at 09:48 in Germany. The landings were made as planned, but against heavy German fire from flak guns and small arms firing from prepared positions as the Germans knew the Allies were coming. All the 17th's designated tasks were carried out; their objectives were taken and cleared within four hours of the first landings. Contact was made with 6th Airborne Division and ground forces to the south and south-east. By daylight next day the 17th had captured 3,000 prisoners and destroyed the German 84th Infantry Division as an effective military force.

The 17th took 1,307 casualties up to midnight on 25 March: 393 killed in action, 834 wounded and 80 missing in action. Planned to the last detail, with complete briefing of every man in the division, and the sheer fighting qualities of the troops, this operation made airborne history. It was the first double tow of gliders into battle and the operation had been accomplished as prescribed without a single amendment or change to the original plan. The way to Berlin was now open and the 17th Division went through it, with the 194th Glider Combat Team capturing Hitler's former diplomat, Franz von Papen, en route.

The other two US airborne divisions, the 82nd and the 101st, continued in battle. The 101st, as a result of their stand at Bastogne, was cited for gallantry and heroism in combat. The 82nd battered the Siegfried Line and the 325th Glider Infantry took more killed in combat in the attack than in any other single day's fighting during the war.

General Ridgeway, commanding 18th Airborne Corps, fighting with the British in the north, requested the assignment of the 82nd to the Elbe river north-west of Berlin. Crossing the Elbe river, the division made its final attack of the war on 4 May 1945, its objective being Ludwigslust. The 325th Glider Infantry and elements of the 82nd overran a concentration camp, accepted the surrender of the 21st German Army and met the Russians at 14:25 on 3 May at Ludwigslust. There, Colonel Billingslea, CO of the 325th Glider Infantry, was awarded the Red Star by the Russians. Three days later the Germans surrendered and the men of the 82nd later marched down the Unter den Linden in Berlin in the Victory Parade.

The 13th Airborne Division, part of 18th Corps, had been held in reserve but had supplied men as replacement to the 17th, 82nd and 101st. It had been assigned combat missions but due to the speed of advance of General Patton's troops the missions were cancelled. With the war in Europe over, the 13th were transferred back to the US ready to go to the Pacific, but Japan surrendered in August.

In the Pacific, the 11th Airborne Division commanded by Major-General Joseph M. Swing, was still fighting the Japanese. The division, which had the 187th and the 188th Glider Infantry Regiments within its establishment, fought mainly as normal infantry but did carry out three airborne operations, two paratroop and one glider. The 11th's final airborne operation included a glider element. On 23 June 1945, at Cagcuyan Valley, Luzon, Phillipines, a unit known as Gipsy Task Force dropped and landed by glider 1,000 troops. Seven gliders were used, six CG-4As and one CG-13 carried in six jeeps, machine guns, ammunition and medical supplies to Camalaniugan Airfield without any enemy resistance. Three days later the airborne forces linked up with the advancing ground forces.

The first and last tactical glider landing in the Pacific had also been the last in the Second World War for the Japanese surrender came shortly afterwards. The 11th Airborne was sent to Japan as part of the occupation forces.

With the Second World War over, a swift run-down of airborne forces began; each man's service record was checked to determine his 'points' for the release from the service programme. One point was given for each month of service with additional points for overseas duty. Five points were given for each battle star and decorations awarded, plus five for dependents back in the US. Indicative of the 'high pointer' was the 325th Glider Infantry Regiment of the 82nd Airborne Division, some of whom had well over 100 points.

The airborne divisions of the United States of America had fought well and gallantly but at a cost. Their casualties were:

Division	Killed	Wounded	Missing	Total
11th	1011	4073	40	5124
13th	9	3	1	13
17th	1119	4214	87	5420
82nd	1581	5544	552	7677
101st	1731	5584	273	7588
Totals:	5451	19418	953	25822

The US had trained 6,000 men to fly gliders of which 14,612 were built. Only one regiment, the 325th GIR, retained several CG-15A transport gliders, their last use being in April 1949, on exercise at Fort Bragg. On 1 January 1953, the use of gliders for carrying combat troops ended. Helicopters took over the role, but lacked the great advantage of gliders: silence.

XII

United States Military Glider Forces Operations

Invasion of France, 1944: USAAF Glider Tug Units

9th Troop Carrier Command, HQ Ascot, Berkshire.
Commanding Officer Brigadier-General Paul L. Williams.

50th Troop Carrier Wing
439th Troop Carrier Group, 91, 92, 93 and 94 Squadrons, Upottery, Devon
441st Troop Carrier Group, 99, 100, 301, and 302 Squadrons, Merryfield, Somerset

53rd Troop Carrier Wing
434th Troop Carrier Group, 71, 72, 73 and 74 Squadrons, Aldermaston, Berkshire
435th Troop Carrier Group, 75, 76, 77 and 78 Squadrons, Welford, Berkshire
436th Troop Carrier Group, 79, 80, 81 and 82 Squadrons, Membury, Berkshire
437th Troop Carrier Group, 83, 84, 85 and 86 Squadrons, Ramsbury, Wiltshire
438th Troop Carrier Group, 87, 88, 89 and 90 Squadrons, Greenham, Berkshire

Scheduled to tow 514 gliders, 292 Waco CG-4A and 222 Horsas, in six glider operations: 'Chicago', 'Detroit', 'Keokuk', 'Elmira', 'Galveston' and 'Hackensack' on D-Day and D + 1.

Landing Zones	'E' Oval area 2,640 yds north–south and 1,760 yds east–west, with the right side bordering on the village of Hiesville, ten miles inland from the Channel coast.
Drop & Landing Zone	'O' oval area north west of St Mère Eglise and west of the Merderet River. Similar in size to 'E'.
Landing Zone	'W' Oval area 2,800 yards north–south and 2,000 yds wide, a mile south of St Mère Eglise with the southern part astride the village of Les Forges.

US Air Movements Table
D-Day 6 June

US Army Unit	USAAF Unit	Glider	Number	Take-off	Airfield	LZ	Load & down time
101st Airborne Division	434th TCG	CG-4A	52	'Chicago Mission' 01:19	Aldermaston	E	Down 03:45 hours. Brig.-Gen Pratt. 155 troops. 16 A/Tk guns. 2½ tons ammunition. 25 vehicles. 1 bulldozer.
82nd Airborne Division	437th TCG	CG-4A	52	'Detroit Mission' 01:59	Ramsbury	O	Down 04:10 hours. 220 troops 22 Jeeps: 16 A/Tk guns. 10 tons supplies. 5 trailers.
101st Airborne Division	434th TCG	Horsa	32	'Keokuk Mission' Evening of D-Day. 18:30	Aldermaston	E	Down 20:53 hours. 157 troops 40 vehicles. 6 guns. 19 tons supplies.
1st Serial 82nd Airborne Division.	434th TCG	Horsa CG-4A	18 8	'Elmira Mission' Evening of D-Day 19:07 19:07	Ramsbury Ramsbury	W W	Down 21:04 hours.
2nd Serial 82nd Airborne Division.	438th TCG	Horsa CG-4A	36 14	18:48 18:48	Greenham Common	W W	Down 21:37 hours.

Both serials carrying 437 troops, 64 vehicles, 13 A/Tk guns, 24½ tons supplies

US Army Unit	USAAF Unit	Glider	Number	Take-off	Airfield	LZ	Load & down time
				'Elmira' Second Wave			
1st Serial 82nd Airborne 319th Fd. Art. Battalion.	436th TCG	Horsa CG-4A	48 2	20:37 20:37	Membury Membury	O O	Down 22:55 hours. 418 troops 31 jeeps. 26 tons ammunition 25 tons supplies.
2nd Serial 82nd Airborne 320th Fd. Art. Battalion.	435th TCG	Horsa CG-4A	38 12	20:40 20:40	Welford Welford	O O	Down 23:05 hours. 319 troops. 12 × 105mm Howitzers. 28 jeeps. 33 tons ammunition 23 tons supplies. Each CG-4A carried one howitzer.
				'Galveston' Mission, D + 1			
1st Serial 82nd Airborne	437th TCG	Horsa CG-4A	18 32	04:39 04:39	Ramsbury Ramsbury	E E	Down 07:55 hours. 325th Glider Inf. Regt. 717 men.
2nd Serial 82nd Airborne	434th 435th TCG	CG-4A Horsa	50 2	04:32	Aldermaston	E	Down 07:01 hours. HQ 325th Glider Inf. Regt. Col. Lewis Abort from 'Elmira'
				'Hackensack' Mission, D + 1			
1st Serial 2nd 325th GIR. 2nd 401st GIR.	439th TCG	Horsa CG-4A	30 20	06:47 06:47	Upottery Upottery	W W	Down 08:51 hours. 968 troopers.
2nd Serial 325th GIR. 401st GIR.	441st TCG	CG-4A	50	07:17	Merryfield	W	Down 08:59 hours 363 troops.

Both these serials carried in 17 tons ammunition, 25 vehicles, 10 tons supplies, 18 tons equipment, 5 trailers, and 12 mortars.

Operations 'Chicago' and 'Detroit'

The gliderborne landing of the US 82nd and 101st Airborne Divisions at dawn on D-Day, 6 June 1944.

Both airborne divisions were to land by parachute and glider in advance of the main seaborne landings, seize ground and hold it to protect the flanks of the seaborne troops, and also to prevent German reinforcements reaching the invasion bridgeheads.

Brigadier James Gavin's 82nd Airborne was tasked to take the small but important town of Ste. Mère Eglise, create bridgeheads over the River Merderet on the two main roads running west from the town and protect the invasion bridgehead from the west. Codenamed 'Detroit', the 82nd's first glider mission would take off at 01:30 and land at dawn on LZ 'O', located north-west of Ste Mère Eglise.

The 101st Airborne, under Brigadier-General Maxwell Taylor, was to seize four vital causeways over flooded ground, which led from the 'Utah' invasion beach, and secure bridgeheads over the River Douve to the south. Its initial glider mission, 'Chicago', would take off at 01:20 and land at dawn on LZ 'E' ten miles inland from the Channel coast at Hiesville.

Both initial glider missions would fly the same route as the first US paratroop drops. Leaving the English coast at Portland, Dorset, code-named 'Flatbush' the route went fifty-seven miles due south at 500 feet over the sea to a point marked by a Royal Navy submarine code-named 'Hoboken' emitting a Eureka beacon signal. There the route made a 90 degree turn to the left, then led fifty-four miles to the German-occupied British Channel Islands, passing between them to avoid enemy fire. Whilst crossing the sea, a ten-mile wide corridor would be used to prevent Allied Naval ships opening fire as they had done on the Sicily operation.

On approaching the French coast on the west side of the Cherbourg Peninsula, the glider combinations would climb to 1,500 feet to avoid German small arms fire. Landfall on the coast would be six miles north of Carteret, code-named 'Peoria', then straight to LZs 'E' and 'O'. All aircraft would be marked on wings and fuselage with three white and two black stripes to identify them to Allied ground, sea and air forces.

At 01:19 on 6 June Operation 'Chicago' began when the first C-47 of the 434th Troop Carrier Group, towing a Waco CG-4A, took off fom Aldermaston airfield. At intervals another fifty-one combinations took off carrying 155 troops, 16 six-pounder guns, 24 vehicles, one bulldozer, $2\frac{1}{2}$ tons of ammunition and 11 tons of equipment.

Forty-four of the gliders carried A and B Batteries of the 81st Airborne Battalion. The other eight gliders carried troops of the 326th Airborne Engineer Company, the 326th Airborne Medical Company, the 101st Airborne Signal Company and Staff of the 101st Divisional HQ, including Brigadier-General Donald F. Pratt, Assistant divisional commander.

The combinations assembled in bright moonlight into column of fours to the right, the standard US flying formation. Shortly after take-off, the glider carrying the SCR-499 (Signal Corp Radio No. 499) broke its tow rope and had to force-land some four miles from Aldermaston. This powerful radio was vital to the

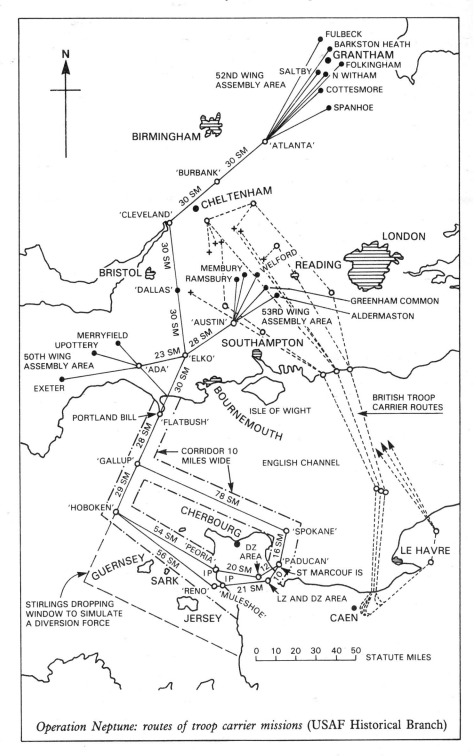

Operation Neptune: routes of troop carrier missions (USAF Historical Branch)

101st's communications network and its loss was felt on the battlefield. However the three NCOs in the force-landed Waco, unloaded the SCR, returned to Aldermaston, reloaded in another Waco and again took off for France in the next serial. Landing in France under fire they set up the radio at the 101st's Command Post.

As the combinations reached Normandy they encountered German small arms fire, one combination was shot down and minor damage was caused to seven other Wacos. One tug lost formation and released his glider eight miles south of the LZ at Carentan.

Forty-nine gliders reached their release area and formed into two landing columns; their LZ was marked by green lights set in the form of a 'T' flashing the code letter identifying the landing zone. Each 'T' had five holophane lights which shone narrow beams of light about two degrees above the horizon in the landing direction and vertically through a lens on top of each light. A Eureka beacon was also placed twenty five yards beyond the head of the 'T'.

The weather over the LZ was cloudy and, as the gliders made a 270 degree left turn to land at 03:54, many of them lost sight of the 'T'. In the poor light only six gliders landed on their LZ and fifteen landed about half a mile away from it. Ten landed in a group near Les Forges and the remaining eighteen were scattered east and south-east of the LZ, but all except one landed within two miles of it. Many of the gliders made crash-landings in the half light including the leading glider nicknamed 'The Fighting Falcon', flown by Lieutenant-Colonel Mike Murphy which had Brigadier-General Pratt as a passenger. Colonel Murphy made a good landing but was unable to stop the Waco sliding on the wet ground and it crashed into a hedgerow. General Pratt was killed by whiplash as the glider smashed through the hedgerow and Colonel Murphy had both legs broken. As some of the Wacos had crumpled on landing it proved difficult to extract their loads but six anti-tank guns and 115 glider troops were in action with the 101st by noon on D-Day. Five of the glider troops, including General Pratt, were dead; seventeen were injured and seven were missing, but Operation 'Chicago' had largely succeeded in spite of the adverse landing conditions.

Operation 'Detroit', the first glider mission of the 82nd Airborne, began at 01:59 on 6 June, when the 437th Troop Carrier Group's C-47s began to tow off fifty-two Waco CG-4As from Ramsbury, Wiltshire, on single tow destined for LZ 'O'. The same type of landing aids used for the 82nd's paratroop drop on DZ/LZ 'O' would be used for the glider mission landing. Carried aboard the fifty-two gliders were part of the 82nd's Divisional Staff, Batteries A and B of the 80th Airborne Anti-Aircraft Battalion, and the 82nd Signals Company, 220 troops in total. Also carried were sixteen 57-mm guns, 22 jeeps, five trailers and ten tons of ammunition, supplies and equipment. By 02:23 all fifty-two combinations were airborne; one C-47 lost its glider and returned to Ramsbury for another reserve glider, then took off again half an hour later for France. Flying the same flight route as the 'Chicago' mission, the entire 'Detroit' mission reached the initial point, 'Peoria', without incident. Encountering cloud over the French coast, the formation climbed to 1,500 feet over the clouds. A few minutes later the combinations began to let down through breaks in the clouds, but their formation was broken by lack of visibility. Most managed to maintain a rough correct heading for

Operation Neptune: air and sea routes of 101 Airborne Division, 6–8 June 1944
(US 101st Airborne Division)

the LZ. During the few minutes in the cloud cover, seven gliders either broke their tow ropes, were cast off by their tugs or came under German fire which cut their tow ropes. As they crossed the Cherbourg Peninsula, the cloud cover thinned, but was still bad in the poor light. Seven more gliders were released prematurely west of the flooded river Merderet, when the tug pilots mistook in the bad light the inundated ground for the sea on the other side of the peninsula. Other tug pilots saw the seven gliders released and thought the LZ had been reached and cast off their gliders. The Eureka beacon on LZ 'O' was operating, but the green 'T' lights were not, causing difficulty for the approaching combinations which by now were coming under German small arms and machine-gun fire.

Some gliders were damaged and casualties were taken among the occupants. Thirty-seven gliders managed to reach the general area of LZ 'O' between 04:01 and 04:10. The disorganised formation managed to cast off in two columns at 400 to 500 feet. Disorientated, the glider pilots put their gliders down where they could in ones and twos on their own initiative. Several came under enemy fire during their descent.

Between seventeen and twenty-three gliders landed on or very near the LZ. Five glider pilots of the 84th Troop Carrier Squadron landed their gliders on the western end of the LZ. Nine more landed within two miles of it. Three more landed near LZ 'E' at Hiesville.

Twenty-two gliders were destroyed and twelve badly damaged. One glider landed on a herd of cows. The heavy landings killed three of the troops and twenty-three more were injured, less than had been feared.

Eleven of the twenty-two jeeps were destroyed but eight of the guns had been landed near the LZ, and were usable by noon and soon in action against the Germans. 'Detroit' had proved costly, at just over 50% effective, but the timely arrival of the gliderborne troops and guns proved invaluable to the paratroops.

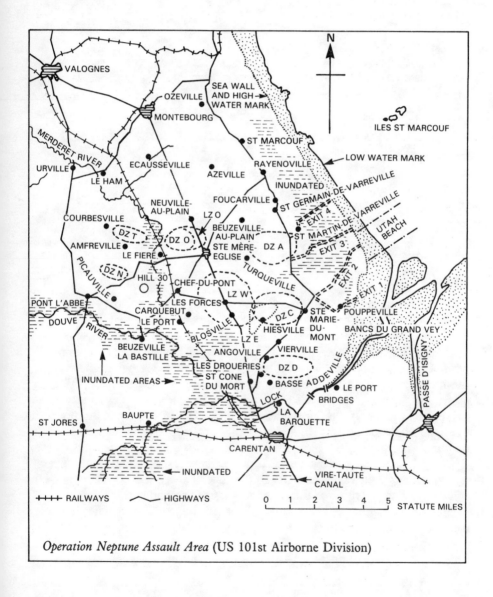

Operation Neptune Assault Area (US 101st Airborne Division)

Operation 'Keokuk'

The second glider mission of the 101st Airborne Division on the evening of D-Day using Horsa gliders.

Operation 'Keokuk' got under way at 18:30 when the first of the thirty-two C-47 Horsa glider combinations took off from Aldermaston airfield; the tugs were from the 434th Troop Carrier Group.

The large Horsas carried 157 troops of the 101st's Divisional Staff, the 101st Airborne Signal Company, the 326th Airborne Medical Company and 40 vehicles, 6 guns and 19 tones of ammunition, equipment and supplies for LZ 'E'.

In daylight and good weather the formations were able to keep station and on course. Approaching the French coast on the east side and flying over the 'Utah' beach, instead of the west coast route taken by the 'Chicago' and 'Detroit' missions, the mission encountered little enemy fire.

On LZ 'E' troops already landed had cleared the zone of trees and marked it with green smoke and a yellow 'T'. Arriving ahead of schedule at 20:53 the combinations found the LZ was still only two miles away from German positions north and south of the zone.

As the gliders cast off, they came under German fire and some glider pilots found that they had been released or cast off a mile short of their objective. Only five landed on the LZ, fourteen gliders landed in fields $2\frac{1}{2}$ miles north-east of the LZ, five in fields several hundred yards east of the zone and another eight came down south-east of the LZ and up to two miles away from it. However, all thirty gliders were down.

Fourteen troopers were killed, either in accidents or by the Germans and thirty more were injured. Ten troopers were missing, believed captured by the Germans, in two gliders that had landed behind the enemy positions.

Little damage was caused to the loads carried in the Horsas, most of which were only moderately damaged, and the cargoes were recovered and soon in use.

Operation 'Elmira'

The 82nd Airborne Division's second glider mission on the evening of D-Day carrying reinforcements to the division in 76 Horsa and Waco gliders.

Owing to the number of gliders involved the operation had to be divided into two waves each of two serials. The first serial of the first wave would consist of eighteen Horsa and eight Waco CG-4A gliders, towed by C-47s of the 437th Troop Carrier Group out of Ramsbury, Wiltshire. The second serial of the first wave was thirty-six Horsa and fourteen Waco CG-4A gliders towed off from Greenham Common by C-47s of the 438th Troop Carrier Group. The two serials would carry 437 troops, 64 vehicles, 13 anti-tank guns and $24\frac{1}{2}$ tons of supplies to LZ 'W', an oval-shaped LZ 2,800 yards long from north to south and 2,000 yards wide, a mile south of St Mère Eglise.

At 19:07 the first of the combinations took off from Ramsbury, followed at intervals by the remainder till at 19:21 all twenty-six were airborne. The Horsas and Wacos flew in different formations to keep the two different glider types separate.

The second serial of thirty-six Horsa and fourteen Wacos had been towed off from Greenham Common between 18:48 and 19:16. As in the first serial the Horsas and Wacos were segregated. Flying at first in high gusting winds the formations headed for Portland on the English Channel coast. There they were greeted with a swarm of US fighters which escorted them across the Channel. Crossing the sea without incident, the glider stream came in over 'Utah' beach and made for the release point of LZ 'W' some six miles from the coast. As they came over, the Germans began to open fire on them with rifle and machine-gun fire.

Unknown to the aircrews the northern part of the LZ was still under German fire although the southern part was held by US troops. For this reason the LZ markers were not placed on LZ 'W' but two miles north-west of it. The 'Keokuk' LZ 'E' markers of green smoke and 'T' were two miles east of Les Forges and in operation. Assisted by radar and map reading, the 437th Troop Carrier Command flew direct to LZ 'W' and cast off their gliders, the first of which began to descend at 21:04. Only two gliders of the first serial managed to land on the LZ but twelve landed within a mile and most within two miles of it.

In the second serial, thirteen Wacos, towed by the 88th Troop Carrier Squadron, landed on or near the LZ. Nine Horsas landed on the zone and six within a mile of it. Another twelve Horsas landed on LZ 'E' and four landed three miles away. Three Wacos and twenty-one Horsas were destroyed mostly by German fire; five glider pilots were killed, seventeen had been injured or wounded and four were missing. Most of the troopers and equipment carried in the gliders that had landed on US held ground were unloaded within a few hours and assembled at the 82nd's Command Post on the north side of Les Forges, and were soon operational.

'Elmira's' second wave consisted of two serials of fifty gliders each. The first serial comprised forty-eight Horsas and two Waco CG-4As towed by the 436th Troop Carrier Group from Membury, carrying 418 troops, mostly of the 319th Airborne Field Artillery, together with 31 jeeps, 26 tons of ammunition and 25 tons of supplies. The second serial of thirty-eight Horsas and twelve Wacos was towed by the 435th Troop Carrier Group from Welford, carrying 319 troops of the 320th Airborne Field Artillery, twelve 105-mm howitzers, 28 jeeps, 33 tons of ammunition and 23 tons of supplies. Each of the Wacos carried one howitzer.

The first combinations of the first serial took off from Membury at 20:37 and that of the second serial at 20:40 from Welford with the aircrews unaware that LZ 'O' was being marked instead of the intended landing zone LZ 'W'. Both serials formed in columns of four with the Horsas and Wacos segregated. One Horsa broke its tow rope and one C-47 had to return to base with electrical trouble; the remaining formation of ninety-eight flew on to the east coast of the Cherbourg Peninsula without incident.

As the glider streams flew over 'Utah' beach the sun began to set causing long shadows on the ground. On the fields below the 82nd had set up a Eureka beacon and landing markers near LZ 'O', as the northern part of LZ 'W' was within range of German guns. As the glider streams approached the landing areas, they came under heavy enemy fire as they passed over German positions. The first serial began releasing its gliders at 22:55 and the second serial at 23:05. Most of the first serial cast off their gliders a mile short of LZ 'O' and six gliders cast off five miles east of the LZ. The bulk of the second serial landed within a mile of LZ 'O' but five landed on LZ 'W'. Two gliders landed north-east of St Mère Eglise.

Most of the gliders made heavy landings; fifty-six out of eight-four Horsas were destroyed; only thirteen were undamaged. All the fourteen Wacos were badly damaged with eight of them being destroyed. However, in spite of the damage most of the loads carried survived; forty-two of the fifty-nine jeeps were serviceable and were off-loaded after night fall when darkness gave cover from enemy fire. Ten glider pilots were killed out of 196 engaged, twenty-nine were injured and seven went missing.

Operation 'Elmira' had been succcessful, in spite of confusion over the LZ caused by lack of radio links between the forces battling on the ground and higher command in England.

Operation 'Galveston'

The further glider mission of D + 1 to reinforce the 82nd Airborne Division with part of the 325th Glider Infantry Regiment.

As in Operation 'Elmira' the 'Galveston' mission was divided into two serials. The first serial of eighteen Horsa and thirty-two Waco CG-4As, towed by C-47s of the 437th Troop Carrier Group from Ramsbury, would carry 717 troopers of the 1st Battalion of the 325th Glider Infantry Regiment, plus 17 vehicles, 9 guns and 20 tons of supplies and equipment.

The second serial of fifty Waco CG-4As, towed by the 434th Troop Carrier Group, would leave from Aldermaston with 251 troopers of the 325th Glider Infantry Regiment, including its CO, Colonel Harry Lewis, and 24 vehicles, 11 guns, 5 tons of ammunition and 1½ tons of supplies. The two Horsas that had aborted from the 'Elmira' mission joined the 'Galveston' mission in the second serial, making a total of 102 gliders involved.

Half an hour before dawn, in squally weather the operation got under way. At Ramsbury the combinations began to take off at 04:39; at Aldermaston, 04:32. One Horsa at Ramsbury was so overloaded that it could not be towed off in the gusty wind and rain. One Waco broke its tow rope over Dorset and had to land.

Once airborne the formations of twenty Horsas and eighty-one Wacos set course for the mouth of the River Douve instead of 'Utah' beach. To avoid German positions, a different route over France would be made to land near LZ 'E' a mile east of Marie-du-Mont. However between the coastline and the LZ both serials encountered German fire.

At 06:55 the first serial from Ramsbury arrived over the LZ, releasing its gliders as low as possible to reduce the time over enemy fire. All but six of the gliders cast off too soon and landed a mile north-east of Ste Marie-du-Mont, some landing between the two causeways to the sea.

Some of the gliders landed east of LZ 'E' and made heavy landings, in which ten Horsas were destroyed and seven badly damaged, killing seventeen troopers and injuring sixty-three more. The Waco gliders suffered twenty-two casualties but no fatalities although nine Wacos were wrecked and many more damaged.

The second serial from Aldermaston came up on its cast-off point at 07:01, ahead of schedule. Instead of landing on LZ 'E', twenty of the gliders landed on LZ 'W', nineteen within one mile and another eight a mile and a half away from it. One other glider landed two and a half miles away and another four and a half miles away from the LZ. Forty-two of the Wacos were either wrecked or damaged and thirteen troopers were injured, but there were no fatalities.

The Germans still had LZ 'W' under fire, but nineteen jeeps, six trailers and seven guns were recovered from the landed Wacos and the troopers of the 325th Glider Infantry managed to reach their assembly point at Les Forges.

'Galveston' had been the most successful glider mission so far, with comparatively light casualties.

Operation 'Hackensack'

The last glider mission of the invasion, flying in two hours behind Operation 'Galveston' on to LZ 'W' on the morning of D+1.

Like 'Galveston', 'Hackensack' was divided into two serials: the first of thirty Horsas and twenty Waco CG-4A gliders was towed by the 439th Troop Carrier Group from Upottery, carrying 968 troopers of the 2nd Battalion 325th Glider Infantry Regiment and the 2nd Battalion of the 401st Glider Infantry Regiment, plus five vehicles, eleven tons of ammunition and ten tons of supplies. The second serial comprised fifty Waco CG-4As towed by the 441st Troop Carrier Group out of Merryfield, carrying more troopers of the 325th and 401st Glider Infantry, plus twelve 81-mm mortars, twenty jeeps, nine trailers and six tons of ammunition.

At 06:47 the first combinations began to take off from Upottery and at 07:17 the second serial lifted off Merryfield in dull rough weather with a 2,000 ft cloud base. Led by a Pathfinder C-47 of Troop Carrier Command, the glider stream flew over the Channel into better weather with a cloud base of 8,000 feet, accompanied by a strong fighter escort.

Making landfall on the east coast of France at 'Utah' beach, the first serial began to cast off tow ropes at 08:51 and the second serial at 08:59. Releasing at 600 feet, the first serial started to descend on LZ 'W'. Twelve gliders landed on the northern part of the landing zone under heavy German fire which took its toll of the troopers. Some gliders landed a mile west of the LZ, and others two and a half miles from it. More gliders landed on the south-west part of the LZ, some landing in the flooded areas close to the actual LZ.

Twenty-nine Horsas were recorded as landing: twelve within a mile of the LZ, seven within two miles, nine between two to four miles away and one nine miles away. Sixteen were wrecked and ten damaged on landing. Fifteen troopers were killed and fifty-nine injured. Seven of the Wacos landed within a mile of the LZ, six within two miles and another six between two to four miles away. Only four gliders were destroyed and ten damaged. Two glider pilots were killed and eleven more injured.

The Wacos of the second serial fared better; releasing at 600 feet, they spiralled down onto LZ 'W' with twenty-five landing on it and another nineteen landing within a mile of it. The remaining six of the fifty-strong serial landed a mile away. All fifty had landed either on the LZ or within a mile of it. One glider pilot was killed and five were injured. One trooper was killed and fifteen injured. Most of the loads carried were serviceable, although eight Wacos were wrecked and twenty-eight damaged. The second serial made the most successful landing of the glider missions, in that it was the most accurate, although it sustained more casualties than 'Galveston'.

Ninety per cent of the 325th and 401st Glider Infantry had assembled by 10:15 and immediately went westwards to engage the Germans at Carquebut, where on arrival they found the enemy had retreated. The glider troops of the 325th/401st then went into the Divisional Reserve of the 82nd Airborne Division. Shortly afterwards they went into action and became the longest serving unit in continuous action against the Germans, winning a Presidential Citation.

In all, 1,030 USAAF glider pilots reached the invasion areas, and twenty-five were known to have been killed. Most of the pilots were evacuated within three days of landing but some, having landed in outlying areas, did fight with the airborne divisions, in spite of having very little military training.

Four more minor glider missions were flown by the 436th Troop Carrier Group out of Membury as follows:

9 June   Two Waco CG-4As   Ste Mère Eglise   Signals Unit.
10 June   Six Waco CG-4As   Ste Mère Eglise   Two jeeps, six tons supplies.
12 June   Five Waco CG-4As   Ste Mère Eglise   Two jeeps, forty two troops.
13 June   Eleven Waco CG-4As   Ste Mère Eglise   Thirteen tons supplies.

Operations 'Bluebird' and 'Dove'

The glider missions of Operation 'Dragoon', the invasion of the south of France on 15 August 1944.

Planning for the invasion of the south of France had begun in December 1943, at the headquarters of 7th Army at Palermo, Sicily, under the codename 'Anvil'; the Planners were given the codename Force 163. Shortly afterwards, however, Force 163 moved to Bouzareah near Algiers, North Africa, where in January 1944 detailed planning commenced under Brigadier-General Garrison H. Davidson, US 7th Army, with General Mark Clark in overall command.

However General Clark was also commanding the 5th Army in Italy which was engaged in heavy fighting, so on 28 February Lieutenant-General Alexander M. Patch was appointed commander of the US 7th Army.

The invading forces were to be principally American and French with a small British presence. The US 6th Corps would consist of three divisions, the 3rd, 36th and 45th, plus the 1st US Special Service Force. The corps would spearhead the seaborne assault and would be followed up by seven French divisions. Two French groups would land on the flanks of the invasion beaches during the night before D-Day.

Specially for the operation, a Provisional Airborne Division under the command of Major-General Robert T. Frederick, was quickly formed and a Provisional Troop Carrier Air Division under the command of Brigadier-General Paul L. Williams was created to air-transport them. Soon the Airborne Division was renamed the 1st Airborne Task Force and comprised a Parachute Regimental

Team, a US Gliderborne Regimental Team, the British 2nd Independent Parachute Brigade Group and the British 1st Independent Squadron of the Glider Pilot Regiment.

The Provisional Troop Carrier Air Division comprised the 9th Troop Carrier Command Pathfinder Unit, the 50th, 51st and 53rd Troop Carrier Wings. The three Wings would use 512 aircraft to drop paratroops and tow 403 Waco CG-4A and Horsa gliders. Pathfinder paratroops were to drop at 03:23 on D-Day to mark three LZs, 'A', 'C' and 'O', with Eureka Beacons and landing signals. 'A' and 'O' would be combined zones for paratroops and gliders, 'C' would be for paratroops only. LZs 'A' and 'O' were between the villages of Le Muy and Le Mitan, ten miles inland from the coastal town of Fréjus, DZ 'C' was south-east of Le Muy.

The main force of paratroops would drop at 04:23 and clear the LZs of the enemy and obstructions for Operation 'Bluebird', the first glider wave of forty Waco CG-4As and thirty-five Horsas due to land at 08:14. The paratroops would also prevent German reinforcements reaching the invasion beaches where the seaborne assault was due to take place at 08:00 on 15 August.

At 18:10 on D-Day another paratroop drop by forty-two aircraft was to be made, with the main glider landings by 332 Waco CG-4A gliders in seven waves on LZs 'A' and 'O' shortly afterwards.

Eleven airfields strung along the west coast of Italy above Rome were to be used for the airborne task force's take-off points. Eight air beacons lettered 'A' to 'H' were placed along the flight route to aid navigation for the Troop Carrier Wings. Each of the Troop Carrier Wings would have an airborne assembly area off the Italian coast where they would form up with their gliders into their respective waves. After assembly all the waves would head for air beacon 'D' on the northern tip of Elba, then steer north-north-west for air beacon 'E' on the northern point of Corsica. Guided by three more air beacons, 'F', 'G', and 'H', on naval ships, the flight path led to the French coast just south of the coast town of Cannes. The last air beacon, 'H', was aboard the Royal Navy ship HMS *Stuart Prince* forty miles off the invasion beaches.

To avoid the errors of the Sicily operation, the route was clear of Allied naval ships and Allied fighter cover was provided from 6,000 feet to 20,000 feet. German radar would be confused by aircraft dropping Window (metal foil) strips and fighter bombers would attack known enemy flak positions. Dummy paratroops would also be dropped between Marseille and Toulon to further confuse the enemy.

Prior to the landings, bombing attacks would be made along the whole of the southern coast line to conceal the intended landing beaches, which stretched from Cap Cavalaire eastwards to the Agay Roads south-west of Cannes. Beginning at 07:30, four bombardment groups of Allied warships would pound the landing beaches until just before H-Hour, 08:00.

Defending the south of France was the German 19th Army made up of the 4th, 85th and 62nd Corps, a total of eight divisions. Two of the divisions, the 148th and 157th, were up to strength but had no combat experience. Another two, the 242nd and the 244th, were at 85 per cent strength but with young inexperienced troops. The other four divisions, 716th, 189th, 198th and the 338th, were being

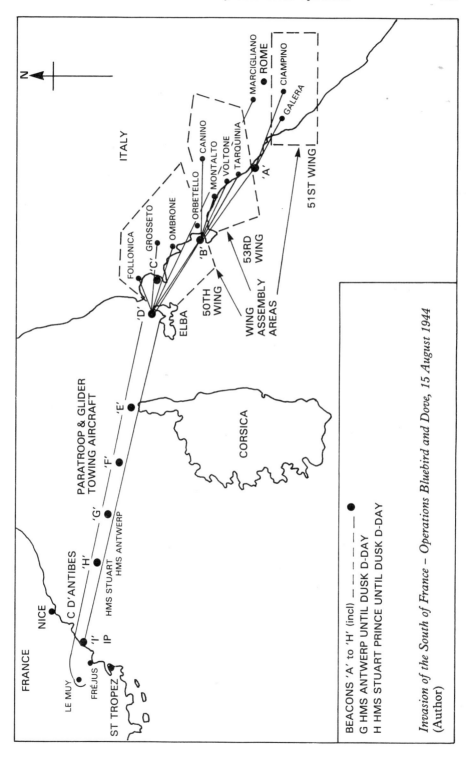

Invasion of the South of France – Operations Bluebird and Dove, 15 August 1944
(Author)

refitted and reformed after heavy losses in Normandy and Russia. Many of the divisions contained a large percentage of non-German nationals impressed into service from German-occupied countries.

Before dawn on D-Day, the first glider mission, Operation 'Bluebird', began; at 05:18 the first Horsas were towed off by the 435th Troop Carrier Group from Tarquina, Italy; by 05:50 hours all were airborne. At Voltone the 436th Troop Carrier Group towed off forty Waco CG-4A gliders loaded with half of the 64th Light Artillery Battalion, Royal Artillery, plus some HQ Staff. Immediately one Waco/tug combination had to return to base with tug engine trouble. The remainder flew on in bright sunshine along the line of beacons below. One Waco disintegrated in mid air over the sea killing all on board – another broke its tow rope but landed safely in the sea.

Off the French coast Allied warships began bombarding the invasion beaches at 07:30 and the 'Bluebird' glider mission was nearing the tip of Corsica. General Williams received a report that the glider LZs were shrouded in fog which would make landing hazardous for the large Horsas so he decided to recall his Horsa wave. A radio message was sent to the lead Horsa combination to return to base with the Horsa wave; the smaller Wacos were allowed to continue with the mission. At 08:20 the Waco combinations began arriving over the fog-covered LZs. For an hour the combinations circled over the area waiting for the sun to burn off the fog.

By 09:26 the fog had thinned enough for the LZs to be seen and the gliders began to release their tow ropes and spiral down to land. The LZs had been largely cleared of obstructions and the enemy by the previously dropped paratroops, and the gliders were able to land without fatality although eight pilots were injured in heavy landings. The glider loads of guns and jeeps were quickly offloaded and soon in action. Thirty-three gliders landed on LZ 'O', four others well outside it.

Meanwhile, the recalled Horsa wave was flying over Corsica when two tug aircraft developed trouble, one with lack of fuel and the other with engine trouble, and had to release their Horsas both of which force-landed safely in Corsica. The rest landed back at base where they were remarshalled and the tugs refuelled. At 14:30, the operation was remounted and within thirty minutes all were airborne once more en route for France. Thirty-five Horsas, carrying 233 troops, 35 jeeps, 30 guns and 31,000 pounds of ammunition, set course for France. Off the north coast of Corsica they were joined by a tug towing one of the Horsas which had landed in Corsica earlier in the day on the recall flight, and then by a Waco towed by the 436th Troop Carrier Group which had mistakenly returned to base when the Horsa wave was recalled. Thirty-seven gliders were now on course for the LZs. This time there was no recall and at 17:45 the combinations arrived over LZ 'O', casting off at 1,200 feet in a visibility of five miles in spite of smoke from the battlefield below, they landed without opposition – some in echelons of three – successfully.

Back at seven Italian airfields, the Waco CG-4A gliders of 'Dove' mission were being loaded and marshalled. Some 2,250 troops of the 550th Glider Infantry Battalion, under Lieutenant-Colonel Edward Sachs, the 596th Airborne Engineer

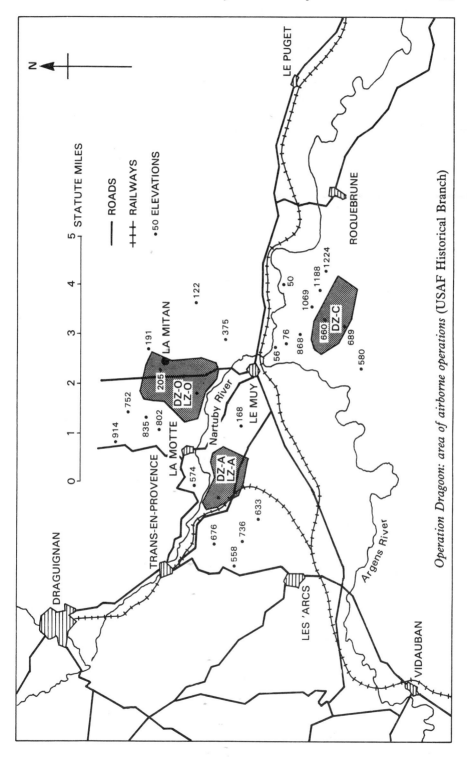

Operation Dragoon: area of airborne operations (USAF Historical Branch)

Company, the 442nd Anti Tank Company, 834th Chemical Mortar Company plus Signals and Medical Units were to be carried in seven serials of forty-seven or forty-eight aircraft/glider combinations. 332 Waco gliders were to be towed by the 442nd, 438th, 439th, 440th, 441st Troop Carrier Groups and the 62nd and 64th Troop Carrier Groups to LZs 'A' and 'O'. The seven serials were scheduled to have a ten-minute flight time interval between them to avoid bunching over the LZs.

At 15:10 the 64th Troop Carrier Group at Ciampino began to lift off its serials, followed by the 442nd at 15:35 from Follonica. Last off was the 440th from Ombrone at 16:10. At first all went well, apart from two gliders that had to abort the mission but landed safely and later were towed off again. Soon, however, the mission began to run into trouble: the leading combinations had to reduce their airspeed to avoid forty-two C-47s carrying the 551st Parachute Battalion who were making for DZ 'C', which intersected their flight route. This reduction of airspeed was followed by a delay caused by a glider of the lead serial having to ditch in the sea due to tail structure weakness. Happily all the occupants were rescued, but the whole group, the 442nd, made a full turn to avoid the released Waco and the next group, the 441st, flew on into the lead.

Before long the vital ten minute flight time interval was lost and confusion set in. Four gliders of the 441st broke their ropes and ditched; most of the occupants were picked up safely. The tug pilots struggled to maintain their position; some had to increase speed, others to reduce speed to try and keep station.

By 18:27 the bunched serials were over the LZs. The 441st and 442nd arrived simultaneously. At 18:40 the 440th arrived, followed eight minutes later by the 439th; a minute later the 438th appeared. At one time four Troop Carrier Groups were over the LZs at the same time. At 18:54 the 62nd came on the scene, followed at 19:05, by the 64th Group.

Considerable congestion ensued: at one time over 180 gliders were in free flight over the LZs. Only the flying skill of the glider pilots prevented catastrophe, the British glider pilots already down on the LZ had to take cover and they recall some Wacos colliding in mid-air and shedding their loads of guns, jeeps, men and supplies over the area.

All the serials and 95 per cent of the gliders reached the area of the LZs and most of the loads carried were intact in spite of the heavy landings some gliders made. Eleven glider pilots were killed and thirty were injured; eight glider troopers lost their lives and 100 were badly injured.

Overall, Operation 'Dragoon' was a success; by 9 September the US 7th Army had linked up with the US 3rd Army in the north. 1st Airborne Task Force had carried out its allotted tasks and no German reinforcements had reached the invasion beaches. Nine thousand men, 221 jeeps, 213 guns plus supplies and ammunition had been delivered to the battlefield.

Both 1st Airborne Task Force and the Provisional Troop Carrier Air Division were immediately disbanded and personnel returned to or posted to other units.

Burma

By May 1942, the invading Japanese Army was on the borders of India, having taken Burma and forced British forces to retreat nearly 1,000 miles in a hard-fought campaign. By July the Japanese had entered India and were menacing Imphal. It was then that the 38-year-old Colonel Orde Wingate was put in command of all guerilla operations in Burma. He proposed that the way to fight the Japanese was by forming Long Range Penetration Brigades to strike deep into Burma and disrupt the enemy.

General Sir Archibald Wavell, Commander-in-Chief India, approved Wingate's plan and the 77th Infantry Brigade was formed. The 50th Parachute Brigade was also raised and, far-sightedly, the use of gliders was considered. In February 1943, 3,000 men with Wingate in command entered Burma, mainly to test his theory that his troops could be maintained by air whilst behind enemy lines. Air drops were successful, but Wingate had to withdraw his forces to India on 27 March 1943. The penetration into Burma had cost dearly: only 2,182 out of 3,000 men who had started out in February returned, and Wingate's ideas were almost scrapped. By now Wingate's men were known as Chindits, a semi-official term derived from the Chinthi, part-lion and part-griffin stone figures which guard the entrances to Burmese temples. Wingate was promoted to major-general and command of a large force, the 3rd Indian Division, which comprised six brigades: the 3rd, 14th, 16th, 23rd, 77th and the 111th.

Early in 1943 Lord Louis Mountbatten, Supreme Commander South-East Asia, decided to mount an offensive against the Japanese to regain occupied Burma. Wingate's brigades would be used; it was proposed to transport 10,000 men by air and that 2,000 should make their way on foot to behind the Japanese lines. The 77th Brigade, commanded by Brigadier Michael Calvert, and comprising 1st Battalion The King's Regiment, 1st Battalion Lancashire Fusiliers, 1st Battalion South Staffords and the 3rd Battalion 6th Gurkha Rifles, would fly in by glider. The USAAF formed a special unit specifically for the operation to transport and support the Chindits. In effect the unit was a self-contained miniature air force. At first named the 5318th Air Unit and code-named Project Nine, the unit soon became known as the 1st Air Commando Group. Equipped with 100 Waco CG-4A and 75 Aeronca TG-5 gliders, B-25 Mitchell medium bombers, P-51 Mustang long range fighters, Douglas C-47 Dakotas, Sentinel L-1 and L-5 light aircraft and six Sikorsky YR-4 helicopters, the Air Commando had 500 men to fly and service the aircraft. US Colonel Phillip C. Cochran was placed in command with US Colonel John R. Alison as his deputy. The command of the 100-strong US glider pilots was given to Major William H. Taylor, an experienced glider pilot. He organized the glider pilots into four flights each, with an experienced officer or non-commissioned officer in charge.

The airborne part of the offensive was to land in several clearings in the jungle code-named Piccadilly, Broadway, Aberdeen, White City, Blackpool and Chowringhee. The first two to be used were to be Piccadilly and Broadway, and the plan was for gliders to be landed with troops and equipment to clear and secure these LZs, then to establish runways for the main forces to land by transport aircraft.

On 5 March 1944, the 16th British Brigade, under Brigadier Fergusson, who were marching overland, reached the River Chindwin. Four Waco gliders loaded with equipment for the river crossing landed by the river while two others landed on the far side to establish a bridgehead to protect the troops crossing.

Sunday 5 March was also the date set for the start of Operation 'Thursday' with eighty Waco gliders assembled at Lalaghat and Hailakandi airstrips in the Silcher valley of India. Forty gliders were scheduled to land at Piccadilly and another forty at Broadway. All gliders would be on double tow, with one glider on a 425 ft tow rope and the other on a standard tow rope of 350 ft, giving a 75 ft clearance to avoid mid-air collisions.

During the afternoon of the 5th Colonel Cochran sent out a B-25 Mitchell of the Combat Camera Unit, flown by Lieutenant Russhon, to take photographs of Piccadilly and Broadway LZs. When Russhon returned with the photographs, it was found that the main LZ, Piccadilly, was obstructed by teak logs laid in rows but the Broadway LZ was clear. Doubts arose as to whether the Japanese knew of the impending landings. H-Hour was postponed and a conference was held which took the view that if the Japanese knew of the landings they would have obstructed both of the LZs; it was therefore decided to put all the gliders down on Broadway.

At 18:06 on 5 March the first combination took off. The lead Waco was flown by Major Taylor, CO of the glider unit, and another of the gliders was flown by Colonel Alison, second in command of the Air Commando. Four more double tow combinations lifted off, making ten gliders en route for Broadway. These gliders were to act as a Pathfinder Force to mark the LZs for the rest of the glider force.

Within two hours six gliders had broken their tow ropes owing to turbulence and the strain of climbing to 8,000 feet to clear the Chin Hills. The remaining gliders led by Major Taylor flew on to the LZ, still in severe turbulence and with visibility reduced by a thick haze. Back in India gliders continued to be lifted off and set course for Broadway but owing to turbulence and overloading several more gliders broke their tow ropes and had to force-land. Five landed near a Japanese HQ and the occupants immediately engaged the enemy, leading the Japanese to believe that the Allies were mounting guerilla attacks on their positions.

As the leading gliders approached Broadway, the haze cleared and the glider pilots could see their LZ in the moonlight. Casting off the Pathfinders began to land without any opposition. Most made heavy landings; some crashed but they managed to set up a signal beacon to indicate the cast-off point and lay a flare path for the following gliders.

Many of the incoming Wacos crashed or made heavy landings on the rutted log strewn LZ, some colliding with each other on the ground in the dark. Casualties began to mount and at 02:30 Brigadier Calvert sent out to India the code-word 'Soya Link', the pre-arranged signal to stop further despatches of gliders. Eight combinations en route to Broadway were recalled to base and the glider operation was suspended. Out of the fifty-four gliders despatched and not recalled, thirty-seven had reached Broadway. Eight had landed in friendly areas and nine in enemy-held ground. In all, 539 troops, three mules and 29,972 lb of supplies had been delivered to Broadway during the night.

At Broadway the US 900th Airborne Engineer Company aided by the Chindits cleared a runway 300 ft wide and 5,000 ft long for transport aircraft to land the main body of troops during the evening of 6 March. With the runway ready, the code-word 'Pork Sausage' was sent from Broadway to India, the signal for the despatch of the main body of troops to Broadway. During the night of 6/7 March, sixty-three Dakotas landed troops and supplies at Broadway.

As this part of the operation was in full swing, twelve Waco gliders had been towed off from Lalaghat bound for another of the LZs, Chowringhree, some 75 miles south-west of Broadway. The purpose of this glider sortie was to act as Pathfinders and lay out a flare path and prepare a landing strip for later inbound transport aircraft laden with troops. Carried in the gliders were three platoons of the 3rd Battalion 6th Gurkha Rifles together with US Army engineers with a two-ton bulldozer. The small force, commanded by US Colonel Clint Gatty, had Flight Officer Jackie Coogan, a former film star, as lead Pathfinder glider pilot whose task it was to lay a flarepath for the other eleven gliders coming in behind his Waco. Flight Officer Coogan landed his glider successfully and his load of Gurkhas fanned out to protect the LZ ready for the US Army Engineers with their bulldozer. Unfortunately the glider carrying the bulldozer crashed, killing all the occupants and destroying the bulldozer.

With the bulldozer destroyed it was difficult to create a runway at the LZ, so a radio message was sent to the Broadway LZ requesting another bulldozer. At 21:00 on 7 March, four more gliders, one carrying a bulldozer, began to arrive at Chowringhree and were quickly at work preparing a 3,000 feet dirt runway. Four hours later, at 01:30, transport aircraft began to land bringing in Brigadier Lentaigne's 111th Brigade. For two nights the Dakotas brought in half of the brigade, until Wingate decided that enough troops had arrived and the LZ was abandoned. Two hours after the last man had left the Japanese began to bomb the airstrip, but the Chindits had gone as had the US Engineers with their equipment, snatched out in gliders.

In six days 9,052 troops, 175 ponies, 1,183 mules and 509,082 lb of supplies had been flown in from India some 150 miles into Japanese-held ground. 121 casualties were sustained, all among the glider pilots and their occupants. Thirty men had been killed at Broadway alone, with thirty-three injured. Not one tug or transport aircraft had been lost.

On 23 March the second half of the operation began when another Chindit brigade was flown into Aberdeen LZ by transport aircraft. By 12 April two brigades had been flown in, but Wingate did not live to see this. The legendary leader had been killed with his American air crew when their aircraft crashed in a storm in the Naga Hills on 24 March. Brigadier W.D.A Lentaigne of the 111th Brigade took over Wingate's command.

At the White City LZ, the Japanese attacked the Chindits and five Waco gliders loaded with ammunition landed there during the battle. Three of the gliders were snatched out from the LZ loaded with wounded Chindits, but enemy fire destroyed the other two gliders whose pilots then fought on the ground with the 77th Brigade. During the 16th Brigade's advance on the ground, its CO, Colonel Ferguson, requested folding boats to ferry his troops over the River Irrawaddy so the 1st Air Commando despatched a Waco glider loaded with four folding boats to the west bank of the river where it landed on a sandbank. Later the same day the Waco was snatched out by a Dakota and flown back to India.

During the fighting, the air ambulance of 1st Air Commando, nicknamed the 'Blood Chariots', was engaged in ferrying out wounded Chindits. Some were snatched out in gliders, others in light aircraft and the helicopters.

On 21 March six Wacos had landed at Aberdeen with bulldozers and equipment to establish a dirt runway for transport aircraft. When the Dakotas landed next day the six gliders were towed back to India. For several weeks the glider pilots continued to fly resupply missions to the Chindits and fly out wounded troops.

By May 1944, US and Chinese troops in Northern Burma were closing in on Mykityina. On the 17th, US forces arrived at Mykityina airfield where, with the Chinese 150th Regiment, they took it by noon. The Allied CO, Colonel Charles N. Hunter, immediately requested reinforcement and supplies to beat off the expected Japanese counter-attack. Ten Waco gliders carrying the 879th Aviation Engineer Battalion troops lifted off from Shingbwiyang airstrip in Northern Burma and landed under fire at Mykityina airfield. Assisted by the native population, the glider loads were discharged quickly and the engineers went to work preparing the airfield to receive Dakota transports. By late afternoon a battalion of the 89th Regiment arrived by air from Ledo and other transports began landing equipment and supplies.

By the end of August 1944, the Japanese were in retreat and Operation 'Thursday' came to an end with the withdrawal of the Chindits to a well-earned rest in India. The glider concept had worked well; the Waco gliders stood up well to the climate, landing men and equipment to prepare airstrips for the main bodies of troops to be flown in by transport aircraft. The only way to get a bulldozer into a clearing in the jungle was by glider.

Operation 'Market' (United States)

The airlandings of the US 82nd Airborne Division near Nijmegen and the US 101st Airborne Division, north of Eindhoven, Holland, fifty miles behind enemy lines in a daylight operation.

As part of Operation 'Market' and the 1st Allied Airborne Army, both US airborne divisions would take and hold ground, secure crossings over canals and rivers, to allow ground forces to pass through to link up with the British 1st Airborne Division at Arnhem. An airborne forces carpet would be laid from Eindhoven to Nijmegen to secure the highway for British tanks to drive to Arnhem.

The mission of the 82nd Airborne Division, under General James Gavin, was to take and hold the bridge over the River Maas at Grave, five miles south-west of Nijmegen, the four bridges over the Maas–Waal Canal between Grave and Nijmegen, and the River Waal bridge at Nijmegen.

As well as the bridges, the 82nd was to take and hold the Groesbeek Heights, two miles south-east of Nijmegen. Some 300 feet in height, these were the only high ground in the area, and it was decided to take them first to prevent the Germans using them to dominate the battlefield. The LZs and DZs would be between three and four miles south-east of Nijmegen on the far side of the

Groesbeek Heights. LZ 'T' and LZ 'N' were joined together in an oblong $3\frac{1}{2}$ miles north to south and $1\frac{1}{2}$ miles east to west.

The 101st Airborne Division was tasked to take the bridge over the Wilhelmina Canal at Zon, five miles north of Eindhoven, the bridge over the River Dommel north of Zon, four bridges over the Aa River and Willens Canal at Veghel, and then the town of Eindhoven. The commanders of the British 2nd Army were confident that their troops and tanks could advance from their start line in Holland and punch through the German lines to reach Eindhoven and link up with the 101st Airborne.

For the 101st's glider landings a large open area of land was chosen; LZ 'W' was $1\frac{1}{2}$ miles north of Zon and west of the north–south main road from Eindhoven to Nijmegen. Two aerial routes were chosen for the flight from England to Holland. The northern route was the most direct, leaving the English coast at Aldeburgh, Suffolk, then straight across the North Sea to Holland. But this meant the Allied aircraft would have to cross eighty miles of German occupied ground. The southern route was longer, leaving the Kent coast at North Foreland then to Gheel in Belgium before turning left to fly the last thirty miles over German-held ground to the LZs.

General Williams, the air commander, found that he did not have enough transport aircraft to deliver all the airborne troops in one lift, therefore the flights would have to be over several days. On being informed of this, General Brereton was forced to plan to deliver the airborne troops and their equipment over three days.

On 16 September, RAF Bomber Command began to pound German flak positions in Holland to reduce anti-aircraft fire the following day on the Allied troop planes. D-Day, Sunday, 17 September 1944 dawned bright and clear over England. During the morning over 1,000 Allied bombers attacked German anti-aircraft positions along the northern and southern aerial routes of the 1st Allied Airborne Army, with over 4,000 tons of bombs. At 10:19 the first of the transport aircraft began to take off from airfields all over the south of England, assemble and set course for Holland.

Following the take-off of the paratroops of the 82nd Division, the 439th Troop Carrier Group at Balderton, Nottinghamshire, began to tow off fifty Waco CG-4A gliders at 11:12. In the first twenty-two Wacos were 86 troops of A Battery, 80th Airborne Anti-tank Battalion, eight 57-mm guns, nine jeeps, and two trailers. The next 28 gliders carried 130 troops of the 82nd Divisional HQ, Signal Company, recce platoon and air support platoon with 18 jeeps.

With the 82nd's paratroop aircraft forming into the American pattern of flying, echelons of four to the right, the fifty Wacos began to assemble at low altitude into the same pattern.

Two gliders broke their tow ropes during take-off and had to be re-marshalled before being towed off again. Flying the northern route, the Wacos crossed the English coast at the Aldeburgh Eureka beacon, then headed for the next Eureka beacon on a ship in the North Sea midway between England and Holland. One Waco carrying a jeep began to break up and had to ditch; the occupants were rescued by Air Sea Rescue.

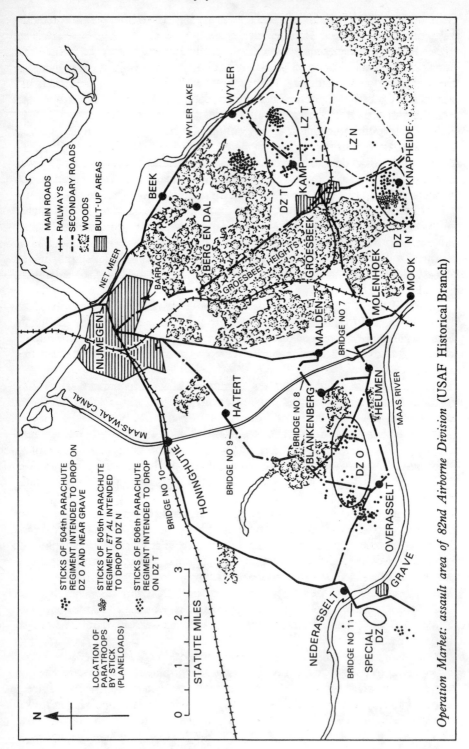

Operation Market: assault area of 82nd Airborne Division (USAF Historical Branch)

On landfall at the Schouwen Islands, enemy anti-aircraft guns opened up on the formations and one combination was brought down. The remainder flew on towards LZ 'N' and began to cast off tow at 13:47 one mile short of their release point. Six gliders managed to land on LZ 'N' and another forty landed a mile to the west. Another Waco landed $1\frac{1}{2}$ miles west of the LZ. A Waco whose load had started to shift in mid-flight had returned to England, but was towed off again and landed some time after the main body.

Fifty gliders had set off from England: one had ditched in the sea and one had been shot down, but forty-eight had managed to reach Holland. Two of the gliders made heavy landings and were wrecked; fourteen were damaged. There were no fatal casualties but fourteen troops were injured. All the guns were in working order but four of the jeeps were damaged.

By 19:00 the 82nd Airborne had seized the Groesbeek Heights, and at 20:30 set off to take the Nijmegen bridge. Assisted by the Dutch, they reached the bridge at 00:15 on the 18th but could not take it against the superior force holding it. However, they seized and destroyed the control house of the bridge, which prevented the Germans blowing up the 1,960-foot steel span bridge. So ended the first day for the 82nd Airborne.

The 6,695 paratroops of the 101st Airborne had been lifted off just after 10:00 from their Berkshire bases in 424 aircraft of the 53rd Troop Carrier Wing and flew the southern route, dropping onto their DZs between 13:00 and 13:40. Following the 101st's paratroop aircraft came seventy Waco CG-4As in two serials, towed by the 437th Troop Carrier Group from Chilbolton at 10:00. Aboard the gliders were 311 troops of the 101st's Signals Company, Recce Platoon, 326th Medical Company and the British Phantom signals Unit, plus 43 jeeps and 18 trailers.

Before the glider serials reached the English coast three had to abort the mission, and flying over the Channel on the southern route, one Waco had to ditch. Over Belgium two more gliders broke their tow ropes and seven more either released as the tow planes were hit by enemy fire or their tow ropes broke between Hertogenbosch and LZ 'W'. Five of the seven gliders' occupants later reached the 82nd but one Waco vanished and one went straight into the ground.

Arriving over LZ 'W' the first serials cast off tow at 13:48, the second serial at 13:55. Fifty-three gliders landed perfectly with 252 troops, 13 trailers and 32 jeeps. Two Wacos collided in mid-air and crashed. Another crash-landed; one glider pilot was killed and five troopers injured.

The leading glider of the first serial came under enemy fire whilst coming in to land and both glider pilots were knocked out and wounded. A trooper in the Waco, Corporal James L. Evans, of the 101st's Divisional Artillery HQ, although wounded himself, crawled into the cockpit and despite having no pilot training, took the controls and flew the Waco. Managing to rouse the first pilot, Evans gave him back the controls, then attended to the second pilot who had a severed artery. The dazed first pilot landed the glider safely. With fifty-three of the gliders safely down, 80% of the troops and 76% of the vehicles and equipment had been delivered to the LZ.

By 16:00 Troop Carrier Command had dropped most of the 101st's paratroops accurately and they had taken the road and rail bridges over the Willens Canal. An hour later Veghel was taken but the road bridge at Zon was blown by the Germans as the 101st reached it.

The 101st was scheduled to capture Eindhoven by 20:00 hours, but could not do so. The British Guards Armoured Division was six miles away meeting strong German resistance so they too were behind schedule. The blown road bridge at Zon still had its piers intact and the 101st's airborne engineers worked all night to repair the central span ready for use next day.

By the end of D-Day the 82nd and the 101st had achieved considerable success, only meeting small numbers of German troops except at Best and Nijmegen.

In England, General Brereton decided to postpone the D+1 second wave arrival time from 10:00 until 14:00, because of fog over England and rain and low cloud over the Channel and Holland. At first it was planned to use the shorter southern route but bad weather set in and the northern route had to be used by all the missions. This meant that 1,336 US aircraft, 340 British aircraft and 1,205 US and British gliders would be airborne in a massive stream over Holland.

On D+1 the 82nd Division came under a strong attack by the Germans who over-ran LZ 'N' between 08:00 and 10:00. With the 82nd's glider reinforcements due to take off at 14:00 that day, the division had to retake the LZ before the gliders came in. The 82nd counter-attacked and retook the landing zone by 13:50 but the enemy dug in close enough to LZs 'N' and 'T' to cover them with mortar and small arms fire.

Back in England, 453 Waco gliders carrying 1,899 troopers of the 319th, 320th and 456th Field Artillery Battalions, B Battery of the 80th Anti-Tank Battalion and HQ Battery of the Divisional Artillery together with 60 guns, 206 jeeps and 123 trailers, were ready for take-off from six airfields towed by six Troop Carrier Groups of the 50th and 52nd Wings.

Bad weather with fog and low cloud still hung over the US airfields and the take-off was postponed for fifty minutes. At 11:09 the first combination took off but with cloud hampering assembly it was nearly two hours before the entire mission was airborne.

The columns of Wacos flew towards the English coast into better weather. One Waco began to come apart in mid air and had to force-land. Another glider was released by a hysterical trooper who lunged into the cockpit and pulled the tow rope release lever. Two more gliders were buffeted by the slipstream of tug aircraft and snapped their tow ropes; both had to ditch but were rescued by an Air Sea Rescue launch.

Making landfall over the Dutch coast the columns began to come under German fire; three C-47s were hit and went down with their gliders, another tug had its wings shot off and went down. It was never established what happened to its glider. Another five tugs went down to German flak. The fate of all the gliders which went down near the Dutch coast is not known but five glider crews and passengers did survive.

The first serial of gliders towed by the 313rd Troop Carrier Group began to cast off tow at 14:31 and spiral down in two columns of pairs from 800 feet to land a mile south-west of LZ 'N'. The landing aids of smoke and panels had been moved as the LZ was under German fire. Landing into a slight north-east wind, most of the Wacos made good landings on the soft ground. Only one glider was destroyed by a heavy landing. Some of the Wacos using their arrester chutes stopped within fifty yards; some came in fast because of the German fire but most came in at about 65 mph. Of 212 Wacos scheduled to land on LZ 'N', 150 landed within half a mile radius of a point a mile south-west of it. Some did manage to land on the actual zone in spite of enemy fire. Of 242 Wacos intended for LZ 'T', only 90 got down on it, with another 52 within a mile away. Another 19 landed a mile west, and 19 more were strewn over German-held ground up to four miles north-west of LZ 'T'. A total of 385 gliders landed on ground held by the 82nd; no glider pilots were killed during landing but two died by German mortar and small arms fire on the ground after landing.

Nine gliders towed by the 61st Troop Carrier Group, carrying B Battery of the 320th Glider Field Artillery, were towed in error into Germany twelve miles east-south-east of LZ 'T' and released. They were never seen again. Another tug squadron overshot the LZ and released nine of their gliders at Wyler; on landing, the glider occupants immediately came under attack by the Germans who destroyed their gliders by shelling. Most of the glider crews and troopers went to ground and during darkness managed to join the 82nd on the Groesbeek Heights.

Another serial of thirty-eight gliders, towed by the 61st Troop Carrier Group, reached the Veghel area and about thirty made their cast-off five miles south of LZ 'T' near Gennef where they came under intense German fire. Landing as fast as they could, the occupants were fired on immediately and had to fight for their lives until darkness. Led by officers of the 320th Glider Field Artillery, they formed into four fighting groups and during darkness made their way to the 82nd lines. In spite of the German attacks on the 82nd's LZ and losses due to human error, the glider missions to supply and reinforce the 82nd Division had been 85% successful.

Meanwhile the 101st Division had reached Eindhoven at 09:00 on D+1 and captured it with its bridges intact. The British tanks were still fighting their way towards the 101st at Eindhoven, but were still five miles away at 12:30. Bitter fighting continued all day for the 101st within 1,000 yards west and south-west of the 101st's LZ 'W', on which that afternoon 450 gliders were due to land with reinforcements.

On six English airfields six Troop Carrier Groups of the 53rd Wing were to tow 450 Waco CG-4A gliders, carrying 2,656 troopers of the 327th Glider Infantry Regiment, the 326th Airborne Engineer Battalion and the 326th Airborne Medical Company. Riding in the first glider of the first serial would be the Divisional Artillery Commander, Brigadier-General Anthony C. McAuliffe. The lead tug of the 434th Troop Carrier Group from Aldermaston was flown by their CO, Colonel William B. Whittaker, who would tow General McAuliffe's Waco. As well as the troops the gliders carried 156 jeeps, 111 loaded supply trailers and two bulldozers.

At 11:20 the 450-strong force of Wacos began to be towed off and to assemble over Greenham Common, Berkshire. Flying in the US formation, the serials headed north-east towards the English coast at Aldeburgh, Suffolk, then onto the northern route for Holland in good weather. Shortly after take-off five gliders broke down in flight and another five broke their tow ropes before leaving English airspace. Three gliders had to ditch in the North Sea and the occupants were rescued by the Air Sea Rescue Service. One Waco became unstable over the Dutch coast and the pilot was forced to cast off and fell onto German positions.

Approaching LZ 'W' the combinations found the German flak was slight and inaccurate but in spite of this three tugs were shot down after casting off their gliders. One glider was hit by flak three miles from the LZ and crashed; three more cast off too soon and were never heard from again.

On reaching LZ 'W' the gliders began to cast off at 14:30; 428 gliders landed safely on or very near the LZ by 16:30. Three Wacos crashed on landing on it. Some gliders came under mortar and rifle fire after landing and the crews had difficulty in off-loading but the majority off-loaded quickly and mustered at a control point east of the main road. A check revealed that 2,579 troopers, 151 jeeps and 109 trailers had been landed; only five jeeps and two trailers had been lost but 54 troops were dead or missing and 23 were injured. The glider mission had been splendidly carried out and was 95% successful.

On D + 2, 19 September, the weather over England and Holland was poor and the planned 219-strong glider mission to carry the 325th Glider Infantry Regiment to reinforce the 82nd Airborne Division was postponed. On the ground in Holland British tanks had crossed the Zon bridge at 06:15 and fought their way through German positions to make contact with the 82nd at Grave.

In spite of the bad weather, the 385-strong Waco glider mission to the 101st began to take-off at 11:30, towed by the 53rd Troop Carrier Wing and assembled over Berkshire. It was carrying 2,310 troopers of the 907th Field Artillery Battalion, part of the 327th Glider Infantry Regiment, the 81st Airborne Anti-Tank Battalion, the 321st Glider Field Artillery Battalion, part of the 377th Parachute Field Artillery and the 101st's Divisional Artillery HQ, plus 136 jeeps, 77 trailers and 68 guns.

Flying in bad weather, the glider formations reached the English coast where they found the weather worse with visibility down to zero. The glider pilots were unable to see their tug aircraft and had to fly by instinct, instruments and the angle of their tow rope.

When over the sea one entire serial was recalled to base and eighty landed back in England. Seventeen gliders had to ditch in the sea but all the occupants were picked up by the Air Sea Rescue Service. Flying over Belgium, thirty-one Wacos had to force-land. Three of these crashed killing five troopers, but the other twenty-eight landed safely.

As the remaining glider columns approached the 101st's LZ 'W', they came under enemy fire and seventeen tugs were shot down but some managed to release their gliders near the LZ. Other gliders had their tow ropes shot away or were released too soon due to the German flak. Fifteen gliders were released ten miles west of LZ 'W'. Twenty-six gliders went missing and were believed to have landed in German-held ground. Another sixteen Wacos landed safely in German areas, but the occupants managed to reach the 101st's lines later.

At 14:37 the first gliders of the depleted mission landed on LZ 'W' and by

16:00, 209 had landed safely. One Waco was shot down over the LZ and three more crashed on the zone, making a total of 213 gliders reaching the LZ. 1,341 troops out of 2,310 made the LZ, eleven were killed and 157 missing, the rest being safely down in England or around LZ 'W'. 79 jeeps, 49 trailers and 40 guns had reached the LZ and within two hours the 377th Field Artillery had twelve 75-mm howitzers in action against a German tank attack. Anti-tank guns of the 81st Airborne Anti Tank Battalion knocked out several of the attacking German tanks and the attack petered out into a German retreat.

At Nijmegen the 82nd Airborne with British tank support tried to take the Nijmegen bridge which was still intact. Meeting strong German resistance, they got to within 400 yards of the bridge but were then brought to a halt. The presence of the 325th Glider Infantry Regiment, grounded in England, was sorely missed in the action.

On D+3, 20 September, the 82nd with British tanks and troops fighting with them, took the vital Nijmegen bridges against heavy resistance. As their LZs 'N' and 'T' were still too close to German fire, the 82nd decided to use their DZ 'O' as an LZ for gliders. However, the 405 Waco glider mission to the 82nd had to be postponed, owing to fog over the English airfields, although one Waco with a ton and a half of supplies was towed by the 53rd Troop Carrier Wing to LZ/DZ 'O' during a resupply mission by the wing during the afternoon.

D+4, 21 September, saw fog still blanketing the take-off airfields in England and the glider missions to the 82nd and 101st were postponed.

The 82nd Airborne had been engaged in four days of fighting and needed the 325th Glider Infantry badly. Although Nijmegen bridge had been taken, the British tanks could not make any progress towards Arnhem to assist the hard-pressed British 1st Airborne Division paratroops. Three miles north of Nijmegen, the British armour was brought to a halt by German anti-tank guns at Ressen.

On D+5, 22 September, the weather was still foggy over England and again the glider missions had to be postponed. On the ground the Germans made a determined counter-attack aimed at the 101st's position at Veghel with its vital bridges. The 327th Glider Infantry and the 321st Glider Field Artillery moved towards Veghel and defended the south-west side against the enemy armour and artillery. Assisted by British armour and artillery which was trying to advance towards Arnhem, the 101st Airborne fought off the enemy attack and stabilised the situation. The 82nd had no major German attacks made against it and consolidated its position on the ground around the Nijmegen bridge.

The British 43rd Division fought its way forward and probed towards Osterhout. At 18:00 a further force was sent towards the Rhine and reached the Polish Brigade at Driel but their amphibious vehicles could not cross the Rhine.

D+6, 23 September, saw the weather clear over England during the morning and the skies cleared over Holland in the afternoon. The huge fleet of gliders grounded by the weather since 18 September was now able to be towed off: it consisted of 490 Wacos, carrying 3,385 troopers of the 325th Glider Infantry, 80th Airborne Anti-Tank Battalion, engineers, military police and a recce platoon with loads of jeeps trailers, guns and supplies for the 82nd Airborne and the 101st Airborne LZs 'O' and 'W'.

US Air Movement Table: Operation Market

U.S. Army Unit	USAAF Unit	Glider	Number	Airfield	Take-off	LZ	Down	Load
				D-Day, 17 September				
101st Airborne Division	53rd TCW 437th TCG	CG-4A	70	Chilbolton	11:10	W	13:48	43 jeeps. 18 trailers. 311 troops. Phantom Signals Unit. Recce Platoon. Medical Coy.
82nd Airborne Division	50th TCW 439th TCG	CG-4A	50	Balderton	11:12	N	13:47	A Battery 80th A/Tk Batt. 8 × 57mm guns. 9 jeeps. 2 trailers.
				D+1, 18 September				
101st Airborne Division	53rd TCW 434th TCG 435th TCG 436th TCG 437th TCG 438th TCG 442nd TCG (50th)	CG-4A	450	Aldermaston Welford Membury Chilbolton Greenham Common	11:20	W	14:30	327th Glider Infantry Regt. 326th Engineers. 326th Medics 2656 troops. Brigadier Gen. McAuliffe.
82nd Airborne Division	52nd TCW 61st TCG 313th TCG 316th TCG 50th TCW 439th TCG 440th TCG 441st TCG	CG-4A	454	Barkston Heath Folkingham Cottesmore Balderton Fulbeck Langar	11:09	N & T	14:31	1899 troops. 206 jeeps. 123 trailers. 60 guns. 319th, 320th & 456th Field Artillery. 80th Anti Tank Battalion. HQ Divisional Artillery.

U.S. Army Unit	USAAF Unit	Glider	Number	Airfield	Take-off	LZ	Down	Load
				D + 2, 19 September				
101st Airborne	53rd TCW 434th TCG 435th TCG 436th TCG 437th TCG 438th TCG 442nd TCG (50th TCW)	CG-4A	385	Aldermaston Welford Membury Chilbolton Greenham Common Chilbolton	14:37 to 16:00	W		81st Anti Tank Battalion 321st Glider Field Artillery 327th Glider Field Regiment 377th Para. Field Artillery Divisional HQ Artillery
				D + 3, 20 September				
82nd Airborne	53rd TCW	CG-4A	1	No record	14:30	O		1½ tons supplies Nijmegen
				D + 6, 23 September				
101st Airborne	53rd TCW 436th TCG 438th TGG	CG-4A	84	Membury Greenham Common	12:00	W		395 troops. 100 tons supplies 15 guns. 13 trailers. 23 jeeps.
82nd Airborne	52nd TCW 61st TCG 313th TCG 316th TCG 434th TCG (53rd TCW)	CG-4A	406	Barkston Heath Folkingham Cottesmore Chilbolton	12:10	O		325th Glider Infantry Regt. 80th Airborne A/Tk Battalion Military Police Platoon Recce Platoon Two Companies Engineers

The 101st's Wacos, towed by the 53rd Wing from Membury and Greenham Common air bases, would fly in two serials between the fifth and sixth serials of the 406 Wacos of the 82nd's mission, making 490 gliders in all. The mission would be towed by the 50th and 52nd Troop Carrier Wing out of seven English air bases and along the southern route to Holland.

At 12:10 the first of the combinations began to take off and assemble over England in good visibility, with a 2,500-foot cloud base. Over the channel a glider had to ditch but the occupants were soon rescued.

The 101st Airborne Division's eighty-four Waco glider mission carrying 395 troops, 23 jeeps, 15 guns and 100 tons of supplies, lost four gliders over England due to tow ropes breaking and one more over Belgium again, owing to tow rope break. The remaining seventy-nine Wacos were towed on towards LZ 'W' without incident apart from slight flak from the Germans. Arriving over the LZ at 16:32 the gliders began to cast off at 600 feet; within four minutes all were down. Two gliders crashed on landing, killing three troopers and injuring nine more. However, 338 troopers, 26 jeeps, 14 guns and 12 trailers were down on the LZ in good shape.

The 82nd's 406-strong Waco glider mission did not fare so well. West of Eindhoven the Germans opened up with small arms fire and five gliders were released. On flying over the highway near Veghel, the glider stream came under more enemy fire and twenty-one gliders in the first serial either had their tow ropes shot away or released too soon and had to come near the highway between Grave and Veghel. All landed safely and their loads were soon in the hands of the 101st Airborne.

Not so fortunate was the second serial; eighteen Wacos released six miles from Veghel and six landed in German-held ground, two gliders in the following three serials released near Veghel.

About 348 Wacos reached the vicinity of LZ 'O', the first at 16:02. Casting off tow at heights from 600 to 1,300 feet the Wacos began to circle and land as the next serial began releasing at 16:03. In spite of the problem caused by two serials being over the LZ at the same time no major mishaps occurred and 75% of the Wacos landed into wind in formation. 210 gliders landed in an oval a mile across by $1\frac{1}{2}$ miles long at Ouerusselt and 100 gliders landed on the river bank opposite Grave.

At 17:03 the 325th Glider Infantry Regiment landed, and by 18:00 had assembled 75% of its troops. 2,900 troopers had been landed with 24 guns, 82 jeeps and 47 trailers. The 325th moved out to occupy positions in the Groesbeek sector on the east flank of the 82nd's area and by midnight had assembled 90% of its men under the command of Colonel Charles Billingslea. Soon after daylight on 24 September the regiment was in action, and 'E' Company took casualties whilst probing the Kiekberg Forest. On 27 September, the 325th went into full scale action against a stubborn enemy,

Other glider missions to the 82nd and 101st were proposed but did not take place. General Brereton ordered that as many Wacos as was possible be salvaged from the Holland LZs for future use and the US 876th Aviation Engineers Battalion constructed airstrips on LZ 'W' from which the gliders could be towed off to Denain, France. Several glider repair teams carried out repairs to the Wacos and eventually a total of 281 Wacos were towed off or snatched out to France out of the 1,900 used on 'Market'.

Officially the USAAF glider pilots were not combat troops like the British glider pilots; their instructions were to return to their take-off airfields as soon as it was possible for them to be evacuated but until this was done they could be used for guard duties or as supply troops. However they acquitted themselves well as infantry in battle. On 20 September 300 glider pilots were used by the 82nd Airborne Division as frontline or reserve infantry. 100 glider pilots from the 61st and 313th Troop Carrier Wing, USAAF, took over a section of the 82nd's front line near Mook for three days and nights in appalling weather conditions under German fire. Under the command of the Group glider pilot leader, Captain Elgin D. Andross, they held their ground until relieved on 24 September by the 325th Glider Infantry. As they were being evacuated, however, Captain Andross and his glider pilots were ambushed by tough German paratroops south of Veghel. Using grenades and sub-machine-guns the glider pilots fought their way out of the ambush taking casualties of three killed, ten wounded and three captured. But they had accounted for over 100 enemy paratroops. For his command leadership Captain Andross was awarded the US Silver Star; his leadership under fire would appear to have merited a much higher award.

One result of Operation 'Market' was that General Brereton ordered that all glider pilots receive more military combat training, but it was clear that the great majority of the US glider pilots engaged on 'Market' acquitted themselves very well in action.

The US 82nd and 101st Airborne Divisions had carried out their allotted missions of Operation 'Market'. They had seized and held a fifty-mile corridor as instructed and fought well and hard against a stubborn enemy fighting to defend the fatherland. The 82nd had 215 troopers killed, 427 missing and 790 wounded. The 101st had 315 troopers killed, 547 missing and 1,248 wounded. This was the human cost of 'Market'.

Bastogne: Operation 'Repulse'

By the end of 1944 the Allies were convinced that it was only a matter of time before German resistance collapsed in the west, but Hitler, still with delusions of victory, thought otherwise and personally ordered a massive counter-attack in the Ardennes sector thinly held by US troops. His plan was to punch through the Allied lines and drive to the essential supply port of Antwerp, thereby cutting British forces off from their American allies in the south, for whom Hitler had scant regard. With a wedge driven between the Allies, Hitler hoped to eliminate British forces in the Low Countries, and then turn to attack the Americans in the south.

For his counter-attack Hitler had assembled twenty-nine divisions behind the Siegfried Line under the command of Field Marshal von Runstedt. 200,000 German troops in three armies, including the 6th Panzer Army, would attack on 16 December 1944, preceded by an artillery barrage which would be followed by an armoured attack supported by infantry.

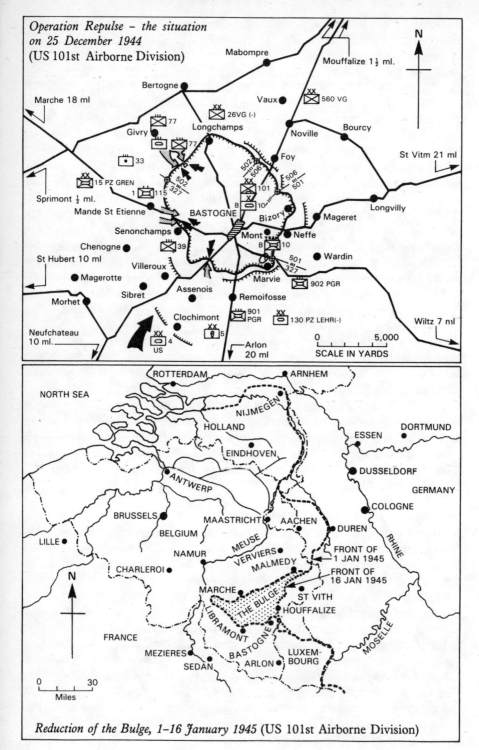

Operation Repulse – the situation on 25 December 1944 (US 101st Airborne Division)

Reduction of the Bulge, 1–16 January 1945 (US 101st Airborne Division)

Opposing this massive German force was the US 8th Corps under Major-General Troy H. Middleton, consisting of the 4th Infantry Division, the 28th Infantry Division and the 106th Infantry Division (which had only entered the line on 12 December), the 14th Cavalry Group of the 18th and 32nd Squadrons, and the 9th Armoured Division. The US front line ran parallel to the German border along an 88-mile stretch through Belgium and Luxembourg called the Ardennes, a thickly forested and hilly area with few roads.

At 05:00 on 16 December the Germans began their offensive in fog and snow with a heavy artillery barrage along the entire US front followed at 08:00 by Panzer and infantry attacks. Against the US 28th Division, the Germans threw six divisions, two panzer, one parachute and three infantry, and made large gains. By the night of 18/19 December the Germans were three miles from the strategic town of Bastogne.

On 17 December at Allied Supreme Headquarters it had been decided to move the 82nd and 101st Airborne Divisions to the Bastogne area, and during the 17th/18th the two divisions began to move out to the battle sector. The CO of the 101st, General Maxwell Taylor, was on duty in America so the 101st was put under the command of its artillery commander, Brigadier General Anthony C. McAuliffe. By 20:00 on the 18th the 82nd Airborne were in position at Werbomont, twenty-five miles north-west of Bastogne, and at 03:00 the next day the 101st were at Bastogne.

By the night of the 20th, the Germans had encircled Bastogne; General Middleton called General McAuliffe to tell him he was in command of all troops within the isolated town.

Try as they might, the Germans could make no impression on the defenders of Bastogne and fighting raged around the outskirts of the town. The Germans even employed the tactic of using captured US vehicles and uniforms to confuse the Americans but without result. Germans captured in US uniforms were shot by US firing squads.

On 22 December the Germans sent two officers to Bastogne under a white flag calling on the Americans to surrender. General McAuliffe gave them a one-word reply: 'Nuts'. It was carried to the German envoys by Colonel Joseph H. Harper of the 327th Glider Infantry Regiment. The German officers did not understand the meaning of the word 'nuts' so Colonel Harper told them in plain English it meant, 'Go to hell'. (Colonel Harper later became a major-general and now at the age of 86 years lives quietly with his wife, Maria, in Atlanta, Georgia.)

By 25 December the Americans had taken heavy casualties and were short of medical staff so General McAuliffe requested medical teams to be sent in by air to the encircled town. It was decided to supply Bastogne by air and the USAAF 9th Troop Carrier Command launched Operation 'Repulse'.

On Christmas Day the weather became so bad that the USAAF 116 aircraft supply drop to Bastogne had to be cancelled. On 26 December a single Waco CG-4A glider of the 96th Squadron, 444th Troop Carrier Group, was towed off from its base at Orleans, France, to Etain, some sixty miles from Bastogne. Volunteers were called for from the 12th Evacuation Hospital and Doctors Henry Mills, Edward Zinschlab, Lamar Soutter and Stanley Weslowski, together with four sergeant medics volunteered. The medics at first thought it was to be a parachute drop but still volunteered, as did the female nurses at the hospital.

The Waco glider flown by Flight Officers Charlton Corwin and Benjamin Constantino with the medical team aboard covered the sixty miles to Bastogne in an hour, landing on a snow-covered field north-west of the town in an area held by the 2nd Battalion of the 327th Glider Infantry. Without delay the medical teams were offloaded into a truck which took them to the hospital where they immediately went to work on the wounded.

With the Germans still attacking Bastogne and the Americans' supplies of ammunition running low, the 101st's G-4 (Chief Supply Officer), Lieutenant-Colonel Carl W. Kohls, suggested that gliders be used to bring in ammunition. Gliders salvaged from the operations in Normandy and Holland had been collected and based in France.

Accordingly ten more Waco CG-4As were loaded with 16 tons, mainly of ammunition, and were towed off from their base at Orleans at 15:00 on 26 December for the 265-mile trip to Bastogne. When they were some thirty miles from their LZ the gliders began to come under enemy fire, and three doctors and four medics were killed. Casting off tow over the LZ which was marked by coloured smoke the gliders managed to land without any further casualties. After unloading, the twenty glider pilots were detailed to guard the 540 German POWs the 101st had captured.

Although the US 4th Armoured Division's tanks broke through to relieve Bastogne on the evening of 26 December, supplies were still needed by the 101st so another glider mission was quickly arranged for the next day. Fifty Waco CG-4As of the 439th Troop Carrier Group from their base at Châteaudun, France, were loaded during the night with 736 rounds of 155-mm howitzer ammunition and petrol in five-gallon cans.

At 10:30 on the 27th, the gliders were towed off from Châteaudun in good weather. Unusually only one pilot was used to fly the Wacos and they wore parachutes. On tow at 500 feet over German positions near Bastogne the gliders came under heavy fire, which claimed fifteen gliders and the pilots. Approaching their LZ at noon the remaining thirty-five gliders delivered 53 tons of artillery ammunition and 2,975 gallons of petrol. Some gliders landed right next to the US gunpits and the glider loads were in use at once.

On 28 December, acting as guards to the 540 German POWs, the glider pilots who had reached Bastogne were evacuated, together with men of the US 28th Division to Neufchâteau, France.

During the resupply operation the US 9th Troop Carrier Command had dropped and landed by glider 1,112 tons of supplies, 94 per cent into the DZ/LZ.

By 18 January 1945, the battle of Bastogne was over, won by the stubborn troopers of the 101st Airborne Division. The Mayor of Bastogne, M Leon Jacqmin, presented to General Taylor the flag of the town which was accepted on behalf of the 101st Airborne Division.

The name Bastogne has now gone down into military history and is a battle honour of the 101st Airborne Division, aided by the pilots and glider pilots of the 9th Troop Carrier Command of the USAAF.

Operation 'Varsity': US 17th Airborne Division

On 6 February 1945, the 17th Airborne Division received notification that it was likely to be committed in an operation to force a crossing of the River Rhine, Germany, about 1 April; at the same time the division was told that it would move by rail and motor transport to Châlons, France, on 10 February. At this time the 17th was engaged in combat along the Our River near Clerveaux, Luxembourg, where it had suffered heavy casualties. The division was about 4,000 officers and men under strength; some rifle companies had less than forty men of their original strength, and some were without officers. Reinforcements and men returning from hospital arrived and an intensive training programme was undertaken. Gliders were obtained and new men given glider training. During the training period equipment was drawn to replace losses, including 400 tons of ammunition.

On 1 March 1945, the 17th Airborne Division was given its mission in Operation 'Varsity':

> To drop during daylight on D-Day; seize, clear and secure the Division Area with priority to the high ground east of Diersfordt in the general area, and the bridges over the River Issel; protect the right (south) flank of the Corps; establish contact with the 1st Commando Brigade, the 12th British Corps and the British 6th Airborne Division. Objectives to be held at all costs.

Movement to the twelve take-off airfields in France began on the evening of 19 March. At each airfield joint briefings between pilots and members of the aircraft and glider pilots and members of gliders were held. In addition each aircraft and glider crew were briefed individually with the latest air photos and sand tables.

Definite missions were assigned to glider pilots. Pilots were to assemble after landing in designated areas under their squadron commanders. Liaison officers were to report as soon as possible to the divisional command post. It was planned to evacuate all glider pilots as soon after D+1 as the situation permitted.

Early on the morning of 24 March 1945, the US 17th Airborne Division began to take off from the French airfields. The entire flying column was 2 hours 18 min in length, and consisted of 226 C-47s and 72 C-46 transport aircraft carrying parachute troops, while 906 gliders were towed by 610 C-47 tugs.

USAAF engaged
9th US Troop Carrier Command.
   50th Troop Carrier Wing.

439th Troop Carrier Group	91, 92, 93, 94 Squadrons
440th Troop Carrier Group	95, 96, 97, 98 Squadrons
441st Troop Carrier Group	99, 100, 301, 302 Squadrons
442nd Troop Carrier Group	303, 304, 305, 306 Squadrons

   52nd Troop Carrier Wing

314th Troop Carrier Group	32, 50, 61, 62 Squadrons

   53rd Troop Carrier Wing

434th Troop Carrier Group	71, 72, 73, 74 Squadrons
435th Troop Carrier Group	75, 76, 77, 78 Squadrons
436th Troop Carrier Group	79, 80, 81, 82 Squadrons
437th Troop Carrier Group	83, 84, 85, 86 Squadrons

US Air Movement Table
Operation Varsity, 17th Airborne Division

Serial No	US Army Unit	USAAF	No of aircraft	No of gliders	Chalk Nos	Airfield	LZ	Remarks
A 8	G2 Divisional HQ Recon Platoon 2nd Batt HQ Coy. 2nd Batt 194th GIR Lt-Col Stewart, Commander	437th TCG	40	1 2 77 (80)	1 2–3 4–80	Coulommiers	S	Double Tow
A 9	HQ Coy 2nd Batt Regt HQ Coy F 1st Batt HQ 1st Batt 194th GIR Colonel Pierce, Commander	437th TCG	40	16 5 59 (80)	81–96 97–101 102–160	Coulommiers	S	Double Tow
A 10	Coy B HQ 1st Batt Regt. HQ Coy A/Tk Coy 194 GIR Lt-Col Schorr, Commander	436th TCG	36	5 29 9 29 (72)	1–5 6–34 35–43 44–72	Bretigny	S	Double Tow
A 11	A/Tk Coy 3rd Batt HQ Coy 3rd Batt 194th GIR Major Rowan, Commander	436th TCG	36	5 67 (72)	73–77 78–144	Bretigny	S	Double Tow
A 12	HQ Coy 3rd Batt Regt HQ Coy Regt Medical Detach 194th GIR HQ Det & Med Det Bty B & Bty E 155th AA Batt Lt-Col Paddock	435th TCG	36	26 12 3 7 21 3 (72)	1–26 27–38 39–41 42–48 49–69 70–72	Melun	S	Double Tow

Serial No.	US Army Unit	USAAF	No. of aircraft	No. of gliders	Chalk Nos.	Airfield	LZ	Remarks
A 13	E Bty 155th AA 681st Glider Fd Art. HQ Bty Lt-Col Keating, Commander	435th TCG	36	9 63 (72)	73-81 82-144	Melun	S	Double Tow
A 14	HQ Bty 681st 680th Glider Fd Art. B Bty & HQ Lt-Col Oswald, Commander	439th TCG	36	7 65 (72)	1-7 8-72	Châteaudun	S	Double Tow
A 15	B Bty HQ Bty & 680th Glider Fd Art Batt. Trans 507th Trans 464th Supplies, Engineer Lt-Col Kuhn, Commander	439th TCG	36	24 8 21 14 5 (72)	73-96 97-104 105-125 126-139 140-144	Châteaudun	S	Double Tow
A 16	Recce Platoon 9th TCC Control 139th Eng Batt Coys C & A Lt-Col Johnson, Commander	440th TCG	45	2 6 37 (45)	1-2 3-8 9-45	Bricy	N	Single Tow
A 17	Coys A & C 139th A Bty 155 AA Major Mason, Commander	440th TCG	45	32 13 (45)	46-77 78-90	Bricy	N	Single Tow

US Air Movement Table:
Operation Varsity, 17th Airborne Division (continued)

Serial No.	US Army Unit	USAAF	No. of aircraft	No. of gliders	Chalk Nos.	Airfield	LZ	Remarks
A 18	Bty A & Batt C 155th AA Battalion Divisional HQ Colonel Liebel, Commander	441st TCG	48	8 21 19 (48)	1–8 9–29 30–48	Bricy	N	Single Tow
A 19	Div Art HQ 517th Signal Coy Colonel Gunby, Commander	442nd TCG	48	20 28 (48)	1–20 21–48	St André	N	Single Tow
A 20	517th Signal Coy 224th Medical Coy Major Kenny, Commander	441st TCG	48	6 42 (48)	1–48	Chartres	N	Single Tow
A 21	224 Medical Coy Trans 513th British Air Support G 4 Supply Ordnance Capt Kelly, Commander	314th TCG	40	8 21 8 3 (40)	1–8 9–29 30–37 38–40	Poix	N	Single Tow
A 22	Trans 466th G 4 Supply QM G 4 Supply Ord Phantom Signals	314th TCG	40	14 6 19 1 (40)	41–54 56–60 61–79 80			
Totals:			570 Aircraft	798 Gliders				

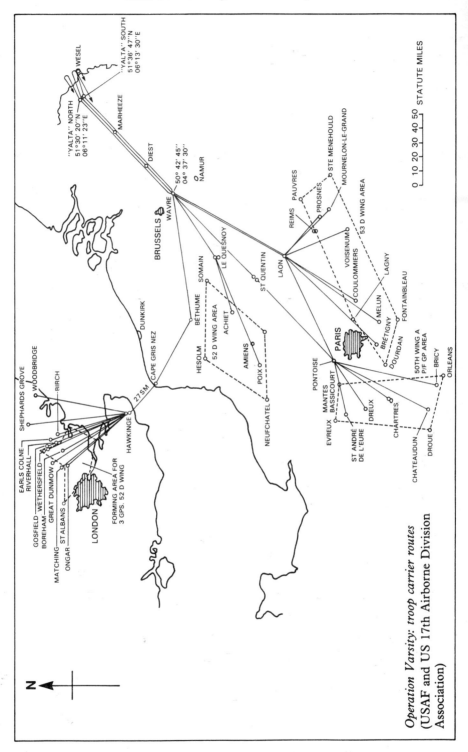

Operation Varsity: troop carrier routes (USAF and US 17th Airborne Division Association)

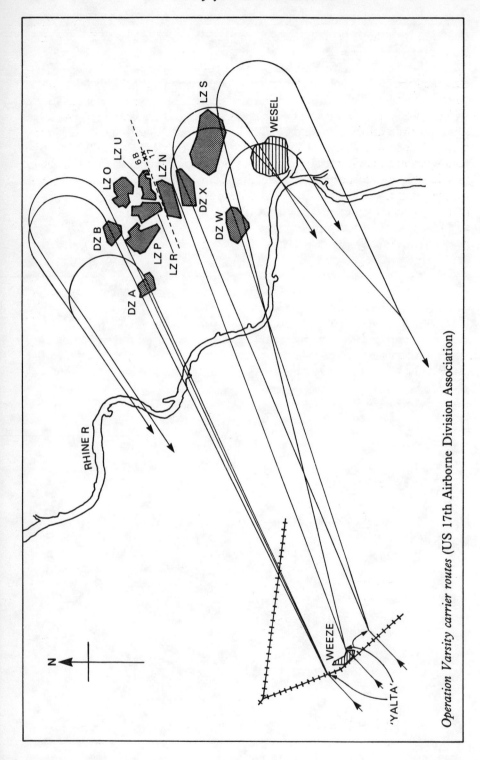

Operation Varsity carrier routes (US 17th Airborne Division Association)

The immense flying column rendezvoused over the battlefield of Waterloo, Belgium, with the British 6th Airborne Division, and side by side the two divisions flew into battle.

At 10:30 the 194th combat team composed of the 194th Glider Infantry Regiment and the 681st Glider Field Artillery, began landing in their CG-4A gliders which had been double-towed. The combat team landed on the previously selected areas except for a small percentage of gliders from each serial. No serial missed the prescribed landing zone. The 1st Battalion of the 194th landed in the correct LZ, except for a small amount of gliders which were scattered. The battalion was able to orient itself immediately and assembled rapidly. The battalion immediately moved north-west from the LZ towards their objectives, with A Company on the east and C Company on the west, leading. The route of the battalion lay generally through areas in which other gliders of the regiment had landed and the battalion occupied its objectives by 14:00 with the exception of C Company. This company, on the left, met very stiff resistance in territory that had not been cleared and they were forced to fight their way toward their assembly area and objective. The 2nd Battalion of the 194th landed in the correct LZ with about 90 per cent of their gliders. A few gliders landed on the east side of the Issel Canal. The gliders were well grouped and this enabled the companies to move off as groups soon after the firefights on the LZs were successfully completed. The heavy weapons and anti-tank platoons were able to support the rifle companies almost immediately according to plan. Within forty-five minutes of landing the battalion had overcome initial resistance in the LZs, had assembled enough per-

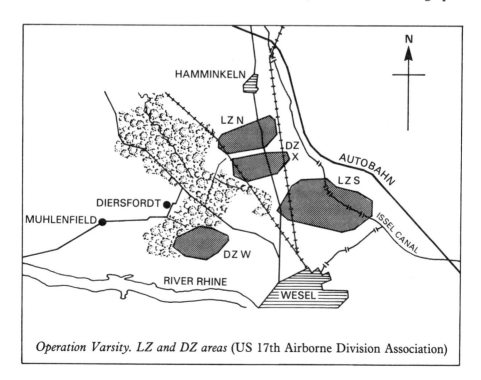

Operation Varsity. LZ and DZ areas (US 17th Airborne Division Association)

sonnel to function as a unit and was on the move towards its objective. By now it had established communications with all companies. By 12:30 E Company, in reserve, had reached its assembly area and the battalion command post was in operation. The battalion knocked out two enemy tanks with bazooka fire en route to its objective, seized all objectives, and repelled four enemy counter-attacks, knocking out two more tanks and damaging one.

The 3rd Battalion of the 194th landed against heavy flak and small arms fire and took heavy casualties on the LZs, but, quickly forming into small units, overcame the resistance and soon reached its assembly area. By 16:00 hours it had reached its objective and contacted the 507th Parachute Infantry Regiment to the west, the 513rd Parachute Infantry Regiment to the north and the British 1st Commando Brigade to the south.

The 194th Glider Infantry Regiment had cleared its LZs and was 75% assembled and under the control of the regimental commander by 12:00. The regiment took all its initial objectives within two hours of landing. During the day it captured 1,150 prisoners of war, four 155-mm guns, two 150-mm guns, four 105-mm guns, eleven 88-mm guns, and destroyed or captured two flak wagons, five self-propelled guns and ten tanks.

The 681st Glider Field Artillery fought its way off the LZs and into its planned firing positions. Upon landing 75 mm pack howitzers were put into action beside their gliders and direct fire was delivered on enemy positions. By 16:00 the 681st had ten guns firing out of twelve brought in and all wire and radio nets were operating to divisional artillery, the 194th Command Post and the artillery on the west bank of the Rhine.

At about 19:00, 100 glider pilots were attached to the 681st and a perimeter defence was organized around the guns so as to give maximum protection to the west flank. At 22:00 the enemy counter-attacked the west flank of the 681st with infantry and tanks. A heavy firefight developed and one tank was destroyed before the enemy withdrew.

The 139th Airborne Engineer Battalion began landing from their gliders on LZ 'N' at 12:00, meeting heavy anti-aircraft fire and ground fire on the LZ. The battalion landed in two serials seven minutes apart on the same LZ. Gliders were widely dispersed on landing and assembly was at first by squad and two squad groups. These groups cleared the LZs and worked their way to the planned areas. By 17:30 the battalion had taken all of its objectives. During the day 80 Germans were killed or wounded and 315 captured along with an entire battery of 105-mm guns.

The 680th Glider Field Artillery Battalion (105 howitzers) began landing west of the Rhine at 11:40. Fifty per cent of their gliders landed in the correct LZs and all gliders landed in an area of 4,000 metres square near the centre of the divisional sector. All elements were subjected to enemy small arms, machine gun, mortar and artillery fire immediately on landing. The battalion cleared its landing area although enemy fire was so intense that forty gliders were destroyed on the ground after landing. Firing by the battalion during this first phase consisted of direct lay on enemy strong points. By 12:45 half of the battalion had assembled and six guns were laid ready to fire, the battalion command post was established and a complete wire net operating at 13:45. At 17:00 nine howitzers were in position and 900 rounds of ammunition had been assembled. By the evening the Germans were beaten, although small pockets of resistance were encountered and trouble was experienced from sniper fire. However the 17th Airborne had won a great victory, under the commander, Major-General William M. Miley.

The divisional mission was accomplished in every particular within a few hours after landing. It was carried out in the face of heavy flak and heavy initial resistance on and around the LZs by enemy troops who had been ordered to sleep at their gun positions during the preceding night. The 17th's mission was carried out almost exactly as planned and with relatively light casualties considering the nature of the operation and the enemy opposition.

Total battle casualties for the period ending 23:59, 24 March 1945 for the 17th Airborne Division in Operation 'Varsity' were:

Killed in action	393
Wounded in action	834
Missing in action	80
Total:	1307

On 26 March, the 17th with the British 1st Commando Brigade attacked east at 09:00 into Germany and secured all their objectives, taking 300 prisoners of war in the process. By 09:30 on 28 March they were in Dorsten, thus flanking the Ruhr valley's military centre and cutting off communications north of the Ruhr. On 2 April they took the city of Munster and the 194th Glider Combat Team captured Franz von Papen, Hitler's former top diplomat, who was later put on trial for war crimes and acquitted. Another capture by the 17th was Colonel Joseph Harpe, commanding general of the German 5th Panzer Army, one of Hitler's top generals.

A month later, Germany surrendered and the 17th remained on occupation duty until August 1945, when they moved to France. On 7 September the 17th left for home and was deactivated but its illustrious record has been written into history.

The US 17th Airborne Division veterans still maintain an association of which I am proud to be a member.

A 'One Point' landing during Operation 'Varsity'
An account, by Bruce C. Merryman of 62nd Squadron, 314th Troop Carrier Group, of the crash at Wesel, Germany, 24 March 1945, which he and John C. Heffner survived:

Our CG-4A glider was loaded with a jeep and medical supplies. The jeep driver was T/C Wallace E. Thompson, a medic and paratrooper in the 17th Airborne division. He told us prior to take-off that he did not want to ride in a glider but had been ordered to, so that he would be with the jeep when we landed. We assured him that there was nothing to worry about as it was just like riding in a bus.

After a rough three-hours (and many disparaging remarks from our paratroop passenger) into the flight from B-44 airfield at Poix, France, we released from the tow plane and started our descent. We deployed our deceleration chute and were within ten to fifteen feet from the ground when we received the first 88 round near the back door of the cargo section. I don't know how many of you [in the British Glider Pilot Regimental Association] either participated in, or were witness to, the CG-4A here in the States that was wired up with a number of plastic explosive charges so that it could be detonated by the glider pilots after landing. The idea was to chop the glider into three or four pieces which the glider pilots could push, pull or roll out of the landing area and clear the way for the other incoming gliders. It worked great when I saw it demonstrated. The reason I bring this up, is that at the same instant I reached up to release the chute and touched the handle, we got the hit from the first 88 shell. The thought that entered my mind at the same instant was, 'which idiot wired this glider'; this round exploded causing the jeep to move forward, break the nose latches and pull the nose section upward where it locked. The jeep, with the medic driver still under the steering wheel, exited the glider through the open front and fell or 'flew' the remaining distance to the ground where it landed upright with no damage or injury to it or the driver.

We crashed immediately behind the jeep in a 'one point' attitude with the tail section pointing to the heavens. This left Heff and me in the nose section still strapped in our seats with our backs on the ground and our feet in the air as though a chair had tipped over backwards. At almost the same instant we touched the ground, the 88 gunner removed our left wing with the next round. We released our seat belts and rolled over looking for a way out. I used my Tommy gun to smash out the plexiglass window. We crawled through it and ran to a ditch alongside the railroad tracks that ran through the LZ. We jumped into the ditch and began to crawl to our right. The 88 gunner, not being able to see which way we had crawled, began to slam rounds into the embankment in an effort to hit us with shrapnel. We continued to crawl for probably 100 yards when we came up on another man lying in the ditch. It was the medic paratrooper who had ridden in with us. He did not seem at all pleased with the way his glider ride had been terminated and assured us that he had taken his last one. His account of the landing was as follows: he was sitting in the jeep inside the glider one instant and the next instant he was sitting out on the ground in the jeep. While he was sitting there more or less in a daze, a German rifleman hit his helmet at an angle with his Mauser. The bullet cut the helmet in the vicinity of the medic's white cross but did not enter it. At that time the driver left the jeep, ran to the ditch and also crawled to his right as we did a few minutes later. That is where we found him.

While we were in the ditch and while the 88 rounds were still hitting the embankment, a piece of shrapnel, rather large from the sound of it, came fluttering up the ditch towards us. We could hear it coming and fell as flat as we could in the ditch. It hit Heff on one of his legs just above the knee and numbed his leg so that he couldn't feel it. It had hit him flat and did not cut his clothing or his skin but ricocheted away. He was quite relieved when he found that his leg was still attached to him. Both of us had been wounded but had not had time to realize it. Heff had a piece of shrapnel lodged in the large knuckle where the index finger joins the hand. It was evidently grating on a nerve as every time Heff moved or breathed he suffered excruciating pain. Either the medic or I gave him a shot of morphine. After a bit this seemed to ease the pain somewhat. I had ran the distance from our crashed glider to the ditch not knowing I had torn the cartilage in my right knee, badly sprained my right ankle, and had received two shrapnel wounds in my upper right thigh. Shows what you can do when you have the proper incentive. I had also sustained a broken nose. We dressed my shrapnel wounds with sulpha powders and a bandage.

The report in the squadron was that we had been slightly wounded by small arms fire. An 88 is some 'small arm'.

While we were in the ditch, a B-24 with the right inboard engine on fire came down, barely clearing the railroad embankment by us and bellied in on the other side. I talked to the pilot later at the aid station and told him that I had felt the heat from his burning engine when he passed over us. He said that he was afraid he was going to hit us at the time but was able to pull it over the tracks at the last minute. There is an interesting story about what happened to them after they pancaked but which will be told at another time.

The medic lay in the ditch with us for a few minutes and then stated that this was not getting his job done. He left the ditch, retrieved his jeep and began picking up wounded and carrying them to the aid station. He returned after an hour or so, picked us up in the same jeep and carried us to the aid station as well. Heff was given another shot of morphine and I received some more sulpha powders. After this Heff was 'in orbit' from the morphine. I don't know how many shots he received during this period but I don't think he remembers much about the rest of Operation 'Varsity'. At one point during the night he disappeared and was gone for a couple of hours. I could not go look for him as by this time I could not stand alone or walk. Later a paratrooper led him back to me and told me that I had better tie him down before he got himself killed. They had found him standing, leaning against a tree watching the 'Battle of Burp Gun Corner'. I was able to keep him with me until sometime after daylight on the 25th when he got up and told me he was going to look for Jimmy (James L. Cox, a tent mate of ours). He took off before I could stop him. After a couple of hours he returned but I could not get anything out of him as to where he had been.

After we got back to our squadron a couple of weeks later – Jimmy told me that early on the morning of the 25th someone sat down on the edge of his foxhole. He looked round and saw it was Heff, so he pulled him into the foxhole as there was a fire fight going on round them. Jimmy said he asked Heff where I was but it did not seem to register with him. He was still in orbit from all that morphine. After a short time Heff left the foxhole and walked away. Jimmy said he figured that was the last time he would probably see Heff alive as there was heavy fighting in that area. That was when Heff came back to where I was. I managed to keep him with me the rest of the time until we were moved back across the Rhine that afternoon.

The next day or two we were sent to different hospitals and did not see each other again until a couple of weeks later back in our home squadron. Another tent mate of ours, Warren Page, was killed on this mission.

So much for Operation Varsity.

Frank Dillon of the US 17th Airborne Division recalls his part in 'Varsity'

After returning from the Battle of the Bulge, the 17th Airborne Division consisting of the 513th Parachute Infantry, the 193rd and 194th Glider Infantry Regiments, were situated in a large tent city near Châlons-sur-Marne, France. Here replacements were received and the two glider regiments were combined into one, the 194th, and retraining and re-equipping occupied those chilly spring days.

Four airborne divisions were assembled in the Rheims area. These were the veteran 82nd Airborne, 101st Airborne and the newly arrived and unannounced 13th Airborne, beside the 17th Airborne which had flow from England to help stem the German thrust through the Ardennes. It was evident that an airborne drop would launch the American drive across the Rhine...which of us would be selected?

Few of us knew during those days when we trained new squads, platoons and companies, ran field problems and rehearsed simulated landings behind enemy lines, that the 17th with the British 6th Airborne would be chosen. The time seemed to be ripe; rumors were exchanged between men of different companies, regiments and even divisions, and the summation of minor activities indicated an operation in the near future. Large stocks of 'C' and 'K' rations came in, replacements were still arriving, practice jumps and flights were made but the first single evidence was the painting out of all organizational designations on our motor vehicles.

On 18 March the entire division was restricted to the respective camp areas. An airborne operation was at hand, and not too far off at that. More clothing, equipment, weapons and ammunition were distributed to the men. Duffle bags containing articles that would not be carried were packed and stored in a large company tent. From now on we would live out of our combat packs. At this time only officers down to the company commanders knew the particulars of the operation. Operation 'Varsity' was the code-name.

Late on the afternoon of 20 March we left by truck for the railroad yard at Châlons. Each man carried his combat load... just what was necessary to sustain him in combat. At Châlons we boarded the well known 40 and 8's in which we travelled to our marshalling area. Detraining at 02:00 21 March we again boarded trucks for the airfield. We were placed in tents that night and early the next morning we made ourselves comfortable for our stay there, such as it would be. That morning while the men did most anything from playing ball to getting haircuts, the officers got their first briefing of the mission.

Here in the briefing tent which was surrounded by high barbed wire and guarded twenty-four hours a day, we knew for the first time that elements of the 1st Allied Airborne Army, the American 17th and the British 6th Airborne Divisions were to drop over the Rhine north west of Wesel, Germany. We saw the situation from the standpoint of armies on large maps down to the action of individual regiments, companies and platoons. We saw aerial maps and photos flown by reconnaissance planes, sometimes at an elevation of only fifty feet. The maps and photos were brought to life by large sand tables with terrain features and man made objects built to scale.

Late that afternoon the men were given their first briefing which embraced the 'big picture'. When briefing for an airborne operation, it is essential that every man knows the overall picture as well as what he, as an individual, must accomplish on landing.

March 22: More briefing, intense study of our landing zones and our company assembly areas and platoon objectives. Company commanders issued their orders and in turn the platoon leaders decided on a plan and oriented their squad leaders. Alternative plans were decided upon should last minute changes in the situation cause the primary plan to be abandoned. In the afternoon various items such as ammo, water cans, shovels, 'K' rations, litters and blankets were broken down into glider loads and lashed securely. Briefing and the checking of individual combat loads consumed the remainder of the day. It was announced that Saturday, 24 March was to be D-Day and H-Hour 10:45. Take-off, 08:00.

March 23: Final preparations! Combat loads checked and rechecked. Weapons disassembled, cleaned, oiled and reassembled. Trench knives whetted to a keen edge; every trooper carried at least one, some two. Some passed the time, while awaiting their turn in the briefing tents, by writing letters that could not be mailed until after the landing, some played ball or just sat and joked or talked about the Ardennes, or tomorrow, or home. Others had their hair completely off, some left a single strip over the top of the head, Iroquois style.

Final briefing today, with aerial photos flown just a few hours ago and rushed to us. There was evidence of anti-airborne elements near Wesel. Did they know we were coming? Rumors spread, 'Come on over 17th Airborne, we're waiting for you', were broadcast by loudspeakers across to the American side of the Rhine.

In the open air theater the Catholic Chaplain said mass late in the afternoon. Protestant services were held shortly afterwards. All were attended very well. Prayer during those days was ever-present; combat veterans relied on it because they knew, the new men because they were going into the unknown.

Briefing was completed that evening to the degree that every man knew where all the elements of the division were to land and what to expect upon landing so that at D-Day minus 12 hours the troopers were in a keen mental attitude for the drop behind the lines.

After chow that evening, word was passed around that three movies would be shown in the open air theater, for it was anticipated that there would be little sleep that night. The first show started at nine and the last one would end around 02:00 the next morning. Those who didn't take in the movies spent the last few hours before going to bed writing a last letter, oiling their weapons putting a razor edge on their trench knives, or having a brief visit with the chaplain, or going over and over with their buddies the plan for tomorrow.

Those of us who did sleep were awakened at 03:30 for breakfast; and, since most of us slept in our clothes, we lost little time getting to the mess tent for a typical army breakfast with a side dish of *steak*. Why is it that a trooper always gets steak as his last meal before going in? Perhaps it's a way of saying, 'So long, trooper, good luck!'

In the mess tent we saw our buddies together for the last time for some hours or days to come. Some we would never see again. Chow over, we walked back to our tents calling out, 'Good luck!' to this one and wise-cracking with that one. In the tents we packed our field bags, put on equipment, hung extra bandoliers of ammo over our shoulders and then helped our buddy into his gear. At 05:00 we lined up in glider loads, checked equipment once more, and then a message from the Commanding General of 21st Army Group which impressed us with the importance of our 'drop'. We were to establish and protect a bridgehead on the east side of the Rhine. The British 2nd Army was to force a crossing several miles below Wesel; and in order to secure that bridgehead, the airborne troops must seize and hold the high ground four miles east of the river and to control all bridges over the Issel Canal and Issel River.

Shortly after 05:00 we started the $1\frac{1}{2}$ mile trek to the airfield. Take a close look at a trooper, like thousands of his buddies who are primed for their mission. He's shod in his jump boots – still shiny as he leaves for combat. Strapped to one leg or both between the ankle and knee is a trench knife. Most men favor this location if the situation calls for hand to hand fighting. Notice his combat trousers are of a green tough material. Characteristic of airborne troops are the large 'cargo' pockets on the trousers on the outer portion of the thighs. In them are carried various items: extra socks, 'K' rations, cleaning kit, grenades or other small articles. The combat coat, usually worn over an OD shirt and woollen sweater has four pockets which bulge with articles each individual deems necessary. Over the coat he wears a rifle belt and suspenders. Attached to the belt are ammo pouches of M1 clips or carbine magazines, a first aid packet, perhaps another trench knife, an entrenching tool, canteen, compass, and some carry an automatic pistol in addition to their primary weapon. A trooper usually carries on his suspenders or other easily accessible spot, several grenades. His pack contains extra socks, underwear, rations, mess kit, toilet articles, towel and sweater. He wears a camouflage net covering his helmet and attached to the net on the front of the helmet is a paratroop's first aid packet containing a tourniquet, morphine syringe, bandage and wound tablets. Of course each man has his weapon, M1 carbine M3 or grease gun, Thompson submachine-gun or M4 or M6 light machine gun. As he left for the field every man carried a blanket on which to sit while over the flak areas. There he goes, the finest man in the Army, the airborne soldier.

At the field we dumped our equipment beside our gliders, met our pilot and co pilot and after a brief conference, we decided on a name for our ship. Some were named after wives or sweethearts: 'Jeanne, Dot, Rosemary.' Some were named after States or cities like 'Kansas Kid' or 'Brooklyn Bums'. Ours was, 'Just one more time'. The visible tension on everyone's face was eased by joking or horseplay. There is no sign of fear. It was strange to think of fear on a peaceful sunny day in France with the fighting many hundreds of miles away.

And yet within three hours we would be dropped abruptly into a hot spot. A few minutes before take off time we had a group picture taken in front of the glider. God only knows who of us will be fortunate enough to see the print of that picture.

As the tug ship, a C-47, moves down the runway the tow rope becomes taut and finally we too started down behind the tug. We gained speed – the tail came up and shortly after we were airborne. We could look to our right rear and see the other glider attached to the same tug, leave the ground. The tug under the great strain of towing two gliders took to the air with just a few hundred feet of airstrip remaining. We circled several times to gain altitude and to take our place in the mighty sky train that could stretch from New York to Cincinnati. We flew northwards towards Brussels where we would rendezvous with the British 6th Airborne Division which loaded in England. It was an uneventful flight; seldom did we talk. Our thoughts turned from our assembly after landing, to prayer, to watching the tremendous sky army, and back to the hell we would drop into.

Over Brussels the British Lancasters and Horsa gliders joined the procession to the Rhine. All around us flew our fighter escort – nothing could break through to disrupt our train. Ahead the planes and gliders disappeared into the clouds – or was it smoke. There was a ribbon of water ahead. The Rhine? No, not yet. On the east side of that small river were the remains of heavy hard fighting.

Over to our right some of the C-47s were coming back, some were in flames and down on the ground was the smoking flaming wreckage of others. That cloud up ahead *was* smoke, all along the Rhine – we were almost there, about five minutes out of our LZ. More flaming planes going back after dropping their human cargoes. The Rhine seems to be passing under us as we roar over – it's gone. Smoke is all around us now – can't even see the ground – impossible to distinguish landmarks. Will we hit our LZ?

There goes a flaming glider over to our right! A dull flat wham, as flak bursts nearby! A rapid but dull crack as machine gun bullets tear through the wings and fuselage. A man stares blankly and open-mouthed as a buddy sitting opposite him slumps forward but is held in his seat by his safety belt. What can you do? What can you say? Nothing!

You look out trying to see the terrain as you saw the aerial photos and sand table back in France. Nothing but smoke, nothing visible from 800 feet. There is a break in the smoke but just a field shows up – no landmarks. Your heart drops, you don't hear the flak or bullets: you see an ack ack position, you can't be mistaken – it is the same one that showed on the aerial photo! We're almost to our LZ. Then the smoke obliterates our view.

Suddenly the pilot reaches up and cuts loose; we bank to the left. All is quiet except for the wind rushing by the struts. The flak is loud; you can hear the machine guns on the ground. There's a triangular patch of woods, a road – you're oriented. We're right over our LZ. A glider comes in from our right, you watch it come closer, and as you shout to the pilot he turns his head and avoids the danger by banking sharply to the left. We're down low now, just a few more seconds. A high tension wire looms up, even though you brace yourself for a crash, the pilot pulls her up and over – except for the tail.

We plunge to the ground as the tail strikes the wires but once more the pilot levels her off but our speed is terrific. Directly ahead is a tree and even though our wings are sheared off, the fuselage is still heading for the tree. We run down a row of fence posts and as that tree looms in front of us we brace ourselves for the crash. It comes – you open your eyes – the whole top is missing. The tree is between the pilot and the co-pilot. No one appears to be hurt as we all scramble through the doors and emergency exits.

We run from the glider lest a machine gun or 88 is being brought to bear on it. The entire crew assembles in a ditch beside a road and before you can check the entire crew you are threatening a prisoner who is pleading for his life. Every one is present. So well briefed were you that you are able to orient yourself as you check your men. You pass the word and lead them to the assembly area. From the sounds up ahead we will have to fight for it – but that is typical of airborne landings, small fights of individuals and small units until larger units can assemble and push off to their own objective.

Luzon Gypsy Task Force

The first and the last US combat glider mission in the Pacific during World War II, on 23 June 1945, at Camalaniugan airfield, Luzon, the Philippines.

By the end of 1944, US forces had driven the Japanese from the southern part of the Philippine Islands, but on the main island of Luzon, the Japanese had over 250,000 men of their 14th Area Army under General Tonoyuki Yamashita. The Japanese knew that they could not match the Americans' superior air power or ground forces fire power, so decided to retreat with 140,000 men to the rugged Sierre Madre mountains in the north of Luzon. There they would fight a delaying action for as long as possible to slow and delay the US advance on the Japanese mainland.

At 09:30 on 9 January 1945, the US 6th Army, commanded by General Walter Kreuger, landed at Lingayen, Luzon. By early March 1945, the Americans had taken Manila, the capital, after heavy fighting against a fanatical enemy who refused to surrender.

One US airborne division, the 11th, commanded by Major-General Joseph M. Swing and comprised of the 511th Parachute Infantry, and the 187th and 188th Glider Infantry Regiments, was in the Philippines but had been used mainly as ground infantry, except for two paratroop drops on 3 and 23 February, at Tagatay and Los Banos. Officially the 11th Airborne had one parachute and two glider infantry regiments, but most of the glider troops became parachute-trained so that all three regiments were interchangeable as paratroop/glider units.

No US gliders had been used in combat in the Pacific although four Waco CG-4As had, on 17 October 1944, carried US Army Engineers with their equipment in New Guinea to construct an airstrip there. Behind the entrenched Japanese in the north of Luzon was the small sea port of Appari, which the Americans considered could be used by the enemy to evacuate his forces. Ten miles south of Appari was Camalaniugan airfield, thought to be in Japanese hands. General Kreuger decided to mount an airborne assault on the airfield using the 11th Airborne Division's paratroops and gliders. At the same time ground forces would attack northwards and link up with the airborne troops as soon as possible.

General Swing, the 11th's commander, assembled a task force to carry out the airborne mission. Gypsy Task Force comprised a reinforced battalion of the 511th Parachute Infantry, C Battery of the 457th Parachute Field Artillery plus elements of the 127th Airborne Engineers, and the 11th's Signal and Medical

Teams. In command of the task force of 1,000 troops was Lieutenant-Colonel Henry Burgess, of the 511th Parachute Infantry. For the first time in the Pacific gliders were to be used in a combat operation. Seven gliders, six Waco CG-4As and one CG-13, loaded with six jeeps, one trailer, ammunition, medical supplies, radios and nineteen men would be towed by C-47s of the 54th Troop Carrier Wing to land on Camalaniugan airfield immediately following the paratroops' drop.

On 22 June US ground forces from the north-west reached Camalaniugan airfield and found it clear of Japanese forces. Shortly after 06:00 on the 23rd the seven gliders were towed off from Lipa airfield in southern Luzon and formed into formation for the mission. The lead glider, a CG-13 piloted by Major Edward Milau and Lieutenant Max Cone, was the only one of its type in Luzon.

As the task force approached Camalaniugan LZ, Lieutenant-Colonel Enis Whitehead's 5th Air Force pounded it with bombs and gun fire. Fighter bombers laid a smoke screen between the airfield and the hills to the south-east to hide the LZ from the enemy. Pathfinders on the ground marked the LZ with coloured smoke and in a twenty-five mph wind the paratroops and gliders began to land at 09:30.

The CG-13 piloted by Major Milau and five CG-4As landed safely, having cast off tow at 400 feet. Four of the gliders landed within yards of each other, three almost line abreast, and two more 200 yards behind them. One Waco collided with a bomb crater and made a heavy landing injuring a passenger.

No Japanese resistance was encountered on the LZ and the glider loads were easily offloaded and in the hands of the 11th Airborne troopers. An hour later the glider pilots were evacuated by C-47 Dakota and returned to Lipa airstrip. Three of the CG-4As were snatched out from the LZ by C-47s but the other four were abandoned on the airstip.

By the 26th the 11th Airborne Task Force had established contact with the advancing US 37th Division from the south.

The first and last US combat glider mission in the Pacific had been a success with no lives lost and all cargo delivered to the LZ.

US records show the following USAAF glider pilots engaged on the Luzon mission: CG-13, Major E. Milau and Lieutenant M. Cone; CG-4As, Lieutenants J.J. Booth and D.E. Drummond; Flight Officers W. Bartz, R. Brook, E. Doty, R.J. Meer, D. Orkney, and H. Wallace.

XIII
United States Gliders

Military

On 8 March 1941, the US Government issued USAAF Specification 1025/2 for military gliders to carry two, eight and fifteen troops. Eleven small aircraft manufacturing companies were invited to built prototypes but only Waco Aircraft, Bowlus Sailplanes, Frankfort Sailplane Company and the St Louis Aircraft Corporation made positive tenders.

In April 1941, the Waco Aircraft Company, Troy, Ohio, US, was awarded the US Government contract to build nine- and fifteen-place military gliders. Waco's chief engineer and designer, A.F. Arcier, produced the XCG-3, an experimental glider, to carry eight men. With 73 ft wooden spar fabric-covered wings and a 48½ ft welded steel tube fabric-covered fuselage, the glider weighed 4,400 lb and passed flight and structural tests at Wright Field. None of the other companies' glider designs passed the USAAF tests.

One of the conditions of the US Government's contract with Waco was that the company had to furnish designs to other aircraft contractors who would build the Waco glider under licence. The object was large scale production by American industry.

Trials of the XCG-3 being successful the Commonwealth Aircraft Company produced one hundred gliders as the CG-3A (CG = Cargo glider).

With the need for a larger troop or cargo-carrying glider contained in their contract, Waco produced the XCG-4, building two prototypes. Able to carry fifteen troops (including the pilot), the glider was in fact a larger version of the CG-3A with an 83½ ft wing span and a 48 ft long fuselage. A specially made wooden floor could support a quarter ton truck – or a 75-mm howitzer and crew of three – or any other combination up to 7,500 lb all-up plus. No flaps were fitted, although trim tabs were incorporated in the ailerons. The entire nose section of the glider including the cockpit, hinged upwards. A lever on the cockpit floor, when pulled, released a catch which allowed the upward hinging. The two steel tubes leading to the lever were marked in large letters 'nose release'. With the nose section in the up position direct access was gained to the fuselage. Loads could quickly be loaded or unloaded – vital for speed into action in war.

First models only had one control column fitted, which could be swung from

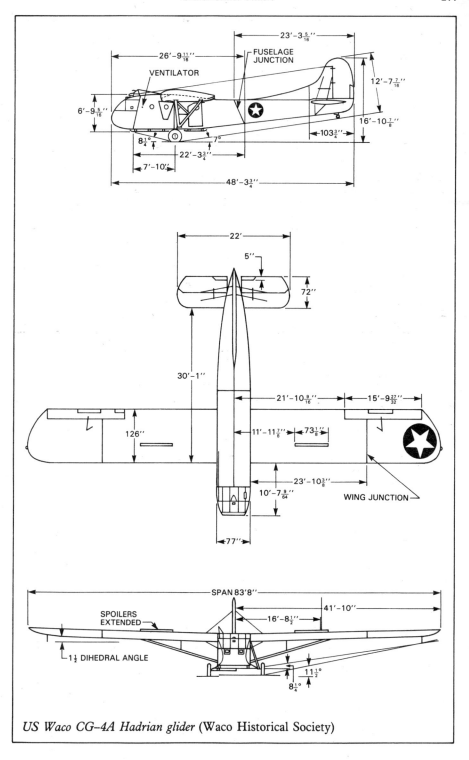

US Waco CG–4A Hadrian glider (Waco Historical Society)

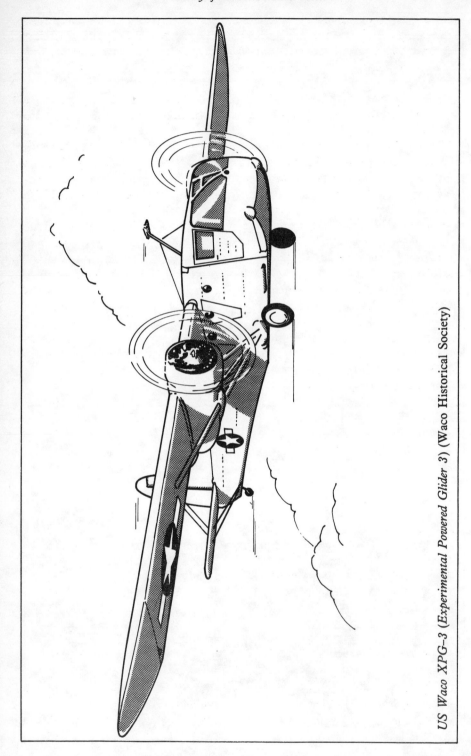

US Waco XPG–3 (Experimental Powered Glider 3) (Waco Historical Society)

pilot to pilot by sitting side by side; later models had two control columns. A bank of five simple flying instruments, turn and bank indicator, altimeter, rate of climb indicator, compass and airspeed indicator, were mounted on a steel tube in front of the pilots. Contact with the towing aircraft was by an intercom line wound round the 300 ft one-inch thick nylon tow rope. Later two way VHF radios were installed. Towing speed was 120–125 mph and after release a landing run of 660 feet was needed, depending on wind speed. Stalling speed in free flight was 48 mph.

The trials of the XCG-4 being satisfactory, on 29 June 1942 the glider was designated the CG-4A and declared ready for mass production. In July 1942, sixteen companies received contracts to build the glider, with Waco supplying design and manufacture details. Production costs of the glider were from 15,000 to 26,000 dollars depending on the builder.

In an effort to extend the use of the glider North Western Aeronautical produced a powered version of the CG-4A by installing two 130 hp engines on the wing struts. Designated the XPG-1 (Experimental Power Glider) the glider was successfully test flown on 13 May 1943, by Colonel Fred Dent, USAAF, but was found to be under powered. On 13 September 1943, the USAAF converted another CG-4A to a power glider equipping it with Ranger L-440-7 engines and designated it the XPG-2. Trials by Major Ernest Lasalle proved satisfactory, and North Western Aeronautical began to produce the glider as the PG-2. Ten were built but no real use was found for them. Ridgefield and Ford produced one prototype each but did not proceed with the project.

The seventeen companies who built the CG-4A were as follows:

Model	Maker	Year	Numbers	Seats
XCG-1	Frankfort	1941	0	8
XCG-2	Frankfort	1941	0	15
XCG-3	Waco	1941/42	1	8
CG-3A	Commonwealth	1941/42	100	9
XCG-4	Waco	1941/42	2	15
CG-4A WO	Waco	1942/43	1074	15
CG-4A BB	Babcock	1942/43	60	15
CG-4A CE	Cessna	1942	750	15
CG-4A CM	Commonwealth	1942	1470	15
CG-4A FO	Ford	1942/43	4190	15
CG-4A G&A	G & A Aircraft	1942/43	627	15
CG-4A GE	General	1942/43	1112	15
CG-4A GN	Gibson	1942	1078	15
CG-4A LK	Laister/Kaufman	1942/43	310	15
CG-4A NA	National	1942	1	15
CG-4A NW	North Western	1942/43	1509	15
CG-4A PR	Pratt & Reid	1942/43	956	15
CG-4A RI	Ridgefield	1942/43	162	15
CG-4A RO	Robertson	1942/43	170	15
CG-4A TI	Timm	1942	433	15
CG-4A WA	Ward	1942/43	7	15

The contracted companies together produced 13,909 CG-4A gliders; the largest of the manufacturers was Ford with 4,190 built, next was North Western with 1,509. The glider became the US standard military glider and was used extensively on operations from Sicily to the Far East. With the CG-4A being a successful design, various companies continued experimental work as follows:

Model	Maker	Year	Numbers	Seats
XCG-4B-TI	Timm	1942/43	1	15
XCG-5	St Louis	1941/42	1	8
XCG-6	St Louis	1941/42	0	15
XCG-7	Bowlus	1941/42	1	8
XCG-8	Bowlus	1941/42	1	15

None was put into production.

In 1942 with the need to produce still larger military gliders, the Waco Company was requested to design and produce, under the same terms of contract as before, a glider to carry thirty troops. Waco came up with the XCG-13 WO in 1943 and built two prototypes capable of carrying forty-two men each, or a cargo load of 105-mm howitzer, a quarter ton truck and gun crew or a one and a half ton truck.

The glider was basically the same as the smaller CG-4A but the wing span was 85 feet and the fuselage 54 ft long. The nose section opened vertically by hydraulics for access and exit. Two ramps carried inside the fuselage allowed rapid loading and unloading when in position. Two doors in the side of the glider gave access for troops. Unladen weight was 8,900 lb and laden 18,900 lb giving a $4\frac{1}{2}$ ton payload. Landing speed was 80 mph and maximum towing speed 190 mph.

A prototype XCG-13 was delivered to the USAAF in March 1942 for evaluation and it passed flight tests satisfactorily so a production order was placed. The following companies produced five gliders designated YCG, all with thirty seats:

Ford	YCG-13 FO	1
North Western	YCG-13 NW	1
Ford	YCG-13A FO	1
North Western	YCG-13A NW	2

The first YCG-13 was test-flown on 2 December 1943, and being successful went into production as the CG-13A. Production numbers were:

Ford	CG-13A FO	48 made	30-seater
North Western	CG-13A NW	47 made	30-seater
Ford	CG-13A FO	37 made	42-seater

The RAF acquired nine CG-13s but never used them operationally.

The Chase Aircraft Company designed and produced two experimental gliders, the XCG-14 and 14A, between 1944 and 1945. The XCG-14 made its first flight on 4 January 1945. This was very successful and led to the XCG-14A, which made its maiden flight on 16 October 1945. Both gliders had rear fuselage access and a tricycle undercarriage. The XCG-14 was of all wood construction and the

14A had a steel tube frame and a plywood covering.

As the USAAF wanted a metal-skinned glider, Chase produced the XCG-18A the world's first all metal glider. This was a high wing monoplane with hydraulically operated rear fuselage door and ramp. The ramp lowered to the ground and the door went upwards, giving quick unimpeded access to the whole section of the fuselage. The Air Force was impressed with these features and, after a flying test of the prototype issued a contract for the XCG-18A.

The all-metal skinned glider had an 86 ft 4 in wingspan and fuselage length of 53 ft 5 in. Payload was 8,000 lb with an all-up weight of 15,500 lb. The large cargo hold was 6½ ft high, 7 ft 8 in wide and 24 ft long.

The glider made its first flight in December 1947; and designer, Michael Stroukoff and his company, Chase Aircraft, had designed, built and test-flown it in a little more than a year.

The XCG-18 was followed by the interim YCG-18A and went into production as the CG-18A of which three were delivered to the USAAF and tested. Shortly afterwards the USAAF made a decision to extend the glider's use and requested a powered version. The second prototype XCG-18A was converted to power by adding two Pratt & Whitney 1450 hp engines under the wings. It was redesignated the YC-122 and flew in November 1948.

Twelve, including the converted XCG-18A, YC-122 aircraft were produced by Chase followed in 1949 by the larger YC-123. Another glider, the XCG-20, was successfully developed by Chase; later designated the XG-20, it was destined to become the last US glider transport. In April 1950 it was decided to power the XG-20 with four General Electric jet engines under the wings and redesignate it the XC-123A, thereby becoming the first US pure jet transport.

The Waco Company continued with its designs and came up with the XCG-15, again a modified CG-4A but with a wingspan of 62 ft 2½ in. The 48 ft long fuselage could carry fifteen men. The design was improved with the Waco XCG-15A of which two were built for trials and the mark went into production in 1944 as the CG-15A. Waco built 385 CG-15As as 15-seat models and forty-two more as 16-seat models. An important modification was the addition of landing flaps to give a better landing run.

Parallel to the Waco Company's production of the CG series other companies continued to build and experiment as follows:

Model	Maker	Year	Number	Seats
XCG-9	AGA Aviation	1942	0	30
XCG-10	Laister	1942	0	30
XCG-10A	Laister	1942/44	1	42
XCG-10A	Laister	1945	10	42
XCG-11	Snead	1942	0	30
XCG-12	Read & York	1943	0	30

In September 1943 the USAAF asked Laister Kaufmann to develop the XCG-10 and the Bowlus Company developed the XCG-16, a 48-seater model which was testflown at Clinton Army Air Field, Ohio, in May 1944. The CG-10A was the second largest glider built by the United States, with a wing span of 105 ft, and was projected as the troop-carrying glider for the invasion of Japan. One thousand were to be built but Japan surrendered in 1945 and the glider was not needed.

The XCG-16 had a wing span of 91 ft with two cabins to carry 48 troops; it was of unusual design having twin booms to carry the single fin tail plane, retractable tricycle undercarriage and with the two tandem-seated pilots' cockpit high above the square section fuselage. However on a test flight the glider crashed, killing four of the crew, including the glider pioneer Richard C. Dupont.

Another odd glider was the XCG-17 developed by the Douglas Aircraft Company in 1944. A C-47 Dakota was stripped of its engines and converted to use as a 25-seat glider towed by a B-17 bomber – or on double tow by two powered C-47s. Only one conversion was made but the plan was dropped and the glider restored to powered flight by reinstalling the two engines.

Interest and design for gliders continued in the United States – experimental designs and planning were carried out on assault, bomber and fuel carrying gliders

Assault Gliders: AG (Assault Glider)

XAG-1	Christopher	1944	8 seats	Two ordered, non made.
XAG-2	Timm	1944	8 seats	Two ordered, Cancelled.

These were one pilot gliders with two machine gun turrets and engine assisted but nothing came of the project; none was built.

Fuel Glider: FG (Fuel Glider)

XFG-1	Cornelius	1944	Two built

54' wingspan – 29' long fuselage containing 677 US gal of fuel. Designed as an expendable flying petrol carrier. Two prototypes were built – flown by one brave pilot with no passengers. The project was abandoned.

Bomber Glider: BG (Bomber Glider) Radio controlled.

XBG-1	Fletcher	1942/43	Ten built to carry 2,000 lb bomb.
XBG-2	Fletcher	1942	None built.
XBG-3	Cornelius	1942	None built.

Training Glider: TG (Training Glider)

XTG-1	Frankfort	1941	3 built	2 seat
TG-1A	Frankfort	1942	42 built	2 seat
TG-1B	Frankfort	1942	4 built	2 seat
TG-1C	Frankfort	1942	3 built	2 seat
TG-1D	Frankfort	1942	1 built	2 seat
XTG-2	Schweizer	1941	3 built	2 seat
TG-2	Schweizer	1942	32 built	2 seat
TG-2A	Schweizer	1942	7 built	2 seat
XTG-3	Schweizer	1942	3 built	2 seat
TG-3A SW	Schweizer	1942	110 built	2 seat
TG-3A AG	Air Glider	1942/43	1 built	2 seat
XTG-4	Laister/Kaufmann	1942	3 built	2 seat
TG-4A	Laister/Kaufmann	1942	150 built	2 seat
TG-4B	Laister/Kaufmann	1942	1 built	2 seat

TG-5	Aeronca	1942	253 built	3 seat
TG-6 (L-2)	Taylorcraft	1942	253 built	3 seat
XTG-7	Orlick	1942	1 built	1 seat
TG-8 (L-4)	Piper	1942/43	253 built	3 seat
XTG-9	Briegleb	1942	3 built	2 seat
XTG-10	Wichita	1942/43	3 built	2 seat
XTG-11	Martin-Schemp	1942	1 built	2 seat
XTG-12	Bowlus	1942	1 built	2 seat
XTG-12A	Bowlus	1942	1 built	2 seat
XTG-13	Briegleb	1942	1 built	2 seat
TG-13A	Briegleb	1942	2 built	2 seat
TG-14	Stieglemeir	1942	1 built	1 seat
TG-15	Franklin	1942	8 built	1 seat
TG-16	ABC Sailplane	1942	2 built	1 seat
TG-17	Stevens/Franklin	1942	1 built	1 seat
TG-18	Midwest	1942	3 built	1 seat
TG-19	Scheyer	1942	1 built	1 seat
TG-20	Goeppingen	1942	4 built	1 seat
TG-21	Notre Dame	1942	1 built	1 seat
TG-22	Melhouse	1942	1 built	1 seat
TG-23	Harper-Corcoran	1942	1 built	1 seat
TG-24	Bowlus Dupont	1942	1 built	1 seat
TG-25	Plover	1942	1 built	1 seat
TG-26	Universal	1942	1 built	1 seat
TG-27	Grunau	1942	1 built	2 seat
TG-28	Haller	1942	1 built	1 seat
TG-29	Volmer	1942	1 built	2 seat
TG-30	Smith Blue Bird	1942	1 built	2 seat
TG-31	Aero Indust	1942	1 built	1 seat
TG-32	Pratt Read	1943	73 built	2 seat
XTG-33 (TG-6)	Taylor	1945	1 built	1 seat

United States Navy Gliders

Both the US Navy and later the US Marine Corps experimented and developed independent glider programmes till the end of World War II; the US Navy began in 1929 with experiments in releasing gliders from airships.

The US Navy's first glider was the Prufling, serial number 8546, which had been built in Germany and bought by the US Navy for experimental use. The glider was attached beneath the airship USS *Los Angeles* at Lakehurst Navy Base, New Jersey, and both lifted off. At 3,000 feet the glider piloted by the then Lieutenant Ralph S. Barnaby, was released into free flight and made a successful landing thirteen minutes later at Lakehurst.

Interest in gliders then waned until the outbreak of World War II in Europe when it sparked again by the successful use by the Germans of gliders at Eben Emael.

Like armed forces all over the world the Navy had to use letter and figure classifications for their gliders and adopted the following: letter 'L' stood for glider, 'X' for Experimental, 'N' for Trainer, 'R' for Cargo, 'B' for Bomb. It was followed by a company letter, as follows:

LB: Bomb Carrying glider		LN: Training glider	
LBE	Pratt Read	LNE	Pratt Read
LBP	Piper	LNP	Piper
LBT	Taylorcraft	LNR	Aeronca
		LNS	Schweizer
		LNT	Taylorcraft

LR: Transport glider			
LRA	Allied	LRN	Naval Aircraft
LR2A	Allied	LR2N	Naval Aircraft
LRG	AGA	LRQ	Bristol
LRH	Snead	LRW & LR2W	Waco

Prufling Training Glider. No USN designation allocated. Serial No. A8546 German built. Wooden construction. High wing monoplane with 32 ft 8 in span. Length 17 ft 9 in. Open single seat cockpit. All-up weight 400 lb.

Franklin PS-2 Trainer. No USN designation allocated. Navy markings. American-built. Steel tube fuselage fabric covered. Open single seat cockpit. Single landing wheel. High wing monoplane with 36 ft span. All-up weight 400 lb. Six gliders bought, serials 9401, 9402, 9614 to 9617.

Pratt Read LNE-1: Trainer, Navy markings. American-built all wooden construction sailplane. Side by side enclosed cockpit. Single landing wheel with landing skid under nose. Wingspan 54 ft 6 in. All-up weight 1,150 lb. Serials 31505 to 31585 and 34115 to 34134.

Schweizer LNS-1: Trainer. American-built all metal high wing sailplane. Dual seats. Wingspan 52 ft, length 23 ft. Serials 02970 to 02980, 04380 to 04389, and 26426.

Taylorcraft LNT-1: Trainer, Navy markings. American-built welded steel tube 25 ft fuselage, fabric-covered. 35 ft wooden spar, fabric-covered wings. All-up weight 1,100 lb. Three seats. This was the Taylorcraft Tandem powered light aircraft with the engine removed and a third seat added in its place. The glider could be flown from any of the three seats. The US Navy bought thirty-five gliders and designated them XLNT-1. Serial Nos. 36428 to 36453, 67800 to 67806. Later, another twenty-five were bought as LNT-1. Serials 87763 to 87787.

Waco LRW-1: Trainer and cargo glider, Navy markings. American-built Waco CG-4As acquired from the US Army. Serials 37639 to 36648, 44319 and 69990 to 69991. Ten were supplied to the US Marine Corps but were never flown by them. On the ending of the USMC glider programme, the gliders were returned to the US Army.

Uniquely, however, the US Navy experimented with two amphibious gliders: the XLRA-1 and the XLRQ-1. In effect, these were glider flying boats designed to take off and land on water.

XLRA-1 Prototypes to fulfil USMC specifications to carry twelve marines and take off and land on water. Two XLRA-1s were built by Allied Aviation. Serials 11647 and 11648. The glider was of all-wood construction with a 72 ft wingspan and was 40 ft in length. The low wing was designed to support the glider when afloat and the hull was shaped like a flying boat hull. An order for one hundred gliders had been made but was cancelled by the US Navy. No XLRA-1s were flown.

XLRQ-1 Prototypes to fulfil same specification as the XLRA-1. Two built, serials 11651 and 11652. The first, a static test model, the second a flight test model delivered to the Navy in May 1943. Flight testing was carried out using a Catalina flying boat as a tug. The contract was cancelled by the Navy.

Still larger glider designs were put out to contract: the XLRG-1 and the XLRH-1; these were to carry twenty-four troops and AGA Aviation and Snead & Company were to be the builders, but again the project was cancelled.

XLRN-1: Troop and Cargo Heavy Glider, Navy markings. Experimental all wooden construction, high wing monoplane. One prototype built by NAF Naval Aircraft Factory at Johnsonville, Pennsylvania. 110 ft wingspan. 67.5 ft fuselage. Said to be comparable with the British Hamilcar heavy glider. Successfully test-flown, towed by a four-engined Douglas R5D Skymaster but the project was abandoned.

United States Marine Corps Gliders

In October 1940, the commandant of the US Marine Corps, General Thomas Holcomb, decided that one battalion of each USMC Regiment would be used as airborne troops. Of the battalion, only one troop would be trained and used as paratroops, the remainder would be air lifted in gliders.

The Navy Department of Aeronautics was requested to obtain suitable gliders, whilst the Marine Corps would be responsible for pilot training. Volunteers in the rank of 2nd Lieutenant were called for as first pilots and enlisted men as second pilots. The call went out in July 1941, for fifty officers and 100 non-commissioned officers to train as pilots at civilian flying schools until such time as the Marine Corps could develop its own flying training schools.

The Marine Corps laid out its glider capability requirements to the Bureau of Aeronautics as follows:

1. A transport capability of twelve marines.
2. A capability to lift off from land and water.
3. A suitability for dropping paratroops.
4. A defensive machine gun capability whilst on tow.

USMC pilot training began in November 1941, when four USMC officers, led by Lieutenant-Colonel Vernon M. Guyon, began a glider pilot course at the Motorless Flight Institute, Hanvey, Illinois. At the same time, eight other USMC officers went to the Lewis School of Aeronautics, Lockport, Illinois, for glider pilot training. The flying training was for thirty hours and included cross-country towing, release and landing in simulation of battle requirements. By mid-

December, 1941, the officers had completed their training at the Schools and were assigned to the USMC Air Station at Parris Island, South Carolina.

By March 1942, six, two pilot, Schweizer LNS-1 and Pratt & Read LNE-1 gliders had been delivered to Parris Island and the recently trained officers began training on them.

At first the USMC Planning Staff envisaged a need for seventy-five 12-seat gliders to transport one battalion, but at this time no such gliders were available in the US and so the US Navy issued contracts for the design and development of amphibious gliders. Two companies, Allied and Bristol, took up the contract with the Allied XLRA-1 and the Bristol XLRQ-1, both low wing designs capable of carrying ten marines and two pilots.

Allied built two prototypes, Nos. 11647 and 11648, and one hundred LRA-1s were ordered. Another glider, the LRA-2, was proposed.

Bristol produced the XLRQ-1 which was similar to the Allied design and built four prototypes, Nos. 11651 to 11654; it received an order for a 100 glider production run. The Howard Aircraft Company also had a contract to produce a glider, the XLRH-1, two prototypes of which were built, Nos. 11649 & 11650; fifty production gliders were ordered.

Training continued during early 1942, the glider pilots unit being equipped with three N3N-3 NAF (Naval Aircraft Factory), one SNJ-2 North American (Texan), one J2F-3 Gruman Duck and one JE-1 Bellanca Pacemaker towing aircraft and five two-seat Schweizer LNS-1s as gliders.

As the twelve-seat gliders were expected to be on delivery by 16 March 1942, the USMC requested the US Navy Chief of Operations for authority to form Glider Group 71 composed of an HQ, Service Squadron 71, and Marine Glider Squadron 711 (VML 711). Authority was granted on 24 April 1942, and Glider Group 71 came into being with an establishment of twenty officers and 218 men, based at Marine Corps Air Station, Parris Island.

A search was undertaken to find a suitable base for gliders in the US. Three were approved; Eagle Mountain Lake, Texas, Edenton, North Carolina, and Shawnee, Oklahoma. A fourth at Addison Point, Florida, was considered but not proceeded with. Of the four sites only Eagle Mountain Lake was developed and used.

By June 1942, the USMC programme looked toward a strength of 1,371 gliders and 3,436 pilots carrying 10,800 men. This was reduced to a maximum strength of 36 officers and 246 men for the Glider Group at its peak.

Glider Group 71 left Parris Island on 21 November 1942, and arrived at Eagle Mountain Lake on 24 November. Training commenced on the available gliders which later included ten Waco CG-4As redesignated LRW-1 which were delivered but never flown.

With the island to island battle in the Pacific war against the Japanese, it became clear that the US Marine Corps would not be able to use gliders as they were unsuited to this type of assault. General Holcomb, with the approval of the US Secretary of the Navy, terminated the Marine Corps glider programme on 24 June 1943. The glider contracts, few of which had been filled, were transferred to the USAAF as were the LRW-1 (Waco CG-4As) which had been delivered.

The US Marine Corps Glider Units had only a short life, from 10 January 1942 to 23 June 1943. Their commanding officers during this brief period were:

Marine Glider Detachment, CO, Lieutenant-Colonel Vernon M. Guyon. 10 Jan 42–24 April 42.
Marine Glider Group 71, CO, Lieutenant-Colonel Vernon M. Guyon. 24 April 42–23 Jun 43.
Marine Corps Glider Squadron, CO, Captain Eschol M. Mallory, 24 April 42–7 Feb 43; Captain Barrette Robinson, 8 Feb 43–23 Jun 43.

XIV

Russian Military Glider Forces History

A s early as 1932 the Russians recognized the importance of gliders for military use. A year earlier the Soviet Government had taken steps to expand the civil sport of sailplane flying by building a glider factory at Moscow, under Oleg Antonov, and engaging in training civil glider pilots.

In 1932 the eighteen-year-old aircraft designer, Boris Dimitiyevitch Urlapov, with others, had designed the world's first cargo sailplane, the G-63. This glider is reported as being the development of an idea of the director, Special Design Department of the Red Army, Pavel Ingatievitch Grokhouskii.

The G-63 was a shoulder-wing cantilever wooden monoplane design with two pilots seated in tandem in an open cockpit. Sixteen to eighteen paratroops were carried prone inside the leading edge of the glazed portion of the wing. Fitted with a spatted undercarriage and towed by an R-5 tug, the aircraft was named the Jakov Alknsis, in then honour of the later to be purged and executed, Commanding General of the Red Army Air Force.

The G-63 was followed by the G-31 the powered version of the G-63 and fitted with an uncowled M-11 engine in the nose. Another version, the G-32, had a 110 hp M-11 engine and was used for stratospheric research. Later the more powerful 500 hp and 750 hp M-25 engines were fitted. The G-31 had a wingspan of 91.9 ft and and all-up weight of 7,054 lb, the payload being 3,968 lb. However the design was abandoned as impracticable.

After the G-63 came the Groshev GN-4, designed by Yuri Groshev in 1934 and built at the Moscow Glider Factory. This was the world's first military transport glider capable of carrying a pilot and five passengers, The glider was a high wing strut-braced monoplane of oval fuselage section. Wing span was 60 ft and fuselage length 27 ft. It was designed to be towed with a payload of 992 lb in a glider train by an R-5 tug at 100 mph. Unladen weight was 1,000 lb.

A little later the Groshev GN-8 was built which was also a five-seat transport glider, with a low cantilever wing. The pilot and passengers sat in tandem in a very long canopied cockpit. All-up weight was 1,984 lb. The glider passed its trials on 26 January 1937, towed by I-50 and I-16 tugs.

The G-14 was also built; designed by Vladislav Gribouski, it was able to carry fuel and act as a tanker for mid-air refuelling – an idea well ahead of its time.

On 23 January 1940, the Soviet Government set up an organisation for the production of transport and troop gliders, under the direction of V.S. Kulikov and with the Chief Engineer P.V. Tsybin and the Shukovski Central Institute for aerodynamics engaging in research work. A project competition was held for the best unpowered aircraft design, and commissions were given to Oleg Antonov to develop the A-7 seven-seat glider: to V.K. Gribouski for the eleven-seat G-11: to D.N. Kolesnikov and P.V. Tsybin for the twenty-seat KT-20 and to N. Kurbala for the heavy transport KG-1 fifty-seat glider. N. Polikarpov was to develop the BDP, which was to carry sixteen troops.

Except for the KG-1, all the glider types were put into production, at the same time a Military Glider Training School for the gliderborne troops of the Red

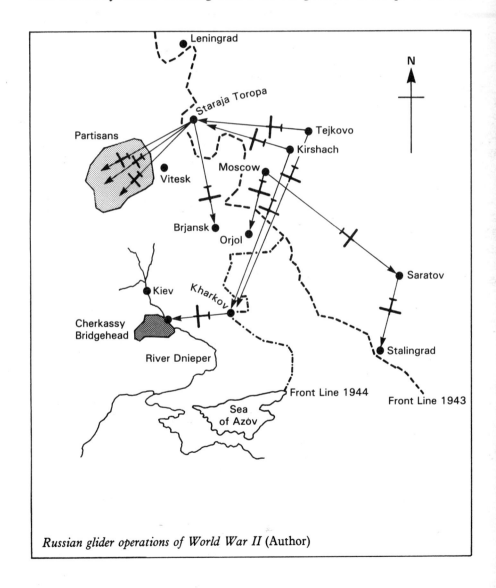

Russian glider operations of World War II (Author)

Army was set up at Saratov, together with two glider training regiments plus repair and servicing workshops.

When Hitler launched his attack on the Soviet Union in June, 1941, the glider training programme was intensified and operational flights began. Essential supplies and arms were flown from Moscow to Stalingrad and other flights were made to supply Russian partisans behind the German lines and front line troops. The gliders were not recoverable and were burnt.

In November 1942, a large scale flight, Operation 'Antifris', was mounted. Very cold weather had frozen the cooling systems of Russian tanks at Stalingrad who were poised to launch an attack against the Germans. Anti-freeze was urgently needed so a fleet of A-7 and G-11 gliders, loaded with cans of anti-freeze, were towed from Medveshii Osero airfield near Moscow, under the command of Dmitri Koshits, to Saratov where they landed under cover of darkness. Further gliders loaded with anti-freeze joined the air train and were towed off towards Stalingrad. Bad weather prevailed over the flight route; low cloud, high winds and low temperatures made the flight difficult, but the air train reached Stalingrad in time for the Russian tanks to begin their successful counter-attack which turned the tide against the Germans.

With large Russian partisan forces fighting behind the German lines and therefore cut off from their source of supplies, it was decided to supply them with arms and supplies by glider. A headquarters, commanded by Brigadier General A. Shcherbakov and controlled by the now Colonel P. Tsybin, was set up at Staraja Toropa, north-west of Moscow, from where glider operations would be carried out.

During early 1943 sixty-five A-7 and G-11 gliders delivered supplies to the cut-off partisans at Begoml. The tug aircraft landed and picked up the glider pilots and returned them back to Staraja Toropa. On 21 March 1943, the glider re-supply flights ended in this sector of Russia.

In April 1943, the partisans requested by radio that the glider supply flights be resumed to the Polotsk-Lepel area. Therefore gliders were towed from Kirshach, Tejkovo and Moscow to the glider base at Staraja Toropa and two other bases at Lushi and Andreapol, to be loaded for partisan supply flights. Bad weather set in and it was not until 21:30 on 2 May that flights began. With only four signal fires in a row as landing aids, six gliders managed to land in the dark at Begoml. No sooner had they landed than the LZ was attacked by German aircraft, but the gliders were unloaded successfully. Next day however the Luftwaffe attacked the LZ in force and the strip had to be abandoned.

In the thickly forested region, LZs large enough were hard to find but a 600 metre by 200 metre clearing was found one mile from the small village of Beresyouka. During the next three weeks over 100 gliders landed with supplies. Some of the tug aircraft also landed to evacuate the glider pilots back to their bases. During July and August 1943, the Germans, who were now in retreat, tried to make a stand on the River Dnieper, but Soviet Forces attacked and succeeded in forcing several bridgeheads across the river by 20 September. On 26 September 6,875 paratroops of the 3rd and 5th Brigades, were dropped into the battle to storm the river.

On airfields at Kharkov 120 A-7, G-11 and KT-20 gliders, loaded with anti-tank guns and troops assembled with their B-25, IL-4 and LI-2 tow planes. Soon they were towed off and into action on the west bank of the river, but a strong wind dispersed them. Nevertheless they managed to link up with the already dropped paratroops and engage the Germans whilst the river was stormed from the east by the Red Army at Cherkassy.

For three days the air landing troops fought against a numerically superior enemy, but by then their ammunition was running out. Another glider resupply mission was mounted and gliders loaded with supplies glided over the Dnieper, landing as and when they could on roads and clearings in the forested area. Some of the glider pilots could not reach landing places and had to land on and in the tops of trees killing or injuring the crews. Through the efforts of the glider crews and troops, other Red Army units were able to cross the Dnieper, some without firing a shot.

The glider operation on the Dnieper, and the second resupply operation to the partisans continued until April 1944, and were the last operations of the Russian glider pilots, although a few were used in various parts of the Front for special tasks. The Soviet Government recognized the achievements of the glider pilots by awarding them the title of 'Guards Regiments'. With the end of major glider operations, most of the glider pilots became fighter pilots until the end of the war. It was said that their towing flights in the dark and in all weathers gave them instinctive flying skills which enabled them to stalk German aircraft up to close range before opening fire.

Each year the former Russian glider pilots meet at Kirshach at a memorial, which is an A-7 glider mounted on a pillar, to the 3rd Guards Regiment of Glider Troops, to remember their dead of World War II.

After the war ended the Glider Training School at Saratov continued to train glider pilots for the Yak-15 and KT-25 gliders but, as in other countries, the glider became obsolete and in 1954 the school became the Suran Officers Institute for powered flight.

XV

Russian Military Gliders

Antonov A-7 (RF-8) Assault glider

One of the most widely used Russian gliders of World War II, the A-7 continued Antonov's award winning 'Rot Front' series of prewar sports gliders and sailplanes. Designed in 1938, the A-7 had a high 62 ft wing span and a 37.7 ft fuselage. Constructed of wood with fabric covering, the glider had one pilot and was capable of carrying eight troops, or a 2,000 lb payload. The two-wheeled undercarriage was retractable and two main and one tail skids could be used for heavy or rough ground landings. The most common tug used was the SB-2 but Il-4 and SB-3 aircraft were also used. Four hundred gliders were produced and delivered mostly during 1942.

The A-7 was used on Operation 'Antifris' and in supplying partisan groups behind the German lines. As it was impossible to recover the A-7s they were burned after landing.

Antonov KT 'Kril'ya Tanka' (Wings of the Tank)

Also known as the A-T and A-40. Tank transport glider.

Designed by Oleg Antonov the KT was unusual in that it was a biplane glider so constructed as to be capable of being attached to a light tank and flying it to battle. Design started in 1941 and in the autumn of 1942 the glider was test-flown by Sergie Nikolayevich Anokhin, a well known glider pilot who held the title of 'Honourable Master of Gliding'. Towed off by a TB-3 tug aircraft, the glider, controlled from the inside of the attached T-60 tank, performed well but the tug's engines were not powerful enough to tow the 18,000 lb glider and it had to be cast off tow. The engine of the tank was started in flight and the revolving caterpillar tracks acted as the undercarriage in a successful landing. As the Russians did not have a powerful enough tug to tow the KT the project was abandoned with only one glider being built. Glider alone weight: 4,418 lb.

Construction and Data: Wing span, 49.2 ft. Single bay constant chord equal span biplane. 37.7 ft twin booms with twin tails. Six-ton T-60 tank slung beneath lower wings. All-up weight 17,205 lb. Towing speed, 100 mph. Landing speed, 70 mph.

BDP (S-1) Boevoi Desantny Planer (Airborne Troop Glider)

Designed by Nikolai Nickolaevich Polakarpov and ordered for production by the OKB (Experimental Design Bureau) in July 1941, the BDP was a high 65.7 ft wing span wooden construction assault glider, which could carry a pilot and twenty troops in the monocoque oval section fuselage.

The first prototype was built within one month of the order being placed and the first air test was in August 1941. Reports differ as to the undercarriage which was believed to be multi-wheel retractable type between twin skids. All-up weight, 7,700 lb, payload 2,630 lb. Seven gliders were built but production was stopped due to the German advance.

MP-1 Motorizovanii Planar

Powered version of the BDP (S-1) with two 145 hp Schvetsov M-11 F engines. Range variously quoted as between 242 and 577 miles depending on load. Maximum speed, 106 mph. Ceiling, 6,560 feet. Test-flown in October 1944. The glider could take off on its own power unloaded, but required tow off when loaded.

PB Planer Bombardirovschik

Projected design for a piloted glider bomber in 1942. Capable of carrying a 4,000 lb bomb. The project was abandoned before any prototype was built.

Gribouskii G-11 Prototype G.29

Transport and assault glider built in quantity and used extensively during World War II. High 59.5 ft wing span and capable of carrying two pilots and twenty troops. Wooden and fabric construction with 32 ft long fuselage and entrance door under port wing. Simple two wheel undercarriage with tail wheel and central skid. Maximum towing speed 173 mph.

G-11M (Prototype G.30)

Motorised version of the G-11 fitted with a small M-11 engine.

Ilyushin IL-32, Large Transport Glider

Designed by Sergie Ilyushin, the IL-32 was a large transport glider with a cargo capacity of 15,432 lb. The high wing, all-metal prototype was completed in 1948 and could carry two pilots and thirty-five troops. Both the nose section and the rear part of the fuselage were hinged for loading and unloading via integral ramps.

Ilyushin IL-34

Prototype rebuilt as powered version of the IL-32.

Jakolev-Cybina

Reportedly designed by A. Jakolev and P. Cybina shortly after World War II and similar in design to the American Waco CG-4A glider.

KT-20

Designed by D. Kolesnikov and P. Tsybin in 1944 as a large transport or cargo glider capable of carrying twenty-four equipped troops or cargo weight 4,410 lb. Constructed of wood and metal the glider had a high 72.6 ft wing span strut braced to the bottom fuselage longerons. Fuselage length 49 ft with rear section hinging upwards behind the wing. The two pilot cockpit was placed on top of the fuselage forward of the wing. Very few were made; most reports state only two were produced.

SAM-23

Designed by A. Moskalev and first produced in 1943, the SAM-23 was a tricycle undercarriage high wing twin boom glider capable of carrying sixteen troops or 3,600 lb cargo. Loading was by an upward hinging door at the rear of the pod like fuselage. Integral loading ramps enabled a small vehicle to be driven in and out of the cargo hold very quickly.

SAM-25

Proposed powered version of the SAM-23 not proceeded with.

TS-25, Transport or cargo glider

Designed by P. Tsybin in 1944/45, the TS-25 was a high 82.8 ft braced wing span transport or cargo glider. Constructed mainly of wood and plywood the glider could carry twenty-five troops, a jeep, small gun or cargo weight 4,800 lb in the 53 ft fuselage. The two pilot cockpit was placed on top of the fuselage slightly foward of the leading edge of the wings to give excellent visibility. The nose section was hinged to starboard for direct access landing. Tricycle undercarriage which could be jettisoned, landing being on skids. Six examples of the TS-25 are reported to have been built.

TS-25M

Powered version of the TS-25 with two 165 hp Schevetsov M-11-FR-1 engines driving two bladed propellers.

According to some reports the TS-25 and the TS-25M were built in quantity and some are known to have been supplied to the Czechs as the NK-25.

YAK 14

Designed by Alexander Yakolev in the immediate post-war period, the YAK-14 was a large box-shaped section wooden glider with a high 85.8 ft braced wing span. The fuselage was 60 ft long and capable of carrying thirty-five troops or 8,050 lb cargo. The two pilot cockpit was on top of the fuselage well forward of the wings giving excellent visibility. The large 26 ft by 7 ft by 7 ft cargo hold could be loaded via the sideways opening nose section. Tricycle undercarriage. 413 YAK-14s were built and some were supplied to the Czechs as the NK-14.

XVI
Japanese Military Gliders

History

Japan entered the Second World War on 7 December 1941, by bombing the US Pacific Fleet at Pearl Harbour in a surprise attack by carrier-based aircraft of the Japanese Imperial Navy.

The Japanese Army Air Corps had been established on 1 May 1925, with a strength of 500 aircraft and 3,700 officers and men. The aircraft were mostly of foreign design or make, but by 1941 the Air Corps had 1,500 aircraft produced by the Japanese aircraft industry. The Air Command structure was: Squadron, Group, Wing, Air Division, Air Army then the Imperial General Headquarters. As required, small independent squadrons and wings were formed for special operations.

The Japanese system for classifying their gliders was confusing: airframe numbers (Kitai or Ki) were used at first but later Guraida (Ku) numbers came into use. In addition an army type number was allocated and a name. In view of this the Allied forces gave a code-name to each Japanese aircraft to aid identification; bird names were given to gliders, and thus the Kokusai Ku-8 twenty-seat troop glider army type 4 was code-named 'Goose' and, later in the war, 'Gander'.

With the use by the Germans of gliderborne troops in 1940, the Japanese Army issued specifications for assault and transport gliders. A large number of designs and prototypes were planned and some flown but the only model to go into service was the KU-8-11.

In December 1941, a Kokusai Ki-59 high wing light transport aircraft powered by two 640 hp radial engines was converted to a glider by removing the engines and undercarriage. Two small wheels and two skids were fitted under the fuselage for take-off and landing. Classified as the Ku-8-1 Army Experimental Glider, flight trials were carried out with success and the design became the Kokusai Ku-8-11 Army Type 4 large transport glider capable of carrying twenty troops or an equivalent weight payload.

Military Gliders

Kokusai Ku-8-11 glider:
Wing span 76 ft Length 43 ft 8 in All-up weight 7,716 lb.

Fuselage constructed of steel tubing fabric covered. Sideways swinging nose section, which contained the two pilots, fitted with a loading ramp. Small two wheel undercarriage and two skids fitted for take-off and landing. Wings and tail plane constructed mainly of wood with the high wing braced to the bottom fuselage. Towing speed, 139 mph, usual tug a Mitsubishi Ki-21-11.

The Ku-8-11 was the only Japanese military glider to be used operationally though only as a transport, not in an assault role. And as far as is known only in the Philippines, where several were found by the liberating US forces.

The other noteworthy Japanese military glider design was the Kokusai Ku-7 'Crane.' This was the largest military glider built experimentally in Japan with a 114 ft 10 in wing span, which made its first flight in August 1944. The design started in 1942, was similar to the German GO-242, having twin booms and a central nacelle which had upwards swinging loading doors at the rear end. Designed to carry thirty-two troops or one eight-ton tank, the loaded weight was 26,455 lb. The four fixed landing wheels were semi-recessed in the streamlined nacelle and a fixed nose wheel was fitted under the nose section for tricycle type tow off and landings. Usual tug was a Mitsubishi Ki-67-1 or a Nakajima Ki-49-11.

A powered version of the Ku-7 was designed and nine prototypes were built. Originally called the Ku-7-11 but was reclassified the Kokusai Ki-105 'Phoenix'. As Japan was short of fuel oil, the aircraft was intended for use as a fuel tanker to carry oil from captured oil wells in Sumatra to Japan. Powered by two 940 hp Mitsubishi radial engines, the Ki-105 had a range of 1,550 miles with a cruising speed of 137 mph. A test programme was begun on the prototypes in April 1945, and production was planned for 300 aircraft. Weighing 1,100 lb more than the Ku-7, the Ki-105 could carry a payload of 7,275 lb. The war ended in August 1945, before production of the aircraft could begin.

Japanese Military Gliders in World War II.

Designation	Maker	Classification
Ki-23	Fukuda	Training sailplane
Ki-24	Tachikawa	Primary Training glider
Ki-25	Tachikawa	Experimental glider
Ki-26	Tachikawa	Experimental glider
Ku-1	Maeda	Army Transport glider-Type 2 twin boom-eight seats. Few made.
Ku-2	Kayaba	Experimental tailless glider
Ku-3	Kayaba	Experimental tailless glider
Ku-5	Fukuda	Two seat training glider
Ku-6	Maeda	Experimental vehicle and troop carrying glider.
Ku-7	Kukusai	Experimental transport glider
Ku-8	Kukusai	Army Type 4 transport glider
Ku-9	Fukuda	Experimental transport glider
Ku-10	Maeda	Special Training glider
Ku-11	Nikon Kogota	Experimental Transport glider

Ku-12	Fukuda	Two seat secondary training glider
Ku-13	Yokoi	Experimental training tailless glider for rocket powered interceptor
Ku-14	Nikon Kogota	Two seat training glider
MxJI (Mx Special Purpose)	Nikon Kogata	Navy primary training glider
MxY-3	Yokosuka	Experimental Target glider
MxY-5	Yokosuka	Experimental Assault glider. 12 built for Navy.
MxY-8	Yokosuka	Experimental tailless glider trainer for rocket powered interceptor
Shinryu	Mizumo	Bomb glider.
K-1	Yokasuka	Glider Trainer for Okha suicide aircraft.

XVII

Other Military Glider Developments

Argentina

I.AE 25 Manque (Vulture)

The only military glider designed and built in Argentina. Built in 1945 by the Industria Aeronautica under the agency of Fabrica Militarde de Aviones (FMA) and, according to them, based on the US Waco CG-4A glider. Designed as a troop transport or cargo carrier, the glider prototype was test-flown on 11 August 1945, but never flew again; the project was abandoned. Only the one prototype was built.

The Manque was built entirely of South American wood – fabric covered with an 82.2 ft wing span and a fuselage length of 48.2 ft. The high wing was braced to the lower fuselage as was the tail plane. The two pilot cockpit could be raised upward for loading and unloading. Payload, 2,474 lb or thirteen troops. All-up weight 7,897 lb; empty 5,423 lb. Simple two wheel undercarriage and tail wheel with two small skids uner the nose. Maximum towing speed 137 mph.

Australia

By 1942 the Japanese Army was threatening the continent of Australia with invasion from the north. The Australian Government realised a need to move its defensive forces to meet this situation. Possessing very few transport aircraft to move the troops it was decided that a troop carrying glider would solve the problem. Early in 1942 Specification 5/42 was issued for a seven seat glider and De Havilland of Bankstown, Australia, took up the specification. The prototype order was placed in March 1942 for the glider.

Having no expertise or experience in building military gliders De Havilland had to start from scratch. Eventually their designers came up with a design which resembled the German DFS 230 and the Waco CG-4A gliders.

De Havilland's produced two prototypes under their company classification: DHA-G1, with registration numbers EG-1 and 2 (Experimental gliders 1 and 2). The nose section of a De Havilland DH 84 Dragon civilian aircraft was used and married to a 33 ft wooden plywood-covered fuselage. The 60 ft span high wing was also wooden but with a fabric covering. A simple single landing wheel and skid served as an undercarriage.

The first prototype flew in June 1942 at Laverton under RAAF serial number A57-1001. The second prototype was RAAF A57-1002.

During early 1943 the Government changed the specification and almost the whole design was changed. Five more G2s were built with a smaller 50.5 ft wing span and delivered to the RAAF for evaluation, but with the threat of invasion receding and the Americans delivering twenty-seven crated CG-4As in February, 1943, to Brisbane, no more gliders were built.

Construction and date: G2
Wing span: 50.5 ft single box spar plywood and fabric-covered.
Fuselage: 33 ft long, wooden, plywood-covered.
Weight: Loaded 3,250 lb. Unloaded 1,450 lb. Payload 1,800 lb.

One G2 serial number, A57-1, was converted after the war to a suction wing test glider, the GLAS 2, using a small engine.

Canada

Canada did not build any military gliders of its own during World War II, but in 1942 bought twenty-two British Hotspur Mark IIs serial numbers:

HH 418, 558, 659	HH 521, 564
HH 419, 559, 667	HH 551, 579
HH 421, 560	HH 552, 580
HH 425, 561	HH 553, 646
HH 427, 562	HH 557, 647

These were for use by the Royal Canadian Air Force on glider training and glider towing. Five Waco CG-4A Hadrian gliders, serials FR 580, KH 994 to KH 997, were also sent by the British to Canada for training and towing training. Post-war the RCAF acquired three Horsas, a few more Waco Hadrians, a Waco CG-15A and a PC-2A, using them on training until 1950.

China

Nationalist China did not produce any military gliders during World War II; it was not until the war ended in 1945 that the Chinese Air Force ordered a military glider design from the Institute of Aero Research, Szechuan, China. At this time the Chinese Air Force was largely influenced by American design and was equipped with various US aircraft and some ex-Canadian DH Mosquitoes.

The Research Institute produced its first prototype in 1947 built of wood with fabric covering. The glider was unusual in that it was of low wing design with pronounced dihedral commencing the fixed undercarriage oleo leg. Extremely smooth and streamlined in appearance it could carry two pilots side by side in the large well glazed cockpit, and twelve troops in the fuselage or a payload of 2,800 lb. Only twelve gliders were produced and in 1949 the Communists took over China and the country came under Russian influence.

Czechoslovakia

The Czech Army Air Force was formed at the Birth of the Nation in 1918, with a cadre of World War I Czech personnel from Russia and France. In 1938 the

Munich Agreement more or less allowed Hitler to take over the small country and during World War II many Czech airmen escaped to the West and flew with distinction with the Royal Air Force. After the war the Czech airforce was re-formed with captured German and surplus RAF aircraft.

In 1947 the construction department of the Czech aircraft company Aero began prototype work on the AE-53 glider, which was designed to carry two pilots and ten troops or a payload of 2,644 lb. During the construction of the prototype many modifications were made, but the project was never completed and was cancelled in 1949. The glider was similar to the US YCG 10A with a wingspan of 61 ft and a length of 37 ft. An estimated high maximum speed of 300 mph was claimed and a minimum of 54 mph.

In 1948 the LD Company in Chocen, led by designer Pavel Benes, began design work on the prototype LD 605 Haban (Mighty One) glider – similar to the US Waco CG-4A but with a 30 troop carrying capacity and two pilots. In 1949 work began on the prototype but the project was cancelled in 1951. The LD 605 had a wingspan of 85 ft and a length of 59 ft. Payload, 7,392 lb. Maximum speed, 186 mph. Minimum speed, 58 mph.

In 1948 the country had come under Russian influence and the Czech airforce was equipped with Russian YAK 14s and Tsybin 25 gliders, under the Czech designations of NK 14 and NK 25 respectively. The Czechs turned their attention to building sailplane gliders and became the largest supplier of them to the USSR.

France

Castel-Mouboussin CM-10

The CM-10 was designed by Castel-Mouboussin as a large military transport glider. The design team was set up by Robert Castello (Technical Director of Etablissement Fouga) and Pierre Mouboussin who had designed light aircraft which were built by Fouga. After designing the CM-7 and the SM-8 sailplanes, the team at the request of the French Air Ministry, designed the CM-10 as a troop carrying or freight glider.

Two prototypes were ordered, the first being delivered for testing in early 1947. In June of that year the first air test took place at Mont de Marson with Captain Leon Bourriay as test pilot. Towed off by an AAC.O (French built Ju/52.3m) the glider performed well and the air test was successful. However on a later test flight the glider broke up in mid-air and the pilot, Bourriay, had to bale out sustaining severe injuries.

As Fouga did not have the capability to build the CM-10, the Air Ministry placed an order with the Société Nationale de Construction Aeronautiques du Nord (SNCAN) for twenty-five gliders. Meantime Fouga had produced a second prototype and five pre-production gliders. As the French were still recovering from the German occupation finance was in short supply and the CM-10 project was cancelled.

To profit from their experience with the glider the French developed the CM-100 and the CM-101 as powered versions of the CM-10. Two 580 hp Renault 12s engines were fitted to the glider but gave poor performance. Two small Turbomeca Pimene jet engines were added but the whole project was abandoned with Fouga concentrating on the Magister training aircraft which they built in large numbers.

Construction and data CM-10: High 87 ft long wing span with a 60 ft fuselage of mixed wood and alloy construction. Fixed tricycle undercarriage. Crew of two pilots and capable of carrying thirty five equipped troops, two jeeps or other combination of the same weight. Payload, 9,000 lb in the 26 ft × 5.8 ft × 7 ft cargo hold which was loaded through the starboard hinging nose section. All-up weight, 15,400 lb. Maximum towing speed 180 mph. A total of seven CM-10s were built, two prototypes and five production line models.

India

Hindustan Aircraft Limited G-1

The Hindustan Aircraft Company, Bangalore, India, was founded on 24 December 1940, and designed India's first military glider, the G-1, during 1941 and 1942. First flown in August 1942, the G-1 had a 56 ft single spar high wing of wooden construction, with fabric-covered flying control surfaces. Spoilers on upper wing surfaces. The 30.5 ft fuselage was of semi-monocoque construction using two-ply moulded plywood for covering. Passenger door rear starboard side. Fabric-covered rudder and elevators. Designed to carry eight troops with light equipment, plus two pilots seated in tandem in the dual control cockpit, access to which was by the hinging cockpit hood. For take-off, a simple jettisonable two wheeled undercarriage was fitted, landing being on a single wooden skid. All-up weight, 4,000 lb. Unladen weight, 1,500 lb. Payload, 2,500 lb. Maximum towing speed of 160 mph.

Being of wood and fabric covered construction, the glider was found to be unsuitable for the Indian climate and only the prototype was made although ten gliders were projected.

Italy

Al-12P and TM-2

During most of World War II Italy was one of the Axis powers, fighting at first with the Germans. In June 1942 they formed their own glider force using German military gliders but in the same year began to design and build their own gliders. *Ambrosini AL-12P Assault and Transport glider*: Designed by A. Ambrosini of the Aerolombardi Company, Como, Italy, and built in 1942 first flying in 1943.

Construction: Fuselage 47 ft long, of wooden ribs plywood-covered. Capable of carrying twelve troops or 2,700 lb payload in the 22 ft long × 5.8 ft wide cargo hold. Wings, 70 ft wooden double spar plywood-covered with fabric-covered ailerons. Slatted spoilers above and below wing surfaces. The two pilots sat side by side in the nose cockpit which was of welded steel tubing covered with plywood, which was hinged to starboard to allow direct access to the troop or cargo compartment. Another small door was fitted to the front port side just behind the cockpit.

A sprung central landing skid ran from just behind the pilot's cockpit to the two wheeled undercarriage. Sixteen of the gliders were built and it was found that the glider was a good design and performed well. A powered version, the P-152, fitted with two 195 hp engines was also made.

TM-2 (Cattm-2)

With a need for a larger military transport glider the Caproni Company designed the TM-2 which was capable of carrying twenty troops or a 4,400 lb payload and two pilots. The glider was of all-wood construction, plywood and fabric-covered with a wing span of 75 ft and a fuselage length of 42.5 ft. The high wing was braced to the bottom of the oval section fuselage which had four loading doors. Two wheel undercarriage with central and rear landing skids.

Only one TM-2 was built and the project ceased with the Italian surrender.

Sweden

AB Flygindustri F1-3

From the period 1941 to 1945 the AB Flygindustri of Halmstaad, Sweden, produced military transport gliders designated the FI-3 for the Swedish Air Force (Flgvapnet). The FI-3 was a high wing wood and fabric glider with a crew of two and capable of carrying eleven troops or a payload of 2,228 lb. All-up weight, 3,970 lb. Wing span, 54.6 ft. Length 30.8 ft. Entry to the glider was via two detachable doors one on either side of the fuselage.

Swedish volunteers fought in the war with Finland against the USSR during 1939-40 but there is no record of gliderborne operations. At the end of the war the Flgvapnet cancelled the glider programme, five FI-3s having been built.

Turkey

THK-1

At the outbreak of World War II the Turkish Air Force (Turk Hava Kuvvetleri) had a strength of 8,500 men and 370 aircraft, supplied mostly by foreign manufacturers, but no military gliders. Turkey remained neutral during the war but did experiment with an all wooden construction military glider, the THK-1, the design of which began in 1941 with the prototype being delivered in 1943.

The THK-1 was a low wing glider of streamlined appearance and capable of carrying a pilot, eleven troops or a payload of 2,400 lb.

Yugoslavia

Sostoric glider

Prior to World War II Yugoslavia had a thriving aircraft industry producing licence-built aircraft for the Yugoslavia Army Aviation Department. When the Germans occupied the country in 1941 most of the Army's aircraft were destroyed as was the aircraft industry.

During the war the only gliders in Yugoslavia were German and the three Waco CG-4A Hadrian gliders used in the Allied clandestine Operation 'Bunghole'. When the war ended the country became a republic in 1945 and a new air force, the JRV, was formed which included a military transport glider.

Designed by Ivo Sostoric the glider was of unusual concept having a high wing braced to a pod type fuselage. The tail plane was carried on a single boom. Capable of carrying twelve troops, a jeep or a payload of 2,800 lb loaded through a door at the rear of the fuselage pod. Landing and take-off was on a fixed tricycle undercarriage. Only one prototype was built and the design was not proceeded with.

Epilogue

The military glider has gone – or has it? In 1948 Francis Rogallo, an American, built a portable folding flexible wing form kite which evolved into the modern hang glider. In July 1963, the United States NASA Department made an award to Rogallo who worked on three gliders for the recovery of space capsules re-entering the Earth's atmosphere. In 1969 the US American Pioneer Parachute Company – with Irvin Industries, worked on and made their Delta Wing Glider. And, of course the US Space Shuttle and the untested Russian Shuttle, are gigantic gliders when re-entering the Earth's atmosphere, the onboard rocket motors being used for control purposes only. During re-entry and landing, it is a glider.

At the present time hang-gliding is in vogue as a sport and pastime. Apart from modern materials the glider is not all that different from Lillenthal's one man 'hang gliders'.

The hang glider, with its quality of silence, has been evaluated by several military units all over the world – not least by Palestinian guerillas. On 25 November 1987, two guerillas from South Lebanon, flying two delta-winged motorized hang gliders, attacked the Israeli camp at Kiryat Shmona. Using the motors to gain height until they reached the Israeli security fence – they then glided in silence with their motors off over the fence and evaded Israeli helicopters. Before being killed themselves they killed six Israeli soldiers with grenades and rifle fire. Israeli Intelligence estimates that 200 guerillas have been trained to fly. 'Silent we Strike' still obtains.

Index